W9-CSD-000

↑om
4

Rappin'
and
stylin' out

■ Rappin' and stylin' out

Communication in urban black America

Edited by Thomas Kochman

University of Illinois Press

Urbana Chicago London

Second paperback printing, 1977

© 1972 by The Board of Trustees of the University of Illinois
Manufactured in the United States of America
Library of Congress Catalog Card No. 75-177896

ISBN 0-252-00413-2

The editor wishes to thank the following publishers, journals, and individuals for
permission to reprint the designated selections. Rights in all cases are reserved
by the owner of the copyright:
"Time and Cool People," by John Horton, copyright by *Trans-action* Magazine,
New Brunswick, New Jersey; "Motion and Feeling through Music," by Charles
Keil, copyright by *The Journal of Aesthetics and Art Criticism,* 1965–66; "Names,
Graffiti, and Culture," by Herbert Kohl and James Hinton, copyright by *The
Urban Review,* a publication of the Center for Urban Education; "The Language
of Soul," by Claude Brown, first published in *Esquire* Magazine, April, 1968,
and copyright by The Sterling Lord Agency; " 'Inversion' in Black Communication,"
by Grace Sims Holt, first published in *The Florida FL Reporter,*
Spring/Fall, 1971; "Street Talk," by H. Rap Brown, reprinted from *Die Nigger
Die,* copyright 1969 by Lynne Brown and used by permission of the publisher,
Dial Press; "Toward an Ethnography of Black American Speech Behavior," by
Thomas Kochman, from *Afro-American Anthropology,* edited by Whitten and
Szwed, copyright 1970 by The Macmillan Company; "Black Poetry—Where It's
At," by Carolyn Rodgers, copyright by *Negro Digest,* September, 1969; "Roles
and Ideologies," by R. Lincoln Keiser, from *The Vice Lords: Warriors of the
Streets,* copyright 1969 by Holt, Rinehart and Winston, Inc., and reprinted with
publisher's permission; "Aspiration," by Melvin S. Brookins, from *The Liberator,*
December, 1967; "Foreword from *Pimp: The Story of My Life,*" by Iceberg Slim,
by permission of Holloway House Publishing Company; "The Game," by Woodie
King, Jr., from *The Liberator,* August, 1965, and by permission of Woodie King
Associates, Inc.; "Lovers and Exploiters," by Elliot Liebow, from *Tally's Corner,*
copyright 1967 by Little, Brown and Company, Inc.

Contents

Expressive role behavior

ACKNOWLEDGMENTS

In the time it took to put this volume together, many people fell in line for special thanks and mention: Jean Phillips, Cathy Weidman, Gloria Mitchell, Sheila Churchill, and Jeannette Lathan for typing of manuscripts; Charlene LaShea, Isabell Klein, and Mildred Hammond for general clerical assistance; Grace Holt and Stan Newman for critical commentary at various stages; and my wife, Alexandra Kochman, for all of the above, and moral support as well.

Thomas Kochman

Preface

Ideology, goals, and perspective

This book is an attempt to get beyond what Albert Murray has called the "fakelore of black pathology" and its corollary, the "folklore of white supremacy," and into what hopefully can be considered part of the texture of everyday experience for most urban black Americans.[1] To realize this aim, published articles were chosen and original articles solicited from researchers and writers whose observations and analyses clearly reflect an awareness of black cultural norms and whose value systems are uncontaminated with traditional notions of black "pathology."

The reason for insisting on these minimum prerequisites as the basis for selection is that black behavior, in the past, has typically been seen through white eyes and interpreted according to white norms; as a result the emergent perspective of black Americans has been tainted with notions of "deviancy" and "pathology," the inevitable consequence of ethnocentric reporting. The opening article by Stephen and Joan Baratz delineates the fundamental white assumptions and biases that have heretofore afflicted social science's and society's view of black culture to the ultimate detriment of black people; it also sets the stage for the following articles, which attempt to represent the "inside" view: black behavior as seen through black eyes, and interpreted according to black norms.

As the title suggests, this book specifically attempts to illuminate the communicative habits and expressive life-style of urban black Americans. In carrying out such a study we have asked ourselves the following basic question: What do adult urban black males and females see and value in various situations that makes a difference in the way they behave?

In our attempt to respond to that question we felt the need not only to describe specific communicative behavior but to reproduce as much as possible of the actual black community contexts in which such behavior occurs, so that those specific elements under study can be viewed and assessed with respect to their functions and the other significant variables of the situation (speaker, setting, audience, topic) that typically influence and account for what is going on.

Identifying these communication features in a way that would be viewed as educational to the unacculturated reader or representative and affirmative to the reader "in the know" became the essential task

[1] Albert Murray, *The Omni-Americans* (New York: Discuss, 1971), p. 143.

and challenge of putting this volume together. Practically, this has meant choosing and soliciting articles for their richly descriptive examples of persons and contexts and subsequently illustrating wherever possible the words of the writers with photographs, cartoon, and other descriptive media. If we have been successful in this respect, the reader should experience a sense of event: presence and action not often felt in a scholarly book. Yet, in addition to catering to the broader aesthetic sense of the reader, re-creating the structure of an event has the perhaps greater benefit of allowing him to observe and participate in the discovery process, as well as enabling him to evaluate the analyses and inferences that the writers have drawn from their material. Too often, in the past, the reader has been denied the empirical data from which a writer has drawn a conclusion. This effectively choked off the evaluative process that would have allowed him to validate or discredit the writer's claims. By being involved in the greater part of the ethnographic process, as in the present text, we would hope also to have enlarged the reader's understanding of it.

Insofar as we began this preface by expressing our concern for the perspective of black people which has emerged from past studies, we would be remiss if we did not show at the outset equal concern over the perspective that is likely to emerge from this collection of articles. That is to say, we are aware of the fact that, by virtue of the contexts that we have chosen—*street* (Horton, Cooke, Brown, Liebow, et al.), *church* (Holt, Powell-Williams), *clubhouse* (Labov, Kochman), *shoe-shine stand* (Maryland), *park* (Mitchell-Kernan), *pool hall* (Brookins), *cafe* (King), etc.—we have represented a kind of behavior significantly different from that which would have been represented had we chosen to study urban black Americans in mainstream interracial institutional contexts, such as the office or school. But this is only to recognize a few of the potent realities of our society. Power relations in communication contexts are expressed through patterns of accommodation; because of the power differential between blacks and whites in America up to now, and the calculated efforts to eradicate ethnicity and force all minority groups into the same "assimilationist" white Anglo-Saxon mold through the imposition of severe social penalties on those who would retain their "other" ethnic character, blacks and members of other minority groups have avoided the known risk of asserting their cultural norms in contexts governed by The Man. Consequently, the character of mainstream contexts is shaped and defined by dominant Anglo norms and is, therefore, not the place to look for ethnic definitions, black or otherwise.

In order to achieve the aim of this book, which is *to identify some of the communicative and behavioral norms of urban black Americans and (wherever possible) their source,* we have deliberately and consistently chosen to examine those contexts where the vernacular culture has been most pervasive and articulated and where mainstream cultural norms are likely to have penetrated *least*—where black people, in short, would feel relatively most free to be themselves. Thus we acknowledge at the outset that the picture represented here is one-sided, as any ethnic portrait in this country must invariably be, and admit that a study which would assess communication and expressive life-style within a range of *bicultural* contexts would be, for the majority of black Americans, a more complete reflection of the social and psychological reality that is their everyday experience.

Organization of the volume

In addition to the editor's preface and introductory essay the present volume consists of four sections, "Nonverbal Communication," "Vocabulary and Culture," "Expressive Uses of Language," and "Expressive Role Behavior," which are traditional subject areas within the disciplines of anthropology and linguistics; they have been typically taught in courses labeled "Language and Culture," "Language and Society," "Socio-Linguistics," "Ethnography of Communication," etc.

But the content in such courses has invariably reflected the global interests of those working in the above disciplines. One might find, in a typical text, "Speech Play and Verbal Art" explored with respect to Thais or Yokuts, or the relationship of vocabulary and culture examined with respect to the Hanunoo, but no text identifying these different areas with regard to the *same* cultural group[2]—with the result that a deeper and broader knowledge of the communicative competence of any specific group has generally been sacrificed, perhaps in part because linguists and anthropologists have felt that the demonstration of proper investigative procedures was primary and the resultant information to more thoroughly know a group was only secondary.

In at least these two respects, then, this volume reverses past patterns. First, the aforementioned subject areas have been investigated with respect to the *same* cultural group: urban black Americans. While still making this volume usable as a text in a language and culture course, this specialized focus should make it especially useful in a black language or studies course, for which it was designed. Second, the validation of the several ethnographic approaches used by our contributors will ultimately be determined by whether the knowledge of black people that these have produced is more complete and accurate than had been provided heretofore. It has seemed to us less important whether such information was acquired via the systematic social science route, through

[2] See, for example, the table of contents in the text often used in such courses: Dell Hymes, ed., *Language in Culture and Society* (New York: Harper and Row, 1964).

the prism of the writer-poet, or through a direct report of the "expert" cultural respondent, based upon his random experience. Our articles reflect the use of all of the above methodologies.

The articles were chosen to represent different aspects of verbal and nonverbal communication. John Horton's article was selected because it gave some insight into how time is structured on the "set," linked to a rhythm and flow of events quite distinct from the way it is structured in mainstream culture.

Benjamin Cooke's article deals with kinesic interaction among Afro-Americans within the urban scene, attempting through words and photographs to capture what optimally needs to be done with film.

Elkin Sithole's contribution, while also related to information-processing, should suggest in a larger sense literacy's limitations in capturing a "happening." It indicates the problems of trying to re-create an oral-event world through the aesthetically diminished world of the printed word. To illustrate this discrepancy, the first two pages, in which Sithole is demonstrating his native language of Zulu, taken verbatim from a tape of his presentation, are included; they should be to the reader visually meaningless.

In contrast to those in the Western compositional tradition who regard expression (performance, output) as entirely accounted for by the structures inherent in form (embodied meaning, competence, input), Keil, drawing from his work in "African and African derived [musical] genres," postulates that there is another aspect above and beyond syntax which needs to be examined (process, engendered feeling) to account for expression which has its roots in the dimension of performance and not in competence. Keil, operating within the jazz genre, attempts to identify the structure of this process with specific reference to the expressive performance style of rhythm performers—drummers and bassists.

Annette Powell Williams's article illustrates some selected physical movements within a black audience and indicates what they mean to the culture-wise. While admittedly brief, her report nevertheless represents a significant beginning in this important area of nonverbal communication.

The second section recognizes that vocabulary embodies and reflects the cultural perceptions and preoccupations of its speakers. The articles in one way or another reinforce this notion, whether they are consciously concerned with *race* (Johnson), *soulfulness* (Brown), *survival* and *power* (Holt), *names* and *being bad* (Kohl-Hinton), or less consciously with *movement, control,* and *contest* (Kochman). Yet, more than that, the articles identify ports of entry for terms in use within the black community, and, in some instances, what may be construed as sources of norms. For example, Dalby's documentations establish African languages as having made a much greater lexical contribution to past and present-day black and American English usage than was previously recognized or accredited. Holt and Johnson's articles clearly manifest the over-whelming and oppressive presence of The Man and the need to deflect or invert the hate labels and caste definitions built into his semantic-social system. Historically, the language of the oppressor has been a power that must be contended with if the black man is to "survive with dignity" (Holt).

If Dalby's article focuses on African sources for terms in black American usage, Kochman's article attempts to explain what keeps the terms alive, through linkage on the one hand to prestigious activities within the cultural field and on the other to values integrated into the cultural system itself.

The Kohl-Hinton text and photographs link names and graffiti to the urban street culture shared by blacks, Puerto Ricans, and other ethnic groups in urban centers throughout the country.

Claude Brown's "Language of Soul" recalls his own usage growing up in Harlem and makes the case for pronunciation ("Spoken Soul") as the essential element in black talk, all else being co-optable by the larger society.

The third section reflects various aspects of verbal art that are part of the black oral tradition. While drawing upon examples from the urban scene, the reader should not infer that its occurrence is restricted to that area. Rather, as the article by Abrahams from the Caribbean area is intended to show, verbal art is a pervasive Afro-American feature, ob-servable wherever black people congregate, appearing in a variety of expressive forms and serving variable functions.

Holt's article deals with preaching style in terms of the role and function of the preacher and the black church. As with many articles in this section, printed words fail to capture the full impact of the oral presentation. Minimally necessary would be a comparative sampler of the diverse preaching styles that exist in the black community. Short of being present at a sermon (or watching a film of it), hearing it is the next-best thing; reading it is only a last resort.

Yet the printed word, even when a substitute for the event itself, can conjure up vivid ideas of what is going on. In addition to Holt's striking portraits, Rap Brown gives a virtuoso sample of street-corner par-lance, as well as testimony for the attraction of street culture. James Maryland, who provided the rich example of "sigging" in the Kochman article, renders an equally descriptive account of a typical scene in a Chicago South Side shoe-shine stand. Abrahams, folklorist and ethnog-rapher, offers samples of "talking broad" from his recent field work in the Caribbean which not only enlarge the "man-of-words" concept but complement earlier published collections on toasts, boasts, jokes, etc., done in urban America.[3]

The Kochman, Labov, and Mitchell-Kernan articles provide a complex of sorts for this volume, since the reader can follow the different treatments of similar speech events from different urban areas in the three articles. One can also see how data drawn from different sources can enlarge concepts. For example, the category of signifying presented by Kochman, conceived essentially from work within the black male peer group, is significantly broadened by Mitchell-Kernan's work within female and mixed adult circles.

Labov's analysis of ritual insults is designed to test the thesis that discourse can only be fully comprehended in terms of the action which follows if underlying cultural propositions known to the participants are revealed. Why one kind of verbal insult will lead to a fight and another will not was the intriguing question that prompted Labov's inquiry and which his analysis attempts to answer.

Rodgers's categorization of certain aspects of black poetic expression is similar in many respects to the categorization of black speech events by Kochman and Mitchell-Kernan; it makes for an interesting comparison of function, motivation, objective, and overall aesthetic purpose.

The section on "Expressive Role Behavior" examines in greater detail the role attributes of the gang-banger and the hustler. Kaiser's two chapters from his book on the Vice Lords, incorporated here as a single piece, provide significant insights into the roles and ideologies of the street warrior, his responsibilities and obligations to himself, his group, and the code he subscribes to.

Ellis and Newman's contribution, the only comparative study in the volume, examines the image projected to outsiders by the black gowster and his white counterpart, the greaser. It offers a composite picture of their role in terms of their code and function in an urban setting.

Charles Keil has described the hustler as one of the "ideal types [along with the entertainer] representing two important value orientations for the lower-class Negro. . . ."[4] The suggestion that hustlers are among those black men who "wear their image in real comfort," and therefore provide logical career models for those who don't,[5] is certainly confirmed implicitly in Brookins's portrayal of Big Time in "Aspiration" and King's portrait of Sweet Mac in "The Game," as well as in the widespread reception the black community accorded Ice-

[3] See Roger D. Abrahams, *Deep Down in the Jungle,* rev. ed. (Chicago: Aldine, 1970).

[4] Charles Keil, *Urban Blues* (Chicago: University of Chicago Press, 1966), p. 20.

[5] Ibid.

berg Slim's autobiography, *Pimp,* and its sequel, *Trick Baby.* The two short stories and the foreword to *Pimp* are included here to reflect this value orientation, as is Liebow's "Lovers and Exploiters" chapter from *Tally's Corner,* as ethnographic confirmation of the influence of the hustler's (specifically, the pimp's) norms on the masculine code shared by his black male street-corner respondents—evidenced, if not so much by their *actual* exploitation of women, in their *verbalizations* "on the corner" of this exploitation.

If the projective image of the hustler is what attracts others, then what contributes to his sense of comfort is worth examining. According to the inside perspective provided by Hudson, the hustler's comfortable self-image is due largely to his regarding himself as successful in beating the system which, through the promotion of the "work ideology," was designed to keep him and other black people poor, powerless, and subservient. If this could be regarded as one of the hustler's basic satisfactions (and perhaps one of his basic motivations as well), then we can see the extent to which role definitions within the community are shaped and influenced by socioeconomic pressures originating outside the community. Ultimately, before any definitive statement of black cultural norms can be made, it is necessary to distinguish the aspects of black life-style which are adaptations to outside (colonial) pressures and those which are manifestations of inner (cultural) forces. While not directly concerned with making that distinction in this volume, much of the communicative behavior represented here—hustling on the one hand, verbal art on the other—will undoubtedly suggest a placement within one category or the other.

All of the articles in this volume view black verbal and nonverbal behavior within the community setting, not only because we feel that the natural context is the only valid situational frame from which one can make accurate descriptive statements about cultural behavior, but also because it is only with reference to the context and the code that we can begin to identify the significant situational and cultural features that are normative with respect to people's actions.

Rappin'
and
stylin' out

■ Black culture on black terms: a rejection of the social pathology model

JOAN AND STEPHEN BARATZ

Joan Baratz is project director of the Education Study Center in Washington, D.C. She was formerly on the staff of the Center for Applied Linguistics and served as an assistant professor at the University of Maryland. She is co-editor, with R. Shuy, of *Teaching Black Children to Read* (1969).

Stephen Baratz is staff associate in the Division of Behavioral Sciences of the National Academy of Sciences. Formerly an executive secretary of the Center for Study of Metropolitan Problems at the National Institute of Mental Health and assistant professor at Howard University, he is concerned with social science and government policy, urban ethnography, and black culture.

This article delineates the fundamental "white" assumptions and biases that have up until now afflicted social science's and society's view of black culture, to the ultimate distress and detriment of black people. As Albert Murray has indicated, a "fakelore of black pathology" easily becomes translated to a "folklore of white supremacy." Within such a translation process,

different behavior (black) becomes *deviant* behavior (black), and, as everyone knows, "deviant" behavior is *pathological,* worse than *inferior: illegitimate!* As such, "deviant" behavior needs to be "normalized" ("white is right") and its "causes" eradicated. Just from the seeds of such characterizations and definitions did the "assimilationist" social and educational policy toward blacks and other ethnic minorities develop. In pointing up how social science research and practice contributed to and sustained these fundamentally racist notions, the Baratz's introductory article formally acknowledges the past, *in order that we may repudiate it,* and present to the public through the articles that follow a view of black culture untainted by notions of white supremacy.

This paper, originally titled "The Social Pathology Model: Historical Bases for Psychology's Denial of the Existence of Negro Culture," was delivered at a meeting of the APA in 1969 in Washington, D.C.

Introduction

This paper is one of a series by the authors seeking to portray the ethnocentrism of the social sciences in studies dealing with the Afro-American. It is a modest attempt to reorient the current demand for relevance in our profession back to the assumptive bases of social science, to the work we do, and to the social policy that is suggested by that work.

We will not suggest here that our prime responsibility as social scientists is to direct social action, but that social science's pressing task is to critically reexamine and reevaluate our scholarly work. We leave the responsibility of social action to individuals. We will concentrate the present discussion on the need for an extensive reevaluation of how social science has and has not dealt with black behavior and culture. The goal is to produce a revolution of ideas, rather than to attempt a revolution of direct action which fails because it is based on old and tired ideas. We believe that a revolution of ideas is a more potent force for the production of social change by social scientists than any other mode of intervention currently available to us. It is an infinitesimal beginning of the much-discussed, but little-thought-through, New Social Science.

We choose to concentrate on the bases for denial of black culture, for we feel that ignorance of this culture has produced a much more distorted and inaccurate view of the Afro-American than most of us would have previously supposed. We believe that the absence of a meaningful conception of black culture has forced the interpretation of almost all psychology's data on the Afro-American into two seemingly dichotomous categories: either that of biological incapacity (genetic inferiority) or social deviance and pathology (environmental deprivation).

We have offered elsewhere[1] a third category based upon the culture of the Afro-American in the United States (cultural difference), and we seek in the present paper to explore the reasons why psychology has never given credence to this concept as a device for hypothesis development and research design.

Briefly stated, the cultural-difference theory asserts that the statistical differences noted by psychologists in intelligence testing, in family and social organization, and in attitude studies of the black community are not the result of pathology, faulty learning, or genetic inferiority. These differences are surface manifestations of the viable, structured culture of the Afro-American—a culture which is a synthesis of African culture in contact with American-European culture under slavery. Such a model does not postulate that the existence of a distinct culture precludes the addition of other cultures. Biculturalism is indeed possible, as is bilingualism. However, it *does* insist that acquisition of new cultural patterns cannot occur without recognition and respect for existing cultural patterns.

Social science and black culture

Although the psychologist has long recognized that behavior is essentially the result of biological, sociological, and cultural factors, there is

---

[1] S. Baratz and J. C. Baratz, "Urban Education: A Cultural Solution," *The Bulletin of the Minnesota Council for the Social Studies,* Fall, 1968, pp. 1–4.

little mention of black culture as an explanation of black behavior except when "culture" is used in a distorted and negative sense. Thus the culture of poverty becomes the focus, rather than black ethnicity. Despite the fact that black behavior has its roots in an African, non-European tradition, social scientists have persisted in viewing Afro-Americans as black Europeans. Why is it that social scientists have failed to recognize a distinct black culture? This failure derives predominantly from four sources:

1. the basic ethnocentrism of social science;
2. the socio-political myths surrounding our conception of assimilation;
3. ignorance concerning the fundamental notion of culture; and
4. embarrassment of the black middle-class and while liberals about dealing with culturally rooted behavioral differences.

The basic ethnocentrism of social science

Since the fundamental social science model is normative, it sets up a criterion of behavior against which individuals and groups are measured. The ethnocentrism stems from the fact that behavioral scientists often attempt to assess behavior using a criterion assumed to be universal to our society, when in fact that criterion is merely one cultural manifestation of the universal human behavior.

The social science literature concerning the language behavior of blacks is a case in point. Social scientists are correct in assuming that language is a universal human characteristic. Linguists have yet to find a human society—no matter how nontechnological, no matter how poor and impoverished—whose inhabitants did not use a highly structured, well-formed grammatical system for communication. It is taken as axiomatic by linguists that all humans develop language (except in those rare individual cases where severe physical and/or psychological traumas occur). Linguists have also learned that, within a large, complex society where individuals from different social classes and different ethnicities live in close proximity, they often speak many varieties (dialects) of the same language. One of these dialects may be considered socially more prestigious than the others; thus it may be used as the standard for the nation. Although one dialect may be chosen as the standard language, it is important to realize that this is an arbitrary (or, at most, social) decision which has nothing to do with that particular dialect's linguistic merits. That is to say, the dialect chosen as standard is no more highly structured, well-formed, or grammatical than any of the other dialects. The evolution of a particular dialect as the standard is due to sociopolitical considerations rather than to intrinsic linguistic superiority. Some social scientists, however, have failed to consider the existence of these language variations and have thus mistakenly equated a single surface manifestation of the universal behavior (that is, the development of the standard dialect) with the universal itself (that is, the development of language). Social scientists' refusal to grant legitimacy to black dialect is a clear-cut example of the discipline's ethnocentrism. At present, we find an entire body of psychological literature, for example, which alleges to assess the language development of black children but nevertheless uses as a criterion for language development the acquisition of standard English—a dialect of the English language that the majority of the black children in this country are *not* developing as their native dialect.[2] Since these psychologists use standard English as the criterion, they wrongly view the child's linguistic system as underdeveloped and filled with errors. He becomes, in the psychological research, verbally defective and conceptually impaired. Such research fails to recognize that the child has a system which is fully developed and highly structured, but different grammatically from that of the standard English criterion.[3]

The language system is but one instance of social scientists' ethnocentrism in dealing with black behavior. One can find and document similar instances in the social science literature dealing with family patterns, interaction styles, belief systems, and test construction.

From social science's ethnocentric position, and without an adequate conception of black culture, the profession has tended to view behavioral differences such as nonstandard black English not as signs of a different cultural system but as defects and deviances from our falsely hypothesized pan-cultural norm. A culture-of-poverty model is not appropriate here because differences observed in such a model are always interpreted *not* as legitimate manifestations of a viable culture, but as an unfortunate pathological reaction to being poor. The culture-of-poverty concept as an insufficient interpretation for linguistic data has been adequately dealt with by Stewart.[4]

In his criticism of the culture-of-poverty model Stewart illustrates that this model cannot deal with the linguistic fact that structurally dif-

[2] C. Deutsch, "Auditory Discrimination and Learning: Social Factors," *Merrill-Palmer Quarterly* 10 (1964): 277–96; V. John, "The Intellectual Development of Slum Children," *American Journal of Orthopsychiatry* 33 (1963): 813–22; C. Stern, "Systematic Instruction of Economically Disadvantaged Children in Pre-reading Skills," U.C.L.A. Research Projects in Early Childhood Learning, unpublished paper; C. Hurst, Jr., *Psychological Correlates in Dialectolalia*, Cooperative Research Project #2610, Communication Sciences Research Center, Howard University, 1965.

[3] J. C. Baratz, "Language and Cognitive Assessment of Negro Children: Assumptions and Research Needs, *ASHA* 11, no. 3 (1969): 87–91.

[4] W. A. Stewart, "On the Use of Negro Dialect in the Teaching of Reading," in J. Baratz and R. Shuy, *Teaching Black Children to Read* (Washington: Center for Applied Linguistics, 1969).

ferent linguistic systems are found among different ethnic groups which are supposedly exposed to the same poverty culture.

The ethnocentrism in social science which sets up norms and declares differences from those norms to be deviances, and which tends to confuse unique manifestations of a universal behavior for the universal itself, is not, however, the only reason why social scientists have tended to ignore the contribution of black culture to the understanding of black behavior.

The sociopolitical myths surrounding our concepts of cultural assimilation

Three particular American sociopolitical beliefs have contributed greatly to the social scientist's denial of the black culture (and, indeed, the culture of other white ethnic groups). The first involves the melting-pot myth and a confusion over the concept of egalitarianism; the second concerns the fact that it was the racists, with their theory of genetic inferiority, who used culturally rooted behavioral differences to support their erroneous theory; the third involves the distortions of black cultural history under slavery which gave rise to what Herskovits so aptly described as the "myth of the Negro past."

The melting-pot myth and the confusion over the concept of egalitarianism. The basic doctrine that all men are created equal has been misinterpreted by egalitarians to read "all men are created equal if they behave in the same manner." This confusion of egalitarianism with behavioral and cultural conformity has been supported by one of the basic components of the American dream—the melting-pot myth. According to this myth, America is the melting pot where peoples from diverse cultures came together and created the American culture which is distinct from the individual cultures that contributed to it. American society, then, according to the melting-pot analogy, is the result of the elimination of the impurities, along with the blending of the best elements of those diverse cultures.

It is interesting to note that until recently there has been little discussion of the contribution of African culture to the American mainstream. This is no doubt due to the supposition on the one hand that Afro-Americans had no culture, and the assumption on the other hand that the different behaviors which they exhibited constituted the greatest of the impurities which the melting pot would eliminate. As a result, those aspects of the mainstream system which blacks share with whites have assumedly been derived from white behavior, rather than resulting from the African contribution to the melting pot. The white Southerner is particularly proud of his "southern hospitality." But Herskovits has noted that certain aspects of polite behavior in the South appear to have no antecedent in European cultures, while they *can* be traced to African patterns of interaction.[5] Again, West African specialist Dalby has pointed out that "uh huh" and "uh uh," formerly assumed to be the result of the typical informal American way, actually appear to be derived from several African languages where "uh huh" is the word for "yes" and "uh uh" is the word for "no."[6] (The verbal-conditioning researchers have yet to acknowledge this contribution!)

The melting-pot myth not only assumed a distinct American culture derived from but not retaining various ethnic styles; it also presumed that the acculturation to the American way occurred by virtue of one's mere residence on American soil. That is, any second-generation American automatically became acculturated into the mainstream of American society. From this a peculiar logic evolved which assumed that to speak of the retention of ethnic differences in behavior was to be "un-American" insofar as any such discussion would contradict the American dream. In addition, it would indicate that the impurities of one's distinct ethnic identity could not be eliminated simply by living in America, the melting pot. This faulty (but nonetheless prevalent) logic postulates that (1) since America is indeed the melting pot, and (2) since the melting pot eliminates all cultural impurities, then (3) the residue of distinct ethnic behavior retained over several generations of living in America must represent the genetic element of behavior. Since the Afro-American has been in this country since the early seventeenth century, this poor logic concludes that to say he behaves differently from whites due to cultural retention of African patterns is comparable to calling him genetically inferior.

This faulty logic, coupled with the fact that racists used the behavioral differences which they observed between blacks and whites to "prove" the innate inferiority of Afro-Americans and to justify slavery, has made it extremely uncomfortable for social scientists to give credence to and explore the behavioral differences between ethnic groups. The difficulty here is that, in rejecting the racists' theory about black behavior, the social scientist also rejected the behavior itself. It is the general thesis of the cultural-difference model that the *intolerance* of ethnic behavioral differences, not their *existence,* is what constitutes racism.[7]

Racist descriptions of black behavior and their interpretation of that behavior. The genetic racists lived for the most part in close proximity

[5] M. J. Herskovits, *The Myth of the Negro Past* (New York: Harper, 1941).
[6] See Dalby article in this volume.
[7] S. Baratz and J. C. Baratz, "Early Childhood Intervention: The Social Science Base of Institutional Racism," *Harvard Educational Review* 40, no. 1 (Winter, 1970): 29–50.

with the black community; they had ample opportunity to study and describe black behavior. The behavior described by the racists was not contrived by perverse minds. The bigot did not have to invent his data —it was there; it abounds. Many Afro-Americans, for example, *do* roll their eyes, perform a little dance when they laugh, speak a distinct dialect, establish extended-family kinship systems, and dress differently. What the bigot did, because he (like today's social scientists) was unaware of the role of culture in determining behavior, was to invent a theory of racial inferiority to explain the differences. Thus Ambrose Gonzales, a white racist and a fluent speaker of the black Creole dialect, Gullah, wrote black folktales down in grammatically accurate Gullah but then erroneously described blacks who spoke this Creolized dialect as using "slovenly and careless speech."[8] In spite of his accurate recording of the dialect he concluded, because of his naïveté about language and his need to explain the differences, that the grammatical differences he observed between standard English and Gullah were due to the "characteristic laziness" of the Negro rather than to the existence of the distinct grammatical system he so aptly recorded.

We have pointed out elsewhere[9] that the pathology-riddled conceptualization of black dialect as given by the racists (despite their accurate recording of that dialect) agrees in many ways with the conceptualization of that language given by contemporary egalitarian psychologists such as Hunt and Deutsch[10]—only the explanation of how he got that way (substitute "inadequate mothering" for "characteristic laziness") is different. One may, therefore, accept the accuracy of the dialect recording (the raw data) but not accept the explanation and conceptualization of that data.

But even when this is done and the existence of these differences is acknowledged, some social scientists have protested the overriding preoccupation of the difference theory with the description of cultural differences. They assert that too much time is spent describing the differences between blacks and whites rather than focusing on their similarities. To this we must clearly assert, as Hannerz and Erickson already have,[11] that it is precisely the differences in cultural behavior that interfere

[8] A. Gonzales, *The Black Border: Gullah Stories of the Carolina Coast* (Columbia, S. C.: State Publishing Co., 1922), p. 10.

[9] Baratz and Baratz, "Early Childhood Intervention."

[10] J. McV. Hunt, "Toward the Prevention of Incompetence," in J. W. Carter, ed., *Research Contributions from Psychology to Community Mental Health* (New York: Behavioral Publications, 1968), pp. 19–45; M. Deutsch, "The Role of Social Class in Language Development and Cognition," *American Journal of Orthopsychiatry* 35 (1965): 78–88.

[11] Ulf Hannerz, *Soulside: Inquiries into Ghetto Culture and Community* (New York: Columbia University Press, 1969); F. D. Erickson, personal communication, 1969.

with the development of true biculturalism in the Afro-American. Further, it is the misreading and misunderstanding of those differences which interfere in our everyday interactions with Afro-Americans and which communicate to the black man our basic ethnocentrism and racism.

Nonetheless, perhaps the social scientist's tendency to dismiss the racist's data was not simply because it was tied to an abhorrent theory of genetic inferiority but, more important, because social science had not developed the methodologies to describe culturally different micro-behaviors and to assess the effect of those microbehaviors on interpersonal contacts. Thus social science could only equate observation of the culturally different behaviors described by the racists with stereotyped expression of prejudice. While it cannot be denied that use of the term "prejudice" is appropriate in this instance, since the interpretation of the behaviors by the racist led to a conception of inferiority, it is interesting to note that the negative concept "stereotype" is the only way that social science has developed to deal with culturally linked microbehaviors. These behaviors are very important, for they are learned early in the child's life and are often out of awareness and most subtle. They appear to be strong evidence for the ethnic identification of the New World Afro-American with his African brother.

The myth of the Negro past. The acceptance of the melting-pot myth and the rejection of the genetic inferiority myth are not the only reasons for social science's failure to recognize and discuss behavioral differences between whites and blacks (and indeed, differences among the various white ethnic groups that constitute American mainstream society). There is one other prevalent American myth which has allowed the behavioral sciences to ignore the role of culture in maintaining distinctive black behavioral patterns; Herskovits has aptly labeled this the "myth of the Negro past." Briefly stated, the myth of the Negro past asserts that the naïveté of social scientists concerning the processes of acculturation has led them to assume that the black man lost all of his characteristic African behaviors merely because he was forcibly removed from Africa and resided on American soil for several generations in slavery. Such a myth invariably leads to explaining black behavior as pathological and due to oppression; the myth can only be perpetuated in the absence of significant inputs from ethnohistorians and microbehaviorists.

Ignorance concerning the fundamental notion of culture

It is this myth of the Negro past coupled with ignorance concerning the cultural process which led Glazer and Moynihan naïvely to assert that "the Negro is only an American and nothing else. He has no values and culture to guard and protect."[12] Because the psychologist and the sociologist did not understand the acculturative process whereby a distinct cultural form becomes transmuted, they assumed, for example, that since Afro-Americans no longer spoke African languages, no longer used African ritual in marriage ceremonies, and no longer wore African dress, they therefore retained no cultural distinctiveness. This assumption left social scientists with no other alternative than to wrongly describe the Creolized black dialect used by the Afro-American as "poorly learned English," the matrifocal family unit so prevalent in lower-class black society as "evidence of male emasculation," the extended kinship systems as "disorganized families," and the clothing choices as "poor taste."

While Afro-Americans are not native speakers of the African languages of their forebears, it is nonetheless true that the dialect of English which many blacks speak includes forms that are substantially similar in structure to the African languages of their ancestors.[13]

As Hannerz has pointed out in regard to interpreting family forms of black Americans, "while specific marriages were broken up [by enslavement] the conscious models of and for marriage could well remain and influence the form of union adopted under new circumstances [during slavery]." Adaptation of new forms is always influenced by existing forms; it does not occur in a "cultural vacuum."

Perhaps the best example of how existing cultural patterns effect the adaptation of new forms comes from examining how Afro-American culture in the United States has dealt with efforts to infuse African styles into the Creolized culture. The "black is beautiful" emphasis in black rhetoric has not simply transferred African hairstyles to the Afro-American community; rather, it has modified them in accordance with certain distinctively New World Afro-American cultural values: namely, that the female should have longer hair than the male. Thus one finds the adaptation of the African bush by Afro-American girls—but with the Americanized aspect of having large, "long hair" bushes as opposed to the typical close-cut bushes of African women. Again, we find that Afro-American women, rather than taking up the dress styles of African women, have instead modified the African male costume—the dashiki— to suit American female dressing patterns. The addition of wire-rimmed glasses and turtlenecks only add to the phenomena described.

It is important for social scientists to understand some basic anthropological concepts in terms of dealing with distinct cultures and the acculturative process. A fundamental anthropological concept is that of

[12] N. Glazer and D. P. Moynihan, *Beyond the Melting Pot* (Cambridge: The MIT Press and Harvard University Press, 1963).

[13] W. A. Stewart, "Continuity and Change in American Negro Dialect," *Florida Language Report* 7 (1968): 1ff.

cultural relativity. The anthropologist approaches his description of cultural differences within a framework of linear rather than hierarchical perspectives. Matrifocal, patrifocal, monogamous, and polygamous societies are merely evidences of the various social structures that groups evolve. One is intrinsically no more valuable a structural ordering than the next.

In addition, as Herskovits and Bascom have pointed out:

> [It is culture rather than social institution that] distinguishes man from the rest of the biological world. Other animals, and insects as well, have societies, but only man uses language, manufactures tools, and possesses art, religion and other aspects of culture. The concern with culture, rather than with society and social institutions thus emphasizes the specifically human elements of man's behavior.
>
> Culture varies from group to group and from one period of time to another within any single group. From this follows a principle of fundamental scientific importance and of equal practical significance: what has been learned can be modified through further learning; habits, customs, beliefs, social structures, and institutions can change.[14]

A perspective that views distinct Afro-American behavioral patterns through this type of cultural framework recognizes that those patterns existing today are not merely the result of oppression but the product of the interaction of distinctly African cultures with the slavery and post-emancipation American society. In fact, perhaps the very strengths of the African culture allowed for successful adaptation and survival of the African under slavery both in Africa and in the New World.

Social scientists have not only been ignorant of the fundamental notion of culture difference as used by anthropologists; they have also confounded the issue by adding a notion of cultural difference which has little relation to that of the anthropologist. Thus, for example, statistically significant differences on standardized tasks between blacks and whites are what most psychologists assume to be cultural differences. But the uniformly lower scores of black children on IQ tests are not cultural differences in the anthropological sense. These scores when viewed by anthropologists are merely a manifestation of actual cultural differences—the dialect, rhetorical style, epistemology, and response styles of the distinctive black culture.

For the social scientist the difference is in terms of his alleged universalistic norm. For the anthropologist the difference is tied to the varying ways in which man has chosen to define his world. As we have

---

[14] M. J. Herskovits and W. R. Bascom, "The Problem of Stability and Change in African Culture," in Bascom and Herskovits, eds., *Continuity and Change in African Cultures* (Chicago: University of Chicago Press, 1959), pp. 1, 2.

indicated elsewhere,[15] IQ scores of black children when viewed within an anthropological framework actually indicate the degree to which they have bought into, or learned, the mainstream culture; they do not indicate the potential of black children for buying into the system, as is the interpretation given to such scores by the psychologist.

Thus, from the perspective advanced here, IQ tests as presently formulated are inadequate measures of black intellectual potential since they are not culture specific. Construction of culture-specific tests of IQ is not an extraordinary task for psychologists. The Binet test originally in French was translated into standard English and modified in accordance with the mainstream American culture. The resulting Stanford-Binet was then retranslated for language and culture differences for use in England. Why, then, do we not have such a translation for use with Afro-Americans? It is the absence of a meaningful conception of black culture, and, as Dillard has pointed out, it is the assumption that Afro-Americans speak defective English rather than a distinctive dialect which has led most psychologists to assume that IQ tests such as the Stanford-Binet could be used on black populations without fear of marked cultural bias.[16] Such a translation is urgently needed and is indeed a priority item for the New Social Science.

Embarrassment of the black middle-class and white liberals about dealing with behavioral differences

The ready availability of a deficit model and its half-sister the culture of poverty model, the belief in certain of the sociopolitical myths of the country, and a naïve view of culture were not the only reasons that social scientists used for not dealing with behavioral differences. There has been a "politeness conspiracy" about not talking of behavioral differences even when they are most apparent. Since these differences have been viewed as pejorative and deviant by most social scientists, to discuss them in great detail was assumed to be rude and tantamount to discussing a hunchback's hump with him.

Another more pressing reason why both middle-class blacks and liberal whites have been reluctant to discuss these differences is fear that such discussions will be used maliciously by racists to support their theories of black inferiority. The difficulty here is twofold: (1) not talking about the differences does nothing to make them disappear, and (2) not recognizing the distinctive behaviors within a cultural model leaves the liberal with only one alternative: that of calling the Afro-

[15] S. Baratz, "Social Science Conceptualization of the Afro-American," in J. Szwed, ed., *Black America* (New York: Basic Books, 1970), pp. 55–56.
[16] J. L. Dillard, *Black English in the United States* (New York: Random House, in press).

American a sick white man—sick in the social rather than genetic sense.

It is precisely this latter train of thought that the black militants use when discussing the racism in social science. We have elsewhere indicated the legitimacy of the claim of ethnocentrism of the social sciences by blacks;[17] however, black rhetoricians' demands that white social scientists no longer do research on the Afro-American is not an adequate solution to the problem. We make this assertion because the absence of anthropologists' insightful views of the ghetto and the overriding deficit orientation of previous research have coincided with the extreme demands of identity denial in the process of integration. These factors in combination have often produced professional black social scientists who have little conception of black culture outside the culture-of-poverty model. Integration, as built into our society and conceptualized by the psychological contact hypothesis of Allport, Pettigrew, and Cook,[18] demands denial of most distinctively black behaviors in order to succeed in the white society. Those blacks who have made it, who have learned to censure distinctive cultural behaviors as the price of integration, have had a stake in disaffiliating themselves from the culture and in denying the legitimacy of these very obvious culturally related behaviors. Indeed, the price of integration for the upward-mobile black man has been continuous tension and anxiety lest distinctively black behavior seep through. The circle here is closed once one realizes that most current black rhetoricians in the social sciences are seeking ways of regaining affiliations with the community which they themselves rejected as a result of this process. Further, one must recognize that this attempt is no small task, for the professional skills that blacks have to offer their brothers are often no more than those characteristic of the deficit model. One need only examine Cobb and Grier's *Black Rage* or Green's comments on black dialect to realize how easy it is for even the most angry militants to fall into the trap of the deficit model.

In a frank and open admission Green, co-chairman of the Association of Black Psychologists, indicates his frustrating work with youngsters in Oakland: "I found that much of the slang terminology was rather incomprehensible to me."[19] It is quite clear that Green saw the dialect system not as a well-structured and lawful system but as an inadequate and substandard form of standard English very much like that described by Martin Deutsch and Vera John:

17 S. Baratz, "Social Science Strategies."

18 G. W. Allport, *The Nature of Prejudice* (Reading, Mass.: Addison-Wesley, 1954); T. Pettigrew, *A Profile of the Negro American* (Princeton, N.J.: Van Nostrand, 1964); S. W. Cook, "Desegregation: A Psychological Analysis," *American Psychiatrist* 12 (1957): 1–13.

19 R. Green, "Dialect Sampling and Language Values," in R. Shuy, ed., *Social Dialects and Language Learning* (Champaign, Ill.: National Council of Teachers of English, 1964), pp. 120–23.

The very inadequate speech that is used in the home is also used in the neighborhood, in the play group, and in the classroom. Since these poor English patterns are reconstructed constantly by the associations that these young people have, the school has to play a strong role in bringing about a change in order that these young people can communicate more adequately in our society.[20]

The middle-class black man, no less than others, has been concerned with stereotypes and not with cultural differences. He has been the one at the cultural crossroads who has borne the brunt of white misreading of black behavior; it is he who has the identity crisis in the black community. Taking all of the above together it is no wonder that discussions of the existence of black cultural differences (such as black dialect) will meet with suspicion of racism, and denial of its existence, and an insistence on its pathology by most middle-class blacks. But one must bear in mind that it is only with the recognition of a culturally different system that we can hope for biculturalism in which the Afro-American can learn the white cultural system without having to reject his own system—and, in so doing, himself. In recognizing a distinct cultural system, we also realize how much whites can learn from black culture. Biculturalism is a two-way street.

The new social science

What, then, is the New Social Science as applied to questions of racism and the problems of Afro-Americans in our society? Our model has been the reevaluation of most research dealing with Afro-Americans in terms of the possibility of intrusion of an ethnocentric bias into data-gathering and interpretation. The model rests on a need for greater description of black cultural and linguistic phenomena and a determination of the adequacy of fit—call it confrontation, if you will—of the existing body of experimental data with these findings. The model also rests on a definition of racism not previously advanced: that is, racism is the denial and/or denigration of cultural differences. Institutional racism, therefore, is the degree to which social policy is based upon social science studies which deny those differences.

We feel strongly that this reevaluation of social science will provide the base for new and different research in the future. We also feel that if social science is to be truly relevant it must begin to understand that it shares responsibility for white racism in this country in a most profound way. The way to correct this previous unconscionable direction of our thinking is not to stop all research, but once and for all to admit the legitimacy of a cultural system too long demeaned and obscured by ethnocentrism. Our call, therefore, is not for less but for more research

[20] Ibid., p. 123.

which will not only produce a better understanding of black culture but above all a better understanding of the process whereby a seemingly value-free methodology could produce gross distortions of the very subject-matter of the methodology. Only when we have understood the culture of the Afro-American can we be in the position to suggest to society and its policy-makers solutions to our current pressing concerns.

Nonverbal communication

■ Time and cool people

JOHN HORTON

John Horton is an associate professor of sociology at the University of California, Los Angeles. His major research interests and publications have been in the sociology of knowledge and expressive behavior and in the sociology of social problems. His current research focuses on ideological interpretation (class, racial, and sexual biases) of social problems in contemporary social science.

Fundamental to the understanding of any group is knowledge of how that group structures time and space. To those outside the group, a different time or space orientation often appears bizarre simply because the outsider doesn't understand the different set of cultural rules regulating and directing the behavior of the insider. In this article, originally published in *Transaction* in April, 1967, Horton explores the meaning of time with reference to the life style and experience of members of a group constituting "the sporadically unemployed young Negro street-corner population," referred to throughout the article as the "set." In contrast to the middle-class "outside" view, which has typically stereotyped this group as having "an irrational present sense of time," Horton, from his vantage-point as participant-observer in set activities, characterizes the perspective of time within this group as being consistent, rational, and logical—in short, consonant with their involvement in the rhythm and flow of events that make up their world.

Time in industrial society is clock time. It seems to be an external, objective regulator of human activities. But for the sociologist time is not an object existing independent of man, dividing his day into precise units. Time is diverse; it is always social and subjective. A man's sense of time derives from his place in the social structure and his lived experience.

The diversity of time perspectives can be understood intellectually, but it is rarely tolerated socially. A dominant group reifies and objectifies its time; it views all other conceptions of time as subversive—as indeed they are.

Thus, today in the dominant middle-class stereotype, standard American time is directed toward the future; it is rational and impersonal. In contrast, time for the lower class is directed toward the present, irrational and personal. Peasants, Mexican-Americans, Negroes, Indians, workers are "lazy"; they do not possess the American virtues of ambition and striving for success. Viewed solely from the dominant-class norm of rationality, their presumed orientation to present time is seen only as an irrational deviation, something to be controlled and changed. It is at best an epiphenomenon produced in reaction to the "real, objective" phenomenon of middle-class time.

Sociologists have not been completely exempt from this kind of rei-fied thinking. When they universalize the middle-class value of rational action and future time and turn it into a "neutral" social fact, they rein-force a negative stereotype: lower classes are undependable in organized work situations (they seek immediate rewards and cannot defer gratifi-cation); in their political action, they are prone to accept immediate, violent, and extreme solutions to personal problems; their sense of time is dysfunctional to the stability of the economic and political orders. For example, Seymour Martin Lipset writes in a paper significantly entitled "Working Class Authoritarianism": "This emphasis on the immediately perceivable and concern with the personal and concrete is part and parcel of the short time perspective and the inability to perceive the complex possibilities and consequences of action which often results in a general readiness to support extremist political and religious move-ments, and generally lower level of liberalism on noneconomic questions."

To examine time in relation to the maintenance or destruction of the dominant social order is an interesting political problem, but it is not a sociology of time; it is a middle-class sociology of order or change in its time aspect. Surely a meaningful sociology of time should take into account the social situation in which time operates and the actor's as well as the observer's perspective. The sociologist must at least enter-tain the idea that lower-class time may be a phenomenon in and of itself, quite functional to the life problems of that class.

Of course, there are dangers in seeking the viewpoint of a minority; the majority stereotypes might be reversed. For example, we might find out that no stereotype is more incorrect than that which depicts the lower classes as having no sense of future time. As Max Weber has observed, it is the powerful and not the powerless who are present-oriented. Dominant groups live by maintaining and expanding their present. Minority groups survive in this present, but their survival is nourished by a dream of the future. In "Ethnic Segregation and Caste" Weber says:

> The sense of dignity that characterizes positively privileged status groups is natural to their "being" which does not transcend itself, that is, to their beauty and excellence. Their kingdom is of this world. They live for the present by exploiting the great past. The sense of dignity of the nega-tively privileged strata naturally refers to a future lying beyond the pres-ent whether it is of this life or another. In other words it must be nur-tured by a belief in a providential "mission" and by a belief in a specific honor before God.

It is time to reexamine the meaning of time, the reality of the middle-class stereotype of itself, as well as the middle-class stereotype of the lower class. In this article, I explore the latter: the meaning of time among a group most often stereotyped as having an irrational, present sense of time—the sporadically unemployed young Negro street-corner population. I choose the unemployed because they live outside the constraints of industrial work-time; Negroes because they speak some of the liveliest street language, including that of time; young males because the street culture of the unemployed and the hustler is young and masculine.

To understand the meaning of street time was to discover "what's happening" in the day-to-day and week-to-week activities of my respondents. Using the middle-class stereotype of lower-class time as a point of departure, I asked myself the following questions: In what sense is street time personal (not run by the clock) and present oriented? What kind of future orientation, if any, exists? Are street activities really irrational in the sense that individuals do not use time efficiently in the business of living? I have attempted to answer the questions in the language and from the experience of my respondents.

Street culture exists in every low-income ghetto. It is shared by the hustling elements of the poor, whatever their nationality or color. In Los Angeles, members of such street groups sometimes call themselves "street people," "cool people," or simply "regulars." Whatever the label, they are known the world over by outsiders as hoods or hoodlums, persons who live on and off the street. They are recognizable by their own fashions in dress, hair, gestures, and speech. The particular fashion varies with time, place, and nationality. For example, in 1963 a really sharp Los Angeles street Negro would be "conked to the bone" (have processed hair) and "togged-out" in "continentals." Today "natural" hair and variations of mod clothes are coming in style.

Street people are known also by their activities—"duking" (fighting or at least looking tough), "hustling" (any way of making money outside the "legitimate" world of work), "gigging" (partying)—and by their apparent nonactivity, "hanging" on the corner. Their individual roles are defined concretely by their success or failure in these activities. One either knows what's happening on the street, or he is a "lame," "out of it," "not ready" (lacks his diploma in street knowledge), a "square."

There are, of course, many variations. Negroes, in particular, have contributed much to the street tongue which has diffused into both the more hip areas of the middle class and the broader society. Such expressions as "a lame," "taking care of righteous business," "getting down to the nitty-gritty," and "soul" can be retraced to Negro street life.

The more or less organized center of street life is the "set"—meaning both the peer group and the places where it hangs out. It is the stage and central marketplace for activity, where to find out what's happening. My set of Negro street types contained a revolving and sometimes disappearing (when the "heat," or police pressure, was on) population of about forty-five members ranging in age from eighteen to twenty-five. These were the local "dudes"—their term meaning not the fancy city slickers but simply "the boys," "fellas," "cool people." They represented the hard core of street culture, the role models for younger teenagers. The dudes could be found when they were "laying dead"—hanging on the corner, or shooting pool and "jiving" ("goofing" or kidding around) in a local community project. Isolated from The Man (in this context the man in power—the police, and by extension, the white man) they lived in a small section of Venice outside the central Los Angeles ghetto and were surrounded by a predominantly Mexican and Anglo population. They called their black "turf" "Ghost-town"—home of the "Ghost-men," their former gang. Whatever the origin of the world, Ghost-town was certainly the home of socially invisible men.

The street set

In 1965 and 1966 I had intensive interviews with twenty-five set members. My methods emerged in day-to-day observations. Identified as white, a lame, and square, I had to build up an image of being at least "legit" (not working for the police). Without actually living in the area, this would have been impossible without the aid of a key fieldworker, in this case an outsider who could be accepted inside. This field worker, Cowboy, was a white dude of twenty-five. He had run with Paddy (white), Chicano (Mexican), and Blood (Negro) sets since the age of twelve and was highly respected for having been president of a tough gang. He knew the street: how to duke, move with style, and speak the tongue. He made my entry possible. I was the underprivileged child who had to be taught slowly and sympathetically the commonsense features of street life.

Cowboy had the respect and I the toleration of several set leaders. After that, we simply waited for the opportunity to "rap." Although sometimes used synonymously with street conversation, rapping is really a special way of talking—repartee. Street repartee at its best is a lively way of "running it down," or of "jiving" (attempting to put someone on), trying "to blow another person's mind," forcing him "to lose his cool," to give in or give up something. For example, one needs to throw a lively rap when he is "putting the make on a broad."

Sometimes we taped individuals, sometimes "soul sessions." We asked for life histories, especially their stories about school, job, and family. We watched and asked about the details of daily survival and attempted to construct street time schedules. We probed beyond the past and present into the future in two directions—individual plans for tomorrow and a lifetime, and individual dreams of a more recent world for whites and Negroes.

The set can be described by the social and attitudinal characteristics of its members. To the observer, these are expressed in certain realities of day-to-day living: not enough skill for good jobs, and the inevitable trouble brought by the problem of surviving. Of the twenty-five interviewed, only four had graduated from high school. Except for a younger set member who was still in school, all were dropouts, or perhaps more accurately kicked-outs. None was really able to use or write formal language. However, many were highly verbal, both facile and effective in their use of the street tongue. Perhaps the art of conversation is most highly developed here where there is much time to talk, perhaps too much—an advantage of the lumpen-leisure class.

Their incomes were difficult to estimate, as "bread" or "coins" (money) came in on a very irregular basis. Of the seventeen for whom I have figures, half reported that they made less than $1,400 in the last year, and the rest claimed income from $2,000 to $4,000. Two-thirds were living with and partially dependent on their parents, often a mother. The financial strain was intensified by the fact that although fifteen of seventeen were single, eight had one or more children living in the area. (Having children, legitimate or not, was not a stigma but proof of masculinity.)

At the time of the interview, two-thirds of them had some full- or part-time employment—unskilled and low-paid jobs. The overall pattern was one of sporadic and (from their viewpoint) often unsatisfactory work, followed by a period of unemployment compensation, and petty hustling whenever possible and necessary.

When I asked the question, "When a dude needs bread, how does he get it?" the univeral response was, "The hustle." Hustling is, of course, illegitimate from society's viewpoint. Street people know it is illegal, but they view it in no way as immoral or wrong. It is justified by the necessity of surviving. As might be expected, the unemployed admitted that they hustled and went so far as to say that a dude could make it better on the street than on the job: "There is a lot of money on the street, and there are many ways of getting it," or simply, "This has always been my way of life." On the other hand, the employed, the part-time hustlers, usually said, "A dude could make it better on the job than on the street." Their reasons for disapproving of hustling were not moral. Hustling meant trouble. "I don't hustle because there's no security. You eventually get busted." Others said there was not enough money on the street or that it was too difficult to "run a game" on people.

Nevertheless, hustling is the central street activity. It is the economic foundation for everyday life. Hustling and the fruit of hustling set the rhythm of social activities.

What are the major forms of hustling in Ghost-town? The best hustles were conning, stealing, gambling, and selling dope. By gambling, these street people meant dice; by dope, peddling "pills" and "pot." Pills are "reds" and "whites"—barbiturates and benzedrine or dexedrine. Pot is, of course, marijuana—"grass" or "weed." To "con" means to put "the bump" on a "cat," to "run a game" on somebody, to work on his mind for goods and services.

The "woman game" was common. As one dude put it, "If I have a good lady and she's on County, there's always some money to get." In fact, there is a local expression for getting county money. When the checks come in for child support, it's "mother's day." So the hustler "burns" people for money, but he also "rips off" goods for money; he thieves, and petty thieving is always a familiar hustle. Pimping is often the hustler's dream of the good life, but it was almost unknown here among the small-time hustlers. That was the game of the real professional and required a higher level of organization and wealth.

Hustling means bread and security but also trouble, and trouble is a major theme in street life. The dudes had a "world of trouble" (a popular song about a hustler is "I'm in a World of Trouble")—with school, jobs, women, and the police. The intensity of street life could be gauged in part by the intensity of the "heat" (police trouble). The hotter the street, the fewer people visible on the street. On some days the set was empty. One would soon learn that there had been a "bust" (an arrest). Freddy had run amok and thrown rocks at a police car. There had been a leadership struggle; Big Moe had been cut up, and the "fuzz" had descended. Life was a succession of being picked up on suspicion of assault, theft, possession, "suspicion of suspicion" (an expression used by a respondent in describing his life). This was an ordinary experience for the street dude and often led to serious trouble. Over half of those interviewed claimed they had felony convictions.

The structure of street time

Keeping cool and out of trouble, hustling bread, and looking for something interesting and exciting to do created the structure of time on the street. The rhythm of time is expressed in the high and low points in the day and week of an unemployed dude. I stress the pattern of the unemployed and full-time hustler because he is on the street all day and night and is the prototype in my interviews. The sometimes-employed will also know the pattern, and he will be able to hit the street whenever released from the bondage of jail, work, and the clock. Here I describe a typical time schedule gleaned through interviews and field observations.

Characteristically the street person gets up late, hits the street in the late morning or early afternoon, and works his way to the set. This is a place for relaxed social activity. Hanging on the set with the boys is the major way of passing time and waiting until some necessary or desirable action occurs. Nevertheless, things do happen on the set. The dudes rap and jive, gamble, and drink their "pluck" (usually a cheap, sweet wine). They find out what happened yesterday, what is happening today, and what will hopefully happen on the weekend—the perpetual search for the "gig" (party). Here peer socialization and reinforcement also take place. The younger dude feels a sense of pride when he can be on the set and throw a rap to an older dude. He is learning how to handle himself, show respect, take care of business, and establish his own "rep."

On the set yesterday merges into today, and tomorrow is an emptiness to be filled in through the pursuit of bread and excitement. Bread makes possible the excitement—the high (getting loaded with wine, pills, or pot), the sharp clothes, the broad, the fight, and all those good things which show that one knows what's happening and has something going for himself. The rhythm of time—of the day and of the week— is patterned by the flow of money and people.

Time is dead when money is tight, when people are occupied elsewhere—working or in school. Time is dead when one is in jail. One is doing dead time when nothing is happening and he's got nothing going for himself.

Time is alive when and where there is action. It picks up in the evening when everyone moves on the street. During the regular school year it may pick up for an hour in the afternoon when the broads leave school and meet with the set at a corner taco joint. Time may pick up when a familiar car cruises by and a few dudes drive down to Johnny's for a "process" (hair straightening and styling). Time is low on Monday (as described in the popular song, "Stormy Monday"), Tuesday, Wednesday, when money is tight. Time is high on Friday nights when the "eagle flies" and the gig begins. On the street, time has a personal meaning only when something is happening, and something is most likely to happen at night—especially on Friday and Saturday nights. Then people are together, and there may be bread—bread to take and bread to use.

Human behavior is rational if it helps the individual to get what he wants, whether it is success in school or happiness in the street. Street people sometimes get what they want. They act rationally in those situations where they are able to plan and choose because they have control, knowledge, and concern, irrationally where there are barriers to their wants and desires.

When the street dude lacks knowledge and power to manipulate time, he is indeed irrational. For the most part, he lacks the skills and power to plan a move up and out of the ghetto. He is a lame in the middle-class world of school and work; he is not ready to operate effectively in unfamiliar organizations where his street strengths are his visible weaknesses. Though irrational in moving up and out of the street, he can be rational in day-to-day survival in the street. No one survives there unless he knows what's happening (that is, unless he knows what is available, where to get what he can without being burned or busted). More euphemistically, this is "taking advantage of opportunities," exactly what the rational member of the middle class does in his own setting.

To know what's happening is to know the goods and the bads, the securities, the opportunities, and the dangers of the street. Survival requires that a hustling dude know who is cool and uncool (who can be trusted); who is in power (the people who control narcotics, fences, etc.); who is the "duker" or the fighter (someone to be avoided or someone who can provide protection). When one knows what's happening he can operate in many scenes, providing that he can "hold his mud" (keep cool and out of trouble).

With his diploma in street knowledge, a dude can use time efficiently and with cunning in the pursuit of goods and services—in hustling to eat and yet having enough bread left over for the pleasures of pot, the chicks, and the gig. As one respondent put it, "The good hustler has the knowhow, the ambition to better himself. He conditions his mind and must never put his guard too far down, to relax, or he'll be taken." This is street rationality. The problem is not a deficient sense of time but deficient knowledge and control for making a fantasy future and a really better life possible.

The petty hustler more fully realizes the middle-class ideal of individualistic rationality than does the middle class itself. When rationality operates in hustling, it is often on an individual basis. In a world of complex organization, the hustler defines himself as an entrepreneur; indeed, he is the last of the competitive entrepreneurs.

The degree of organization in hustling frequently depends on the kind of hustling. Regular pimping and pushing require trusted contacts and organization. Regular stealing requires regular fences for hot goods. But in Ghost-town where the hustler moves, he usually moves alone and on a small scale. His success is on him. He cannot depend on the support of some benevolent organization. Alone, without a sure way of running the same game twice, he must continually recalculate conditions and people and find new ways of taking—or be taken himself. "Free enterprise for the poor and socialism for the rich" applies only too well in the streets. The political conservative should applaud all that individual initiative.

Clock time vs. personal time

Negro street time is built around the irrelevance of clock time, white man's time, and the relevance of street values and activities. Like anyone else, a street dude is on time by the standard clock whenever he wants to be, not on time when he does not want to be and does not have to be.

When the women in school hit the street at the lunch hour and he wants to throw them a rap, he will be there then and not one hour after they have left. But he may be kicked out of high school for truancy or lose his job for being late and unreliable. He learned at an early age that school and job were neither interesting nor salient to his way of life. A regular on the set will readily admit being crippled by a lack of formal education. Yet school was a "bum kick." It was not his school. The teachers put him down for his dress, hair, and manners. As a human being he has feelings of pride and autonomy, the very things most threatened in those institutional situations where he was or is the underdeveloped, unrespected, illiterate, and undeserving outsider. Thus he knows that whatever "respectable" society says will help him will actually oppress him, and he retreats to the streets for security and a larger degree of personal freedom. Here his control reaches a maximum, and he has the kind of autonomy which many middle-class males might envy.

In the street, watches have a special and specific meaning. Watches are for pawning and not for telling time. When they are worn, they are decorations and ornaments of status. The street clock is informal, personal, and relaxed. It is not standardized or easily synchronized to other clocks. In fact, a street dude may have almost infinite toleration for individual time schedules. To be on time is often meaningless, to be late an unconsciously accepted way of life. "I'll catch you later," or simply "later," are the street phrases that mean business will be taken care of, but not necessarily now.

Large areas of street life run on late time. For example, parties are not cut off by some built-in alarm clock of appointments and schedules. At least for the unemployed, standard time neither precedes nor follows the gig. Consequently, the action can take its course. It can last as long as interest is sustained and die from exhaustion or from the intrusion of some more interesting event. A gig may endure all night and well into another day. One of the reasons for the party assuming such time dimensions is purely economic. There are not enough cars and enough money for individual dates, so everyone converges in one place and takes care of as much business as possible there, doing whatever is important at the time—sex, presentation of self, hustling.

Colored people's time

Events starting late and lasting indefinitely are clearly street and class phenomena, not some special trait of Afro-Americans. Middle-class Negroes who must deal with the organization and coordination of activities in church and elsewhere will jokingly and critically refer to a lack of standard time sense when they say that Mr. Jones arrived "CPT" (colored people's time). They have a word for it, because being late is a problem for people caught between two worlds and confronted with the task of meshing standard and street time. In contrast, the street dudes had no self-consciousness about being late; with few exceptions they had not heard the expression CPT. (When I questioned members of a middle-class Negro fraternity, a sample matched by age to the street set, only three of the twenty-five interviewed could not define CPT. Some argued vehemently that CPT was the problem to be overcome.)

Personal time as expressed in parties and other street activities is not simply deficient knowledge and use of standard time. It is a positive adaptation to generations of living whenever possible outside of the sound and control of the white man's clock. The personal clock is an adaptation to the chance and accidental character of emotion and feeling.[1]

Chance reinforces personal time. A dude must be ready on short notice to move where the action is. His internal clock may not be running at all when he is hanging on the corner and waiting for something to do. It may suddenly speed up by chance: someone cruises by in a car and brings a nice stash of weed, a gig is organized and he looks forward to being well togged-out and throwing a rap to some boss chick, or a lame appears and opens himself to a quick con. Chance as a determinant of personal time can be called more accurately *uncertain predictability*. Street life is an aggregate of relatively independent events. A dude may not know exactly what or when something will happen, but from past experience he can predict a range of possibilities, and he will be ready, in position, and waiting.

In white middle-class stereotypes and fears—and in reality—street action is highly expressive. A forthright yet stylized expression of emotion is positively evaluated and most useful. Street control and communication are based on personal power and the direct impingement of one individual on another. Where there is little property, status in the set is determined by personal qualities of mind and brawn.

The importance of emotion and expression appears again and again in street tongue and ideology. When asked, "How does a dude make a rep on the set?" over half of the sample mentioned "style," and all could discuss the concept. Style is difficult to define, as it has so many referents. It means to carry oneself well, to dress well, to show class. In the ideology of the street, it may be a way of behaving. One has style if he is able to dig people as they are. He doesn't put them down for what

[1] For a discussion of CPT which is close to some of the ideas presented here, see Jules Henry, "White People's Time, Colored People's Time," *Trans-action*, March/April, 1965.

they do. He shows toleration. But a person with style must also show respect. That means respect for a person as he is and, since there is power in the street, respect for another's superior power. Yet one must show respect in such a way that he is able to look tough and inviolate, fearless, secure, cool.

Style may also refer to the use of gestures in conversation or in dance. It may be expressed in the loose walk, the jivey or dancing walk, the slow, cool walk, the way one "chops" or "makes it" down the street. It may be the loose, relaxed, hand rap or hand slap, the swinger's greeting which is used also in the hip middle-class teen sets. There are many refined variations of the hand rap. As a greeting, one may simply extend his hand, palm up. Another slaps it loosely with his finger. Or one person may be standing with his hand behind and palm up. Another taps the hand in passing, and also pays his respect verbally with the conventional greeting, "What's happening, Brother." Or, in conversation, the hand may be slapped when an individual has "scored," has been "digging," has made a point, has got through to the person.

Style is a comparatively neutral value compared to soul. Soul can be many things—a type of food (good food is "soul food," a "bowl of soul"), music, a quality of mind, a total way of acting (in eating, drinking, dancing, walking, talking, relating to others, etc.). The person who acts with soul acts directly and honestly from his heart. He feels it and tells it "like it is." One respondent identified soul with ambition and drive. He said the person with soul, once he makes up his mind, goes directly to the goal, doesn't change his mind, doesn't wait and worry about messing up a little. Another said soul was getting down to the nitty-gritty—that is, moving directly to what is basic without guise and disguise. Thus soul is the opposite of hypocrisy, deceit, and phoniness, the opposite of affective neutrality and instrumentality. Soul is simply whatever is considered beautiful, honest, and virtuous in men.

Most definitions tied soul directly to Negro experience. As one hustler put it, "It is the ability to survive. We've made it with so much less. Soul is the Negro who has the spirit to sing in slavery to overcome the monotony." With very few exceptions, the men interviewed argued that soul was what Negroes had and whites did not. Negroes were soul brothers, warm and emotional—whites, cold as ice. Like other oppressed minorities these street Negroes believed they had nothing except their soul and their humanity, and that this made them better than their oppressors.

The personal dream

Soul is anchored in a past and present of exploitation and deprivation, but are there any street values and activities which relate to the future?

The regular in the street set has no providential mission; he lives personally and instrumentally in the present, yet he dreams about the day when he will get himself together and move ahead to the rewards of a good job, money, and a family. Moreover, the personal dream coexists with a nascent political nationalism, the belief that Negroes can and will make it as Negroes. His present-future time is a combination of contradictions and developing possibilities. Here I will be content to document without weighing two aspects of his orientation: *fantasy personal future* and *fantasy collective future*. I use "fantasy" because street people have not yet the knowledge and the means—and perhaps the will—to fulfill their dreams. It is hard enough to survive by the day.

When the members of the set were asked, "What do you really want out of life?" their responses were conventional, concrete, seemingly realistic, and—given their skills—rather hopeless. Two-thirds of the sample mentioned material aspirations—the finer things in life, a home, security, a family. For example, one said, in honest street language, "I want to get things for my kids and to make sure they have a father." Another said, jokingly, "A good future, a home, two or three girls living with me." Only one person didn't know, and the others deviated a little from the material response. They said such things as, "For everyone to be on friendly terms—a better world . . . then I could get all I wish," "To be free," "To help people."

But if most of the set wanted money and security, they wanted it on their own terms. As one put it, "I don't want to be in a middle-class bag, but I would like a nice car, home, and food in the icebox." He wanted the things and the comforts of middle-class life, but not the hypocrisy, the venality, the coldness, the being forced to do what one does not want to do. All that was in the middle-class bag. Thus the home and the money may be ends in themselves, but also fronts, security for carrying on the usual street values. Street people believed that they already had something that was valuable and looked down upon the person who made it and moved away into the middle-class world. For the observer, the myths are difficult to separate from the truths— here where the truths are so bitter. One can only say safely that street people dream of a high status, and they really do not know how to get it.

The collective future

The Negro dudes are political outsiders by the usual poll questions. They do not vote. They do not seek out civil rights demonstrations. They have very rudimentary knowledge of political organization. However, about the age of eighteen, when fighting and being tough are less important than before, street people begin to discuss their positions in society. Verbally, they care very much about the politics of race and the future of the Negro. The topic is always a ready catalyst for a soul session.

The political consciousness of the street can be summarized by noting those interview questions which attracted at least a 75 percent rate of agreement. The typical respondent was angry. He approves of the Watts incident, although from his isolated corner of the city he did not actively participate. He knows something about the history of discrimination and believes that if something isn't done soon America can expect violence: "What this country needs is a revolutionary change." He is more likely to praise the leadership of Malcolm X than Lyndon Johnson, and he is definitely opposed to the Vietnam war. The reason for his opposition is clear: Why fight for a country which is not mine, when the fight is here?

Thus his racial consciousness looks to the future and a world where he will not have to stand in the shadow of the white man. But his consciousness has neither clear plan nor political commitment. He has listened to the Muslims, and he is not a black nationalist. True, the Negro generally has more soul than the white. He thinks differently, his women may be different, yet integration is preferable to separatism. Or, more accurately, he doesn't quite understand what all these terms mean. His nationalism is real as a folk nationalism based on experience with other Negroes and isolation from whites.

The significance of a racial future in the day-to-day consciousness of street people cannot be assessed. It is a developing possibility dependent on unforeseen conditions beyond the scope of their skill and imagination. But bring up the topic of race and tomorrow, and the dreams come rushing in—dreams of superiority, dreams of destruction, dreams of human equality. These dreams of the future are salient; they are not those of authoritarian personalities, except from the viewpoint of those who see spite lurking behind every demand for social change. They are certainly not the fantasies of the hipster living philosophically in the present without hope and ambition. One hustler summarized the Negro street concept of ambition and future time when he said: "The Negro has more ambition than the whites. He's got farther to go. The Man is already there. But we're on your trail, daddy. You still have smoke in our eyes, but we're catching up."

Nonverbal communication among Afro-Americans: an initial classification

BENJAMIN G. COOKE

Benjamin G. Cooke is presently an instructor of speech at Howard University. A graduate of Chicago State University and Northeastern Illinois University's Center for Inner City Studies, Cooke brings to his various present academic roles of instructor, lecturer, and consultant a rich and varied experience reflecting many abilities and interests, among which is that of professional musician (drummer).

Verbal communication has received a great deal of attention and analysis by linguists, but much less consideration has been given to the systematic nature of nonverbal communication. Here, following the direction of such forerunners as Hall (proxemics) and Birdwhistell (kinesics), and using the latter's notational system, Cooke has identified, illustrated, and classified some significant nonverbal kinesic features which, within designated contexts, convey a number of different meanings to Afro-Americans. Cooke's article is included here because he provides illuminating discussion and analysis that makes meaningful one of the more expressive aspects of black in-group communication, because he shows how kinesic interaction is integrated into the overall black cultural communication system, and finally because he demonstrates the success with which people can study *themselves*. The last-named point contradicts the myth often heard in anthropological circles which states that being part of a culture prevents one from being objective when studying it. On the contrary, one could argue that by already having attained the insider's perspective as a native cultural participant, one avoids what John Willis has called the "blind empiricist approach" of the outsider who, not knowing what is culturally *significant* of what he sees, must record *everything*.

Some of the photographs accompanying this article are by Collis H. Davis, Jr., of the Hampton Arts Institute, Hampton, Virginia.

Introduction

Recent research has increasingly stressed the need to investigate nonverbal communication, the importance of which can no longer be ignored or overlooked in any comprehensive theory involving language and its relation to culture, learning, and psychology.

This article initiates such a study with respect to Afro-Americans by (1) describing the basic components of certain gestures and showing how these are altered to achieve variation in different social contexts, and (2) explaining the functions of these gestures along with other bodily movements.

Such a descriptive analysis illustrates the systemic nature of such communication, as well as illuminating something of the black cultural context in which nonverbal communication operates, especially that which might shape or reflect the world view of black people. Additionally, it might increase the reader's awareness of the significance of this channel and mode of communication and his appreciation of the integral part it plays in the Afro-American communication system.

Field study technique

Field study consisted of informal interviews with several members of the black community in Chicago. Interviews were held in the summers of 1968 and 1969. Several of the informants were friends of the researcher and were chosen because of their diverse backgrounds and experiences. The occupational backgrounds included musicians, youth workers, ex-hustlers, artists, semi-skilled workers, educational persons, and teenagers. The teenagers consisted of two different groups: one group from the West Side (middle-lower socioeconomic status) and the other group from the Southeast Side (upper-lower socioeconomic status). The various informants helped to describe and define the gestures considered herein. The major factors considered in the interpretation and differentiation of the forms of nonverbal communication were:

(1) the motives, attitudes, responses, conflicts, and personalities of the people involved in the communicative event;

(2) the context of the message;

(3) the entire social setting; and

(4) the communicative event itself.

Because of the importance of visual cues in nonverbal communication, illustrations assist in the discussion and help clarify certain points considered; motion pictures would, of course, be the most effective way to analyze the total expression. While some of the illustrations were posed, it was also possible to capture some spontaneous movements; these are always preferred because of their communicative value for conveying overall body movement and configuration. Whatever their imperfections, the illustrations give the reader a general idea of the features involved in nonverbal communication, since the study of kinesics—the area incorporating the present study—basically explores how man *sees* rather than how he *hears*.

Skin—giving and getting

The gestural expressions of "giving skin" and "getting skin" are very common in the black community. Harry Edwards, leader of the Olympic boycott, was recently quoted as saying: "Black people are communal by culture. They prepare communally. They dance, they play games communally. That slap on the hand you see Lew Alcindor give Mike Warren, or vice versa, that means something to those brothers. It means something to the brothers in the stands. It means something to the brothers who are watching the TV sets."[1]

In this paper the gestures of giving and getting skin shall be considered as *kinemes* according to Birdwhistell's classification. They derive their meaning from the analysis of the entire range of components involved in a communicative act—sender, receiver, channel, code, setting, etc. The kinemes of giving and getting skin can be combined with facial expressions to produce *kinemorphs*. The variations within each of the kinemes represent subtle, individual *allokines* of giving skin.[2]

Figures 1, 2, and 3 illustrate three regular kinemes of giving and getting skin. These gestures are tools used by individuals for their own specific needs, and there are as many varieties and styles of doing these simple acts as there are individual personalities. Figure 1 illustrates the palm-to-palm kineme of giving skin; it involves palm contact between two people with no significance attached to left-handedness or right-handedness. In other words, "skinning" can be accomplished with a right hand/right hand contact, a right hand/left hand contact, a left hand/right hand contact, or a left hand/left hand contact. Figure 2 illustrates the back-of-hand-to-upward-facing-palm kineme; it involves a back-of-hand contact with an upturned palm. The person receiving the skin can either cup his hand slightly or hold it straight out. One informant regularly uses these two kinemes together in a one-two sequence. As an example of how it is possible to achieve variation the informant related the following: When especially tired or "beat" he may just use the first kineme in a lazy palm-to-palm contact, omitting kineme two completely. In this instance his walking and shoulder movements would reinforce the skinning comprising an entire kinemorpheme, and he would have effectively communicated that he was tired and in a weary mood without saying a word. Its function here would be *expressive* —that is, the focus is on the sender of the message.

Figure 3 illustrates the use of the first regular kineme (i.e., palm-to-palm contact) in a context of agreement between two people; but it should be remembered that the second kineme (i.e., back-of-hand-to-palm) could also have been used to indicate the same amount of agreement. Giving skin is often used as a gesture of agreement and approval;

[1] "The Black Athlete—A Shameful Story," *Sports Illustrated*, July 1, 1968, p. 18.
[2] For a more complete explanation and discussion of the terms, see Ray L. Birdwhistell, "Some Relations between American Kinesics and Spoken American English," in *Communication and Culture,* ed. Alfred G. Smith (New York: Holt, Rinehart and Winston, 1966), pp. 182–83, and Alfred S. Hayes, "Paralinguistics and Kinesics," in *Approaches to Semiotics,* ed. T. Sebeok, A. Hayes, and M. Bateson (The Hague: Mouton & Co., 1964), p. 159.

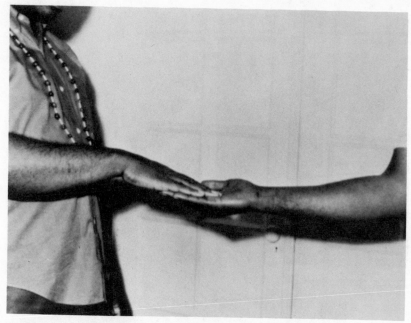

1. Giving skin: Palm-to-palm contact

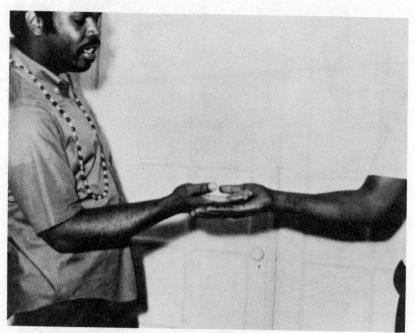

2. Giving skin: Back of hand to upward-facing palm

3. Agreement skin (a) (b)

(c)

4. Complimentary skin

it can also be used to pay a compliment, as in 4. In these situations its functions are both expressive and directive. What determines the minimal distinctions between complimentary skin and agreement skin is a function of the social interaction taking place between the two individuals and is *not* determined by any particular skin kineme.[3]

Giving and getting skin are also used as gestures of greeting or parting; here again there are innumerable individual variations. Figures 5a and 5b are two informants' examples of greeting skin from a distance, perhaps to a friend across the street. This is not a part of any traditional waving motion associated with saying hello or good-by. It is a direct outward-and-upward thrust of the arm, exposing the skin of his palm to his comrade. Figures 5c and 5d illustrate greeting skin at close range. These same illustrations could be used to show parting skin,

[3] More recently the palm-to-palm pattern of skinning illustrated in Figure 3 is being replaced by a fist-to-fist sequence. This variation has evolved out of the Black Power salute, which incorporates an upraised clenched fist as part of its message (see Figure XXI).

5. Greeting skin (a)   (b)

(c)   (d)

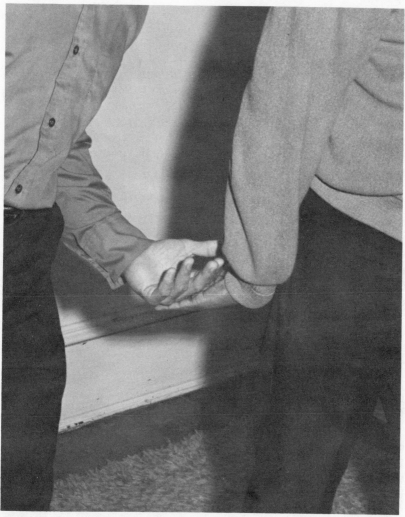

6. "Five on the sly"

which is consistent with earlier statements that the kinemes of skin assume their total meaning from the consideration of the entire social context in which they occur.[4]

Figure 6 illustrates "five on the sly." This sort of contact would serve to heighten intimacy and rapport between two individuals. In this situation it would be a gesture of agreement or compliment concerning

[4] Within the greeting phase, giving and getting skin has generally been replaced by the Black Power handshake. (See discussion and illustration below for the latter.) Skin is still operative within other phases of black interaction, however, as noted.

some facts or factors in the external environment, whether it be the comments they are hearing from someone (perhaps a speaker), or another event they are viewing together. For example, two "cats" are "digging" some speaker who is "tellin' it like it is."[5] Being in an unfamiliar environment, they are concerned with "keeping their cool."[6] However, they may also want to express inconspicuously their mutual agreement with some statement the speaker is making. They would then utilize this method of giving skin on the sly so that they could express the agreement between themselves and what the speaker has said and thus reestablish their solidarity. Its function in this case would be mainly expressive.

This manner of giving skin on the sly could also be utilized in a situation where complete secrecy or privacy would not be of prime necessity; in such a case it would be used for the element of style gained by using it. As for example, when Cat A is "cappin' on"[7] Cat B, Cat A has been so extra witty that a third Cat C is compelled to give him some skin on the sly to show his approval. Its function now would be directive. Another instance of this manner of giving skin can be seen in the following episode:

Several cats are standing together, digging a pretty girl walk by.

Cat A: Hey, baby; what's happenin'?

Pretty Girl (stops, turns around, and smiles approvingly to his "rap"[8]): Everything!

Cat A quickly turns his hand inward toward his friend so that the girl can't see, and Cat B encouragingly lays some "sly skin" on him. Whereupon Cat A takes off in hot pursuit of his would-be prey.

Skin can also be used as an exclamation mark for the purpose of emphasis. For example, if you really agree with someone and you want to accentuate this agreement more than usual, you might use some emphatic skin. In this case the arm might be raised quite high and brought down with a great deal of exaggerated force; the contact is usually palm-to-palm in this situation. Although the contact seems to be hard, it is actually a quick, crisp movement. Emphatic skin derives its meaning from the total communicative event and must be analyzed with the social context in which it is being used. Its function is both expressive and directive.

One other variation observed in field study was the use of both hands

[5] Any words which have been borrowed from the black idiom and which may need clarification will be footnoted and defined the first time they appear in the text. Thereafter any occurrences of the word or phrase will not be footnoted. "Cats" is a term for "men"; "digging" can mean listening to, observing, watching, or enjoying; "tellin' it like it is" means telling the truth.

[6] "Keeping their cool" means staying calm, unexcited.

[7] "Cappin' on" means engaging in one-ups-manship or winning a verbal contest.

[8] "Rap" means to talk in a highly stylized manner.

7. Emphatic skin (a)

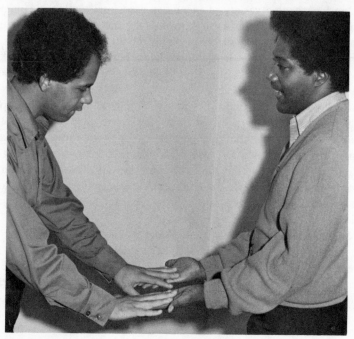

(b)

cupped together to receive two hands full of skin in a superlative manner. This gesture expresses an added amount of happy agreement with a proposed suggestion by another. The other person might use one or two hands, depending on his mood. Although this is not the only way to express it, this kind of skin can be termed superlative skin. The complimentary skin and the agreement skin kinemes can be combined with the emphatic, superlative, or sly kinemes; that is, you can compliment or agree in an emphatic, superlative, or sly manner.

Another variation of skinning designed by drummers is as follows: (1) back-of-hand-to-palm, (2) palm-to-palm, (3) elbow-to-palm, and (4) palm-to-palm. This 1-2-3-4 sequence must be executed with lightning speed—something impossible to achieve without practice and something well-suited to drummers, who are concerned with hand and arm speed in relation to their playing. One variation includes elbow-to-elbow contact, reminiscent of the actions that accompany certain kinds of rhyming slang which are said for fun:

"You my frien'? Then gi' me some skin."
"How's it feel? Then gi' me some heel."
"If you a swinger, gi' me some finger."
"If all tha's so, then gi' me some elbow."
"Since all this has come to pass, now gi' me some ass."

The functions of these kinds of variations are expressive.

One look at this variety of meanings associated with the kinemes of giving and getting skin is enough to indicate that the only way to interpret the act in any one situation would be to analyze the entire communicative event. When a cat approaches his friends, he gives skin to say hello; when he "cuts out,"[9] he gives skin to say good-by. When an athlete makes a touchdown or a basket, his teammates give skin as approval; when a cat plays a "groovy"[10] solo or makes a fine speech, he gets complimentary skin; when two or more people agree to something, they give emphatic or superlative skin to accentuate their agreement. Girls and women also use the kinemes of giving and getting skin, but not to the same extent that the men do. When you give skin, you have to feel it; your style and body motion become a part of the way you give the skin because you cannot separate how your body moves and feels from how your hands move and feel.

We have considered four major kinemes of giving and getting skin: (1) greeting skin, (2) parting skin, (3) complimentary skin, and (4) agreement skin. In addition, four major means of execution have been considered: (a) on the sly, (b) emphatic, (c) superlative, and (d) regular. When any of the four kinemes of greeting, parting, compli-

---

[9] "Cuts out" means to leave, depart.
[10] "Groovy" means fine, excellent.

ment, or agreement is "regular," it is not in combination with any of the others. In addition to these four possibilities, there are twenty-eight other combinations that could conceivably arise in social situations. These possible combinations are shown in Table 1.

Table 1. Possible combinations of seven basic kinemes of giving and getting skin.

Interaction	Greeting G	Parting P	Complimentary C	Agreement A
Emphatic E	G+E	P+E	C+E	A+E
Superlative S	G+S	P+S	C+S	A+S
Sly Sl	G+Sl	P+Sl	C+Sl	A+Sl
Emphatic + Superlative	G+E+S	P+E+S	C+E+S	A+E+S
Emphatic + Sly	G+E+Sl	P+E+Sl	C+E+Sl	A+E+Sl
Superlative + Sly	G+S+Sl	P+S+Sl	C+S+Sl	A+S+Sl
Emphatic + Superlative + Sly	G+E+S+Sl	P+E+S+Sl	C+E+S+Sl	A+E+S+Sl

Standing stances: male

Standing stances are also communicative in the black community. Figures 8 represents, in a general way, the stance of a player. According to one informant, players are distinguishable from pimps in that the pimps have many lady-friends for financial reasons, whereas the players have many lady-friends for pleasurable reasons. Figure 8a also illustrates the use of the lowered-shoulder kineme which is common in the stances and walks of most males. One informant noted that usually a cat stands with one or both hands behind him. However, the hands-in-pocket is also a currently popular gesture associated with players and pimps (see Figure 9). Either one or both hands can be in the pocket or tucked underneath the belt; usually the back of the hands show so that actually only the fingers are inside. According to another

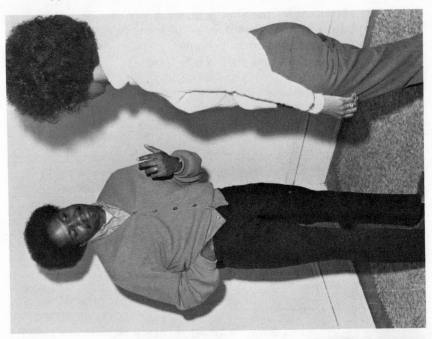

(b)

8. Player stance (a)

informant, pimps usually stand with their legs spread apart—especially in bars, which are the centers for a great number of activities. They are the marketplaces for exchanging ideas and wares, socializing, finding out the happenings, checking out new styles, and making business deals of various sorts. Figure 9c illustrates a typical pimp stance; notice the hands are placed behind. The informant commented, "You seldom see a pimp with his legs close together." Figure 9d illustrates a regional variation of the pimp stance found in Virginia and the Carolinas.

Figure 10 illustrates bodily motion associated with watching a girl walk by. The hands-in-pockets gesture can be seen here. This illustration is especially good for demonstrating the use of shoulder and spine motion, which is felt by this researcher to be the backbone of most bodily gestures. Also noticeable is the lowered-shoulder kineme, and the use of the eyes in the total facial expression to indicate pleasurable attention and interest in an approaching person (in this case, a pretty girl). The look on his face was readily identifiable among various informants as peeping, which is often associated with digging a girl's "action" (watching how she moves her derriere).

Figure 11 illustrates the use of the lowered-shoulder kineme in dancing. The lowered-shoulder kineme is often associated with "rapping"[11] stances, and although it has no unique or special meaning in this particular illustration, the young man interpreted his dance as being his way of showing the girl he digs her. Compare Figure 11 with Figure 12 for a variation of the forward-lower-shoulder kineme. Contrast Figure 11 with Figure 10 for the difference in the lowered-shoulder kineme. Figure 12 illustrates a rapping stance in a sequence which usually involves moving in toward the girl, closing the space between the two people. Contrast Figure 12 to Figure 13, which is obviously *not* rapping! First of all, the distance between the two is too great, and second, the stance of the cat lacks any characteristics thus far described for rapping (lowered-shoulder, facial expression, etc.).

Figures 14a and 14b are illustrations of rapping in a woofing fashion. "Woofing" is a style of bragging and boasting about how "bad" one is and is sometimes used by males and females when rapping to each other. This would be a sincere self-image, and the attitude is very emphatic, as, "I'm bad and I know I'm bad!"[12] This illustration is included to demonstrate the importance of interpreting an expression within the context of the whole event. Some may not see woofing and notice only the hair style which is expressive of black pride (see discussion of hair styles below). The informants in Figure 14a and 14b may look as though they are angry, possibly due to the extension of

---

[11] "Rapping" in this situation means the kind of personal talk a man engages in with a woman.
[12] "Bad" means excellent.

(b)

9. Pimp stance (a)

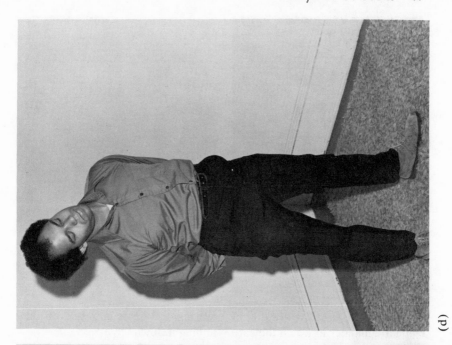

(d)

(c)

10. Peeping

11. Lowered-shoulder kineme

the lower lip, but this gesture of lowering the lip is a result of the emphatic manner in which they are "running it down."[13]

Although rapping is most frequently associated with verbal adroitness, there exists a "silent rap" in which a cat may indicate what his desires are with his facial expression and intensity of eyes, etc. Figure 15c illustrates a cat digging a chick in such a way as to express his feelings without verbalizing. The silent rap can be used effectively across the distance of a room; this is actually one of its best features. In addition, it can be utilized when there are a great deal of noise and a great many people in the environment that would interrupt the flow of a verbal rap. The girl can respond to a silent rap with her own silent rap; or she can communicate lack of interest, also nonverbally.

Figure 15 illustrates the use of eyes in a directive function to focus on a particular person. Notice the lowered-shoulder of the person in the background. Figure 16 shows a girl's use of eyes in talking to her boyfriend. Figure 16b shows the use of the hands to achieve intimacy and privacy between two individuals, although in this case he is not necessarily rapping. The use of the eyes to communicate with cats is frequently employed by females as in the following examples: A girl may be in a crowd and see a cat she digs (i.e., one she finds attractive). To draw his attention she will give him a persistent stare. When he finally looks her way he will notice her persistent look, read her silent rap, and she will then smile and indicate with her facial expression a

[13] "Running it down" is a manner of talking or rapping.

12. Rapping stance (a) (b)

(c)

13. Conversation

14. Rapping styles: "Woofing" and silent rap (a)

(b)

(c)

15. Use of eyes: Male

"ready"[14] look. When two girls are together and they want to attract some cat's attention, they will look him up and down intensely and when he turns their way they will whisper to each other about how fine he is. The cat may not hear what they are saying, but he will know they are talking about him and are interested in him. On the other hand, if a girl in a lounge does not want to be bothered when a cat comes up to rap, she might lift up one shoulder and sneer slightly, rolling her eyes upward in her head as though saying, "What a drag!" Her use of nonverbal communication is highly effective in all such cases.

Styles of walking: male

Each of the various walks described here has its own message when used in a particular social context; most blacks can alternate their walks depending on what the situation calls for. Perhaps the walks most noticeable to people outside the ethnic group are those commonly termed "catting" walks; they come under various individuals names in different sections of the country and are constantly changing in style and method of execution. However, the function of the walk remains

[14] "Ready" means psychologically and emotionally prepared for a given confrontation.

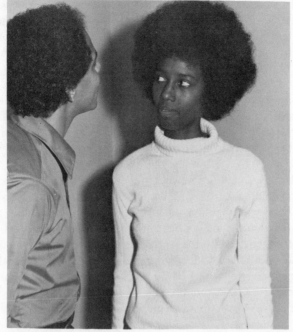

16. Use of eyes: Female (a)

(b)

basically the same: to attract attention and admiration, especially from females. One informant compared it to the strutting of the peacock and his subsequent broad display of fine feathers. This seems to corroborate Hall's recent remarks on the adumbration features of a communicative event which indicates to others some notion of what is to follow.[15] Strutting and display among various fowls and fish have been reported by animal behaviorists for some time; it is also known that disruptions or alterations in the patterns or sequences of these displays can lead to abortive interactions between members of the species. When dealing with man, however, care must be taken not to oversimplify any seeming correlation.

The walks in general are more a matter of individual preference than of socioeconomic background, although those who aspire to be middle-class and white will abandon the ethnic walks and walk like the white folks—less rhythmical, or, as one informant said, "Like a robot." It is certainly erroneous to ascribe a certain combination of walking style, clothes, and vocabulary with just one role or type of personality. This results in a gross stereotyping of the blacks (similar to the Sambo myth) which ignores the true diversity and richness of communicative patterns which exist in the Afro-American culture. Herein possibly lies one of the pitfalls of "ethnic studies."

The chicken walk which Sammy Davis sometimes uses in his version of "Heah come de Judge" has an interesting history and possibly may connect to the catting walks. Similar to the peacock strut, the chicken walk derived its overall strutting apearance and name from its similarity to the strutting of the rooster at mating time. The rooster's mating strut consists of spreading one wing straight down, leaning toward that side, and then circling round the chicken just prior to copulation. The chicken walk consists of a lowered-shoulder kineme (either right or left side) and a simultaneous stiffening of that arm which is held close to the body and leg. When moving, the leg on the lowered-shoulder side bends abruptly and springs back into position abruptly; this results in a bobbing motion. It was suggested that this walk was first used as a catting walk; when black entertainers began to incorporate this strut into their performances, the white people were so amused by it that it gradually became associated with "Uncle Tomism."[16] Today it is not a current walking style, although some entertainers (such as Sammy Davis) still use it for a laugh. The chicken walk is similar to the more animated gowster walk of the bebop era of the early 1950's.

The Slu Foot is another walk which dates back some time. One in-

[15] Edward T. Hall, "Adumbration as a Feature of Intercultural Communication," *American Anthropologist* 66 (December, 1964): 154–63.

[16] "Uncle Tomism" from *Uncle Tom's Cabin:* a black person who is obsequious to the whites; currently called a "Negro."

formant who used the walk regularly referred to it as a "down-home"[17] walk. The feet are turned outward; if the heels were placed together to form the vertex of an angle, it would measure about 150°. The foot lands on the side of the heel, and the weight of the body is actually carried on the sides of the feet. It is possible that this type of walk was first employed by people who had bad feet (perhaps from standing on their feet a lot, such as waiters, soldiers, etc.). However, others not suffering from foot ailments adopted it as a manner of style. This walk can also be seen among classical dancers. It is not currently popular among the teenage set.

The basic soul walk consists of placing one foot directly in front of the other, the heel hits first and the leg drops loosely which results in a bended leg effect. The shoulders sway very slightly and naturally, with a slight dropping of the shoulder which moves forward (the lowered-shoulder kineme). The overall motion is a gentle swing; the stride is rhythmic and graceful.

The cool walk (one informant uses this walk on Sundays only) involves the same leg movements as the soul walk. The difference lies in the movements of the arms and hands. With some, the hands are tucked under the belt or inside the pants in front (the hands-in-pockets kineme discussed under "Standing Stances"). The shoulders sway in a subtle forward-down and backward-up motion. With others, as is customary, individual variations of the cool walk develop. Compare Figure 17a with Figures 17b and 17c.

The pimp walk presently consists of the basic soul walk with some additional gestures. A cat using such a walk is described as pimping off. One arm swings completely free, crossing over in front of the trunk of the body. The other hand is tucked in the side of the pants, either under the belt or in the pocket; some variations keep both hands in the pockets. A regional variation of this type of walk can be seen in Figure 17d.

The hands in the pocket can be used to facilitate pulling up the trousers. According to one informant, this action results in revealing the outline of the genitals, which is again a recurrence of the display associated with the peacock strut. Whatever individual style a pimp adopts, usually when he walks into a bar everyone "hip"[18] to the culture can tell. Before rapping to a chick, a cat's walk would indicate to the chick what his "game" was so that any chick going for his game and interested in hearing his rap could then make her presence known to him. In this sense the walk could be considered adumbrative in nature and function.

[17] "Down-home" referring to the South; since most blacks have roots there, this also refers to "soul."
[18] "Hip" means aware of what's happening, of what's appropriate.

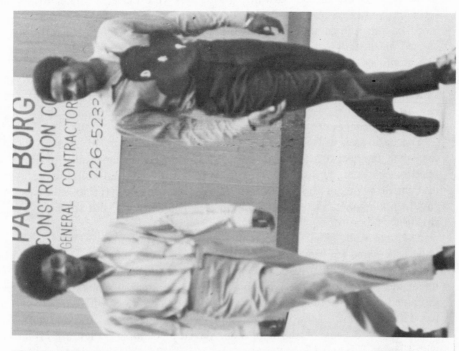

17. Styles of walking: Cool walk and pimp walk (a)   (b)

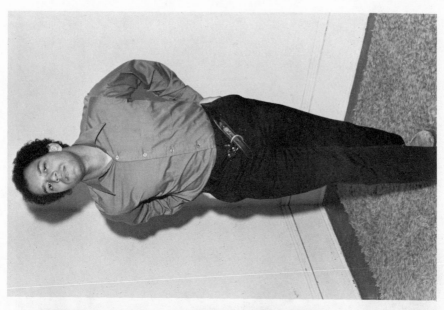

(d)

(c)

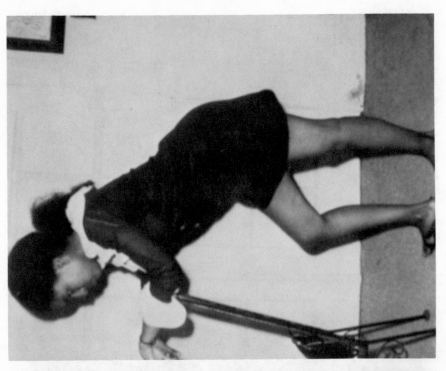

19. Female stances (a)

18. Style of walking: Female

(c)

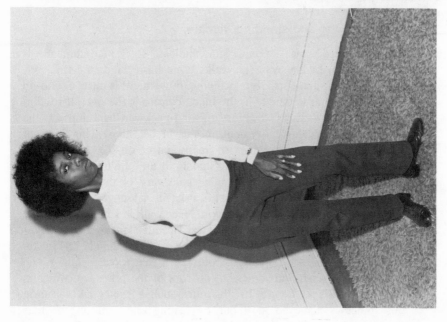

(b)

20. Introducing a bass player

Styles of walking and standing: female

There are several ways a female may indicate to a man that she is interested in him by the way she walks. One basic kind of jaunt consisting of a back-and-forth hip-swinging movement is also found in other cultures. What is unique in the black culture is the overall rhythm of the walk, as well as the forward-and-backward motion of the shoulders which creates movement in the breast area. This kind of walk, which involves movement of many parts of the body (hips, shoulders, breasts), is referred to as "shaking it up." Figure 18 indicates such a walk; notice in this the swinging backward of the shoulder. To indicate her availability and interest to a cat in a lounge, a chick may jaunt up to the juke box to play a record. Her walk is sufficient to draw attention. While at the juke box, there are various stances she may employ to further indicate her mood. Standing with her hands resting on the juke box and her derriere thrust outward ("ass tooched out"), she bends one leg forward and somewhat in front of the other leg, which is held straight in back. Figure 19 illustrates such a stance. A variation of this stance is achieved at a bar by resting one arm on the bar, tooching out the hip and placing the other hand on the hip. Again, one leg may be bent in order to accentuate the tooching of the hip (as in Figures 19b and 19c), although other variations of this stance can be seen in places other than bars.

Figure 20 is illustrative of another use of gestures in the black community. This particular interaction occurred spontaneously in a social situation involving the introduction of two people. The man in the middle, during his introduction of his musician friend to his buddy, makes the motions of playing a bass fiddle. This communicated to his buddy that the cat was not only a musician but that he was a bassist, yet nothing was said about music. This particular illustration does not capture the spontaneity of the original movements, but it is possible to see in it the use of such types of gestures to assist communication. Other motions used to indicate musicians and their "axes"[19] would be (1) a quick movement of the first two fingers up near the mouth area to indicate a trumpet player, (2) a quick wrist-shaking for drummers, and (3) an imaginary running the fingers up and down the keyboard for a pianist.

The Black Power handshake or greeting can be divided into five components executed in a given sequence. These components are illustrated in Figure 21; each is shown first from a distance and then at close range. They are:

1. mutual encircling of the thumbs, interpreted as meaning *togetherness;*
2. grasping each other's hands with bended fingers, interpreted as meaning *strength;*
3. mutual grasping of wrists and hands, meaning *solidarity;*
4. placing hands on shoulders with a slight amount of pressure, indicating *comradeship;*
5. raising of the arm, flexing the biceps, and making a fist. This last gesture incorporates the meanings of the first four and symbolizes all of them: black pride, solidarity, and power. Sometimes Step 5 is elaborated by holding up both arms and fists simultaneously for emphasis.

These five steps are often abbreviated by just using Step 1 for close-distance contacts and just Step 5 for greater distances.

Hair and clothing

Other aspects of nonverbal communication are hair and clothing. Originally what was known in Chicago as the Ranger Bush was worn by a Ranger leader and then adopted by other Rangers as a sign of their membership in that particular group. But the style became popular, and now there is no clear distinction. It consists of a thick bush of hair

---

[19] "Axes" is a term for musical instruments.

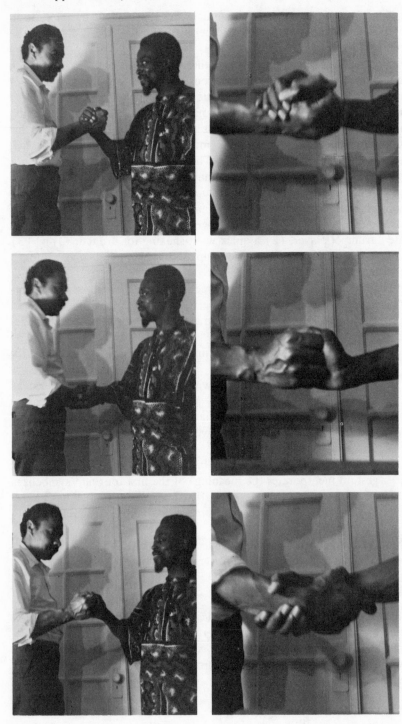

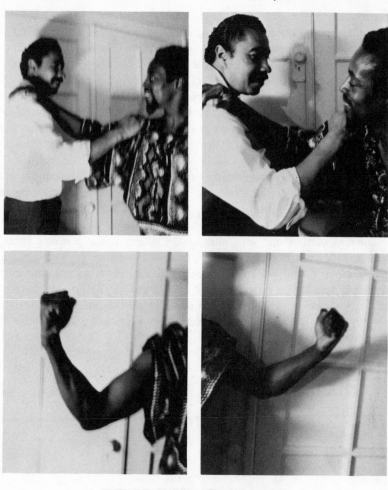

21. Black Power handshake

on top of the head tapered on a slant toward the back of the head and cut close on the sides of the head. Thus bush on top of the head was used before the "naturals" became popular; one informant suggested that the gang members found it helpful to have a "bush" on the top of the head to cushion the blows received in fights or from police.

As mentioned in the discussion of Figure 14, the natural hairstyle is a symbol of pride in self and heritage. This is a current trend of self-assertion of blackness among the males and females of the black community who, because of white racism, have been heretofore systematically separated from and kept unaware of their true identity. The "process" of hair straightening is now considered demeaning; most black brothers have abandoned it. Also symbolic of the emerging new Afro-American identity are the African-styled clothes and jewelry (dashikis, tikis, and dresses).

Just as clothes and hair consciously affirm black people's strength and unity of purpose for the achievement of control of their lives and destinies, so do the selected kinesic forms of nonverbal communication depicted here act on a deeper level of awareness. The greater awareness and appreciation of nonverbal communication created by this article should make intracultural communication even more meaningful and purposeful.

Photo credits: Figures 1, 2, 3, 5c, 8a, 9a, 9b, 10, 11, 12, 13, 14a, 15, 16b, 17b, 17c, 18, 19a, 19c, 20, 21 by Benjamin Cooke; Figures 4, 5b, 5d, 6, 7, 8b, 9d, 14b, 14c, 16a, 17a, 17d, 19b by Collis Davis, Jr.; Figures 5a, 9c by Thomas Kochman.

■ Black folk music

ELKIN T. SITHOLE

Elkin T. Sithole, a native Zulu, was born and raised in South Africa, where he was educated and taught high school before resigning to take scholarships in England and later in the United States. He is instructor in ethnomusicology and anthropology at Northeastern Illinois University's Center for Inner City Studies. His special fields include African cultures and the music of Africa and social change. For example, his master's thesis from Wesleyan University, "Zulu Music as a Reflection of Social Change," was the product of many years of involvement and research in tribal, school, and church music of the Zulus throughout Zululand and Natal.

In addition to his many academic achievements, Mr. Sithole has many personal accomplishments to his credit. He is the author of several songs, one of which was commissioned by the Natal Education Department to celebrate a Zulu festival in Zululand; he speaks fluent Zulu, Africaans, and Xhosa (and a "little German and Sotho") and has made several recordings.

This article reflects an enlightened analysis of one of the most vital and prolific areas of African and Afro-American nonverbal expression (namely music) as it also demonstrates Sithole's extensive knowledge of ethnomusicology, especially in the area of African and African-derived (Afro-American) musical genres. In establishing an African prototype for many of the norms of Afro-American musical expression, Sithole provides us with an all-important source for non-Euro-American norms *in general* within the black community—norms influencing black expression not only in music, but in dance, language (see Dalby), and other channels and idioms (see Cooke, Holt, et al.). Finally, taken with but slight revision from one of Sithole's oral presentations, which can best be described as a combination of a lecture and a performance, this article serves to demonstrate the inadequacy of print in capturing various aesthetic aspects of an oral culture. Try appreciating the "click" song, for example, with which Sithole generally begins his lecture, via the visual medium of the printed page, which was deliberately included to make that point.

First I would like to introduce my language to you. Zulu, like Xhosa and other southern African languages, is characterized by subtle features which add to the beauty of the language, as the following extracts from Zulu poetry illustrate:

> We mfaz'ongaphesheya[1]
> Asambe sotheza
> Mina angiy'ukuya
> Ngagxotshwa isife
> EMazibukweni
> Kwaphuma ngingila
> Yangangoxamu

[1] Zulu dialogue which Zulu children learn from the oral tradition before they go to school at age six.

UXamu lafeceza
Amadod'adlubulongwe
MaSasasa vuka
Ngivuke kanjani
Ngibulewe-nje
Amakhwenkw'akwaThabede
Thabede muphi?
Yena l'osenhla.

Translation:

You woman friend across the river
Come let's go to gather wood
No! Not I
Already I've been trapped
At the Mazibukos
Out came my heart
As big as an animal
An animal big and tall
Like men who eat cowdung,
Wake up MaSasasa!
How can I wake up
When I'm almost dead
Having been killed by Thabede's dogs
Which Thabede?
The one on the north.

The second extract comes from Zulu praise songs. The presentation would normally take place at the king's kraal, where the tribe would have assembled awaiting the arrival of the king. Upon his emergence they would all salute with a tremendous roar of "Bayethe UyiZulu!"— equivalent to "Hail Caesar!" Thereupon a professional orator would sing the following praises to King Dingane, who reigned over the Zulus in 1828:

UVezi uNonyanda kaMgabadeli[2]
Owagabadel'inkundla yakwaBulawayo
Odonswe ngezintaba ezimakhelekethe
UVezi wakwaSimanganyawo
UMbombosh'omnyama
UVemvane lukaPhunga noMageba
UVemvane olumabal'azibhaqu
Ngibe ngiyaluthinta luyahwaqabala
LunjengoPhunga waseBulawini
LunjengoVuma, kubaNgoma
Obuz'amanz'eMbozamo andukuwela
Amanz'eMbozam'asal'ebabaza

[2] Sibusiso Nyembezi, *Izibongo Zamakhosi* (Pieter Maritzburg, Natal: Shuter & Shooter, 1958).

Owel'iMbozam'umtakaJama
Wawel'iMbozamo kwash'iziziba
Ebigezwa uDukuza neNkisimana
Beyigeza bebheke kithi kwaZulu
Nanamhlanje abanini beMbozamo basamangele
Kumangele uManqondo wakwaShiyabanye
Kwamangal'uPhampatha wakwaNkisimana
Isiziba esimavevane Dingane
Isiziba esinzonzo sinzonzobele
Siminzise umuntu eth'uyageza
Waze washona nangesicoco
Ngob'uCoco yena ngimbonile
Obephuma lapha kwaSodlabela

Translation:

Vezi Nonyanda Mgabadeli
The conquerer of Bulawayo
As he crossed the mountain cliffs.
Vezi of Simanganyawo
Black Mbomboshe
Butterfly of Phunga and Mageba
The multi-colored butterfly
Whose colors change upon touch
Like Phunga's of Bulawini
Like Vuma at the Diviners' place
One who drank water at Mbozamo
Water which hailed him
As he, Jama's son
Crossed, leaving a dry Mbozamo river behind,
Having been cleansed by Dukuza and Nkisimana
On their way to Zululand.
The Mbozamo owners remain puzzled.
Among them is Manqondo of Shiyabanye
Phampatha of Nkisimana.
Dingane, the deep deep waters
Full of tranquility and calmness
Yet you drowned a man
Drowning even his head-top
Yes! Coco I did see
As he came out from Sodlabela.

But the beauty of the Zulu language is in the alliteration provided by the click sounds:

(a) Ca ce ci co cu
     Nca nce nci nco ncu
     Gca gce gci gco gcu

Cela uCetshwayo alethe icici lami lelo.
Translation: Tell Cetshwayo to bring my earring.

(b) Xa xe xi xo xu
Nxa nxe nxi nxo nxu
Gxa gxe gxi gxo gxu
Amaxoxo ayaxokozela
Translation: The frogs make noise.

(c) Qa qe qi qo qu
nqa nqe nqi nqo nqu
Ngqa ngqe ngqi ngqo ngqu

Umdlalo kaQa[3]
Uqaq'olwehl'oQaqeni,
Lwaqangqatheka,
Lwagqabul'uqhoqhoqho
Kwaqaqek'isiququlu
Ebesiqashelw'eqomeni,
Ukuqaqwa ngumqaqongo
Ezosiqhaqh'emqaleni
Sisaqhuma amaqhuqhuva
Engiwaqale ngaqhaqhazela
Kwagqabuka nengqondo
Njengenqondo likaNqandela
Eqhwandel'amaQadasi.

Translation:

The Play with the Clicks
The polecat came down from Qaqeni
Ran for life and death
Exercising every little muscle and bone
Tied to some part
Untied by Mqaqongo
As if untying the neck bones
Which already were becoming tight
And scared me
As if brains were opening up
Like those of Nqandela
As he tried to help the Qadasi people.

Perhaps the above extracts will illustrate to the reader how limited the printed page is in communicating ideas, and the aesthetic that was meant to be heard rather than seen—or, better still, heard *and* seen—at the same time (with action).

[3] Reader Stewart, *Eyendima Yesibili* (Shuter & Shooter, 1941).

The topic "black folk music" is vague, not only because it lacks geographic orientation which "African," "Afro-American," or "Carribean" would immediately establish in our minds, but also because such concepts as "music" and "folk music" exclude other forms of music and ethnic groups. If I had chosen "music" as my topic and omitted "black folk," you would have expected me to write about the music of Bach, Beethoven, and Brahms and not about Koto music (Japan) or Ravi Shankar's sitar music (India) and certainly not about the art of drumming in Ghana. "Folk music," as a title, makes people think of the music of Bulgaria, Yugoslavia, and Hungary—or of such names as Cecil Sharp and Pete Seeger.

Definitions and characteristics of music are as varied as the world cultures themselves. First, music is defined as the science or art of incorporating intelligible combinations of tones into a composition having structure and continuity. Second, music is vocal or instrumental sounds having rhythm, melody, or harmony. An interesting definition, however, is that music is an agreeable sound (Webster). Questions may then be asked: Agreeable to whom? Which culture determines what is music and what is not?

Black peoples' music now goes with such labels as "primitive," "popular," exotic," "tribal," "jazz," and "soul." Whatever the labels, the music itself has not been recognized by universities—as evidenced by its absence in their curricula, especially in music conservatories.

It is ironic that in the United States, where black people have pursued a music culture of their own for almost four hundred years, where they have contributed more to the music culture of the nation than any other ethnic group, universities recognize the music of Java, Japan, and India for inclusion in university curricula rather than black peoples' music. The University of California (Los Angeles), University of Michigan (Ann Arbor), and Wesleyan University (Connecticut) confer Ph.D. degrees in Oriental music in addition to owning Gamelan orchestras directed partly by visiting instructors and dancers from the Orient. Recently, however, to compound the irony, Ken McIntire, a black jazz musician, was hired at Wesleyan University (the first northern university to increase black students' enrollment to 10 percent) to teach Afro-American music when Central State University (Ohio), a Negro university, had no need for him.

At U.C.L.A. the Ghanian school of drumming is the sole representative for the whole continent of Africa. Beginning in the spring of 1969 Professor Nketia from Ghana University joined U.C.L.A. to conduct seminars in African music on a six-week contract basis.

To my knowledge there is no university in the United States at which a student can study for a Ph.D. degree in Afro-American music, especially in the field of performance. Credit, however, should be given to the anthropology departments of a few universities (including North-western, Michigan, Illinois, Indiana, and Columbia) for their interest in the religious music of black America. Perhaps it is the popularity of the black peoples' music, with its influence in show business and com-mercial circles, that makes it less appealing to academia.

The main characteristics of black folk music listed in order of pri-ority are: (a) rhythm, (b) harmony, (c) melody. The reader should note that in Western culture the order is as follows: (a) melody, (b) harmony, (c) rhythm.

Rhythm to the black man is a natural phenomenon. He appreciates the rhythm of his speech and retains it in his songs by avoiding the melisma (many notes to one syllable of a word), as most of the Negro spirituals illustrate: "Little David Play on Your Harp"; "And I Couldn't Hear Nobody Pray"; "Oh! What a Beautiful City."

An African musical performance, which still persists among the Afro-Americans, is analogous to the art of conversation where a com-pany of eight people sit in a room and converse freely amongst them-selves without a moderator. The participants may share in the discussion, with each member joining in or not joining in at his will. Two members may begin a conversation of special interest to themselves and therefore deviate from the main discussion. One person may decide to smoke, while another may request a glass of water. Three or more mem-bers may grasp a joke and laugh while others may miss it altogether. Two people may decide to leave as three additional members are being greeted with enthusiasm. This is the essence of an African song, ex-pressed in rhythmic phrases of long and short duration, simple or com-plex rhythmic counterpoint, resulting in polyrhythms unknown in other cultures.

Although black people use all kinds of instruments, their special in-terest lies in percussion instruments. The drum forms the basis of the pulse in their music. Those black folk who have been denied the use of drums by missionaries (as in Africa) or by lack of good material to manufacture drums (as in southern Africa) or through domination by foreign cultures (as in the United States) do not hesitate to substitute the hymn book or the Bible for the drum. In other words, everything available can be used as an instrument, including pens and pencils, pots and pans, etc. In schools it is not uncommon for children to beat rhythms on desks—much to the teacher's dislike, especially if the teacher does not share cultural values with his pupils.

In the following song, taped from Warwick Avenue in Durham (South Africa), Zulu workers use the pick-axes as if they were cymbals in the Western symphony orchestra.

Ayagwazan'amaCele[4]

Ayagwazan'amaCele
Ngemikhontw'emibi

Translation:

Cele people kill one another
With dangerous spears.

The above song is a road-digging song in which the workers raise their pick-axes at the same time and strike only after a couple of musical phrases have been sung. The leader of the song is automatically promoted to assistant to the white foreman. This arrangement becomes necessary, since the amount of work done is determined by the pace of the song. In the past Roads Department personnel tried to hurry the workers by suggesting fast-moving songs, whereupon cooperation between the workers and the leader disintegrated and the entire work output decreased. Today, however, it is accepted that the work songs will be slower and, therefore, allow the workers to dance as they slowly raise their pick-axes, rest a little as they make two or three jabs in the air, and then finally allow their pick-axes to strike the ground. Of

[4] Recording by Elkin Sithole, 1965.

course, with all the energy that the song and dance generates, strenuous work becomes lighter and easier.

If the leader wants to give the workers rest, he simply stops the music. Then they can joke, smoke, and relieve themselves until the leader starts the song again; then they all pick up their pick-axes and the whole process starts again. The song does not have a cadence but a continuous flow of melody which can be stopped at any time, as David Rycroft shows in the following song:

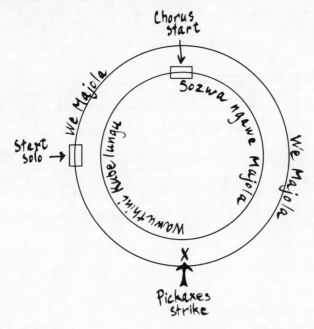

Zulu Work Song[5]

Translation:

> Hey you, Majola!
> Give an account of yourself!
> Hey you, Majola!
> What did you tell white men about us?

Should the leader extend the song beyond what the workers regard as normal duration, they warn him by incorporating such words as "vala" (close it up) in their phrases. He dares not extend the song beyond a couple of seconds after this warning without risking sanctions from the workers. Sanctions range from delay in picking up their tools to dire hatred for his leadership (which might lead to his demotion).

[5] David Rycroft, "Nguni Vocal Polyphony," *International Folk Music* 19 (1967):91.

There is a great similarity between work songs in Africa and those of black America, as the railroad song and "Sound of Thunder"[6] illustrate.

While work songs are generally at a slower pace, especially if working for a white man, African songs for dances are, on the contrary, generally faster.

One of the least expensive instruments is the hand. In addition to being portable, hand-clapping and finger-snapping provide peculiar percussive effects not possible with other regular instruments. Since audiences participate in hand-clapping, each member brings his own instrument. The bigger the audience, the greater the percussive effect. Many a black performer has been frustrated by European audiences which remain passive and fail to provide the handclap percussive response. However, such performers as Tom Jones and the Beatles have worked hard to make audiences participate and respond to performances.

As far as audiences are concerned, there are two kinds: amateur and professional. Amateur audiences are required to clap only at the strong beats; with more professional audiences, hand-clapping can be a complicated rhythmic manipulation. For example, Rev. A. M. Jones[7] found the following hand clap rhythms to be very common throughout the Bantu in Africa.

Another example of how complicated hand-clapping can be occurs as soon as the Operation Breadbasket choir in Chicago sings "Sometimes I Feel Like a Motherless Child."[8]

Besides varieties in rhythm, hand-clapping can also give a variety of sounds. For example, open hands give a greater, hollow sound with more volume than does flat hand-clapping, with less volume and a pointed sharp tone. The size of the hand, too, is a very important influence on the type of sound produced. The bigger the hand, the more volume produced; hence children usually supplement their less-carrying tones with shouts or expressions such as "Ha!"

---

[6] Bernice Reagon, *Sound of Thunder,* Kin Tel Records TK1001 SON47362.

[7] A. M. Jones, *African Music in Northern Rhodesia* (Manchester: Rhodes-Livingstone Museum, 1958), p. 13.

[8] Operation Breadbasket Choir and Orchestra, "The Last Request."

In "Isicathulo Dance"[9] among the Zulus (called Gumboot Dance by Europeans in order to avoid the click) the performers combine hand-clapping and foot-tapping to produce a drum-like effect as they dance to the music of the guitar. The writer has yet to find music students in America who can differentiate the foot-tapping or boot-tapping sound from that of the drum.

The dance songs of the black people abound in rhythm, since every dance song aims at controlling not only the movement of the feet but also the movement of the toes, knees, hips, stomach, neck, head, eyes, hands, and fingers. Each of these parts moves independently of others, yet simultaneously. The beauty of the Western waltz, for example, depends on the erect posture which keeps all parts of the body neutralized from the abdomen to the head, i.e., in a straight line to allow long strides of the legs as the rhythm remains static, as in "Tennessee Waltz," for example.

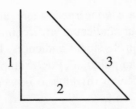

Conductor's Beat

A contrast from "Tennessee Waltz" by Pattie Page or by Lloyd Price[10] would show that in the latter one can dance "twist," "boogaloo," "popcorn," etc., while swinging the stomach from left to right as the head makes jerky up-and-down movements as fast as possible.

Africans move almost imperceptibly from song to speech and vice versa. The melody follows the natural flow of speech tones. In Zulu, for example, there are very few, if any, speech phrases which can be used in an ascending major scale as found in Western music.

A descending scale might be preferred or tolerated in a few cases. When this scale was forced upon Zulu children in South Africa, it did

---

[9] Recording by Elkin Sithole, 1965.
[10] Lloyd Price, *Tennessee Waltz*, Liberty Record #714 C.

not take them long before they sang, as a protest, the following words with the Western diatonic scale:[11]

Africans do not sing scales, nor have they ever considered scales very important in their music. Any succession of intervals would be acceptable, as long as it does not violate language patterns. This approach, of course, is consistent with the theory that a culture with rhythm as its priority over melody does not need a melodic line based on a tempered scale.

The Reverend A. M. Jones found several note sequences which approximate what a Western man would consider some form of scale:[12]

As a Western man himself and therefore bound and obligated to find a scale[13] in any music he studies, Jones resolves the question of scales in Africa as follows (in reference to the above): "Each of these groups is a different scale; they are different because they each have different emphasis notes, – – –. These emphasis notes are the chief notes of rest in the melody or the focal points round which the melody moves."[14]

[11] Swelihle Secondary School students, Umlazi Township, Durban, South Africa, 1964.

[12] A. M. Jones, *African Music,* p. 10. Translated by author from tonic solfa for the sake of consistency in this article. Emphasis notes referred to are at the beginning and end of each four-note phrase.

[13] Any African analyzing scales in African music would do so not for scholarship, but to satisfy Western scholars.

[14] A. M. Jones, *African Music,* p. 10.

Actually there are as many scales in Africa as there are ways of improvising. The nearest equivalent of this approach in contemporary art music (avant-garde) is an arbitrary selection of notes in serial music. In other words, every composition in African music has its own scale, with notes which may be found in other compositions but not necessarily in the same sequence.

People of African descent who became victims of slavery carried these scales with them to their respective countries; some disappeared through disuse, but many remained to influence the trend of music in North America to this day. One of these scales is the pentatonic scale on which most Negro spirituals are built, as in the following:

Swing Low, Sweet Chariot

Look also into the scales of "And I Couldn't Hear Nobody Pray" and "Sinner Please Don't Let Dis' Harves' Pass."

Although the African does use occasionally the seventh note of the major scale, it is, however, usually flattened because it is conceived not as a leading tone up (music ficta) but as a leading tone down, which, if approached from the Western harmonic thinking, would bring us closer to the tonality of the subdominant (F major). But Africans simply pass without establishing the subdominant. In their process of thinking down, they will flatten a number of notes, including the third.

The flattened seventh and the flattened third, usually referred to as the "blue notes," form the foundation of the blues in America. Both these notes have a tendency to create an intimate relationship between the performer and his music or his wife, and may even create memories of a lover who left or who never was.

Combining the pentatonic scales and the principal notes in the blues, we get the following scale:

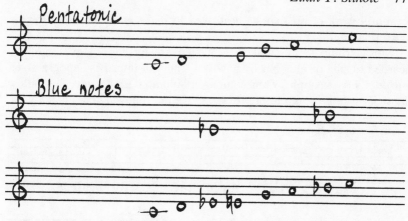

Just as anything could be used as a percussion instrument, any type of voice could be used for singing. In jazz, Louis Armstrong has demonstrated how a rough quality of voice could be used with excellence. This is not a return to primitivism, but an intelligent exploitation of various shades which thereby confirm that beauty and ugliness are not absolutes. In other words, every culture has its own concept of what is beautiful and what is not. For example, blond and blue-eyed beauty applies to European cultures and not to African cultures.

In the same vein, the screams of James Brown and Wilson Pickett add to the beauty of soul music and enhance the performance of an ordinary song by making it part of human experience. In Africa women will listen to a performance of dance and song and suddenly burst into high-pitched, shrill sounds known as Ukuyiyiza (Zulu) as soon as a performer or performers have reached a certain level in their performance. The writer is convinced that the Beatles have not only imitated the black peoples' art but have been good students of it, as evidenced by their "Hey Jude,"[15] where, after satisfying the Western world by giving a gorgeous melody, they suddenly burst into meaningless la-la-la-la where the level of involvement is raised not only by continuous high-pitched tones but also by the freedom of what goes into that part of the song. Most radio stations cut short the second part of "Hey Jude" because they are Western oriented and therefore melody conscious. In other words, their share of the song is over. Wilson Pickett, however, gives the Western world the melody in installments (i.e., in short broken melodic lines) beginning seconds after the main beat has been sounded and quickly gets to what he really wanted to do: *the scream.*[16]

The genius of black folk music lies in the art of improvisation. The creative act is the essence of art, not the finished product. Hence a

[15] The Beatles, "Hey Jude," Apple Corp., 1968.
[16] Wilson Pickett, "Hey Jude." Atlantic SD8215.

beautiful work of art may be destroyed to make an opportunity for the creation of another.

Musicianship in this culture is judged not by how many songs you learned to sing or play but by how well can you improvise upon a given melody. For example, Zulu composer Solomon Linda gave his fellow musicians the freedom to improvise above the following bass melody:

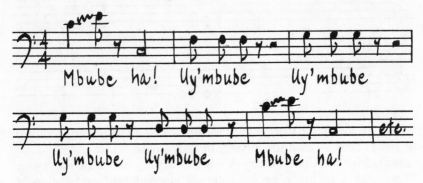

Mbube ha!
Uy'mbube.[17]

Translation:

Hey Lion!
You're a lion.

The result was a polyphony whose complexity increases according to the number of people performing.

The separatist churches in southern Africa as well as the Baptists in the United States refused to join or broke away from Catholic, Anglican (Episcopalian), and Lutheran churches because these institutions denied black people responses of free and spontaneous expressions.

The Reverend C. L. Franklin of Detroit's New Bethel Baptist Church has maintained the African elements of unrehearsed and uninhibited performances, as the following extract shows:

PREACHER:	Son of man,
CONGREGATION:	Yes my Lord
	Yes my Lord
	Oh yeah
PREACHER:	I wish you could hear him say that,
CONGREGATION:	Oh yes
	Ahah
	Go ahead
	(*desk drumming*)

---

[17] Miriam Makeba, *Mbube*, RCA #LPM-2267. ("Mbube" is also known as "Wimmoweh" or "Whim Away.")

PREACHER:	Son of man,
CONGREGATION:	All right
	Yeah—(*hummed*)
	Go ahead
	My Lord
	Ahah
PREACHER:	Can these bones live?
CONGREGATION:	Yes my Lord
	Go ahead
	Yeah—(*hummed*)
PREACHER:	That son of man seems to be reminiscent,
CONGREGATION:	That's right
	My Lord
	Yes! Yes!
	Yeah—
PREACHER:	Of man's limitations,
CONGREGATION:	All right
	Yes! Sir!
PREACHER:	Reminiscent of man's finiteness,
CONGREGATION:	My Lord
	Yeah—
	Yes Lord
PREACHER:	Man's humanity,
CONGREGATION:	Yes Lord
	Yes Sir
PREACHER:	Son of man,
CONGREGATION:	Yes Lord
	My Lord
	(*six drum beats on desk*)
PREACHER:	Son of man you are a scholar,
CONGREGATION:	Yes!
	Ahah!
PREACHER:	You are an educator,
CONGREGATION:	Yes Sir
	Yes Lord
PREACHER:	Son of man, you are a scientist,
CONGREGATION:	Ahah
	Yeah—(*hummed*)
	My Lord
PREACHER:	Can these bones live?
CONGREGATION:	Ahah
	Yes
PREACHER:	Son of man, you are an engineer,
CONGREGATION:	Yes
	Show the light
PREACHER:	Can these bones live?
CONGREGATION:	Yes

Yeah—
All right
Oh—(*hummed*)
PREACHER: Son of man you are a heart specialist,
CONGREGATION: Ahah
All right
Yea! Great
Yes
PREACHER: Son of man you are a geologist,
CONGREGATION: Yeah
Yes! Lord
Preach
Take your time
Come on up
PREACHER: You are a botanist,
CONGREGATION: Yes, my Lord
Yes Lord
PREACHER: You, you are a specialist,
CONGREGATION: Ahah!
Yes
PREACHER: In various phases of the human body,
CONGREGATION: Woo—
Yes Lord
Go ahead brother
PREACHER: You are a psychologist and psychiatrist,
CONGREGATION: Ahah
Yea—
Yes my Lord
PREACHER: You know all about drives and reactions and responses
and tendencies
CONGREGATION: Yes, my Lord
Come on
PREACHER: I want to know with all of this knowledge, can you tell
me, can *these bones live?*
CONGREGATION: Oh Yeah!
All right
Yes my Lord
Yes Lord
Come on
Ha, ha, ha, ha, ha
(*cascading laughter*)
Yeah—(*prolonged and hummed*)
Look out now
Go ahead.
(*Long extended pause, etc.*)[18]

    [18] C. L. Franklin, *Dry Bone in the Valley, Son of Man,* Chess Sermon Series
#36.

Can you imagine what would happen if this preacher delivered his sermon in a Catholic cathedral in Rome or in the Cathedral of St. John the Divine in New York?

Can this Baptist preacher afford to read his sermon or his congregation read the responses in the form of "Lord have mercy on us"?

Soul music has its strong foundation in the baptist tradition, not only because Aretha Franklin[19] is daughter and student of C. L. Franklin, but also because soul music is an art of involvement first with art itself and second with the culture it expresses.[20] It would be incorrect to say black people have the monopoly on soul but, unlike others, the black man does not separate his art from the life lived here and now; from his total experience of being, a dramatic human being emerges, relating both to himself and to his natural and human environment.

Soul music is founded on improvisation combined with a call-response technique. An introduction to a soul performance might start, "Thank you very much ladies and gentlemen," in response to shouts, whistles, and hand-clapping to welcome the performer on the stage. If he is really good, he would then continue the dialogue by asking (*call*) "You wanna soul music?" (*response*) "Yeah! Yeah, do your thing!"

Whether it is Martin Luther King, Jr., with his theme "I Have a Dream!" or Jesse Jackson, it is mandatory for a soul performer or preacher to establish rapport with his audience by such call-response formula as inherent in:

> "I am, *somebody*
> I may be black
> But I am, *somebody*
> I may be poor
> But I am, *somebody*
> I may be unemployed
> But I am, *somebody*
> I may be on welfare
> But I am, *somebody*
> I'm black, and I'm proud
> I'm black and beautiful
> I am God's child." (*etc.*)[21]

Anywhere along the performance, should the response be minimal, the performer will solicit more response with "You understand what I am saying?" or "You dig that?"

To other cultures this style of performance seems oversimplified and abhorrent; yet it is the most complicated and natural in all communica-

[19] Aretha Franklin, "Dr. Feelgood," Atlantic #8139.
[20] James Brown, *Say It Loud, I'm Black and I'm Proud,* King 5-1047.
[21] Jesse Jackson, introductory theme to Operation Breadbasket meetings on Saturday mornings at the Capital Theater, 7941 South Halsted, Chicago.

tions, whether it is conversation or a telephone call. In the latter, for example, one never tells the other party what to say or when to say it; yet no chaos or disaster ever occurs. Of course, disaster may occur if the other party remains silent or passive throughout the telephone call.

Stripping black people of call, response, and improvisation, whatever the rationale, is like taking fish out of water. Schools, though not beyond redemption, have successfully turned many a black child off by denying him the option of interjecting "Yeah! We hear you," or "Yes! Tell us more," during the teacher's lectures.

Finally, leadership among black folk, in church, politics, band-directing, or even court defense, has always been based on the ability of the leader to improvise upon a given theme. Confidence in the art of improvisation encourages creativity, which in turn builds charisma, a necessary ingredient of soul performance. Comedians, black and white, thrive on this art. Whereas Bob Hope and Johnny Carson make one laugh merely by *what* they say, Flip Wilson and Scoey Mitchill put emphasis on *how* they say it. Without the call-response formula allowing spontaneous laughter from the audience, humor is dead—and so is black folk music.

■ Motion and feeling through music

CHARLES KEIL

Charles Keil is an associate professor in the program in American studies at the State University of New York at Buffalo. A graduate of Yale and the University of Chicago, Keil was a research fellow in the Foreign Area Fellowship Program (1964–67), where he studied Tiv language, culture, music, and aesthetics, and Yoruba urban music, and collaborated with A. V. Keil on a study of Tiv dreams, stories, and folktales. His publications include *Urban Blues,* several articles and reviews, such as "Musical Meaning: A Preliminary Report," in *Ethnomusicology* (1966), and a review of a Tiv dance film in *American Anthropologist* (1969). The article anthologized here originally appeared in the *Journal of Aesthetics* in 1966. His work in progress includes a dissertation on Tiv songs, and an anthology of black lyrics entitled *Spirit in the Dark* (with David Ritz).

"Motion and Feeling through Music" has theoretical significance, as well as importance in the continuing controversy over whether meaning is to be accounted for entirely in terms of *composition* (competence, syntax), or whether one needs additionally to look within the dimension that constitutes the realm of *performance* (process and engendered feeling) to account for the total significance of a musical work. In analyzing the expressive performance style of rhythm performers (drummers and bassists) within the jazz genre, Keil is in effect identifying for us the structure of another aspect of Afro-American nonverbal communication: namely, the improvizational spontaneity that is the trademark of Afro-American musical expression and is a characteristic feature of the relationship between the black performer and his audience.

In *Emotion and Meaning in Music,* Leonard Meyer[1] has managed to fill a great deal of the gap in our knowledge defined by the question, What is a musical experience? In attempting a very short sequel to his work, my primary purpose is to discuss an aspect of music that I feel has been neglected in his studies.

To do this effectively, I find it convenient to define my general position vis-à-vis the positions delineated so clearly by Meyer at the outset of his book and in his more recent articles, "Some Remarks on Value and Greatness in Music" and "The End of the Renaissance."[2] To begin with, I am primarily concerned, as is Meyer, with teleological or goal-directed music,[3] although I will try to demonstrate that the goals to which music may direct itself are not always as circumscribed as he would have us believe. Second, we share an emphasis (in this discussion,

[1] Leonard Meyer, *Emotion and Meaning in Music* (Chicago, 1956).

[2] Leonard Meyer, "Some Remarks on Value and Greatness in Music," *Journal of Aesthetics and Art Criticism* 17, no. 4 (1959), and "The End of the Renaissance," *Hudson Review* 16, no. 2 (1963).

[3] Meyer, "End of the Renaissance," pp. 172–73.

at least) on understanding music itself, irrespective of any referential or extramusical content it may possess.

At this point, however, our positions begin to diverge. Among those who are interested in "the understanding of and response to relationships inherent in the musical progress," Meyer distinguishes two points of view: "the formalist would contend that the meaning of music lies in the perception and understanding of the musical relationships set forth in the work of art and that meaning in music is primarily intellectual, while the expressionist would argue that these same relationships are in some sense capable of exciting feelings and emotions in the listener."[4] *Emotion and Meaning in Music* demonstrates quite effectively that formalist and expressionist points of view tend to be complementary rather than conflicting, "for the same musical processes and similar psychological behavior give rise to both types of meaning." Meyer develops this thesis with materials from the Western compositional tradition, using the concept of syntax and certain corollary concepts such as norm-deviation and tendency-inhibition; the net effect is impressive. The thesis established, he attempts (with somewhat less success, I think), to transpose the theory into the musical systems of other cultures.

Meyer's relative failure to extend his generalizations to styles outside the Western stream stems at least partly from the fact that syntax and syntax alone provides the core of his theory; that is, he develops his thesis by first examining the form of music—a succession of tones—and then relating this form via psychological principles to meaning and expression. This procedure assumes that for analytic purposes music can be fixed or frozen as an object in a score or recording, and it implies not only a one-to-one relationship between syntactic form and expression but a weighting in favor of the former factor to the detriment of the latter. This tight equation of form and expression that for Meyer equals "embodied meaning" yields excellent results when applied to the generally through-composed and harmonically oriented styles of our own Western tradition, and in fact it is with only a few reservations that we can extend the equation to the evaluation of this music, saying, "Music must be evaluated syntactically."[5] But when this equation and the corresponding evaluative criteria are applied to non-Western styles or to certain Western compositions *in performance,* we often find that something is missing. It is that something, or at least an important part of it, that I will attempt to specify in some detail.

All music has syntax or embodied meaning; indeed, perhaps the analyst's primary obligation is to elucidate the syntax or grammatical rules of the musical system or style with which he is dealing. Consider, however, the system or style in action—music as a creative act rather than

4 Meyer, *Emotion and Meaning in Music,* p. 3.
5 Meyer, "Some Remarks," p. 496.

as an object—and remember that outside the West musical traditions are almost exclusively performance traditions. In some music, and I am thinking specifically at present of African and African-derived genres, an illumination of syntactic relationships or of form as such will not go very far in accounting for expression. The one-to-one relationship postulated by Meyer will not hold; syntactic analysis is a necessary condition for understanding such music, but it is not sufficient in itself.

In addition to embodied meanings we must talk about aspects of the on-going musical progress that can be subsumed under the general heading of "engendered feeling." For the sake of brevity and, hopefully, greater clarity, these aspects will be listed at the outset. In making this list of polarities my primary reference points are Meyer's theory (as formulated for the Western composition tradition) and the musical idiom that I am best acquainted with, jazz. I hasten to add that these contrasts are loose and fuzzy; they are meant to be thought provoking rather than precise, hence the logical interconnectedness of the notions in either column is conjectural, to say the least.

There are a number of valid objections to be met and ambiguities to be clarified with respect to this preliminary and rudimentary chart of the musical experience. Though I would much prefer to remain suggestive rather than explicit, I will try to delineate point by point what is meant by "engendered feeling."

Table 1. Table of contrasts.

	Embodied Meaning	*Engendered Feeling*
1. Mode of construction	composed	improvised
2. Mode of presentation	repeated performance	single performance
3. Mode of understanding	syntactic	processual
4. Mode of response	mental	motor
5. Guiding principles	architectonic (retentive)	"visual drive" (cumulative)
6. Technical emphases	harmony/melody/ embellishment (vertical)	pulse/meter/rhythm (horizontal)
7. Basic unit	"sound term" (phrase)	gesture (phrasing)
8. Communication analogues	linguistic	paralinguistic (kinesics, proxemics, etc.)
9. Gratifications	deferred	immediate
10. Relevant criteria	coherence	spontaneity

In an effort to meet some objections head-on, first let me repeat that every piece of teleological music involves both syntax and an elusive quality designated here as "process." For example, a good composer gives some spontaneity to his form and, conversely, a good improvisor tries to give some form to his spontaneity (see #1 and #10). In any case, whether the notes are written or improvised, whenever music is performed, the processual aspect becomes important.[6] Second, it may appear that the columns of concepts here simply reassert the formalist-expressionist split so carefully patched up by Meyer. Again, let me reiterate that my ultimate aim is to reveal just that part of expression not inherent in form or syntax—hence the accent on just those aspects of music that are in one sense, yet to be specified, less syntactic.

Third, the metaphysical specter of mind-body dualism seems to emerge from these polarities, specifically at #4 on the list. Although hardly a philosopher or physiological psychologist, I would agree with Meyer that the mind-body duality is something of a false chicken-and-egg sort of issue. Yet it would seem that the dualism dilemma was resolved a little prematurely along Christian Science mind-over-matter lines. I would particularly take issue with the following paragraph:

> On the one hand, it seems clear that almost all motor behavior is basically a product of mental activity rather than a kind of direct response made to the stimulus as such. For aside from the obvious fact that muscles cannot perceive, that there seems to be no direct path from the receptors to the voluntary muscles systems, motor responses are not as a rule made to separate, discrete sounds but to patterns and groupings of sounds. The more order and regularity the mind is able to impose upon the stimuli presented to it by the senses, the more likely it is that motor behavior will arise. Such grouping and patterning of sounds is patently a result of mental activity.[7]

Common sense and day-to-day observation of children learning by doing as much as by thinking would seem to cast considerable doubt on some of the statements above, but recent experiments have demonstrated quite convincingly that our muscles are perceptive.[8] Could it be that in some cultures children learn to dance before (or even while) they learn to listen? Watching an African father support his infant while it pumps its legs up and down to the "high-life" coming over the radio, one is tempted to think so.

[6] Performance and process are synonymous in the sense that the "embodied meaning" column relates to a Beethoven cello sonata while the "engendered feeling" list refers to a Casals performance of that sonata. In this light the "presentation" contrast (#2) may seem confusing, but I am arguing that in music composed for repetition, "engendered feeling" has less chance—or, conversely, the more the music is left in the hands of the performer (improvised), the more likely it is that "engendered feeling" aspects will prevail.

[7] Meyer, *Emotion and Meaning in Music*, p. 81.

[8] Richard Held and Danford Freedman, "Plasticity in Human Sensorimotor Control," *Science* 142, no. 3591, pp. 455ff.; Wilder Penfield and Lamar Roberts, *Speech and Brain Mechanisms* (Princeton, N.J., 1959); D. O. Hebb, *The Organization of Behavior* (New York, 1959).

Which leads to another possible objection: the right-hand column above seems to be flirting seriously with referentialism in that a music-for-dancing or choreographic reference is implied throughout. Far from being a mere flirtation, there often seems to be an out-and-out romance going on between music of the "engendered feeling" type and the dance. If this were a court of law, I would have to sustain this objection, I suppose; but there are three counterstatements and a summation to be made. (1) In many cultures music and dance are so tightly intertwined that a clean separation of the two seems not only impossible but fruit-less—like separating myth from ritual, or mind from body, for that matter. (2) Styles of music designed for dancing have a way of evolving into music for listeners only, e.g., modern jazz. Although Thelonious Monk[9] regularly leaps from the piano to choreograph a chorus or two, and other jazzmen have their characteristic stances and movements, the jazz audience now remains immobile save for some head-bobbing, toe-tapping, and finger-popping. Yet the music persists, and though its choreographic or motor element is less visible, perhaps, it is still essential to an adequate analysis. (3) No less an avowed formalist than Stravinsky states, "The sight of the gestures and movements of the various parts of the body producing the music is fundamentally necessary if it is to be grasped in all its fullness."[10] Can we then dismiss choreographic expression as extramusical?

Toward the end of his book Meyer paradoxically manages to make the point of this sequel while missing the point altogether:

Unfortunately little of the extensive research done in the field of primitive music is of value for this study. First, because the primitives themselves do not make musical creation a self-conscious endeavor, they have neither a theory of music nor even a crude "aesthetic" which might serve to connect their musical practices to their responses. It seems clear that on the most primitive level music is, on the one hand, so intimately connected with ritual and magic that its aesthetic content is severely restricted and, on the other hand, that it is so closely associated with bodily effort that its shape and organization are to a considerable degree products of the physical activities connected with ritual, labor or expressive behavior.[11]

May I suggest, first of all, that it may be our notion of an aesthetic that is rather crude and restricted, not necessarily that of the primitives? Need an aesthetic be exclusively verbal? Can we not infer a great deal from choreographic responses or "symbolic action,"[12] from the "con-

[9] Barry Farrell, "The Loneliest Monk," *Time,* February 28, 1964, pp. 84–88.
[10] Quoted in Meyer, *Emotion and Meaning in Music,* p. 80.
[11] Ibid., p. 239.
[12] Kenneth Burke's works are well worth reading for anyone interested in elaborating a theory of music along the lines presented here. J. L. Moreno's

versation" between dancers and musicians (the stimuli and responses go in two directions, I suspect), not to mention from the relationship between man and instrument? If music "is so closely associated with bodily effort," why not build a bodily aesthetic adequate to the task? John Blacking in his brief discussion of Hornbostel's[13] "motor theory" of African rhythm has asked essentially the same questions, and I strongly second his motion that greater attention be paid to this problem.

Having answered objections with queries, let me return now to some of the above-mentioned terminological ambiguities.

Contracts #1 and #2 are well amplified by the exceptionally articulate (musically and verbally) jazz pianist Bill Evans; the liner notes he has written for a recent Miles Davis album are worth citing at length.

There is a Japanese visual art in which the artist is forced to be spontaneous (#10). He must paint on a thin parchment with a special brush and black water-paint in such a way that an unnatural or interrupted stroke will destroy the line or break through the parchment. Erasures or changes are impossible. These artists must practice a particular discipline, that of allowing the idea to express itself in communication with their hands (#7 and #8) in such a direct way that deliberation cannot interfere (#4).

The resulting pictures lack the complex composition and textures of ordinary painting (#5 and #6), but it is said that those who see well find something captured that escapes explanation (#9).

This conviction that direct deed is the most meaningful reflection (#4, #7, and #9), I believe, has prompted the evolution of the extremely severe and unique disciplines of the jazz or improvising musician.

Group improvisation is a further challenge. Aside from the weighty technical problem of collective, coherent thinking, there is the very human, even social, need for sympathy from all members to bend for the common result. This most difficult problem, I think, is beautifully met and solved on this recording.

As the painter needs his framework of parchment, the improvising musical group needs its framework in time (#5 and #6). Miles Davis presents here frameworks which are exquisite in their simplicity and yet contain all that is necessary to stimulate performance with a sure reference point to the primary conception.[14]

Psychodrama (New York, 1946) is also recommended in this connection, especially for its treatment of spontaneity.

[13] John Blacking, "Some Notes on a Theory of African Rhythm Advanced by Erich von Hornbostel," *African Music* 1, no. 2 (1955): 12–20; Erich M. von Hornbostel, "African Negro Music," *Africa* 1, no. 1 (1928), reprint from International Institute of African Languages and Cultures, *Memorandum* 4:1–35.

[14] Bill Evans, "Improvisation of Jazz," liner notes to *Miles Davis: Kind of Blue*, Columbia, LP-1355.

The numbers inserted in this discourse on jazz essentials refer to other points in Table 1; in fact, this brief text might easily stand by itself as an expanded definition of process (#3). Further definitions of process can be culled from a recent interview with another outstanding jazz pianist, Paul Bley. Although talking about music in general, many jazzmen would find his imagery particularly appropriate to describe a successful piece of music in their idiom:

> Basically the body of music that exists is like a river meeting a dam— constantly accumulating. It'll find the weakest spot, and finally it will break through and continue—but it will still be a river. . . . You can approach a piece as an anti-piece for example. But whatever you use, there has to be *a groove to get into*. That's the hard part. Once you're into it, you don't have to keep deciding whether or not the next phrase is going to be good or not. A soloist can usually tell by the first phrase whether it's going to be a good solo. When you *get into something* to start with, don't worry about the rest of the set; it's going to be beautiful. If anything, just hold back, because it'll all come out eventually anyway. The important thing is getting on the *right track*—the *right pattern*—in the *right way* and exerting the control and practice necessary to get it.[15]

The phrases I have emphasized in this statement, the extended river simile, and Evans's analogy to Japanese art do not add up to a very concrete definition of process, simply because, as used in this context, it is an abstract concept covering an infinite number of "vital drive" principles—which brings us to contrasts #4, #5, #6, and #7 and the empirical problems about which this theory revolves.

What is this groove, track, pattern, or something that Bley and other jazzmen feel is so important to get into? What is this thing called swing, vital drive, or process? Aside from a close examination of the music itself, we have only a brief chapter from a book by French critic André Hodeir to help us. It is from Hodeir, in fact, that I have borrowed the term "vital drive." Although he designates the phenomenon and stresses its importance, he goes no further: "There is another element in swing that resists analysis and that I would hesitate to mention if my personal impressions had not been echoed by many jazz musicians. What is involved is a combination of undefined forces that creates a kind of 'rhythmic fluidity' without which the music's swing is markedly attenuated."[16] All we have then from Hodeir is one more ambiguous term to add to our burgeoning catalogue. In all fairness, he offers a number of important insights into process that will be incorporated here before admitting defeat at the strategic moment. His general failure evolves from a misordering of the elements in swing which, in turn, is related

---

[15] Paul Bley, interviewed by Don Heckman, *Downbeat,* March 12, 1965, pp. 16–17. Italics mine.

[16] André Hodeir, *Jazz: Its Evolution and Essence* (New York, 1956), p. 207.

to his initial denial of what I feel is a fundamentally sound assertion made by Joost Van Pragg as far back as 1936—"Swing is a psychic tension that comes from the rhythm's being attracted by the metre."[17] The word "psychic" here might involve us in more mental-motor (#4) controversy, so for the sake of nonargument may I offer "organismic" as a temporary surrogate—a term sufficiently general, but with strong motor connotations. The focus of attention that this definition gives us is crucial: the tension generated by a complex relationship between meter and rhythm. But here again a qualification must be made by defining meter, à la Meyer, as "an awareness of the regular recurrence of accented and unaccented beats," thus leaving room for a primary pulse, "an objective or *subjective* division of time into regularly recurring, equally accented beats."[18] Quite clearly, it is to the pulse that the rhythms in Van Praag's definition of swing are attracted. It is a subjective pulse that Richard Waterman is speaking of when he uses the concept "metronome sense" as the ordering principle in the polymetered rhythms of West African ensembles.[19] In jazz groups polymeter or even a sense of polymeter may or may not exist, but the subjective pulse or metronomic sense remains the center from which all vital drives derive.[20]

Vital drive may be generated in a number of different ways, and a more detailed look at the mechanics of this process as exemplified in jazz may prove serviceable in explicating contrasts #5, #6, and #7.

The best starting-point is probably rhythm-section attack:[21] the inter-

[17] Joost Van Pragg, "Etude sur la musique de jazz," in *Jazz Hot,* January, 1936; quoted in Hodeir, *Jazz,* p. 196.

[18] Meyer, *Emotion and Meaning in Music,* pp. 102–3. Italics mine.

[19] Richard Waterman, "African Influence on the Music of the Americas," in *Acculturation in the Americas,* ed. Sol Tax (Chicago, 1952).

[20] Marshall W. Stearns, *The Story of Jazz* (New York, 1956), pp. 11–14.

[21] Although not concerned with vital drive or swing per se, Hornbostel and Blacking justly place strong emphasis on attack. Hornbostel states: "African rhythm is ultimately founded on drumming. Drumming can be replaced by hand-clapping or by the xylophone; what really matters is the act of beating; and only from this point can African rhythms be understood. Each single beating movement is again twofold: the muscles are strained and released, the hand is lifted and dropped. Only the second phase is stressed acoustically; but the first inaudible one has the motor accent, as it were, which consists in the straining of the muscles. This implies an essential contrast between our rhythmic conception and the Africans'; we proceed from hearing, they from motion; we separate the two phases by a bar-line, and commence the metrical unity, the bar with the acoustically stressed time-unit; to them, the beginning of the movement, the arsis, is at the same time the beginning of the rhythmical figure" (p. 26). Elaborating upon this statement, Blacking feels that "the contrast which Hornbostel suggests is therefore not so much one of procedure as of *attitudes* towards movements and the productions of sounds." Blacking documents this shift in emphasis by comparing the technique of a Chopi xylophone player with that of a concert pianist. "One has a similar impression of downward 'attacking' movements when one watches the performance of a virtuoso pianist. . . . Closer analysis of his movements will usually reveal that there is a constant lift, which makes the down-

play between bass and drums. By attack[22] I mean simply the type of contact the player makes with his instrument in the initial production of a note. Every drummer has what is known in the jazz argot as a distinctive tap,[23] that is, a manner of applying stick to cymbal. The basic tap may be notated approximately as in Example 1, or somewhat more accurately as in Example 2. But the fact is that taps cannot be notated.[24]

For syntactic purposes we might write down a reasonable facsimile of a tap with all its variations (and there are many) vis-à-vis the improvisations of a soloist, noting how the rhythmic structures of the two patterns complement each other and interact, but we would only be talking about a small part of what the drummer contributes to the music. For the primary goal of his characteristic and internally consistent tap is to create as much vital drive as possible, to build a groove or track for the soloist to get into—and this is done by pulling against the pulse.

Although each drummer has his own way of doing this, for heuristic purposes we may distinguish two common approaches or attacks: those who play "on top" of the pulse, and those who "lay back" behind it. The former school (e.g., Kenny Clark, Roy Haynes, Billy Higgins, Jimmy Cobb, Frank Dunlop, Osie Johnson) attacks the cymbal so close to the pulse as to almost be ahead of it or "above" it when dealing with those notes in the tap that fall on 1, 2, 3, and 4 or a 4/4 measure. It is

---

ward 'thrust' more of a downward 'drop.' Some piano teachers insist that all the muscular effort must be made when preparing to play each tone, so that the note is actually struck during a moment of muscular relaxation. The fingers are allowed to fall on the keys rather than compelled to hit them: thus, contrary to what may seem natural, the louder one plays the more relaxed one is" (p. 15). The Adler system of drumming so popular with today's jazz percussionists is derived from the same foundation of note preparation.

[22] Characteristically, Hodeir relegates the crucial notion of attack to a footnote: "the rhythmic phenomenon is not simply a question of *time values;* the succession of *attacks* and *intensities* is also an important part of it" (p. 196).

[23] I am speaking of jazz since the introduction of the "ride cymbal," during the 1930's.

[24] Of course, no rhythm can be notated *accurately*—there is always performance tradition which gives "life" to the notes (see footnote 10)—but it has often been observed that the standard notation system is particularly ill-suited to the transcription of jazz (or African) rhythms.

primarily by "playing" with the syncopated beat in between the pulses (see Examples 1, 2) that "on top" drummers generate vital drive. Some drummers eschew the "middle" beat altogether on occasion, playing "straight four" on the cymbal and elaborating the pulse with sporadic accents on the snare or bass drum. In the hands of a master (e.g., Louis Hayes, who uses rotary draw-away motions when applying this tap), this "straight four" technique may be dull as dishwater syntactically but electrifying as part of a process. Although it is difficult to generalize about the attacking motion, "on top" drummers tend to keep the stick close to the cymbal, arm fairly stationary with the stroke moving perpendicular to the cymbal, such that each beat lands on the cymbal in the vicinity of its predecessor.

Conversely, drummers of the "lay-back" school (e.g., Max Roach, Philly Joe Jones, Art Blakey, Pete LaRoca, Elvin Jones) seem to attack horizontally, so to speak, placing each beat on a different part of the cymbal as the arm moves back and forth slightly. In the pattern given in Example 2, the lay-back drummer places a slightly delayed accent on the notes marked plus, letting beats 1 and 3 "lay back" still farther behind the pulse, so that only notes 2 and 4, the offbeats, seem to coincide with the metronome.[25] In keeping with the motion described, the "plus 1" and "plus 3" parts of this tap are played on one side of the cymbal and the 2's and 4's on the other. Clearly "lay-back" drummers take more drastic (or less subtle, if you prefer) liberties with the pulse than their "on-top" compatriots.

This dichotomy by no means exhausts the typology of taps. For example, Connie Kay employs what might be called a "flattened-out" tap in which the syncopation is almost but not quite eliminated; Frank Isola is perhaps the only other drummer that uses anything like the same attack. More recently some drummers (notably Sonny Murray, who uses thick knitting needles in place of sticks) have developed a tap that might be described as "reflex-textural." Murray seems to let his hand respond by itself to the music (provided by pianist Cecil Taylor), and while it is sometimes difficult to pick out any recognizable rhythmic pattern in his playing, the resultant echo-effect is certainly tension-producing.

As far as bassists are concerned, a similar broad division can be made on the basis of attack or, in this case, pluck. This distinction is not formally recognized by jazzmen in their argot, but I think it exists nonetheless. The opposition will be described here as "stringy, light, sustained, and basslike" versus "chunky, heavy, percussive, and drum-like." The former school (e.g., Paul Chambers, Scott LaFaro, Ron Carter, Steve Swallow) plucks higher on the strings, away from the bridge, usually with the full side of the finger, and the tone "emerges." The latter

[25] In actual practice beats 2 and 4 are usually reinforced by the "chap" of the sock-cymbal apparatus manipulated by the left foot.

group (e.g., Wilbur Ware, Henry Grimes, Percy Heath, Milt Hinton, Ahmed Abdul Malik, Gene Ramey, Eddie Jones) plucks lower on the strings, nearer the bridge, usually with the tip of the finger, and the tone "bursts."

Classifications of this sort are tenuous, for no jazz bassist or drummer attacks "time" in quite the same way as any other. Nevertheless, I would like to take the discussion a few steps further by examining briefly the various bassist/drummer combinations (see Table 2), relating these

Table 2. A Set of Bassist/Drummer Combinations.

	Bassists	
	chunky	*stringy*
Drummers on-top	A. Malik/R. Haynes P. Heath/K. Clark M. Hinton/O. Johnson J. Ore/F. Dunlap	P. Chambers/K. Clark
lay-back	W. Ware/P-J. Jones	P. Chambers/P-J. Jones S. LaFaro/P. Motian S. Swallow/P. LaRoca R. Carter/T. Williams

("Four-fold table schemes" are very much in vogue with social scientists but this one is simply illustrative and not statistically significant.)

rhythm teams to the "comping" or chording instrument (piano, guitar, etc.) found in most jazz groups and to the soloists. In general, chunky bassists and on-top drummers combine effectively, while stringy bassists and lay-back drummers work well together. Although there are certainly some notable exceptions to this rule, the groups of Thelonious Monk and Miles Davis, two outstanding leaders in contemporary jazz, illustrate this contrast very nicely. Monk consistently prefers chunky bassists, and almost invariably they are coupled with on-top drummers[26] (Pettiford/ Clark, Malik/Haynes, Ore/Higgins, Warren/Dunlop, Sam Jones/Art Taylor), the exceptions being some excellent earlier recordings in which lay-back drummers Art Blakey and Shadow Wilson are coupled with chunky bassists Percy Heath and Wilbur Ware respectively. Miles Davis's rhythm teams are organized on the complementary principle— that is, he invariably employs stringy bassists and shows a marked preference for lay-back drummers (for many years Paul Chambers/ Philly Joe Jones[27] and more recently Ron Carter/Tony Williams), although at one point Jimmy Cobb (a predominantly on-top drummer) and

[26] *Monk's Dream: The Thelonius Monk Quartet,* Columbia CL 1965.
[27] *Round about Midnight: The Miles Davis Quintet,* Columbia 949.

Chambers made up the rhythm team. Miles, too, has occasionally brought a group into the recording studio that had a "Monk-type" rhythm section (Heath/Clark, Pierre Michelot/Clark). These rhythm section preferences are guided, I think, by the manner of phrasing used by the leader-soloists (in these examples, Miles and Monk). Not only is Monk's syncopation (phrases #7 in Table 1) remarkably irregular ("predictably unpredictable," as one writer puts it) even for a jazzman, but he places his notes (phrasing, #7) against the pulse with vicious consistency; hence his preference for a firm, even heavy, rhythm team whose pulse is relatively explicit and (in the case of the bassist, at least) sometimes openly objective. Miles Davis is primarily a melodist; his lyrical phrasing is inconsistent in the sense that during a given phrase some notes may fall behind the pulse, others ahead of it, still others directly on it. He often tends to float around and above the pulse rather than to attack it directly and thereby contribute cumulatively to the vital drive. In other words, he needs a rhythm section that can swing well on its own, with or without him.

I should point out here that in my opinion a *good* stringy/lay-back team can generate considerably more vital drive *by itself* than the best chunky/on-top combination, although the latter teams are better in terms of consistency. For example, when a jazz soloist wants to make a record in New York and has not been working regularly with any particular rhythm team, he can be more confident of making a good showing by bringing together a chunky bassist, typically Milt Hinton or George Duvivier, and an on-top drummer, usually someone like Osie Johnson or Roy Haynes, even if the two men have played together infrequently prior to the recording. The three other possible combinations (cf. Table 2), if made impromptu, are somewhat risky: a chunky/lay-back team sometimes generates a sluggish vital drive (e.g., some Wilbur Ware/Philly Joe Jones recordings), a stringy/on-top team usually doesn't lack for drive but may rush as fast tempos (Kenny Clark/Paul Chambers),[28] and when a stringy bassist and lay-back drummer get together, anything can happen.

The foregoing examples are extremely oversimplified, for the best jazzmen are incredibly adaptable when faced with the task of generating a vital drive around a common pulse; in the words of Duke Ellington, "It don't mean a thing if it ain't got that swing." Charles Mingus, bassist extraordinaire, and Danny Richmond, drummer, have been known to create a number of different vital drives within a single piece;[29] Mingus shifts his attack and Richmond adjusts accordingly, or vice versa. One thinks also of Roy Haynes, a thoroughly on-top drummer, replacing Elvin Jones (who likes to lay back his tap as far as it will go)

[28] *Bohemia after Dark,* Savoy MG12-17.
[29] *Mingus Presents Mingus,* Candid 8005.

with the John Coltrane Quartet for a month or so; after a few nights'
work his playing became practically indistinguishable from that of his
predecessor, at least as far as the overall "engendered feeling" of the
group is concerned. The Coltrane group,[30] by the way, features a unique
yet prototypical process that deserves a full monograph of analysis, if
only we had an adequate theory and method to meet the challenge.
For when we add a third variable to the picture—a pianist whose placement of chords has a great deal to do with vital drive—and begin to
talk about rhythm sections rather than simple teams, processual permu-
tations become very complex indeed. Introduce more variables—that
is, soloists whose placement of notes may be just as important to process
as the contributions of any rhythm section member—and one can begin
to see why jazz critics, with the noteworthy exception of Hodeir, have
studiously avoided the very essence of their subject matter.[31]

Returning to the table of contrasts (#5 and #6), the foregoing examples should facilitate the clarification of terms. In composed music
the structure or architecture is obviously of great importance; broadly
speaking, melody rests upon harmony and embellishment upon melody.
For example, to the extent that an artfully embellished melody inhibits
the tendency toward an expected harmonic resolution, we have embodied
meaning. Furthermore, retention is important, for to properly understand a variation or deviation one must remember the theme or norm;
it pays to know the score.

In improvised music, the fitting analogy is not to a building but to a
train (or to the above-mentioned river): "Swing is possible . . . only
when the beat, though it seems perfectly regular, gives the impression
of moving inexorably ahead (like a train that keeps moving at the same
speed but is still being *drawn ahead* by its locomotive)."[32] To the extent that the rhythms conflict with or exhibit the pulse without destroy-
ing it altogether, we have engendered feeling, and for a solo to grow the
feeling must accumulate. Pursuing the contrast, it pays to keep careful
track of the pulse.

Finally, to comprehend syntax thoroughly it is necessary to focus on
the vertical dimension, to examine the constituent notes of each chord,
to be able to distinguish the various architectonic levels at any point in
the progress, to delimit the range of melodic variations possible over
a given ground base. Something approaching complete comprehension
of the processual aspect will only be possible when we are able to
determine accurately the placement of notes along the horizontal di-

[30] *Coltrane: The John Coltrane Quartet,* Impulse Mono-A21.

[31] Realizing, I suppose, that purely syntactic evaluations do not really do the
music justice, this sort of criticism is also avoided and, excepting the sometimes
insightful semi-sociological work of Nat Hentoff, Martin Williams, and LeRoi
Jones, jazz criticism is largely in limbo.

[32] Hodeir, *Jazz,* p. 198.

mension. Where is each musician placing his notes in terms of the subjective pulse? This is a difficult question to answer, but some progress
might be made by gathering a group of competent musicians and asking
them to match their perceptions and intuitions with respect to a given
rhythm section stimulus. Although the thought is somehow distasteful,
it may be that instruments something like the melograph or the device
used by A. M. Jones[33] can be used to measure objectively the tensions
between the attacks of drummer A and bassist B. How far can the beat
be laid back, or is this phenomenon some sort of illusion? Quite
obviously our explorations of this processual nexus have hardly begun.

A section of Meyer's text provides a good introduction to contrasts
#7 and #8:

> A sound or group of sounds (whether simultaneous, successive, or both)
> that indicate, imply, or lead the listener to expect a more or less probably
> consequent event are a musical gesture or "sound term" within a particu-
> lar style system. The actual physical stimulus which is the necessary but
> not sufficient condition for the sound term will be called the "sound
> stimulus." The same sound stimulus may give rise to different sound
> terms in different style systems or within one and the same system.[34]

Meyer goes on to develop a language analogy—the meanings a word
may have in different contexts, the meaningful relationships between
sentences in a paragraph, and so on—but a stricter analogy to linguistics
can be made with equal or greater profit, for Meyer's "sound term" corresponds quite closely to the notion of a morpheme, and a sound stimulus seems clearly to be on the phonemic level: notes may be considered
as phones, and so forth. This analogy could be carried further, but I
think the suggestion, made often before, that musicologists primarily
concerned with syntax might add considerable rigor and new insights to
their studies by collaborating more closely with linguists should be taken
seriously. On the processual side, a kinesic analogy can readily be made,
and it is with the researchers exploring this field that collaboration may
be of inestimable value. Birdwhistle, Hall, and others have demonstrated that a vast amount of communication is nonverbal, bodily, and
largely unconscious.[35] The problems they deal with in segmenting a
continuum of body movement into significant units on the general
linguistic model—kines, kinemes, and gestures—are very much like
those faced in a processual analysis of music. When a man winks while
gazing at a pretty girl, is he attempting to cope with a piece of dust

---

[33] A. M. Jones, *Studies in African Music* 1 (1959): 13.

[34] Meyer, *Emotion and Meaning in Music*, pp. 45ff.

[35] Ray L. Birdwhistle, *Introduction to Kinesics* (Louisville, Ky., 1952); Edward T. Hall, *The Silent Language* (New York, 1959) and "A System for the
Notation of Proxemic Behavior," *American Anthropologist* 65, no. 5 (1963):
1024–26.

in his eye—or is he making a pass? The answer depends upon what happens next. Similarly, when a jazz saxophonist comes up with a triple forte screech, is he having reed trouble—or is it the climax of his solo? Only the gesture's place in the overall process can determine the answer. This illustration is gross and subject to distortion but suggestive, I think. The analogy between music and both kinesics *and* linguistics may be confusing at first, for while in face-to-face interaction a wink is a wink and a word is a word, in music the same note or set of notes may be both a "sound term" and a "sound gesture." I am insisting on this relatively abstract distinction because in jazz, it seems to me, the net effect of an entire piece may focus on one or two significant gestures; indeed, a vital drive may be seen as a device for holding our attention and increasing our involvement so that a single phrase that is "weighted just right" will have maximum impact—e.g., a good "break" in the earlier jazz styles, the few seconds of "squatting and tooting" that inevitably climax one of John Coltrane's half-hour solos, the soloist whose phrasing is consistently behind the pulse and then for one dramatic instant squarely on top of it. The "gesture" suddenly bursting forth from the midst of "process" may be something of an illusion, for in some instances (those in which the jazzman is more a stylist than an innovator) it may be possible to show how an apparent bolt from the blue has actually been prepared for syntactically by the improvisor. In general, however, an analyst who attempts to cope with the sound and fury of a contemporary jazz solo (e.g., one by Cecil Taylor, John Coltrane, Ornette Coleman) in purely syntactic terms will be forced to quit in frustration; there is little in the way of a consistent terminology to be grasped, and the usual criteria of clarity, unity, and order are largely irrelevant. Careful, even microscopic, observation of the movements associated with music-making, particularly the motions of those entrusted with the creation of vital drive, paying attention to the manner of phrasing used by each participant, noting the characteristic "sound gestures" of the soloist—in short, employing the processual approach advocated here with as much precision as our elementary knowledge allows—will lead eventually, I hope, to more intellectually and emotionally satisfying results.

If the primitive theory that I have attempted to evolve here has any validity, it follows that we must be willing to employ two sets of criteria in evaluating music, depending upon whether the processual or syntactic aspect is dominant. In classical Indian music, to use a difficult example, syntactic criteria seem most applicable to the initial phases of a raga's development, whereas the accelerating rhythmic interplay between sitar and tabla during the concluding portion calls for a processual evaluation.

In order to specify more concretely the relevant criteria for processual music, a discussion of gratifications seems unavoidable. In one sense, there are certain obvious parallels to be drawn from Meyer's discussion of value in music wherein he bestows the label "masterpiece" upon those works in which resistances, uncertainties, tensions, and the overcoming of obstacles manifest themselves most markedly; in good music, if I may paraphrase Meyer, resolutions must be anticipated and patiently awaited; gratifications must be deferred. His citation of Robert Penn Warren's definition of a good poem is apt: "A poem, to be good, must earn itself. It is a motion toward a point of rest, but if it is not a resisted motion, it is a motion of no consequence."[36] In syntactically organized music the points of rest are largely harmonic and the resistances and uncertainties are the product of melodic elaborations, usually reinforced with rhythmic deviations, to be sure. On the processual side, the pulse provides the resting points; the rhythms (in the sense not only of syncopations but of note placement) provide the resistances. There are at least two levels of feeling to be distinguished, for to the extent that vital drive is constant throughout, as it usually is, the resting point is reached only at the conclusion of the music, while the soloist "landing on" the pulse at scattered intervals can release some tension at points within the piece as well. In improvised music uncertainty would also seem to be more constant; you never know from one performance to the next what shape a solo will take or when the significant gestures will emerge. Paralleling Meyer, then, the greater the processual tension and gestural uncertainty a jazz piece has, the higher its value.

In an important sense, however, music which has engendered feeling rather than embodied meaning as its primary goal also stresses immediate gratifications to the detriment of delayed or deferred satisfaction. Somewhat paradoxically, I must admit, the pulse-meter-rhythm tensions of jazz are immensely gratifying, even relaxing[37] in themselves, in a way that extended arpeggios in composed music are not. To the extent that you feel like tapping your foot, snapping your fingers, or dancing, gratification is also constant, and when a jazz fan does not feel like doing this, he begins to question the merits of the group that provides the stimulus. Similarly, when a jazz buff wants to convince you that a particular performer is great, he is likely to point to a single gesture or a portion of the music in which the musician is playing with the pulse in a particularly perverse manner, asking simultaneously, "Isn't that bit a gas?" To exaggerate slightly, a classics fan will wait respectfully until the piece is finished or, better still, put a score in your lap and ask, "Do you see how beautifully it all fits together?"

[36] Quoted in Meyer, "Some Remarks," p. 489.

[37] Hodeir quite correctly stresses the fact that "relaxation plays an essential role in the production of swing" as well, although his argument that a great many Negroes are naturally endowed with "complete neuromuscular relaxation" while white men invariably have to work very hard to attain it, leaves something to be desired (*Jazz*, pp. 206–7).

In music where good process and spontaneity are the avowed goals, it seems unfair if not ludicrous to frame an evaluation exclusively in terms of coherent syntax and architectonic principles. Meyer's remarks with respect to this problem are particularly pejorative and reveal a restricted view of Freud that, as Meyer himself admits, borders on the puritanical. For example, "The differentia between art music and primitive music lies in speed of tendency gratification. The primitive seeks almost immediate gratification for his tendencies whether these be biological or musical." Or, "One aspect of maturity both of the individual and of the culture within which a style arises consists then in the willingness to forego immediate, and perhaps lesser gratification, for the sake of future ultimate gratification. Understood, generally, not with reference to any specific musical work, self-imposed tendency-inhibition and the willingness to bear uncertainty are indications of maturity. They are signs, that is, that the animal is becoming a man. And this, I take it, is not without relevance to considerations of value."[38]

In Meyer's defense it must be added that by primitive he means music that is dull syntactically (repetitive, cliché-ridden, of small tonal repertoire)[39] and not necessarily the music produced by nonliterate peoples. Nevertheless, such statements are first of all rather silly from an anthropological perspective, for every culture demands varying sorts of conformity, toleration of uncertainties, and deferment of gratifications from its members; these demands are no greater for participants in our civilization than those made upon Kalahari Bushmen, though they may be somewhat different. Second, why should we assume that immediate gratifications are evil and brutish? Meyer insists that value correlates with the inhibition of natural tendencies and the overcoming of obstacles, and for syntactic music in which intellectual control is at a premium this may be so. But what of music where inhibition itself is the primary obstacle? In our culture (and perhaps in others where hyperconformity must be fought) it may be that music whose goal is engendered feeling, spontaneity, and the conquest of inhibition is of far greater value than music which aims to reflect our civilization and the repression–sublimation–Protestant-ethic syndrome upon which it is based simply because, like much great art, it offers an antidote, a strategy for dealing with our situation[40] rather than reinforcing it. I suspect, as do other critics, that we admire many modern painters—Picasso, Klee, Kandinsky, Miro, Chagall, Pollack—more for their sophisticated childishness than for their maturity. Many modern jazz-

[38] Meyer, "Some Remarks," p. 494.

[39] Even this qualified definition of "primitive" reveals the analyst's syntactic blinders; in music concerned with process, constant repetition, the use of clichés, and exceedingly small tonal repertoires can sometimes be employed to create great tension and vital drive.

[40] See footnote 13.

100 Rappin' and stylin' out

men, notably Thelonious Monk, Sonny Rollins, and Charles Mingus, are equally serious about being infantile. At the very least, art of this sort deserves to be evaluated by canons other than those associated with a Meyerish concept of maturity (i.e., unity, control, clarity, variety), although admittedly such general concepts can be twisted to at least partially fit music of the processual sort. In a long, involved, and erudite sequel to Freud's *Civilization and Its Discontents*,[41] Norman O. Brown offers some interesting notions that may be suggestive in concluding this attempted sequel to Meyer's work. Although any crystallization of his thought into a few neat slogans does Brown a grave injustice, he argues generally for release from repression, resurrection of the body, and a return to the perverse, polymorphous playfulness (and immediate gratifications) of childhood. The latter qualities of childhood alliterated so playfully by Brown (and Freud before him) strike me as a peculiarly appropriate set of criteria for establishing value, if not greatness, in jazz. Just how one goes about measuring perversity or playfulness I am not at all certain. But where process and spontaneity are the ends in view, I think we must make the effort to analyze and evaluate in these terms, for, as Brown notes in speaking of art, "Its childishness is to the professional critic a stumbling block, but to the artist its glory."[42]

Finally, I must ask myself the same nasty question that I have directed to Meyer: Will a theory based almost exclusively on one musical idiom, in this case jazz rather than classical music, have any validity when applied to the music of other cultures? I am convinced, of course, that ultimately the answer will be an emphatic Yes. My conviction rests on two assumptions: first, that the vast majority of cultures the world over have musical styles that are performance-oriented, dance-derived, and at least partially improvised; and second, that a processual methodology will be developed in the coming years so that this rudimentary theory can be tested, elaborated, and refined accordingly.[43]

[41] Sigmund Freud, *Civilization and Its Discontents* (London, 1930).

[42] Norman O. Brown, *Life against Death* (Middletown, Conn., 1959), p. 58.

[43] I wish to thank Leonard Meyer (composer, critic, and teacher), Rozwell Rudd (jazz trombonist), Louis Feldhammer (perceptive layman), and Angeliki Keil (psychologist and wife) for the comments which have helped me revise this paper and which have also been instrumental in generating an excessive number of footnotes!

◼ Dynamics of a black audience

ANNETTE POWELL WILLIAMS

Born in Chicago, Annette Powell Williams combines a research interest in linguistics and communication with an experience gained from growing up, living, and working in Chicago's South Side black community. A graduate of Chicago State University, she was enrolled as a graduate student at Northeastern Illinois University's Center for Inner City Studies at the time she wrote this paper, one which reflects her considerable perceptivity and interest in this nonverbal aspect of black communication. With only scant allusions to black audience dynamics in the literature, her contribution is welcome as an introduction, however brief, to a significant area of black communication—one which every black speaker/performer knows and relies upon as he presents himself before a black audience, yet a knowledge scarcely articulated in print up to the present time. Optimally, as with other aspects of nonverbal communication, audience dynamics should be systematically studied with film within the context of an actual event. In lieu of the optimal, selected photographs have been incorporated within the text, with the hope of making the author's descriptive analysis more meaningful.

In *Thinking on Your Feet,* Louis Nizer advises his readers that "the art of persuasion is a complex combination of psychology, hope, prejudice, emotion, fear, facts, purpose, and beauty. The vehicle on which they are all propelled is rhythm." According to Nizer, a speaker can expect certain conduct from his audience. It is considered improper to do anything that disturbs either the speaker or your fellow listeners. Included in the infractions are such things as talking to your neighbors, slouching in your seat, and laughing or snickering when the speaker has made a mistake embarrassing to himself.

Such "courtesy" is expected and is generally given to speakers by white audiences. It is not the case with black audiences. What constitutes courtesy to a white person may not, in fact, constitute courtesy to a black person. Courtesy is relative to the group one finds oneself with. To turn one's back when greeting an old friend is a courtesy to a black person; it acknowledges that the two friends still maintain a binding trust with one another. Such a gesture to a white person would be discourteous.

Very often, if a white speaker appears before a black audience, he experiences anxiety and frustration. He finds that the audience does not respond in the usual, courteous manner. An examination of the audience would reveal a good deal of activity during the speech. Commenting to neighbors, constant adjustment of the position in the seat, and turning around are frequent.

This kind of activity constitutes inattention and disrespect to the white speaker, the worst thing that could happen. To a black speaker it means something else. It means that he is communicating with his audience and that they are communicating with him. He is stirring their emotions and they are reacting to what he has to say.

In examining a black audience, certain patterns seem to unfold. Before the program begins, the audience is relaxed. Many people are sitting with their arms and/or legs crossed; they are conversing with friends and neighbors. They may be found walking, talking, or just standing along the sides looking at others.

When it is time for the program to begin, the audience composes itself. Conversations with neighbors and friends cease. People begin to find the seats they previously selected for themselves. Those seated unfold their arms, sit up straight in their seats, and uncross their legs. For the most part this movement is self-directed. As the appointed hour approaches, the ritualistic activities cease out of respect for the occasion. If one arrives at the point when most of the people are seated and quiet, then he knows the program is about to begin.

The movement which follows depends on what the speaker has to say and how he says it. Black audiences react to speakers more with their movements than with their applause; this is more prevalent when the person speaking is unfamiliar to them. If the opening remarks made by the speaker antagonize his audience, they react by keeping their arms folded during the entire speech. Some will not applaud. Some will cross their legs again, slouch in their seats, and wait until the speech is over.

When what a speaker has to say is acceptable to most members of the audience, they sit forward in their seats, or bend forward slightly. Some have their arms resting on their legs and their hands folded. In this position a person can watch the expression of others sitting around him. It is also a position which indicates that he is giving his full attention to the speaker.

Certain positions assumed by black people have their special reasons and meanings. Black people carry expressions on their faces which communicate acceptance or rejection, boredom, agreement or disagreement, embarrassment, indecisiveness, belief or disbelief. Most black people can read these facial expressions, and it is therefore important to them to be in a position where they can watch others. This probably accounts for most black people's preference for sitting in the middle of the audience.

Black people have many ways of indicating boredom. For example, cupping the chin in one's hands can signal that attention is being given —or it might indicate boredom, depending on the facial expression. Another indication of boredom appears in a person who is observed with his head slightly to the side, arms folded, in a statue-like position. Still another is in a person who repeatedly turns his head up to the ceiling and sighs an extended sigh.

Black people show agreement by nodding the head—but then, most people do. But if a speaker brings out a point that that person has never thought about, the nodding is replaced by a change of position in the seat, arms are folded, and the person rocks back and forth before assuming his original position. Before this person resettles himself, he will glance around the audience to see how others are reacting.

Some people close their eyes to indicate agreement. Others look at the persons next to them. If the person smiles at his neighbor, it indicates approval of what has been said. If the neighbor does not smile back, it indicates that he did not approve of what was said, or that he did not agree with it.

When something said sounds ridiculous to a black person, he generally will turn to another black person and give him a very hard stare when he catches his eye. Such stares translated into words would say, "Does this sound real to you?" or, "That's a bunch of shit!" or, "This cat is out of his mind!" Usually this movement is simultaneous, which makes it a source of amusement between the parties, as well as indicating that the two are of the same mind.

When a speaker says something that is embarrassing to himself, certain movements are elicited from black people. Many of them will slowly bring their hands up to rest on their cheeks until the embarrassing moment is over. Others will bend their heads back, touch their cheeks, and close their eyes. Still others will change their positions in their seats, turning around at the same time to look at the other members of the audience. In doing this, they can catch the eyes of several people and communicate a thought.

When black people are not sure whether what the person has said is believeable, some of them give one another very quick glances to ascertain what others think about that point.

When the audience does not understand what a speaker is discussing, most of them turn around nervously, glancing from side to side. An indication of total rejection is shown by turning one's head away from the speaker with eyes closed.

Some illustrations of these points as well as others can be shown in the following photographs.

Photo I was taken outside an administration building in Springfield, Illinois, when the Reverend Jesse Jackson was leading the march on Springfield to protest the threatened cutback of welfare payments. The group clearly presents a united front and common purpose, yet note the variable eye focus of different members of the audience checking out the "haps" (happenings) elsewhere even as they listen *attentively* to

what Jackson is saying. Black cultural norms for attentive listening do not require eye contact.

In contrast, consider Photo II, of a white audience taken when William Kunstler spoke at the University of Illinois at Chicago Circle. The eye focus of the audience centers directly on Kunstler. Attentive listening is manifested not only by being within hearing distance but through direct eye contact with the speaker. Variable eye focus, as depicted in the photograph of the black audience, would signal *inattentiveness* to a white speaker. Failure to interpret correctly the cultural signals of members of others groups always has an adverse (and at times disastrous) effect on attempts at cross-cultural communication.

Cultural "understanding" can only come about after a long period of involvement with a group. The subtle ways in which black people communicate with each other, unperceived by the outsider—or, if perceived, likely to be misinterpreted—are nevertheless the cues that make for effective communication. Their correct interpretation by black speakers adds greatly to their ability to communicate with black audiences.

Photo credits: Kunstler photo by John Burlinski; Jackson photo by Paul Walker.

Vocabulary and culture

■ Names, graffiti, and culture

HERBERT KOHL
PHOTOGRAPHS BY JAMES HINTON

Herbert Kohl is the author of *The Age of Complexity, 36 Children, Teaching the "Unteachable,"* and *The Open Classroom.* A graduate of Harvard and Teachers College, Columbia, and a Henry Fellow at Oxford in philosophy, Kohl also served on the staff of the Center for Urban Education in New York and was a public schoolteacher for several years in Harlem. He is presently directing "Other Ways," an experimental program in the Berkeley, California, schools.

James Hinton, photographer and filmmaker, formerly taught photography at the Afro-American Total Theatre Arts in New York and film-making in the "Other Ways" project in Berkeley. A free-lance photographer for the Associated Press, *New York Times,* Random House, Macmillan, IBM, and *Cultural Affairs Magazine,* and cameraman for WNDT-TV for the documentary film *The War Is Over* (1967), Hinton was director-cameraman for the WNDT-TV, New York (1968), Huntley-Brinkley news program covering the Columbia University student revolts, Poor People's March, and black politics in Newark, New Jersey. His film-making credits include *The New-Ark,* by Leroi Jones. In addition to the present publication, Hinton and Kohl have collaborated on a forthcoming book, *Anthony Cool as Golden Boy* (Dial Press).

"Names, Graffiti, and Culture" originally appeared in the *Urban Review* in April, 1969. It successfully utilizes and reaffirms the traditional link between vocabulary and culture in the anthropological discipline, and it exhibits knowledge and insight gained about urban street life from an application of this method. It has been established that one of the best ways to get to know a group is to identify and examine the vocabulary (names, terms, and expressions) habitually used within the group. By applying this basic understanding and approach to the public written language (graffiti) of black and Puerto Rican urban youth in New York, much significant cultural information was revealed. The information is there, proclaimed from building to building or inscribed on school desks, *public*—and yet *private,* because adults don't read the walls and teachers ignore desk inscriptions except as something to erase. Yet it is this "other" world, oral, vernacular, induced and unsanctioned, that is the antithesis (and at times the antidote) to the formalized, academic, imposed, and legitimated world of adults and institutions, one from which adults can learn a great deal about culture, learning, and life.

Johnny Rodriquez is fourteen and lives with his mother, three brothers, and two sisters in a poor, predominantly Puerto Rican neighborhood. Last year he stopped going to school. It probably doesn't make much difference to the authorities, since he was thrown out of junior high school and put in a school for "socially and emotionally disturbed children" where truancy is hardly unusual. Accepting the official definition of himself as a disturbed and different child, he withdrew from all contact with public authorities. He stays in his building from nine in the morning until three in the afternoon, taking care of his pigeons. He has over 100 birds—tumblers, flights, homers. He knows which birds fly best in windy winter skies and which in the still summer air. He built a basement winter quarters for his birds and is known as a pigeon expert in the neighborhood. It is only after three in the afternoon that his life with other people begins.

I met Johnny in a strange way. At Christmas, 1966, I had a party for some former pupils who had been in my sixth-grade class five years before and were now in high school. Two of them brought Johnny and asked us in private if I would teach him to read. He wanted to learn badly, they told me, and was messing up by memorizing the signs in the neighborhood and thinking that's all there was to reading. There was no one to help him at home and he was ashamed to ask me himself, so they were doing it for him. I had taught them to read, they reasoned, so why couldn't I teach Johnny?

I accepted Johnny as a pupil, and beginning in January, 1967, he came to my apartment punctually at 4:00 every Monday and Friday afternoon. We both pretended for the first few months that he couldn't have lessons any earlier than 4:00 because he was in school every day until three.

About the time Johnny became my pupil I began to notice the word "Bolita" scrawled across the elevator doors and halls of my apartment building. Under each inscription of the name was a date. It took me over a month to figure out that all the dates were Mondays and Fridays. I mentioned my discovery to Johnny and asked him to stop documenting his visits in this manner since my neighbors didn't appreciate it. The next week he came to the lesson with "Johnny Bolita" written boldly across the cover of his notebook and "Bolita 2–10–67" scrawled in ballpoint on his left palm. The writing in the halls and elevators stopped.

"Bolita" is Spanish for "little ball." Johnny explained to me that his mother gave him that nickname because he was so small and full of energy and mischief.

I forgot about the matter until several weeks later, when I noticed Johnny's handwriting on a wall several blocks from my building. The wall was overrun with layers of names and nicknames, declarations of love and hate, boasts and insults. On one corner was "Bolita as Johnny Cool."

I looked at the wall more closely and was able to find other signs of Johnny under the layers of graffiti. I could discern the worn-out declaration "Johnny and Anita—Don't Mess!" and an anagram:

Bolita
nestor
g
Jaime
Larry

Next to the anagram was another one that read:

Maria
n
titi
t
Anna

and between the two anagrams were the initials T.L.F.E. scratched into the brick on the wall and then carefully traced over in blue and yellow magic marker.

That wall fascinated me, and I often returned to search for new additions or to unravel the many layers of writing it held.

There were many things that were puzzling:

Golden boy as Anthony Cool
Edgar as José
Gilbert as Fire Box
Anna as Brillo
Willie as Papo

Other things began to fit into patterns:

Johnny of 93
Jaime of 89 as Batman
Marie the Black Queen of 89th

I could make out that at one time Titi and Nestor were enclosed in the same heart and that at another (or perhaps the same) time Larry claimed Titi as his one-and-only.

The form the graffiti took was as interesting as the content. There was deliberate overwriting and sly dialogue. "Fat shit" was scrawled across "Billy the Great" and "Johnny Cool" had "or cold" appended to it in another hand. The media used for the inscriptions were as varied as contemporary mixed-media work in the graphic arts. There was writing and drawing in multicolored magic markers, crayons, pencils, and paints. There were also things scratched into the wall with pen knives, and chipped away from the wall with stones.

The more I attended to that particular wall, the more I felt like a voyeur spying on the lives of children who were strangers to me. I found myself looking closely at children in the neighborhood, identifying their faces with names and nicknames from the wall, manufacturing intrigues and adventures for them. Johnny's friends were special targets for my imagination—Maria, the black queen, Jaime Batman. . . .

Johnny appeared in a different perspective to me because of the way he was described on the wall. During reading lessons he was shy and reserved. He appeared scared and ashamed because he couldn't read. At the same time he was a serious and persevering student who, despite his shame, was willing to start from the very beginning and learn the alphabet and elementary phonics even though he was over fourteen. He arrived punctually for each lesson and impressed me as a remote, inarticulate, and probably unpopular boy.

"Johnny Cool"—I watched Johnny more closely on the street after discovering his nickname. It was easy since he was a delivery boy for a tailor across the street from me. I saw him bopping down the street with plastic bags full of clean clothes swinging over his shoulder. He would stop and rap with some girls for a while, then continue on, followed by at least one of them. In fifteen minutes he would return, his arms, empty of cleaning, hanging casually about the girl's shoulders or waist. They would be chatting away, laughing. Johnny seemed like another person on the streets; or perhaps it would be more appropriate to say that he was another person with me during lessons. I stumbled onto a rare view of a youngster as he is most naturally with his friends and felt sad at how artificial is even the best of teaching situations.

The discovery of Johnny's two faces led to a change in our relationship. I told him about finding "Bolita as Johnny Cool" written on a wall; although he blushed, he began to talk about it and other nicknames. He explained that some kids had as many as four nicknames: a first from their parents, a second from their friends, a third from their teachers, and a fourth they chose for themselves. I mentioned Jaime as Batman; Johnny laughingly made it clear to me that this was Jaime's fantasy about himself. Maria was called the Black because of her attitude, and he was called Johnny Cool because he had nice vines and a good rap. He elaborated for my benefit that vines were clothes and that a rap was a line you gave a girl.

We became closer and Johnny became more relaxed during lessons. He seemed more like the Johnny I'd observed on the streets. Often the lessons were taken up with talking about writing on the walls and what it tells of the life of the child. When I mentioned that I was thinking of writing a book on graffiti, he offered to help. Once I asked him why he put his names on the walls of buildings in his neighborhood. He replied, "Because all the kids do," and when I pressed him, he had no response. Yet as he thought more about it he talked of the joy of knowing that other people see one's name and the sense of satisfaction he felt in seeing his own name next to those of his friends.

As Johnny began looking more intensely at the writing on walls, he told me of secret things writtten on rooftops and of a favorite wall where all the kids had been inscribing their names for years ("at least five," as he put it). He even explained to me that the small tattoo between the thumb and forefinger of his left hand was the symbol of his gang, and that they put it on the walls whenever they were about to challenge another gang.

One day I asked Johnny to write down for me all the names he knew by heart and could spell. He produced this impressive list:

Nestor	Maria	Freddie	Lydia
Angel	Titi	Hector	Julie
Jaime	Anna	Betty	Wanda
Larry	Anita	Cookie	Wilfredo
Johnny	Victor	Bewitch	Joseph
Milta	Letty	Nora	Louy
Tito	Slim	Millie	Fernando
Miguel	Lefty	Joseph	Marta

Johnny could read and write all of those names and probably others that hadn't occurred to him that moment. Yet at that time he was reading on a first-grade level.

I spoke to Johnny of my fascination with what I was learning of his life and his friends. It went beyond their inscriptions on walls, though it started there. I began to take graffiti tours of my neighborhood, stopping in halls or in front of walls, poking in alleyways and vacant lots. I tried to trace the territory occupied by different groups of youngsters, looking at notebooks, casts, autograph books, the backs of jackets, and tattoos.

Occasionally I showed Johnny some of the things I'd copied, and once told him I felt embarrassed and somewhat guilty spying on the lives of children that way, as if I were invading the privacy of strangers and returning with their secrets.

Johnny looked puzzled and told me, "Mr. Kohl, they're no secrets— that's why we write them on the walls. Only grownups don't read them."

They're no secrets

The documents on walls are there to be read. It's a question of what we take seriously and what we choose to notice. But generally we are a visually tired people, worn out by the movement in cities and the freneticism of television. It is of little interest to busy and harassed people that kids write their names on walls, and that, in doing so, they reveal a great deal about themselves.

On the other hand, clever comments, underground jokes, and toilet repartee are a relief to the weary. People notice "Even paranoids have enemies," or "Beethoven scares little kids," scrawled over billboards, toilet walls, or subway ads, yet they pay little attention to the names and nicknames, declarations of love, hate, and confusion that appear on the same walls. It's a question of what we are able to take seriously and what we are willing to take the time to notice.

There is a prehistoric cave in the Dordogne region of France called the Cave of the 1,000 Bison. On the walls and ceilings are hundreds of prehistoric drawings and paintings of bison. The cave was rediscovered during our century; gates have been put over the prehistoric impressions, which are now illuminated by spotlights. The guidebook praises the bison elaborately and deplores the defacement of much of the cave by pre-twentieth-century tourists. It seems that the latest rediscovery of the cave is only the most recent of a series extending over several centuries.

A close look at the ceiling reveals not merely the hundreds of bison but thousands of names and dates, jokes, boasts, insults, and witticisms written over the past three centuries at least: drawings and scratchings, lists of names and esoteric symbols. None of these is illuminated by spotlights; rather, they are concealed in the darkness and damned in the guide books. Again it is a question of what we take seriously and what we choose to notice. How much may be there, unread, on those walls?

I am not suggesting that people shouldn't preserve prehistoric documents and take care to keep them unsoiled. I *am* suggesting that when documents exist we pay attention to them because they don't fit into our preconceptions of what is "serious" and what is not. We may learn more of nineteenth-century French secret societies or fraternal organizations, or of the style and content of graffiti over three centuries, from the walls of the Cave of 1,000 Bison than we learn of prehistoric man. Such modest knowledge is not to be scorned. In fact, it may reveal more of the everyday life of times past than do documents that are considered historically "significant."

Not all walls go unscrutinized. People in our society seem to be well acquainted with the walls of public toilets and quite familiar with that literature. The recent books on graffiti are little more than collections of writings transcribed from the walls of toilets.

Some of what is written in toilets is funny; much of it is nasty. But the most general characteristic of public-toilet graffiti seems to be expression of thoughts, feelings, and ideas that are usually left unsaid in "polite" conversation. Toilet graffiti is the medium of a doubly anonymous dialogue—an anonymous audience with equally anonymous writers (drawn from that audience) responding to each other. Robert Reisner in *Graffiti* describes the writing on the walls of toilets of interracial bars, congenial liberal places. It is often racist, full of hate and confusion, self-degradation and self-aggrandizement.

One finds such things as:

Congo coons rape nuns

卐

Juden raws!   Jews out!
Black Power—want white women
Burn, baby, burn.

In the toilet the patrons of these bars are alone in a public place where they can snicker at truths they can't face or participate in feelings that terrify them.

Johnny Bolita may have written a furtive "The teacher is a faggot" in the toilet of his school, but he was being neither furtive nor secret when he proclaimed "Bolita as Johnny Cool" on the wall of a building on his block. Nor was he being anything but public when he declared on another wall: "Johnny and Anita—True Love For Ever."

Johnny knew who his audience would be when he wrote the last two things. It would be his friends and enemies, the kids on the block. The walls of buildings are thoroughly public, and people who write on them (mostly children and teenagers) do it to reveal, even to proclaim themselves, and not to conceal themselves.

There are pleasures in writing about toilet graffiti. People display so much suppressed or hidden cleverness, brilliance, irony, and humor in public toilets that the mere quotation of what they produce is impressive and entertaining. This cleverness and brilliance acknowledged, there are reasons to forego writing about toilet literature and look more closely at public walls to discover what they can teach us of life in our cities.

Little is known about the way children come to terms with the cities they are forced to inhabit. It is usually the novelist or poet and not the social scientist who is interested in discovering and re-creating the lives youths lead outside the ken and supervision of the adult world. Yet for many children, life on the streets is as influential in the formation of adult personality as any other psychological or sociological factors. The way children choose to identify themselves to friends and enemies, to declare love or hate, or to associate themselves with groups of their peers is a crucial aspect of their growth. The way they and their friends stake out and defend the territory they inhabit is no less important.

In all of this, children make constant use of symbols and marks which proclaim and are often part of their activities. When a gang writes: "Defenders Turf—Junkies Keep Out" on a supermarket wall, they are not merely labeling a wall that is already theirs, but actually claiming that wall as a boundary of their territory through the act of leaving their mark on it.

When a boy writes his name, that of a girl, and T-L-A (to love always) on a wall, he is committing himself to certain feelings and ways of acting. He may not be committing her, however, and this is often reflected in someone else's disavowal of the boy's affection written on the same wall.

Wall graffiti provides material for a glimpse at the life of urban youths. But the same material one finds on walls can be discovered in other places—scrawled in notebooks, on casts and skin, or in slam books and slang books. It can be uncovered by looking at rings and tattoos, the backs of jackets, and inscriptions on sidewalks. There is nothing unusual about these things or places; we see them all the time, though we hardly ever attend to them. Urban iconography is too often ignored. It may well be worth the effort and concentration to discover what young people reveal about their lives from the marks they leave on things and themselves.

What's in a name?

"Johnny as Johnny Cool" and "Bolita as Johnny Cool" turned up in Johnny's handwriting on walls throughout his neighborhood. The "as" in these inscriptions puzzled me, and I noticed that it kept cropping up in strange ways. On one particular wall it appeared in the following contexts:

Negro as Jim
Clarence as Lefty
Edgar as José
Juan as Fire Box
Golden Boy as Anthony Cool
Anna as Brillo
Alice as Slick

On some of my pupil's notebooks the same "as" appeared on their title pages:

Rafaella as Titi
Helen as Tiny
Gloria as Babyface
Frankie as The Monster
James as Boy

Once I asked Johnny what this "as" signified, and his explanation was simple: "It means sometimes I'm Johnny and sometimes I'm Johnny Cool."

We all have many public identities and behave in different ways with different groups of people. We also develop ways for these identities to be known by the proper people. We have business cards, pins, secret handshakes, badges, etc. In the case of youngsters from poor neighborhoods, they use the walls that surround them to document and make public several of these identities. This is not true for children of the middle class, since the walls in middle-class neighborhoods are usually kept scrupulously clean of graffiti by superintendents, landlords, zealous parents, and other graffiti-destroyers.

There is an interesting characteristic of the "as" form of graffiti: it is reflective. One discovers "Clarence as Lefty" as well as "Lefty as Clarence"; "Alice as Slick" as well as "Slick as Alice." It does not differentiate a proper or legal name from a nickname; rather, it places various types of names in interchangeable positions and may signify that the authors of such graffiti choose to display two of their identities side by side as coequals.

On the surface, adults would not regard the two types of names as coequal. The given name (Clarence or Alice, for example) would be thought of as primary and essential, while the nickname (Lefty or Slick) would be thought of as secondary and incidental. The given name is received from one's family and remains unchanged throughout life. This contrasts with the secondary name or nickname, which is usually a name the youngster chooses for himself or receives from his peers. It identifies him as a member of the peer group, which can be as important to him as membership in his family. The "as" locution declares that the child wants public acknowledgment of the fact that he lives in a world of his friends which is, to him, coequal to the world of his family.

The "as" phenomenon is not the only curious one found on walls. Often accompanying it, or with a single name alone, one will find the specification of a locality. Thus, Papo, a common Puerto Rican nickname, may be scrawled by itself; but it will also appear as:

Papo of 87
Papo of 91
Papo of 114

Another example of such specification of locality is:

to distinguish him from other Killer Als.

The author of "Papo of 87" is saying "I am a Papo, one of many, and am that specific one that lives on 87th Street." The name Papo is both specific and general in function and the "of 87" functions very much like Smith and Williams in names John Smith and John Williams. Nicknames are often very much like first (or given) names; they beg to be qualified to place the individuals that bear them in specific social contexts. At present there is probably very little that all the Johns or Peters in the United States have in common, except their names. But think of "Peter," for example, which derives from a word meaning "stone" or "rock"—how much like the nickname that sounds! It is not farfetched to speculate that given names may have had their origins in the identification of people with things or characteristics of personality.

Which came first, the name or the nickname?

Take the Puerto Rican nickname Papo. According to etymological dictionaries of the Spanish language, the prime meanings of *papo* are variously: thistle down, a fowl's gizzard, the fleshy part that hangs down from the chin of a fowl, the quantity of food given to a bird of prey, and the crest of feathers about a bird's neck and breast that he fluffs up during courtship and combat. In colloquial language *hablar de papo* (to speak from one's papo) means to boast or talk big. From here it is a short step to calling a braggart or boaster a papo and, by extension, Papo.

Over the years Papo seems to have become a nickname which only retains the most tenuous ties to its original meanings. I have spoken to a number of Puerto Rican friends about the nickname Papo; they all knew at least one Papo, yet they claimed that the word "Papo" itself had no meaning beyond its use as a name.

One girl told me that Papo was the nickname given to the oldest or youngest or favorite son of the family—perhaps the one parents boast, deriving from "my papo" (my boast). Another friend said it was used on the streets to designate people who thought they were big or special. Most people were content with the explanation, "It's just a nickname, that's all."

Why all this concern with names? How important are they to the individuals who bear them? Aren't they just tags attached to people for their own and other people's conveniences? Why do youngsters bother to write their names on walls at all?

When one scrutinizes wall inscriptions, discerning the recurrence of certain forms of expression and the energy and art with which they are inscribed, it becomes clear that name graffiti does not represent attempts to deface walls. Nor is it a simple way of showing off. There are too many regularities in the forms in which wall graffiti manifests itself not to suspect that what one is dealing with is a complex cultural phenomenon. Inscribing one's name on a wall involves more than the immediate pleasure of writing where one is not supposed to. It may have to do with the important roles names play in our lives and, in a larger sense, in the whole fabric of life in the society of men.

Why do the youngsters whose energy created the wall graffiti shown in the accompanying pictures need to look around for new names? This may be a suitable point to inquire into the structure and function of naming in our society.

What's my name?

Recently a teacher was assaulted in a Manhattan junior high school because he refused to address several of his pupils by the names they considered their own. He insisted that the boys answer to their "legal" names: that is, the names listed in his roll book. They laughed, ard when he waved the roll book at them, they grabbed it and tore it up.

The teacher was probably astonished by the boys' reaction and may have felt that it was out of proportion to the lightness of his offense. All he did was insist upon calling the boys by the names they had to use on legal documents; the classroom is no place for nicknames. Besides, why should anyone take the matter of names so seriously that it leads to violence?

The puzzled teacher may even have laughed in private at the boys' exotic choices of names and thought the whole thing silly and superstitious. Akmir, Arkbar, Rabu—weren't Thomas Jackson, John Robinson, and Robert Lee more suitable names?

It's not that the teacher was altogether against changing names, for he could understand the logic of going to court and legally changing Cohen to Cole or Schwartz to Black. He may not have sympathized with those who were ashamed of their family names, but it probably made sense to him that some people would want to fit in with the majority of people in the society and give up the stigma of bearing names that differentiated them. What he couldn't understand was that his pupils were moving in the opposite direction. The names they chose for themselves were intentionally bizarre in the context of their society because they wanted to differentiate themselves from it. They laughed at his notion of "legal" names because they considered the society illegal.

To the three boys the names Thomas Jackson, John Robinson, and Robert Lee were slave names, names that came to their families in ways that identified them as descendants of slaves. They were not wrong; their forebears, once free men, did not bring those names from Africa. They were acquired during and after the period of American slavery. The frequency of Anglo-Saxon names among black youth is a living symbol of the suppression of African culture and identity in the United States. Once this symbol is recognized for what it is, it is not surprising that some individuals attempt to destroy it. In fact, some black people are now giving their children legal African first names such as Jomo, Sekou, and Lumumba.

Akmir, Arkbar, and Rabu recently discovered Africa—not the Africa of school textbooks, the white man's burden, but a proud continent with a complex cultural history. They have identified with much they learned, and in the process they have developed a new sense of who they are. They are proud of their newly discovered origins, through which they are learning to be proud of themselves as black men. This is not an intellectual experience, not a question of learning a few new facts or seeing a new facet of life. It is much more like the phenomenon of conversion. The boys once accepted a world without hope where they were resigned to being inferior. Now they have been converted to a new and different vision of things. With it, they have assumed new identities that must be named and displayed to the world. Akmir, Arkbar, Rabu— these names are not merely symbols of new identities but also confirmations of them.

If someone accepts the boys' claim and uses their new names, that is tantamount to accepting their new identities. On the other hand, to deny these names is to refuse to acknowledge their conversion and to force the boys to defend their new identities. The teacher did not understand what he was doing by refusing to use his pupils' new "original" names. He felt their violent reaction was out of proportion to his action. It isn't hard to imagine his rationalizations of the affair—racism, delinquency, defiance, hatred of the school. After all, what's in a name?

The early Christians received new names upon conversion—Simon as Peter, Saul as Paul, etc. These names were symbols of the new lives they were assuming and were often received in ceremonies (such as baptism) that marked the passage from one life to another, purer one. In the Ceylonese Buddhist initiation ceremony the initiate formally renounces his family ties and received a new name. In our own country Cassius Clay assumes a Muslim name, Muhammad Ali—although few sports writers have accepted the change.

The new names are not mere symbols of conversion but proof of it as well. To bear a strange name differentiates one from the rest of society. If the strange name is also one of a series belonging to a certain sect, the name both differentiates the individual from the majority and identifies him with a specific minority. To refuse to respond to an old and common name and insist on being addressed by a new, less familiar one is a proof of one's conversion and the degree to which one wants to make it a public issue.

This leads to an interesting psychological (or perhaps sociological— the boundary fades here) phenomenon. People may respond in a variety of ways to a person's claim to having a new name based upon a personal conversion to a new way of life. They may react negatively and mock the name, satirize it, insult it, or refuse to acknowledge it. Or they may react positively and acknowledge the name, overusing and praising it. In either case the effect will be the same on the new convert: it will increase the intensity of his commitment to the conversion. Insult supports the convert's views of the philistine, uninitiated world; acceptance supports the value of the conversion. Both positive and negative responses to the most social sign of conversion, the use of a new name, reinforce the conversion itself. This is a curious phenomenon, one in which the range of possible reactions—from positive though indifferent to negative—produces positive reinforcement. Any reaction one makes to a convert's use of a new name reinforces the strength of belief the convert has in his new life.

With conversion as a case in point, one can see that naming is not an arbitrary or simple phenomenon. It is not at all like tagging a suitcase or numbering a group of identical objects. Nor is it simply giving a unique designation to an individual to distinguish him from others. To receive a certain name or to choose a new one is to be articulated into some human institution or system of relationships among men. In this sense being named at birth, changing a name at marriage, and receiving a title (M.D. or Ph.D., for example) are not as different as one might suppose.

The conferring of a name is often considered a privilege, the denial of which can lead to great pain. Not everyone in Western societies, for example, has the right to a "legitimate" family name. There are some children in our society whom we choose to call illegitimate. Children born out of wedlock are denied their fathers' family names and the rights and privileges conferred by belonging to a family. The most common word used in English to designate such illegitimate children is "bastard." It is also used as a curse word signifying someone who is mean, nasty, untrustworthy, inferior, unnatural. The word itself seems to come from the Old French *fils de bast,* where *bast* means a barn or granary. The bastard is a child of the barn.

Yet what is illegitimate about an illegitimate child? It is not the child who is illegitimate, but the circumstances of his birth as related to the structure of marriage and family life in our society. It is not hard to imagine a society where a child is legitimate merely by virtue of being born; there he is conferred full rights, because paternity is not a social issue.

Traditionally in Western society the fact that a bastard has no family name makes full membership in our society impossible. It is not possible to separate his illegitimacy, his having no recognition from his father's family, and his being denied their name. His namelessness is his stigma. The importance of having a name is most dramatically reflected in the tragedy of not having one.

Still, there is a temptation to say "It's only a name," that the name itself merely labels deeper, more significant phenomena. From there it is only a step to an opinion like the one James Frazer expressed in *The Golden Bough:*

> Unable to discriminate clearly between words and things, the savage commonly fancies that the link between a name and the person or thing denominated by it is not a mere arbitrary and ideal association but a real and substantial bond which united the two in such a way that magic may be wrought upon a man just as easily through his name as through his hair, his nails, or any other material part of his person. In fact, primitive man regards his name as a vital portion of himself and takes care of it accordingly. Thus, for example, the North American Indian regards his name, not as a mere label, but as a distinct part of his personality, just as much as are his eyes or his teeth, and believes that injury will result as surely from the malicious handling of his name as from a wound inflicted on any part of his organism (p. 284).

We, too, are insulted and injured by the "malicious handling" of our names. There are phrases in our language that reflect this: using someone's name in vain, soiling his "good name," insulting the name of his parents. Our names are not "mere labels" but part of our beings. The distinction between primitive man and ourselves, if it has any meaning at all, certainly has none in the realm of naming.

Having a name in our society is no less than having a family and being identified as an individual *within* that family. It may also be more. Receiving a name at birth is not an arbitrary happening, and the choice of name for a newborn child is often a complex affair. First of all, there are male names and female names; the choice of name is partially determined by sex. (This needn't be the case, but it reflects the importance we place on distinguishing the sexes.) Other phenomena come into play, the range of which reflects the diversity of our society. There are children who are hereditary "juniors" and "II's" and "III's."

In the Jewish community newborn children are traditionally named after recently deceased members of their family and cannot receive the same name as living relatives. It is Scottish tradition, on the other hand, that someone named after a dead person is cursed and bound to be "a bit off." Catholics give their children saints' names; some Protestant sects use Old Testament names exclusively. Even the most "modern" way of naming a child, with disregard of tradition and family, is considerably less than arbitrary; it still required choice made in a cultural context.

Name

Last	First	Middle
(Family)	(Christian)	Initial

We have all filled out innumerable forms during our lifetimes. Last name, first name, middle initial. In our society each individual is expected to have at least two names which he receives at birth and carries with him to the grave. One name, the family name, identifies the individual as a legitimate member of a certain group (his father's family) and the other "proper" name identifies him as a specific individual within that family. It also usually identifies the sex of the bearer. Other names may be added, but—as the request for middle initial rather than middle name indicates—they are secondary and often only important to small groups of individuals (e.g., within a family rather than in the society at large).

The name received at birth constitutes a legal name, and one must go to the courts to change it; otherwise it does not change through the course of one's life. Yet we change many times and in many ways. Our names identify us primarily within our family groups, yet we participate in many more groups as we mature and move further and further from this primary identification. Often we want the associations we develop to be publicly acknowledged, or at least to be evident to the initiated. We seek ways of describing, symbolizing, defining ourselves to others. We resort to buttons, secret handshakes, lapel pins, dress, written documents, and—in the case of some youngsters—writing on the walls. In our society there are no publicly sanctioned or legal ways of incorporating these changes and identifications into our names, yet the name is so potent a medium of identification and differentiation that we invent informal methods. People give themselves and others names and nicknames. As they become part of groups other than the family, they undergo changes of names and identity. It is not a matter of acquiring a new label, but of being a different person involved in different things.

The importance of names and the act of naming throughout the cultures of the world illuminates the seriousness with which much naming graffiti is produced, and it allows us to see that the creation of graffiti is more than ego indulgence or public display. For example, entering the life on the streets is the equivalent in urban ghetto society of the passage from one stage of life to the next. With such a change in one's life it is only appropriate that one assume a name appropriate to that aspect of life. The name must be one acceptable to one's peers and must fit into an accepted series of possible names. This may be why gangs with similar structures often have similar nicknames for their members. Also it is why some youngsters will be at pains to identify themselves as Spider of 117 or Papo of 87. They realize there is no uniqueness to their bearing that name in their own gang or peer group. To declare one's name on a wall is to claim that name for oneself; it can also be a public announcement of one's role in a peer group. If there are no "legal" ways to proclaim these important aspects of our cultural life, we invent extralegal procedures.

The "as" phenomenon makes sense here too. "Johnny as Johnny Cool" says in effect that Johnny has two identities (at least) which he acknowledges in this case, one legal and one with his peers.

The inscription "Johnny as Johnny Cool" has a further significance. A peer name is not something that one can choose arbitrarily; the name must be accepted by one's peers. If Johnny's friends feel that "Johnny Cool" doesn't fit Johnny and refuse to use the name, he must find another one. He may even be given another name by his friends, and it may stick to him whether he likes it or not. The acceptance and use of peer names implies a community of users who can agree upon the use of names.

There are some groups on the streets that require greater allegiance than others. For example, there may be a loose-knit group of people who identify with each other simply because they happen to live on the same block. Such a block group is likely to be loosely structured: the members hang out together, but otherwise they have little loyalty or allegiance to each other. Another kind of block gang is more tightly structured and resembles a fraternity. An even tighter organization is the gang that makes many demands on its members. Membership in a gang is usually a complex affair, and an individual's assuming a gang name only comes after acceptance and initiation by the gang.

Belonging to a gang is not a part-time affair. The gang often insists that members renounce other loyalties, familial and societal. Fights by one member of the gang involve other members according to the obligations of membership. Sexual liaisons are restricted to members of brother and sister gangs. Safe territory is defined by the limits of the gang's turf. It is no small thing to announce publicly, by inscribing one's name on a wall under a gang roster, that one has just become a member.

And it is dangerous to put one's name on a gang roster if one is not actually a member.

On gang rosters one sometimes sees inscriptions such as "Clarence as Lefty." However, they are not common; the "as" phenomenon is more often found on lists of names of people from the same block or of boys and girls who hang out together. It is more likely that "Lefty" would stand alone on the gang roster. The name Clarence, identifying Lefty as the son of his parents, is more thoroughly renounced through gang membership than through becoming part of a more loosely structured and less demanding peer group. In some instances, gang names are the only ones permitted their members, and conflicts often arise within families over the name a young man is to bear.

Membership in a gang is not as total a conversion to a new life as is religious conversion. Prior identities still have certain claims in one's life; there are still times when Clarence will be Clarence (in school, perhaps, or in court). It is interesting to note, however, that social workers, when they persuade youngsters to leave gangs, speak of having converted the youngsters.

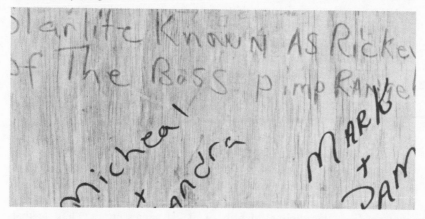

Recently in many urban ghettos another grouping of teenagers has developed with a more religious and ideological basis. In some areas Muslim and black nationalists groups have replaced the gangs; in others they exist alongside the gangs, drawing on a different group of youngsters than those tapped by the gangs—a group more politically and socially aware and, generally, more interested in school and learning. Akmir, Arkbar, and Rabu, the boys I referred to earlier, are members of such a group. For them membership involves conversion and means total loyalty. They would never think of writing "Thomas as Akmir" or "John as Arkbar." Akmir and Arkbar suffice. These young men answer only to their new names, for their old names do not refer to them anymore. That is why the trouble developed with their teacher.

Yet the line between membership and total commitment is not that sharp. There are degrees of loyalty that groups demand of their members. Some permit dual loyalties and encompass only a part of their members' lives, so it is possible for the group to accept Clarence *as* Lefty and Johnny *as* Johnny Cool. Some organizations claim the entire lives of their members; Cassius Clay *is* Mohammad Ali—"Cassius Clay as Muhammad Ali" is an insult.

Peer identification may explain another feature of wall graffiti. The inscriptions examined included no family names that were the works of children or teenagers. At most a last initial was appended to a first name or a nickname. This is too consistent a phenomenon to be accidental. Not only does wall graffiti display the strength and solidarity of peer culture; it seems to deny the strength of family culture and, in doing so, gives a glimpse of the breakdown of family loyalties experienced by many youngsters in urban ghettos. "Nickname" has been stretched far beyond its original meaning and is not very useful for an understanding of the phenomenon subsumed under it. The original sense of the word seems to have implied a certain form of insult which "nicked" a person's character. It probably referred to such nicknames as Stinky, Big Head, Bad Breath, and Fatso, which identified a person with some unattractive quality or habit attributed to him. Some nicknames used behind people's backs might not be known by those who bore them.

"Nickname" has expanded its meaning to incorporate names that are affectionate, praising, or boasting, such as Bolita, Anthony Cool, or Spider. It now covers almost the entire range of nonlegal names from Umbrella Man, Saint, Boy, all the way to diminutives such as Johnny, Ken, Phil, Babs, Dee Dee, and the like. It reflects so many social modes and identification that it would be better to forget "nicknames" and look at different groups of names and their relationships without that concept in mind. A more useful way of looking at the range and variety of things we call ourselves and others would be to see what they add or subtract from the minimal identity our legal names imply. Thus, to that whole body of names called nicknames it would be useful to add other forms of address (such as Mr. and Mrs.) and titles (such as Dr.), and to study them as a series of verbal forms that function within our social and cultural system.

But names can never harm me

I'm called "Mr. Kohl" by my pupils, "Herbert" by my parents, "Herb" by my wife, "Herbie" by childhood friends, and "Kohl" by some colleagues. The differences are not so slight as they may seem. They embody a whole range of social relationships which we all participate in, ranging from the most intimate to the most formal. We may not institutionalize forms of address as rigidly as some cultures (e.g., the Japanese), yet violations of the conventions of which name to use in which social situation are often regarded by us as serious, even insulting. To be called "Herbie" by a stranger or "Kohl" by a close friend are both insults and signs of the disruption of ordinary social relations.

I remember being struck by the whole business of what names are appropriately used in different social circumstances when I first began teaching. My last month of student-teaching was at the Walden School, a progressive private school in New York City, where the students and teachers were on a first name basis with each other. It took several weeks to get used to this convention, having attended traditional public schools. Yet I realized that the school was deliberately attempting to change the traditional teacher-pupil relationship, and that the use of the familiar form of address by all people in the school was an effective way of doing it. After a month I felt easy introducing myself to children as "Herbert" and responding to their using my first name. At that point my student-teaching ended, and I got my first job as a teacher in a predominantly Puerto Rican public school in Manhattan. The day before I began teaching, I observed my future class. They had a substitute teacher who seemed beaten and indifferent. The children paid no attention to her and walked up to me and around me, looking me over. After a while one boy got up some courage and came up to me and introduced himself.

"I'm Narciso, who are you?"

"I'm Herbert, I'm going to be your teacher."

"Herbert . . . hey, Hughie here's Herbert."

He looked at me and laughed. I blushed and found myself angry and hostile. I remembered my place.

"Mr. Kohl to you and don't forget it."

Narciso seemed relieved by my anger and the issue was never brought up in class during the term. On the other hand, he would test me by using my first name after school. I didn't know what to do about that. It didn't seem wrong to me; yet I was having trouble with the class, feeling very unsure of myself and afraid that a general use of "Herbert" in the class would destroy my uncertain authority altogether.

Children are aware of the social power of names and are very sensitive to the names they receive from their peers and to the reception their peers give to names they choose for themselves. I know a boy who chose to call himself Albert the Great and who found himself victim of the following graffiti variations:

<pre>
              stink
Albert the Great fagit (faggot)
              hua   (whore)
</pre>

to which he responded:

Albert the Great ~~stink~~ ~~fagit~~ lover
~~bua~~ fighter

Some names are merited, and these are often acknowledged publicly. An Alice could have given the Slick to herself and have it acknowledged by her friends (to acknowledge a name of this sort is simply to use it). The name could equally have been given to her by her friends, either as praise (because she is slick) or as an insult (because she thinks she's slick and she's not).

Another peer given name (which I shall call a peername) is Chino. In Puerto Rican and black teenage groups a boy is usually called Chino because of the yellow tint of his skin. This can be considered an insult (because he's a half-breed) or a compliment (because he approaches an ideal of whiteness).

There are names such as Lil Man and Half Pint which are usually given in admiration of the strength and guts of individuals who happen to be short. On the other hand, Half Pint could also be given to someone derisively, or given to a huge person affectionately.

Peernames such as Squeaky, Lefty, and Rocky are self-explanatory.

There are Spanish equivalents of many of the English peernames mentioned above (Chino is actually a Spanish peername). "Feo" means ugly and can be taken as an insult or a compliment (as meaning an ugly temperament: that is, someone not to mess with). "Flaco" is Spanish for skinny.

The subtleties of naming are not lost on young people, however dull they may seem in a school setting. A simple reading of wall graffiti gives one a sense of the range of irony, cynicism, ambiguity, praise, and insult at the command of individuals whose significant lives may be led on the streets.

The use of peernames, besides identifying the bearer with certain human qualities or characteristics, gives each individual a unique designation within his peer group. There may be many José's in a gang or on the same block, but not more than one will bear that name for gang members. This is analogous to the fact that within a family no two children are given the same first name. Not all individuals need receive peernames. There can be a José whose first name is accepted both on the streets and within family. However, he may have to qualify this first name to identify himself with his friends and prevent himself from being confused with another José. In this sense the "Papo of 87" functions in a similar way to Rodriguez and Gonzalez in José Rodriguez and Papo Gonzalez.

Negro as Jim, Clarence as Lefty

As children pass into adolescence, they move toward independence from their families. In poorer urban areas this means moving into a life on the streets that has different rules, rituals, and obligations than those of family life. This is not to imply that young children don't play on the streets or that middle-class teenagers don't also begin to develop independence. But there is a difference between these last two and the street life reflected by public wall graffiti. Young children usually play in the streets under the eye of an adult and are expected not to stray too far from their own buildings; a block is usually the limit of their territory. Middle-class teenagers, accustomed to participation in supervised activities, have greater mobility (especially in the suburbs, where cars are omnipresent) than ghetto youth and are not so oriented toward life in a neighborhood.

The ghetto adolescent's life is centered on his neighborhood; even if he leaves it for school or work, it is to the neighborhood that he returns. His life there is essentially free of adults and is one in which rules and rituals evolve from his peers. The ties of the neighborhood and its streets can be so strong as to make it impossible for someone to leave. Recently, for example, a group of teenagers in one of New York City's ghettos decided to take revenge on someone they considered responsible for the death of a friend of theirs. The accused, who was from the same neighborhood as the others, fled to Baltimore. When I asked one of the youths whether they intended to go to Baltimore, he replied that it wasn't necessary since all they had to do was wait for the accused to return. No one from their neighborhood could ever stay away, he said.

The boundaries of a neighborhood are difficult to define; there are so few natural markers. Occasionally a park, railroad tracks, or a particularly large street will bound a neighborhood at one or two places. But neighborhoods melt imperceptibly into one another at most points. Therefore, a need develops to mark out the boundaries of the neighborhood—and what better way to do it than to post boundaries on the walls? This applies not only to gangs but to more loosely affiliated groups of boys and girls. One often comes upon such proclamations as:

Imperials Turf—Walk Cool

You are Now Entering Dragons Territory—No Junkies Allowed
Young Imperial Rangers
> Boys of 89th St. only
> Reggie as Angel
> Sam as Spider

These boundary markers do not indicate the limits of a preestablished territory but are often claims to the space they bound. On some walls one can see the boundaries of neighborhoods change hands. Dragons will be crossed out and replaced by Sharks, which will be crossed out and replaced by an even larger and bolder Dragons.

Some territory is difficult to claim. There are parks, for example, which border on several different turfs; possession of them is constantly contested. In New York, Tompkins Square Park was fought over by Puerto Ricans, Polish, and hippie groups before some truce was agreed upon. Each tentative victory in the war for the park was marked by some public graffiti. The Puerto Rican and Polish groups marked their conquests by inscribing gang, block, and personal names. The hippies countered with signs of their own hand imprints, hearts, and the word "love." (The hippies have created an interesting variation on graffiti. Many of them are artists; they tend to elaborate their graffiti, using the surfaces they discover in ingenious ways. Their graffiti is much closer to a conscious form of artistic creation than the usual wall graffiti.)

Sometimes a territory claimed by one gang is specifically prohibited to another. Thus, for example, one finds such inscriptions as:

> Dominicans Not Allowed
> No Sharks, You Dig

Other groups provide strangers with general warnings that they are going to be held responsible for their movements in the territory the gang controls. Thus in Chicago the Blackstone Rangers have assumed the authority to enforce their own code of behavior on anyone who enters their turf, and they let visitors know it.

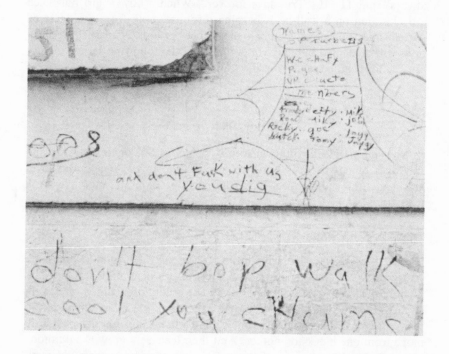

The walls not only serve to mark out territory and identify individuals within the context of certain peer groups; they also serve as a means of communication for these groups and individuals. One notices a series of initials and messages ranging from DTK, DTKLAMF, TLFE, and TLA to "Don't mess" and "Walk cool" that are used for making public declarations on the walls.

DTK means "Down to kill" and DTKLMF goes one better, meaning "Down to kill like a mother fucker." These sets of initials are found appended after gang names or individual names and are public commitments to fight.

"Sharks DTK" written on a wall commits members of the Sharks to be ready to fight; DTKLAMF commits them further, calling for provocation. When the enemy is specified—for example, "Sharks DTK Imperials"—then a Shark and an Imperial must confront each other or lose face.

Individuals can make their own declarations of warfare, and their friends know what to look for if they find someone pasting his name and DTK on a wall. There is an audience for such declarations, and they do not go unread.

TLA and TLFE are declarations of love, just as the previous three were declarations of war. TLA means "True love always" or "To love always" and TLFE, "True love forever." When a boy or girl puts such a declaration on a wall he is begging response, both from the declared partner and from other members of the peer group. Often such declarations will be denied publicly via graffiti, and the following series of communications can be read from the wall:

Hector as Spider and Ana TLFE
Angel—Ana   Ana is a hua
Hector DTK Angel

In translation: Hector, known to his friends as Spider, loves Ana, and she loves him. Ana does not love Hector; she loves Angel, who loves her. Angel thinks he's wise, but Hector will get him and moreover Ana is a whore.

These are our walls

Graffiti is not a particularly durable form of expression. Names are crossed out or replaced by other names; layers of graffiti develop, and often it is hard to make out what was once boldly proclaimed on a wall. In the streets life itself is not durable. There are too many enemies, too many pressures forcing gangs and clubs to break up, forcing people to move from one block to another. And then teenagers grow to adulthood and their loyalties change. If they are lucky, they leave their old territory. Graffiti forms make their appearance and fade, reflecting the tenuousness of a gang's hold on its territory and more generally the fluidity of life in an urban ghetto.

It is different for the rich and powerful who express their territorial claims and social identities in more durable forms. A gang can paint its name on the walls of its turf, but that is nothing compared to a corporation that stamps its emblem on its buildings or a rich man's club that embodies in stone its claim to power and importance. The stone yacht carved onto the front of the New York Yacht Club's building performs the same function as the name "Lancers" scrawled across a wall. Only the yacht club sculpture is more durable, as the yacht club presumes itself to be, than the inscription "Lancers" and the gang itself.

But things are changing and new forms of graffiti are emerging, bolder and more assertive than gang and block inscriptions. Hippie graffiti is one example. Summer antipoverty projects have developed in urban ghettos, bringing artists together with young people and fusing art with public declaration. In one such project, "Summer in the City," artists and teenagers declared possession of some public walls and painted on them. The substance of the graffiti on these walls was the same as on the furtively decorated walls described so far—names, nicknames, claims of territory, declarations of love and hate—but the elaboration of themes and the decoration of the walls was not the same. It was as if the youth said "These are our walls" and for the first time believed it. It is as if the makers of graffiti emerged from an underground existence and proclaimed in more durable paints with bolder images and a prouder form that the life of the streets had value and that the adult established world which cared not to recognize it would not be able to ignore it any longer.

But antipoverty projects are just that—projects. There is something artificial about bringing people together to legitimize graffiti, even if the intent is to legitimize the lives of the youngsters as well. Yet once the idea of possessing the walls in one's environment, regardless of who legally owns them, is concerned, it is not likely to stop there. In Chicago a group of black artists and youngsters, perhaps some of them members of the Blackstone Rangers, stated on the walls of several buildings, in words and images three stories high, that the neighborhood they happened to live in was in fact their own.

It is no longer a matter of what people take seriously or what they choose to notice. Anyone passing through that block has the paintings on the walls thrust before him. Here wall graffiti, once a furtive expression of the lives of the poor, young, and disenfranchised, becomes a public monument which presents a challenge and a warning to the makers of stone, glass, and steel monuments. To paraphrase Johnny Bolita, there are no secrets on these walls, and it is only a matter of time before people will have to read them.

■ The language of soul

CLAUDE BROWN

Claude Brown is best known for his autobiography, *Manchild in the Promised Land,* which depicts his and others' daily experiences, hazards, crises, and frustrations of "growing up black" in New York's Harlem. "Language of Soul" appeared originally in *Esquire* in April, 1968, and is especially valuable for its description and analysis of various words, expressions, and pronunciations by one who has habitually used such terms, was on the scene when they were in vogue, and was able to assess their impact firsthand within the wider black community. Clearly word- and language-conscious, Brown also offers the thesis that it is essentially pronunciation stress and intonation which form the basis of black ethnic speech ("soul talk"), all other aspects of black speech (such as vocabulary and grammar) being readily cooptable by the larger white society.

Perhaps the most soulful word in the world is "nigger." Despite its very definite fundamental meaning (the Negro man), and disregarding the deprecatory connotation of the term, "nigger" has a multiplicity of nuances when used by soul people. Dictionaries define the term as being synonymous with Negro, and they generally point out that it is regarded as a vulgar expression. Nevertheless, to those of chitlins-and-neck-bones background the word nigger is neither a synonym for Negro nor an obscene expression.

"Nigger" has virtually as many shades of meaning in "Colored English" as the demonstrative pronoun "that," prior to application to a noun. To some Americans of African ancestry (I avoid using the term "Negro" whenever feasible, for fear of offending the Brothers X, a pressure group to be reckoned with), "nigger" seems preferable to "Negro" and has a unique kind of sentiment attached to it. This is exemplified in the frequent—and perhaps even excessive—usage of the term to denote either fondness or hostility.

It is probable that numerous transitional niggers and even established ex–soul brothers can—with pangs of nostalgia—reflect upon a day in the lollipop epoch of their lives when an adorable lady named Mama bemoaned her spouse's fastidiousness with the strictly secular utterance, "Lord, how can one nigger be so hard to please?" Others are likely to recall a time when that drastically lovable colored woman, who was forever wiping our noses and darning our clothing, bellowed in a moment of exasperation, "Nigger, you gonna be the death o' me." And some of the brethren who have had the precarious fortune to be raised up, wised up, thrown up, or simply left alone to get up as best they could, on one of the nation's South Streets or Lenox Avenues, might remember having affectionately referred to a best friend as "my nigger."

The vast majority of "back-door Americans" are apt to agree with Webster—a nigger is simply a Negro or black man. But the really profound contemporary thinkers of this distinguished ethnic group—Dick Gregory, Redd Foxx, Moms Mabley, Slappy White, etc.—are likely to differ with Webster and define "nigger" as something else—a soulful something else. The major difference between the nigger and the Negro, who have many traits in common, is that the nigger is the more soulful.

Certain foods, customs, and artistic expressions are associated almost solely with the nigger: collard greens, neck bones, hog maws, black-eyed peas, pigs' feet. A nigger has no desire to conceal or disavow any of these favorite dishes or to restrain other behavioral practices, such as bobbing his head, patting his feet to funky jazz, and shouting and jumping in church. This is not to be construed as meaning that all niggers eat chitlins and shout in church, or that only niggers eat the aforementioned dishes and exhibit this type of behavior. It is to say, however, that the soulful usage of the term "nigger" implies all of the foregoing and considerably more.

The language of soul—or, as it might also be called, "Spoken Soul" or "Colored English"—is simply an honest vocal portrayal of black America. The roots of it are more than three hundred years old.

Before the Civil War numerous restrictions were placed on the speech of slaves. The newly arrived Africans had the problem of learning to speak a new language, and slave-masters and overseers placed inhibitions on the topics of the slaves' conversation. The slaves made up songs to inform one another of, say, the underground railroad's activity. When they sang "Steal Away," they were planning to steal away to the North, not to heaven. Slaves who dared speak of rebellion or even freedom usually were severely punished. Consequently, Negro slaves were compelled to create a semi-clandestine vernacular in the way that the criminal underworld has historically created words to confound law-enforcement agents. It is said that numerous Negro spirituals were inspired by the hardships of slavery, and that what later became songs were initially moanings and coded cotton-field lyrics. To hear these songs sung today by a talented soul brother or sister or by a group is to be reminded of a historical spiritual bond that cannot be satisfactorily described by the mere spoken word.

American Negroes, for virtually all of their history, have constituted a vastly disproportionate number of the country's illiterates. Illiteracy has a way of showing itself in all attempts at vocal expression by the uneducated. With the aid of colloquialisms, malapropisms, battered and fractured grammar, and a considerable amount of creativity, "Colored English," the sound of soul, evolved.

The progress has been cyclical. Often terms that have been discarded from the soul people's vocabulary for one reason or another are reaccepted years later, but usually with completely different meanings. In the 1930's and 1940's "stuff" meant vagina. In the middle 1950's it was revived and used to refer to heroin. Why certain expressions are thus reactivated is practically an indeterminable question. But it is not difficult to see why certain terms are dropped from the soul language. Whenever a soul term becomes popular with whites, it is common practice for the soul folks to relinquish it. The reasoning is, "If white people can use it, it isn't hip enough for me." To many soul brothers there is just no such creature as a genuinely hip white person. And there is nothing more detrimental to anything hip than to have it fall into the square hands of the hopelessly unhip.

White Americans wrecked the expression "something else." It was bad enough that they couldn't say "sump'n else," but they weren't even able to get out "somethin' else." They had to go around saying "something else" with perfect or nearly perfect enunciation. The white folks invariably fail to perceive the soul sound in soulful terms. They get hung up in diction and grammar, and when they vocalize the expression it's no longer a soulful thing. In fact, it can be asserted that "Spoken Soul" is more a sound than a language. It generally possesses a pronounced lyrical quality which is frequently incompatible to any music other than that ceaseless and relentlessly driving rhythm that flows from poignantly spent lives. Spoken soul has a way of coming out metered without the intention of the speaker to invoke it. There are specific phonetic traits. To the soulless ear the vast majority of these sounds are dismissed as incorrect usage of the English language and, not infrequently, as speech impediments. To those so blessed as to have had bestowed upon them at birth the lifetime gift of soul, these are the most communicative and meaningful sounds ever to fall upon human ears: the familiar "mah" instead of "my," "gonna" for "going to," "yo" for "your." "Ain't" is pronounced "ain' "; "bread" and "bed," "bray-ud" and "bay-ud"; "baby" is never "bay-bee" but "bay-buh"; Sammy Davis, Jr., is not "Sammee" but a kind of "Sam-eh"; the same goes for "Ed-deh" Jefferson. No matter how many "man's" you put into your talk, it isn't soulful unless the word has the proper plaintive, nasal "maee-yun."

Spoken soul is distinguished from slang primarily by the fact that the former lends itself easily to conventional English, and the latter is diametrically opposed to adaptations within the realm of conventional English. Police (pronounced pō'lice) is a soul term, whereas "The Man" is merely slang for the same thing. Negroes seldom adopt slang terms from the white world; when they do, the terms are usually given a different meaning. Such was the case with "bag." White racketeers used it in the 1930's to refer to the graft that was paid to the police. For the past five years soul people have used it when referring to a person's vocation, hobby, fancy, etc. And once the appropriate term is given the treatment (soul vocalization), it becomes soulful.

However, borrowings from spoken soul by white men's slang—particularly teenage slang—are plentiful. Perhaps because soul is probably the most graphic language of modern times, everybody who is excluded from Soulville wants to usurp it, ignoring the formidable fettering of the soul folks that has brought the language about. Consider "uptight," "strung-out," "cop," "boss," "kill 'em," all now widely used outside Soulville. Soul people never question the origin of a slang term; they either dig it and make it a part of their vocabulary or don't and forget it. The expression "uptight," which meant being in financial straits, appeared on the soul scene in the general vicinity of 1953. Junkies were very fond of the word and used it literally to describe what was a perpetual condition with them. The word was pictorial and pointed; therefore it caught on quickly in Soulvilles across the country. In the early 1960's when "uptight" was on the move, a younger generation of soul people in the black urban communities along the eastern seaboard regenerated it with a new meaning: "everything is cool, under control, going my way." At present the term has the former meaning for the older generation and the latter construction for those under thirty years of age.

It is difficult to ascertain whether the term "strung-out" was coined by junkies or just applied to them and accepted without protest. Like "uptight" in its initial interpretation, "strung-out" aptly described the constant plight of the junkie. "Strung-out" had a connotation of hopeless finality about it. "Uptight" implied a temporary situation and lacked the overwhelming despair of "strung-out."

The term "cop" (meaning "to get") is an abbreviation of "copulation." "Cop," as originally used by soulful teenagers in the early 1950's, was deciphered to mean sexual coition, nothing more. By 1955 "cop" was being uttered throughout national Soulville as a synonym for the verb "to get," especially in reference to illegal purchases, drugs, pot, hot goods, pistols ("Man, where can I cop now?"). But by 1955 the meaning was all-encompassing. Anything that could be obtained could be "copped."

The word "boss," denoting something extraordinarily good or great, was a redefined term that had been popular in Soulville during the 1940's and 1950's as a complimentary remark from one soul brother to another. Later it was replaced by several terms such as "groovy," "tough," "beautiful," and, most recently, "out of sight." This last expression is an outgrowth of the former term "way out," the meaning of which was equivocal. "Way out" had an ad hoc hickish ring to it which made it intolerably unsoulful; consequently, it was soon replaced by "out of sight," which is also likely to experience a relatively brief period of popular usage. "Out of sight" is better than "way out," but it has some of the same negative, childish taint of its predecessor.

"Kill 'em" has neither a violent nor a malicious interpretation. It means "Good luck," "Give 'em hell," or "I'm pulling for you," and originated in Harlem between six and nine years ago.

There are certain classic soul terms which, no matter how often borrowed, remain in the canon and are reactivated every so often, just as standard jazz tunes are continuously experiencing renaissances. Among the classical expressions are: "solid," "cool," "jive" (generally as a noun), "stuff," "thing," "swing" (or "swinging"), "pimp," "dirt," "freak," "heat," "larceny," "busted," "okee doke," "piece," "sheet" (a jail record), "squat," "square," "stash," "lay," "sting," "mire," "gone," "smooth," "joint," "blow," "play," "shot," and many more.

Soul language can be heard in practically all communities throughout the country, but for pure, undiluted spoken soul one must go to Soul Street. There are several. Soul is located at Seventh and T in Washington, D.C.; on One Two Five Street in New York City; on Springfield Avenue in Newark; on South Street in Philadelphia; on Tremont Street in Boston; on Forty-seventh Street in Chicago; on Fillmore in San Francisco; and in dozens of similar locations in dozens of other cities.

As increasing numbers of Negroes desert Soulville for honorary membership in the Establishment clique, they experience a metamorphosis, the repercussions of which markedly influence the young and impressionable citizens of Soulville. The expatriates of Soulville are often greatly admired by the youths of Soulville, who emulate the behavior of such expatriates as Nancy Wilson, Ella Fitzgerald, Eartha Kitt, Lena Horne, Diahann Carroll, Billy Daniels, or Leslie Uggams. The result—more often than not—is a trend away from spoken soul among the young soul folks. This abandonment of soul language is facilitated by the fact that more Negro youngsters than ever are acquiring college educations (which, incidentally, is not the best treatment for the continued good health and growth of soul); integration and television, too, are contributing significantly to the gradual demise of spoken soul.

Perhaps colleges in America should commence teaching a course in spoken soul. It could be entitled "Vocal History of Black America," or simply "Spoken Soul." Undoubtedly there would be no difficulty finding teachers. There are literally thousands of these experts throughout the country whose talents lie idle while they await the call to duty.

Meanwhile, the picture looks dark for soul. The two extremities in the Negro spectrum—the conservative and the militant—are both trying diligently to relinquish and repudiate whatever vestiges they may still possess of soul. The semi-Negro—the soul brother intent on gaining admission to the Establishment, even on an honorary basis—is anxiously embracing and assuming conventional English. At the other extreme, the "Ultra-Black" is frantically adopting everything from a Western version of Islam that would shock the Caliph right out of his snugly fitting shintiyan—anything that vaguely hints of that big, beautiful, bountiful black bitch lying in the arms of the Indian and Atlantic Oceans and crowned by the majestic Mediterranean Sea. Whatever the Ultra-Black is after, it's anything but soulful.

■ The vocabulary of race

KEN JOHNSON

Ken Johnson brings a varied background to his research interests. Born and raised in Chicago's South Side black community, he worked in the post office for five years and served two years in the army before attending Wilson Junior College. A graduate of Chicago State University (Chicago Teachers College–South), the University of Chicago, and the University of Southern California, Johnson is an associate professor of education and ethnic studies at the University of California at Berkeley. Author of the SRA series *Teaching the Culturally Disadvantaged: A Rational Approach* and several articles dealing with the education of minority children, his special interest is in the teaching of black children who speak black dialect, and in those social, cultural, and linguistic factors that affect learning, especially within institutionally defined contexts such as the classroom.

Insofar as the article deals traditionally with the relationship of vocabulary and culture, it is a product of the author's general research interest in sociolinguistics. Yet it almost goes without saying that the motivation for writing this article comes as much from his being black as it does from his pursuit of scholarship, especially as the racial terms discussed herein are a well-established part of his own lexicon and usage. That black people in general should possess and use a different vocabulary from whites is understandable, given the respectively different nature of the black and white experiences in this country. In this respect, by discussing racial terms with reference to the social situation in which they are used, Johnson's article succeeds in illuminating the collective perspective and state of mind of black people which has evolved from the black experience, and which has given rise to those perceptions that are at the root of word creation and dissemination.

"Culture" is the term used to refer to a shared way of life. Behavior patterns, values, and attitudes achieve cultural (in addition to individual) dimension when they are shared. The basis for a collective or cultural world-view is invariably experiential. Individuals perceive the reoccurrence of an event in which they played a part. They remark to their peers about the nature of the event and the parts various people played in it. Other individuals note having participated in a similar event. Comparisons are made, essential features of the event are noted and general parameters drawn. Among other things, roles are identified. If the situation was potentially dangerous, successful maneuvers which avoided unpleasantness or escaped punishment were carefully learned and catalogued to be used when a similar situation reoccurred. Successful escape or avoidance maneuvers become accomplished coping mechanisms or survival techniques.

In the United States, historically, a black-white context has invariably been potentially fraught with peril for the black man. Avoiding difficulty generally depended on an accurate assessment of the kind of white man with whom the black man was dealing with respect to at least one basic criterion: his attitude toward blacks as a group. The importance for the black man of correctly identifying this attitude gave rise to the occurrence within the black lexicon of a wide variety of racial identity labels for whites. These labels briefly designated the attitude of the white man or woman toward them and consequently the predictable behavior pattern that would occur within any given black-white context.

It ought to be clear that the terms emerged within the black vocabulary as a consequence of black people's uniquely disadvantaged position in white society. Whites, dealing with blacks in those contexts from a position of dominance, did not feel that they needed to differentiate among blacks according to their attitudes toward whites in order to manipulate the black-white situation to their advantage. Therefore, racial identity labels for blacks in the white American lexicon fall into a different semantic category, one generally describing black physical features and overt black behavioral mannerisms like "spade," "spook," "jigger-boo," etc. Consistent with their respectively different experiences in the United States, black people have many racial labels which characterize themselves; significantly, whites have no racial labels of self-reference. This is because racial self-consciousness was never a factor that mattered in the white people's contexts.

In a general sense, then, one can see that there exists a relationship between vocabulary and culture, that vocabulary terms serve as an index to the cultural world-view of a group. Traditionally, the number of "snow words" in Eskimo have been cited to indicate the importance of snow in Eskimo culture. However, it must be remembered that while the *number* of words in a language forms a *general* index of importance, a semantic analysis of these synonyms would more precisely identify the perceptions underlying their abundance and reveal the larger cultural significance of these terms. For example, words for "snow on the ground" and "heaving falling snow of long duration" are not only descriptive of natural phenomena; in a deeper cultural sense they signify the options or decisions that the Eskimo could make, given the set of snow conditions designated by these terms ("I can't go hunting today," etc.). Underlying vocabulary items or names (labels), therefore, are perceptions that are ultimately linked to options and imperatives which have an impact on our existence, survival, or preferred way of living.

So the number of racial identity labels that blacks have for whites or for themselves might reveal generally that racial awareness is a primary concern among blacks. A more detailed analysis of these terms reveals a differentiation among them which reflects not only a range of finer perceptions but also, linked to them, a different set of options and imperatives that are available to the black person as a consequence of the situation that the perception and name defines. So identifying a white person as a "cracker" introduces a definition of situation which structures for the black person a behavior pattern (act and response) which is different from the pattern introduced by the term "blue-eyed soul brother."

The purpose of this paper is to examine one area—race—in which experience differs between the dominant American culture and American black culture, and to point out the "lexicon of race" that has developed in black culture. Specifically, the purpose of this paper is to point out and discuss the labels black people have formulated to indicate racial identity. These racial-identity labels are part of what can be called "the black lexicon" (words that are used exclusively by black people) formulated to designate concepts derived from the unique experiences of black people within their culture.

Racial-identity labels for white people which blacks have formulated can be divided into negative, neutral, and positive categories. Negative labels are derogatory; neutral labels carry no value judgments; positive labels are complimentary. The following words for white racial identity are divided into these categories; a meaning for each word is given and discussed.

Negative

Blue-eyed devils or *Devils*. Clearly a derogatory label for white people because it equates them with the greatest character of evil, Satan. This label is usually used in a collective sense and is usually pluralized (even when the plural ending is not pronounced, the plural meaning of the label can be inferred from context—many blacks who speak black dialect do not pronounce the plural ending "-s"). The adjective "blue-eyed" clarifies to whom "devil" is applied. This label for white people was first used by the Muslim leaders Elijah Muhammad and Malcolm X. After they introduced the term, it gained wide use in black culture.

O-fays or *Fays*. Pig Latin pronunciation of "foe." The label refers to the combatant nature of race relations in which all white people are seen as the enemies or foes of all black people.

The Man. Particularly interesting because of the connotations the word "man" has in American culture. Black men have had a difficult time achieving manhood in American society because of the emasculating effects of racism. Therefore, "man" can only be used to refer to white men. The use of "The Man" to refer to whites implies the bitterness that black people—especially black men—have because of the denial of black manhood. The label can also be used to refer to white policemen.

Honky. Not exactly a black word because it was originally used by whites to refer to immigrants from Eastern Europe. It is a shortened version of "Bohunk." It became a black word when it was first used by Stokely Carmichael to refer to all whites. Also, the particular pronunciation of the word is black: honky instead of hunky. The pronunciation change indicates the intensity of the hate black people have for white people. The pronunciation of the first syllable has been changed to conform to the pronunciation given to the word "hungry" when one is intensely hungry—hungry is to be just hungry; hongry is to be famished.

Peckerwood. Originated in the South, and refers to all whites. When white people do strenuous work in the hot sun, there is a tendency for their necks to turn red. Their red necks resembled the red necks of woodpeckers; thus "peckerwood" was coined to refer to whites. This label is similar to the white label "red neck," which was probably coined for the same reason.

Cracker. Did not originate in the black culture; however, the meaning black people give to the term has been derived out of the black experience, and that is the reason it is included here. According to McCall and Scott, "cracker" has two probable sources,[1] the first deriving from the use of the whip during the herding of cattle which was used by early Georgia settlers. The whip made a cracking sound; those who used it were called crackers. The second meaning could have been derived from the Georgia settlers' staple diet of grits, or cracked corn; anyone who had this as a diet was called a cracker. When black people use the term, however, it takes on an extra dimension. Black people use it to refer to all white people who are especially prejudiced (not only prejudiced residents of Georgia). This extra dimension is consistent with the two probable etymologies of the label, since the white people to whom the label applies according to both etymologies are the most prejudiced against black people. "Cracker," then, is a derogatory term especially referring to any prejudiced white person.

Captain. Stems from slavery, when black people were under the charge of an overseer who was often referred to as "Captain." The label continued to be used after slavery whenever black people worked under the supervision of white man. It is especially used in prisons throughout the South to refer to the white supervisor of black work gangs. The label is included under the negative category here because it implies the superior-inferior relationship of white and black men, and because the

[1] Bevode McCall and Taylor C. Scott, "Georgia Town, U.S.A.," *Synergist*, Spring, 1970, pp. 1–13.

captain who commands black work gangs during slavery, in prison work gangs, and in other work situations is usually a hated and feared person.

Mr. Charlie. Any white man who is in a supervisory position over a black man in a work situation. It especially refers to the boss or foreman on a job, although it is sometimes used to refer to any white person. It is derogatory because black people resent the superior-inferior nature of work situations with whites usually in the superior role. The use of the term "Mr." in the label also carries a loaded meaning: black men are frequently referred to without the use of "Mr." and using this word with the first name "Charlie" emphasizes the superior position of white men. In addition, "Mr." always preceded whatever name (first or last) black people called white people during and after slavery, especially in the South.

Chuck. Used in the same way that "Mr. Charlie" is used; however, the use of the nickname for "Charles" is particularly derogatory because black people do not like to be called by their nicknames until they are acquainted with persons over a period of time. (The use of "Mr. Charlie" instead of "Mr. Charles" also emphasizes the derogatory nature of the label.) The nickname "Chuck" implies a familiarity that places a white man in the same position as black men.

Charlene. Feminine version of "Mr. Charlie"; refers to a white woman who is in a position of authority (particularly in a work situation) over a black person.

Miss Ann. Usually refers to white women who have a supercilious attitude toward black people. It especially refers to the white woman who has black people working for her as servants, although it can be used to refer to all white women. Like the use of "Mr." in "Mr. Charlie," "Miss" in this label emphasizes the relationship between black people and white women.

Neutral

Paddy. Neutral label that refers to all white people.

Republican. Interesting because it implies the Democratic affiliation of black people: a black Republican is so rare that the word can be synonymous with "white people."

Whitey. Neutral descriptive label that refers to all white people; it can be used in a derogatory sense as well. The inflection or the context usually indicates whether the label is being used in a neutral or a negative way.

Gray. Implies the "dead" nature of white people in their physical appearance and actions. Black people equate the lack of pigmentation with lifelessness. Also, the actions of white people—especially the moderate unimpassioned behavior of middle-class whites—are seen by black people as lacking life. "Gray" implies all of this, and in this sense the label is slightly negative.

Positive

Blue-eyed soul brother or *Blue-eyed soul sister.* This is the most complimentary label black people have for whites. "Soul brother" (or "soul sister") is used to refer to black. "Soul" is anything indigenous to black culture; "brother" (or "sister") connotes kinship. Thus "blue-eyed soul brother" or "blue-eyed soul sister" is used to label whites who understand and appreciate black culture, and whose actions toward black people are without the reservation, strangeness, and racism that characterize the actions of many white people.

Pearls. Metaphoric label referring to attractive white women, especially to young, attractive white girls. The complimentary label equates these attractive white females to a gem.

Blondie. Descriptive label referring to any white woman; connotes the color of hair that is considered most desirable, according to the white culture's beauty standards. The label is clearly one for white women, because blond hair is not natural for black women. "Blondie" can also be used as a neutral label for white females.

Stars. Refers to white women in movie terms, connoting all the glamour associated with movie stars. The term can be used only to label white women, because there are almost no glamorous black female movie stars.

Golden Girl. Refers to the hair color of white women; "golden" connotes value, and the label is complimentary.

Pinkie. Refers to the skin color of white women.

This list of black labels for white people was collected in Chicago; however, most of the labels are used in other parts of the country. Some labels are used much more than others, and these are certainly known by black people in any area of the country, "Blue-eyed devil," "o-fay," "fay," "The Man," "honky," "peckerwood," "Mr. Charlie," "Miss Ann," "paddy," "whitey," "gray," and "blue-eyed soul brother" or "sister" are the ones commonly used to refer to white people; other labels have a more restrictive geographical currency occurring in the usage of southern or Chicago-area blacks only. Most blacks, however, would know the referent when these labels are used in context.

The significance of black people's labels for white people lies in their abundance and the types of white persons characterized. For example, the number of negative or uncomplimentary labels for white people in the black lexicon exceeds the number of neutral and positive labels.

This greater number of negative labels indicates that black people see white people as an enemy or an oppressive force most of the time. In fact, "o-fay" and "fay" clearly refer to white people as the foe. "Blue-eyed devils" implies that life for black people is a kind of hell ruled by white devils.

Other negative labels reflect the inferior social position which black people occupy in relation to white people. For example, the negative labels "captain," "Mr. Charlie," "Chuck," "Charlene," and "Miss Ann" all refer to the inferior social status of black people.

The neutral labels do not connote the meaning of foe or refer to the inferior social status of black people. Instead, they relate to the dominant physical difference between white people and black people (skin color), as in "gray" and "whitey"; other labels (like "Republican") refer to an extensional characteristic that is predominantly white. It must be pointed out, however, that all of the labels that have been included here in the "neutral" category can be used in a negative context. This implies that it is difficult for black people to think of white people in a neutral way. (Some of the "positive" labels, too, can be used in a negative way.)

Only one label—"blue-eyed soul brother"—favorably refers to white men. On the other hand, a number of labels for white women can refer to them in positive ways: "blue-eyed soul sisters," "pearls," "stars," "golden girls," "blondie," and "pinkie." This means that white men are seen as a much greater threat than white women. Only two labels, "Charlene" and "Miss Ann," refer to white women in a negative way.

In addition, the positive labels for white women refer to physical characteristics. The positive labels refer to white women on the basis of eyes (blue), skin (white), and hair (blond). This may mean that the beauty standards of the dominant white culture have been accepted by black people, and this acceptance is reflected in the use of labels referring to the physical traits which are considered beautiful to the dominant culture. However, the acceptance of white beauty standards as the *only* beauty standards is changing. The black revolution has caused black people to develop standards of beauty based on black physical characteristics. "Black is beautiful" is a reflection of this change in attitude, as is the recent connotation given to one of the labels black people use to refer to black women: "sapphire." Originally the label referred to any black woman. Now, with the additional positive attitude toward themselves that blacks have gained from the black revolution, the label can refer to an *attractive* black woman.

This list of black people's labels for white people is still evolving. As new relationships between black and white arise, and as new situations in the racial crisis emerge, the black subculture will generate new labels to refer to white people.

Black racial labels of self-reference

Black people also have many words to refer to their own racial identity, which indicates the significance of blackness for themselves. This can be understood, even expected, by virtue of the fact that in almost every social context where black people have interacted with whites in America—whether in seeking employment, or housing, or pursuing social relations in general—their own race has always been a factor that blacks have had to consider in evaluating or understanding the white response to their initiative. Because of this many labels which black people have for themselves are descriptive of the postures maintained in their relationships with whites in those contexts. In addition, other labels identify the physical characteristics of blacks that they themselves have been taught by whites to notice and disparage, or they refer to the sense of group cohesion or brotherhood that blacks have developed because of a common black experience.

Like the labels that black people have for whites, these labels of self-reference can also be divided into negative, neutral, and positive categories. The following list of words for black racial identity are divided into these groups. Like the list of white identity labels, this list was collected in Chicago. All of the labels, however, are used throughout the country and are well known to black people.

Negative

Uncle Tom or *Tom*. Derived from the character in *Uncle Tom's Cabin*. He was docile and always subservient to white people. When the term is used to refer to a black person, it means that he follows the wishes of white people, never acts aggressively toward white people, and accepts the inferiority status imposed on him by white people. The most negative connotation of the term applies to black persons who betray other blacks to whites. "Uncle Tom" or "Tom" is the most negative label black people can apply to other blacks.

Dr. Thomas. Same connotations as "Uncle Tom" or "Tom," but applied to professional, middle-class persons—especially those who are intellectuals with degrees.

Handkerchief Head. Refers to the headband or kerchief worn by rural blacks in the South, especially while picking cotton. The label can be used with all the connotations of "Uncle Tom" or "Tom." In addition, the label refers to black people whose behavior is unsophisticated, uncouth, or rural ("country," in the black lexicon).

Oreo. Brand name for a cookie made of two chocolate wafers with a white sugary paste between them. It is "black on the outside, white on the inside," and this is the meaning of the term when it is used to describe black persons. An "oreo" is a black person who is physiologically black but mentally white—that is, a black person who thinks like white people on social issues. The label is used especially to refer to middle-class blacks and other blacks who are not militant or who are not in sympathy with the goals of the black revolution and the strategies for reaching these goals.

Mose. Derived from the biblical character, Moses, and refers to old black men—especially to those whose behavior is that of the stereotyped rural black. The term is often used as a collective noun, in spite of its singular form. Also, the label is often used in a humorous context.

Sam. A common name of black males, it is used to refer to any black male. In addition, the story character, Sambo, was black; perhaps the label derives from "Little Black Sambo."

Jig. A label in the white lexicon used to refer to black persons. Black people, however, took the white label "jig" and added "boo" to make "jigger-boo." The added term "boo" in this context is probably the black dialect pronunciation of their term of self-reference, "boot," with loss of final "t." The second part of the term, with the "black" pronunciation, by merging with the conventional interjection "boo!," absorbs the connotation associated with things spooky or frightening when designating black. These "frightening" connotations are also part of the terms "boogie-man," "booger-bear," and "boogie-woogie."

Booger-bear. Any ugly black woman.

Boot. Metaphoric label referring to the black skin of black people, which is like the black leather of a boot.

Shine. Derived from the sheen that the skin of some black people has.

Slick. Derived from the plastered hair that many blacks have. The hair is greased to make it straight, in an attempt to attain the beauty standards of whites.

Neutral

Spook. Because of their skin coloring, black people are difficult to see in the dark. "Spook" is probably derived from that—like spooks, black persons can be heard but not seen. The label may also have been derived from the black servants or domestic workers who perform their duties around white people without making their presence felt.

Spliv or *Splib.* Can be pronounced either way; "spliv" was probably the original pronunciation. Some black people who speak black dialect change the final "v" to "b"; thus the secondary pronunciation.

Head. This label probably derived from the exaggerated concern over hair. Kinky hair has often been a stigma for many blacks, and they have constantly attempted to hide or disguise the stigma by straightening it.

Positive

Soul brother or *Soul sister; Brother* or *Sister.* The most complimentary label one black can use to refer to another. The label implies a situation which creates a *family* relationship in which all black people are brothers and sisters. "Soul" in the label emphasizes that the relationship is black, because "soul" refers to anything indigenous to black culture. In referring to each other as "brother" or "sister," black people recognize the kinship that they derive from the struggle against racism. The use of the labels "soul brother" or "soul sister" verbalizes and makes this struggle conscious. Stated another way, black identity is attained from the relationship all blacks have with white America. Black identity is forged in the heat of the fight against white racism, and this identity makes each black a brother or sister of every other black.

Club member or *Member.* Also connotes the kinship or "all-in-it-together" aspect of being black in white America. The label is complimentary, because the struggle against white racism is viewed favorably by black people. To recognize another black as a "club member" or "member" is to recognize that black person's membership in the group which is waging a noble struggle.

Blacks. Although this label is used by both whites and blacks, it is included in the black lexicon of racial labels because it originated in black culture. The label acquires increased interest when contrasted with connotations and interpretations of "black" *before* the black revolution. Prior to the black revolution, to call a black person "black" was an insult, because black skin was looked upon as a thing of shame. The increased use of "black" is a healthy sign; it means that black people have accepted the identifying label as something positive—a desirable quality and something to be proud of, not ashamed of. The adoption of "black" to refer to themselves in a positive way means that black people have accepted their physical appearance—their deviation from white-skinned America—as something beautiful. This is what is implied by "Black is beautiful." Calling themselves "black" was the first and most important step in raising the self-concept of black people.

Afro-American. Prior to the black revolution in America black people denied their African heritage and ancestry, and they did everything to hide it. With the increase of pride in being black accompanying the black revolution, African heritage is looked upon as a positive quality of black identity. Thus many black people, especially the more militant ones, refer to themselves as "Afro-Americans" to emphasize their African roots.

Sapphire. Refers to black women and can be used in a positive or negative way. In its positive use, the label refers to a black woman, especially an attractive black woman, as a gem (attractive white women and girls can be gems, too; the label for them is "pearls"). In its negative use the label refers to an overbearing, dominating black woman similar to Kingfish's wife in the Amos and Andy series.

"Negro" and "colored" were not included in the list of racial identity labels, although many black people refer to themselves and other black people in those terms. These two labels were not cited because they are not *exclusively* black—they are used by both black and white. Another reason they were not included is that these two labels were not generated out of the black experience or black culture. Instead, these labels are part of the white lexicon of racial identity labels.

"Black," on the other hand, was included because it was generated by the black experience and black culture. Admittedly, "black" was used by whites in the past to refer to black people. When used by whites, it was solely a descriptive label; it did not connote the identity meaning as when it is used by blacks.

"Nigger" has also been omitted from the list of racial identity labels which black people have for themselves because it did not originate in black culture. Black people often refer to other blacks as "niggers." They don't, however, use this label in the exclusively negative sense that whites use it. "Nigger" can be a derogatory label, a neutral label, or a positive label—a term of endearment—when used by black people. Black comedian Dick Gregory once stated that he resented being called "nigger" by whites because they "didn't say it right." What he meant is that the way whites used the word "nigger" could not have a neutral or positive meaning as it can when blacks use it.

In addition, "colored," "Negro," and "black" have acquired new connotations with the impetus of the black revolution. The three labels identify three kinds of black people: colored people are those who are docile, who don't meet white racism head on, and who have some of the qualities of an Uncle Tom; Negroes are those who don't like the status of black people in America and who don't accept the situation between white and black, but don't do much to change the situation—in other words, the traditional Negro; blacks are those who refuse to accept the situation between whites and blacks and who actively and militantly attempt to alter the situation. The three labels are somewhat age-graded: older black people often conform to the meaning of "colored"; middle-aged black people often conform to the meaning of "Negro"; young black people often conform to the meaning of "black."

The number of labels which black people use to refer to each other indicates that the identification of types among themselves has been an important determination for black people to make. As with the creation of labels for white people, there is an experiential basis for the creation of racial terms for blacks. Said another way, it has been important for black people to know exactly what kinds of other black people they encounter, just as it has been important for them to know exactly what kinds of white people they encounter.

Significantly, most of the racial identity labels of self-reference fall within the negative category. This is because traditionally it has been difficult for black people to think of themselves in positive terms (which is understandable, given the racial situation of America, where black people have traditionally occupied an inferior status to whites). As the black revolution progresses, however, black people will find it less and less difficult to think of themselves in positive terms, and the number of positive labels should increase. Nevertheless, the greater number of negative labels blacks have developed for black racial identity is a sad and tragic reflection of the American racial situation.

Of the negative labels of self-reference several refer to the inferior-superior status relationship of blacks to whites: "Uncle Tom," "Tom," "Dr. Thomas," "handkerchief head," and "Oreo." These labels imply the combatant nature of race relations in which traitors can develop to surrender the cause of black people. These labels also imply the inferior status of blacks to whites in the same way that the white racial identity labels, discussed above, imply the inferior status of blacks.

The negative labels such as "shine," "slick," and "boot" refer to the physical characteristics of black skin that identify black people in a negative way. At the same time, however, the later "black" also refers to the physical characteristic of black skin that identifies black people— but it has a positive meaning. This points out the fact that black people have traditionally viewed their black skin as an inferior mark, even a mark of stigma. "Black," however, is a new label, and it connotes the positive feeling toward blackness which black people have acquired during the black revolution. The same is true for the positive label, "Afro-American."

The two positive labels, "soul brother" or "soul sister" (or "brother" and "sister") refer to the kinship feeling blacks have acquired in their struggle against white racism.

It is clear that racial identity labels are directly related to the experience black people have had within black culture and when interacting with whites in the larger cultural context. These racial identity labels in the black lexicon are an index of the antagonistic nature of the contact between blacks and whites in America. They are suggestive of the roles that all members assumed in their dealings with each other, ultimately reflecting the attitudes that blacks have toward themselves and toward whites.

■ "Inversion" in black communication

GRACE SIMS HOLT

Grace Sims Holt has deep "down home" roots; born in South Carolina, she is a product of southern black culture, experiencing in early childhood intimate contact with the inland speech of blacks and whites, the Gullah speech of Sea Island blacks, and the Geechee speech of lower coastal blacks (found, for example, in Charleston, South Carolina).

The author is currently an associate professor of speech at the University of Illinois at Chicago Circle, as well as consultant and lecturer. Her major research interests revolve around black communication and educational theory and practice, especially as it affects the schooling of minority children. "Inversion in Black Communication" is a product of this interest, as well as a most illuminating example of how powerless minority groups protect their individual and cultural identity against the powerful caste definitions imposed on them by the dominant culture within the larger society.

The perspective for "Stylin' Outta the Black Pulpit," her second article in this volume, comes from the author's religious experience and education. She is a product of the preacher-educator sector of black culture, her mother being a schoolteacher, her father a Baptist minister (preacher) and an educator (principal of a then all-black high school which bears his name).

A graduate of Spelman College in Atlanta at the age of eighteen, her graduate study was undertaken at Cornell, the University of Chicago, and Northeastern Illinois University's Center for Inner City Studies. She credits her experience as a schoolteacher in Chicago's ghettos as one contributing to the most significant aspects of her education. There she found interwoven the strands of "down home" and black urban culture which she attempts to illuminate in her articles.

This is a shortened version of the original article, which appeared in the *Florida FL Reporter,* Spring/Fall, 1971, pp. 41–43, 55.

Introduction

Much of the recent literature concerning black language and communication is limited in perspective and reveals either a deliberate omission or ignorance of black cultural norms or a symptom of our profound theoretical and conceptual dilemmas in the discipline. Oversimplified analyses and approaches overlook the complexity of the problem.

Linguists have provided needed structural analysis and reinterpretation of black language, but because they have been unable to include much social, cultural, and historical information, their focus is excessively narrow and distorted. From the black perspective, this "half-truth" represents an old pattern in a new dress.

In an effort to begin to provide the larger focus that is needed, this paper will discuss a relatively unknown aspect of black communication and its relationship to black experience. The feature of black communication that I will attempt to identify is a linguistic survival process functionally related to the conflicts implicit in American caste, class, and race. This process I have called here "inversion." Though only one of many components present within the evolution of black American communication and culture, inversion is significant in its own right.

Historical factors

Analyzing "Afro-cum Black" culture, Touré suggests that the total culture of a people is composed not only of its arts and philosophy, but also of its tools, work habits and *survival patterns*.[1]

Slavery in America dictated that Blacks behave circumspectly and timorously if they were to survive with some degree of integrity intact. Karon points out that "the American Indian, in offering physical resistance, was practically exterminated by the whites. The Negro had to find a different type of resistance in order to continue to multiply and grow in spite of every sadistic effort to destroy him in some areas."[2] The Indian possessed; the slave *was* possessed. One was an adversary; the other was chattel. Adapting to an unbearable and unbeatable system therefore necessitated the production of a special form of communication interaction between master and slave. Blacks were clearly limited to two responses: submission and subversion, since overt aggression was punishable by death. There was no process by which grievances could be redressed. White verbalizations defined Blacks as inferior; whites rewarded only black responses acceptable to them.

Blacks gradually developed their own ways of conveying resistance using The Man's language against him as a defense against sub-human categorization. The sociocultural context formed the basis for the development of inversion as a positive and valuable adaptive response pattern. As Cobbs and Grier state, "The slaves turned the language as it was presented to them to their own purposes, and in fact to the precise purposes which their owners sought to prevent."[3] The phenomenon of inversion is a practical necessity for people in subordinate positions. The sociohistorical progression of slavery went from physical restraint to legal restraint, followed by a de facto restraint and succeeded by a psychological restraint. Superordinate language was designed to maintain, reinforce, and perpetuate the enumerated existing restraints. Language is the common thread running through these stages. It is safe to

[1] Harold Cruse, "Black and White: Outlines of the Next Stage," Ch. 1 in *Black World*, January, 1971, p. 38. See also Sekou Touré, "A Dialectical Approach to Culture," *The Black Scholar* 1, no. 1 (November, 1969). "Afro-cum Black" culture means African culture continued through black culture; it also means black American culture which praises African culture.

[2] E. Y. Williams, review of *The Negro Personality* by Bertram P. Karon, *Mental Hygiene* 44 (1960): 592–93.

[3] William H. Grier and Price M. Cobbs, *Black Rage* (New York: Basic Books, 1968), p. 103.

remove the physical chains of bondage if legal chains are substituted. One may securely remove the legal chains when the de facto constraints are just as effective. But legalized subordination is meaningless without the subjugation of the will to be free. De facto subordination is ineffective unless accompanied by the victim's belief in his own inferiority. Once the physical chains are removed, language becomes the major vehicle for perpetuating the legitimation of the subsequent stages of oppression.

The function of white verbal behavior toward Blacks was to define, force acceptance of, and control the existing level of restraints.

Blacks clearly recognized that to master the language of whites was in effect to consent to be mastered by it through the white definitions of caste built into the semantic/social system. Inversion therefore becomes the defensive mechanism which enables Blacks to fight linguistic, and thereby psychological, entrapment.

The traditional process of inversion was based on the concept that you can't disguise black skin but you can disguise speech which permits you to verbally "turn the tables" on an unknowledgeable opponent.

Many Blacks took the material of stereotyped utterances and used it to their own advantage. Words and phrases were given reverse meanings and functions changed. Whites, denied access to the semantic extensions of duality, connotations, and denotations that developed within black usage, could only interpret the same material according to its original singular meaning. White interpretation of the communication event was quite different from that made by the other person in the interaction, enabling Blacks to deceive and manipulate whites without penalty. This protective process, understood and shared by Blacks, became a contest of matching wits, the stake in the game being survival with dignity. This form of linguistic guerrilla warfare protected the subordinated, permitted the masking and disguising of true feelings, allowed the subtle assertion of self, and promoted group solidarity. The purpose of the game was to *appear to but not to.*

The heart of the process of inversion is the contrast in referential and contextual functions. In essence, the idea is to make any word of denigration used by the power group take on shades of meaning known only to the inverter. As a consequence, the most "soulful" terms of referents in black usage today are those which traditionally have been the symbols of oppression. Take the word "nigger" as the prime example. When used by whites it has only one meaning, though the degree of degradation may vary with the users. When used by Blacks, the word is often used as a term of affection, admiration, approval; it is a word of positive connotation, a contradiction of original intent. It is also used by Blacks to convey feelings synonymous with the meanings given the word by white users. Here are a few of the many examples I could use to illustrate these points. One Black will say to another: "You're my kind of nigger." When speaking of whites, Blacks often show their admiration by making such statements as: "He's as slick as a nigger."[4] In a 180° switch, Blacks will use the term in the same manner as it is used by whites: "nigger business," "Niggers ain't——(use your own four letter word)." Thus the word becomes a model of deception, taking shades of meaning that would be misinterpreted by that segment of society which originally coined the word. I have been frequently asked by whites why Blacks use "nigger" among themselves when its use by whites would amount to a declaration of war. The answer is obvious; the word has an inverted meaning when used by Blacks.

The dynamics of semantic reconstruction

English uses *black* to denote a quality not considered desirable by white society. When used by whites in reference to Negroes, it is appended to some other term of approbation or disapprobation. An example of the former is, "He's a black dentist." An example of the latter is, "He's a black——(use your own four letter word)." Blacks invert the word and it becomes a noun, not describing an attribute, but naming a group. Blacks' adoption of the noun *Black* represents a determination to call themselves by any name other than that used by whites. Whites, by virtue of their power, define black as representing all that's bad. Blacks wrest from whites the power to define; ergo, the term *Black* is made respectable and good.

Gordon Allport has indicated that "primary potency" labels lose their intensity when converted from nouns to adjectives.[5] So identifying someone as "Jew" or "Negro" devastates the category of Negroness or Jewishness more so than saying Negro *writer,* Jewish *doctor.* By adding a noun, one defuses the prejudicial potency of the adjective. However, the process of inversion with respect to *black* does just the opposite. It converts the adjective *black* into the noun *Black,* making the label *more* potent, not less. This is to recognize that the most universally hateful and denigrating English word used by whites *is* the term *black,* which, for Blacks, symbolizes the continuing chain of semantic bondage built into the connotative system of English.[6] Therefore, by making the verbal weapon more potent (through means of grammatical change) and its use obligatory within the context of public confrontation, i.e.,

[4] This kind of language behavior is called "soul talk," "soul language," or "spoken soul" by Blacks. It is not to be confused with what educators and linguists are currently calling Black English.
[5] Gordon Allport, "Prejudice: Linguistic Factors," in Anderson and Stageberg, *Introductory Reading on Language* (New York: Holt, Rinehart and Winston, 1962), pp. 168–75.
[6] Ossie Davis, "The English Language Is My Enemy," *American Teacher* (April, 1967).

demand that you be called Black, you force an equation on The Man that essentially compels him to come to grips with his own hatefulness. Put more concretely, forcing the "mainstream man" to use the term "Black" (noun) in its more potent form, you create in him uneasiness, discomfort, and embarrassment, and hopefully, as a result of that, a realization of the full derogatory/discriminatory effect of the term as he uses it and a realization of changes in the value, force, authority, and honor of the term. In this way, through convergence of the terms, the derogatory connotation of *black* (adjective) within the semantic system becomes equatable and comparable to the despised and powerless situation of *Blacks* within the social system. (This complex maneuver goes on even as Blacks' definition of the term as it applies to them is in the process of being changed.) In taking The Man's strongest weapon and using it to your advantage, you have denuded him of verbal power, and by implication freed yourself from the psychological bondage that "hate" labels impose. Freedom from psychological bondage forces a change in power relations which presages a drive for self-determination and status. Liberation begins with language.

The white-black opposition which generates the inversion process has many amusing aspects. I am reminded of being stopped in Asheville, North Carolina at 3:00 A.M. a few years ago. My husband was the driver, and we had committed absolutely no offense. A white officer sauntered to the car, casually pulling back his uniform to reveal two pistols. Without stating what violation we could possibly have committed, he demanded the registration papers for the car. After being satisfied that the car wasn't stolen—an unlikely fact since the occupants were two men, two women and a child, and since it bore Illinois license plates—he "let us go."[7] The car was a white Cadillac convertible with a black top. My husband was furious; the "arrest" was totally unwarranted. The other male passenger laughed and said, "You'd have been OK if you'd been driving a black Cadillac with a *white* top. What the cop couldn't take was *anything* where black was on top of white!" Sometimes the only way to live with it is to laugh with it. Inversion is one of the bases of the humor of Blacks who have traditionally laughed about "Putting on Ole Massa," or in current terms, "Tell the man what he wants to hear," or "He don't know what time it is."

Functions of inversion

Playing verbal games with whites developed such aesthetic forms as "The Put-on" "Tomming," "Mocking the Sender," and more recently

---

[7] A Black male traveling South ("goin' down home") knows better than to risk his family to the possibility of jail and maltreatment at the hands of southern white law-enforcement officers. Therefore, the mere idea of the car being stolen was a ridiculous if not absurd idea to us all.

"Doing the Tom Jones" and "The Gamesmanship of Muhammad Ali" (Cassius Clay). Manipulation was possible because whites would not believe that Blacks were capable of out-thinking them or, if they did believe it, would not admit it. Blacks knew this, and many used that knowledge to verbally change the power relationship, for power is the ability to redefine. The subordinated assumed an attribute of power by redefinition of white terms. Blacks intentionally behaved in ways which whites perceived as inappropriate but by which they were flattered, elevating "whitey" to a status they both knew he didn't occupy, invoking praise and ridicule in the same terms. The patrolman became a police "chief," the ex-private was elevated to "cap'n," the ex-captain to "colonel." As the joke goes, "It was so flattering, whites didn't have the heart to deny it." The practice of cunningly attacking a white antagonist by admiring him is of long duration and function.

However, the inversion process operated here, too; by raising the status of The Man, Blacks were also emphasizing in a mocking way their own lack of status. In practicing inversion, the skillfulness is in the creation of the manipulator. The burden of interpretation is always on the person receiving the image reversal—the person denied, mocked, put down, or put on.

As previously discussed, the term "nigger" as an in-group term was inverted by Blacks, this process being a semantic device allowing survival with dignity. The adjective *black* was not only inverted to a noun by Blacks within their group, but also in dialogue between white and Blacks, forcing whites to accept the inversion. In the latter case, the semantic device deals with Blacks' self-definition in the context of racial confrontation with the total (wider) society. Blacks' adoption of the noun *Black* represents a determination to call themselves by any name other than that used by whites. The developmental and functional aspects of inversion furnish an interesting and significant sociolinguistic development in contemporary America.

Quasi-inversion

Quasi-inversion of the word "Black" is the translative norm in the conception of white society. Whereas the inversion of *Black* is total in black society, the inversion adopted by white society is only partial. Bereft of the multiple meanings in black society, white inversion has been truncated to become synonymous with Negro. For example, in its inception, *Black* as used by Blacks in referring to other members of the group was intended exclusively to be used, understood by Blacks for Blacks. The originators of the self-appellation *Black* had absolutely no regard for the opinions, approval, tolerance, acceptance, or rejection of the term by white society. The connotative meanings were intended for black minds only. When whites became familiarized with the term, they perceived that this was a nonobjectionable way to talk to Blacks about Blacks, and with this perception the nuances of the black inversion were unrecognized. Thus the white use of the noun *Black* is strictly limited and circumscribed. Generally, when whites use the noun "Black," they just substitute the noun Negro. The fit is perfect. As a by-product it is worthwhile noting that the adoption of the noun *Black* by white society solved a knotty problem for most whites who spent much of their time in racially mixed company pondering over the monumental question of "what to call these niggers without openly offending."

Socio-political contest and functional change

As is frequently the case with other linguistic phenomena, function remains—after the original cause disappears or is minimized—and reinforces the perception of danger. Replacement with more subtle ones of the old physical bonds which operated in the creation of the process has produced continuously developing variations of the phenomenon. Currently there exist, in addition to historical remnants, new additions according to collective functional need. The black struggle for collective survival and for social, economic, and political power (commonly called the "Black Revolution") utilizes the criterion of blackness as an imperative of unity, a catalyst which cannot be lost, stolen, preempted, or devoured by white society. Black is a unifying term, pro-black and anti-colonialist. It crystallizes self-awareness, ideological direction, and solidifies bonds of the national black experience in confrontation with white domination. Affirmation of self, of blackness, raises levels of commitment to resistance to subordinate status and colonialistic oppression, establishing a feeling of identification with nonwhite people of the world, thereby linking Black America as a colony to the heritage of African colonies.

The reconstruction and idealization of blackness as a force for generating black cultural unity and social power has been espoused by W. E. B. Du Bois and successively by Malcolm X, Lerone Bennett, and Imamu Amiri Baraka (Le Roi Jones).

Universal acceptance and use of the inverted term "Black" in the ideological creation of a new social order are a verbal rejection of the American Caucasian perception of global realities and objectives, and a repudiation of American structural systems and conditions. Promotion of this ideology through language serves as an impetus to changes in behavior and responses, establishing new power relationships both within and outside the group. The expedient was a necessary one for mobilizing and intensifying forces in the continuing historical black-white confrontation.

Superficial resemblances of forms and meaning present a problem for the teacher when inversion occurs. Blacks use "double meaning" as a verbal device to deceive whites as they also abandon black in-group terms as "dead" as soon as they become current among whites. For example, "bad" when used by black children may mean either "good, attractive" or "bad, unattractive," etc. "Uptight" may mean either "beautiful, together, happy, favorable," etc., or "tense, afraid, angry, unfavorable." Numerous examples of this kind provide evidence that the process continues to function in black communication. These examples attest to the very efficient transmission of this subtle process in black culture. Though its function is self-assertive, the process is a hidden dimension which remains quantitatively reduced but qualitatively great. By this I mean to say that when this process of inversion was initiated, the primary objective was survival with dignity, and numerous words were subject to the process of inversion in connection with this objective; the inversion process has been reduced, and their quality and character have changed. The objective is no longer mere survival, but cultural and racial self-assertiveness.

■ The kinetic element in black idiom

THOMAS KOCHMAN

Thomas Kochman, editor of this volume, has for several years been looking at communication within natural settings in order to discover the inside perspective: what the communicating parties know about the situation that affects the way they behave. With his background and training in linguistics and special interest in sociolinguistics, Kochman has also explored the relationship of language to culture and society. In analyzing various ethnic expressions of black people, for example, he has discovered a few "hidden" underlying semantic areas (crypto-sememes) that appear closely linked to black cultural norms (movement, contest, control) which influence the use of such terms. As a thesis, it may also explain what keeps certain terms in use over a period of time. Hence the "kinetic element" article appears here. The ethnography article is the product of the study of speech events within Chicago's black community. It is included here because it demonstrates how sharply instrumental the various types of speech behavior are for those who use them, as well as showing the high level of oral expertise that black cultural norms develop among black people. The descriptive examples in this article are eloquent evidence that black people are among the most original and expressive users of the English language—a point publicly unrecognized heretofore, yet one directly or indirectly substantiated by this and every other article in the volume.

A graduate of City College of New York and New York University, Kochman is associate professor of speech and theatre at the University of Illinois, Chicago Circle. He has published articles on cross-cultural communication, on the rationale and strategies for language intervention in the public schools, and on various aspects of the language arts curriculum.

Introduction

An analysis of black English has yielded an interesting discovery: namely, that words which possess the quality of rapid and unrestricted movement ("dig," "hustler," "swinger," "groovy") or have the potential for such movement ("hip," "boot," "cat," "wheels") have favorable connotation in black usage. Conversely, words which contain a quality of stasis or impeded movement ("scuffler," "lame," "stiff," "busted") have unfavorable connotation.

This paper proposes to do two things: to list and discuss some items from the black lexicon sufficient to justify the above finding, and to relate the connotation of such words to community values and attitudes.

Procedure

In attempting to order the words and citations that follow, I have tried to establish a cultural frame of reference for various groups of words, starting with those that themselves refer to activities in the culture which involve varying degrees of movement or which center around pursuits, goals, and norms that the culture clearly views as favorable.

Discussion

Acquiring the status of a high "rep" (reputation) and being accepted as part of the street scene is a prime motivation for the black street youngster. At an early age he discovers that by engaging in and being successful in action activities—those which might be tentatively defined as involving a certain amount of rapid movement—such as sports, fighting, and dancing, he builds himself up in his own eyes and those of his peers. Words and phrases which refer to this activity, or to the person engaging in the activity, frequently embody a kinetic element—as if speakers, in retaining the sense of movement in the *expression* of the activity, were seeking to reexperience the sensation of the activity itself. Some of the terms are new, and others old and some no longer in use; but the kinetic presence appears to have existed within the culture for some time.

Some words and expressions referring to fighting embody purely kinetic elements, such as "swinging out" and "jitter-hopping" (New York); other terms, such as "bopping" (an onomatopoeic term from the comic strip), "gang-banging," and "rumble" are "noise" terms which suggest violent and rapid movement as underlying causes (cf. the conventional slang phrase, "to start with a *bang*").

Dance terms and expressions such as "stepping" ("I start to step with Miss Jibbs, she'll hip you to that"),[1] "sock it to me," and names for dances (Rock and Roll, Twist, African Twist, Locomotion, Charge, Jerk, and Black Power Stomp) all embody kinetic elements.

Later the black youngster discovers that it adds to his rep to be a good talker, to have a heavy rap that one can throw to a girl for the purpose of becoming intimate with her, or to establish himself among his peers through a lively "rundown" (narration) of some past event, or by "mounting on" someone through verbal contest.

An everyday movement such as walking becomes infused with kinetic and rhythmic elements which are reflected in the terms used to designate it: "bop" and "bop-slouch" (originally from "bebop" or "rebop." "The two-syllable word was merely a way of describing the staccato two-note phrase that became the trademark in its playing").[2] Citations for each term emphasize the kinetic and rhythmic elements noted above: "He bopped . . . dipping the right shoulder low and pushing off on the ball of the left foot to get that rhythmic hop in his walk,"[3] and "Shrimp

[1] Clayton Riley, "Now That Henry Is Gone," *The Liberator*, July, 1965, p. 28.
[2] Robert S. Gold, *A Jazz Lexicon* (New York: Knopf, 1964), p. 32.
[3] R. Ernest Holmes, "Cheesy, Baby," *The Liberator*, April, 1968, p. 14.

said . . . as he dug both hands deep into his pockets and walked on, his body swaying from one side to the other in a kind of bop-slouch."[4]

People whose common goal seems to be pursuit of "bread" (money) are generally viewed kinetically: peddlers of narcotics are "pushers"; persons acting as intermediaries between the consumer and the next higher-up, dealing either in numbers or narcotics, are "runners"; thieves, especially shoplifters, are "boosters." The admired and successful hustler always has something going for him, as evidenced by his affluent appearance. Conversely, you have nothing going for you if you have no scheme or hustle to provide you with money. Other operators on the street who are looking for a chance to "whup" (Chicago) or "run" (Los Angeles, New York) "a game" (trick someone out of some money) are known as "slicks" or "slicksters," by virtue of the ease with which they operate their deceptive maneuvers. ("All the Muslims now felt as though 125th Street was theirs. It used to belong to the hustlers and the slicksters.")[5] Also, "Tell me something slick" is used in Chicago to mean, "Tell me how to make some *quick* money."

"Bread" and "wheels" (money and car) are the high value-symbols for unimpeded movement to where the action is. "Wheels," a synecdoche for car, while not embodying a kinetic element per se, has an obvious *potential* for movement. Money is conceived of as an edible: "bread," but also "cakes" ("Let me run this broad down, and I'll give you the cakes"),[6] and can be construed within the structure I am outlining as fuel, a necessary ingredient for movement or action. As Horton put it: "Bread makes possible the excitement—the high (getting loaded with wine, pills, or pot), the sharp clothes, the 'broad,' the fight, and all those good things which show that one knows what's happening and has 'something going for himself.' "

I view such terms as "pluck" for wine and "taste" for liquor as embodying an action element retained from its more conventional use as a verb. "Pluck" is probably a metonymical form derived from plucking grapes, as "taste" is from taste of liquor.[7] The process of taking drugs is expressed kinetically ("getting high," "turning on," "shooting up"), as is the effect of drugs on the person ("nodding," "flying"). Some kinetic terms referring to the sex act are "pulling" ("If you gon pull a bitch, you can get excited and let her know that you want that pussy so bad you about to go crazy"),[8] *jamming* ("guzzle some 'Hombre' and

[4] Betty Washington, "Summer Fun: A Concert Issue, a Black Vignette," *The Daily Defender's World of Ideas,* May, 1968.

[5] Claude Brown, *Manchild and the Promised Land* (New York: Macmillan, 1965), p. 343.

[6] Woodie King, Jr., "The Game," *The Liberator,* August, 1965, p. 24, and in this volume.

[7] Gold, *Jazz Lexicon,* p. 316.

[8] Brown, *Manchild,* p. 244.

maybe even jam a few broads"),[9] *turning* (in the expression "to turn a trick"), and "run" or "pull a train" (several fellows alternately engaging in the sex act with the same girl: "They thought that I was one of the guys who had pulled a train on their sister in the park the summer before").[10]

A term used to refer to a member of a peer group is "cat" (from a reduced form of "alligator" and perhaps merging with Spanish *gato* [cat], reinforced in black usage by "tomcat"), someone who is always chasing "pussy" (women, especially when viewed as sexual objects). Gold suggests that *cat* may also be related "to the itinerant nature of early jazzmen."[11] The term is clearly one embodying a quality of potential movement. Another term such as "ready" is descriptive of the person who "has his diploma in street knowledge,"[12] which means knowing what's happening, taking advantage of opportunities, avoiding pitfalls, and being prepared to move to where the action is.

Understanding something, with the added connotation of being able to get basic enough to enjoy it, is to "dig" it. Enjoyment typically is expressed in kinetic terms: "I'm finger-popping," "It grabs me," "I'm up in heah (here)," or "Groovy." If someone is giving you information, he is "pulling your coat," "turning you on," or "running it (on) down."

If you "hit" on the numbers you were successful, and if you were "hittin' on" a few women you had expectations of success in your efforts to become intimate with them.

Opposing power groups that one respects are also viewed kinetically: policemen are "headbreakers" and the white power structure is the "whips," the latter an acronym derived from *whi*te *p*ower *s*tructure ("He was cynical about the motives of the white power structure—the Whips")[13] and appropriate to my scheme, like "cat" and "wheels," referring to an object which has the capacity for rapid and unimpeded movement.

A "happening" begins from the "git-go" ("Henry . . . was there from the git-go"),[14] which is reminiscent of the track starter's command, ". . . *get* set, *go*." The place where the movement can occur is appropriately termed the "track," whether the place is a dance hall ("I dig you holding this all-originals scene at the track"),[15] the street ("I

[9] Holmes, "Cheesy, Baby," p. 17.

[10] Brown, *Manchild*, p. 16.

[11] Gold, *Jazz Lexicon*, p. 48.

[12] John Horton, "Time and Cool People," *Trans-Action*, April, 1967, p. 5, and in this volume.

[13] Robert Conot, *Rivers of Blood, Years of Darkness* (New York: William Morrow, 1968), p. 34.

[14] Riley, "Now That Henry Is Gone," p. 28.

[15] I.e., Rockland Palace in Harlem. Malcolm X, *Autobiography* (New York: Grove Press, 1965), p. 310.

went to sleep wondering what to do to solve the fast track"),[16] or, as used figuratively, the life span ("You get on junk and you on a fast track, baby").[17]

All of the above examples are words or expressions whose referents in conventional usage have the quality of or capacity for rapid or unrestricted movement; they all have favorable connotations in black usage. The converse of this also holds: words whose referents embody a quality of stasis or impeded movement have unfavorable connotations in black usage.

A statement by Henry Williamson in *The Hustler* nicely illustrates this distinction. Williamson distinguishes the hustler from his unsuccessful counterpart, the scuffler. "He didn't have no hustlin ability. He would just stay around the neighborhood and beg. . . . He said he was a hustler, but he really wasn't nothing but a goddamn scuffler."[18] "Scuffling" in the idiom means barely making it from day to day, generally by engaging in nonprestigious—because they are unrewarding!—activities such as begging, collecting and returning pop bottles for the deposit, working at odd jobs for minimum wages, etc. It is significant that Williamson also added what for him was the basic cause for the difference in status: the scuffler just stayed around the neighborhood, whereas, as implied, the hustler moved around. Scuffling, in terms of movement, suggests friction: "to walk without lifting the feet."

The "swinger" or "down stud" also has his opposite counterpart, that of the "lame," one who does not do well in any of the action activities and who is easily deceived and victimized. Earlier terms such as "square" and "cube" also reinforced the settled and immobile quality of the persons so designated. Another static term, "stiff," is also used to describe such a person ("You a trick Dan—a stiffy. . . . You so square Little Orphan Annie could put game on you,"[19] or "Negro artists who find their way into white concert halls still find it necessary to "hip" those 'stiffies' in the audience who insist on clapping their hands together in a martial manner.")[20] "Lame" is also used to describe something dull and uninteresting, as a party ("We make it and at first it's a lame set.")[21] Similarly, something that you do not enjoy is a "drag"; if you have problems that you can't solve, you are "hung up"; if you are victimized by another person, you are "put down"; and if you are victimized by heroin, you are "strung out" ("Butch, Danny, Kid were

[16] Iceberg Slim, *Pimp: The Story of My Life* (Los Angeles: Holloway House, 1967), p. 174.

[17] Earl Shorris, *Ofay* (New York: Dell, 1967), p. 44.

[18] Henry Williamson, *The Hustler* (New York: Avon, 1968), pp. 136ff.

[19] King, "The Game," p. 23.

[20] Charles Keil, *Urban Blues* (Chicago: University of Chicago Press, 1966), p. 118.

[21] Riley, "Now That Henry Is Gone," p. 28.

all strung out. They were junkies all the way.")[22] If you are victimized by love, you either "have your nose open" or, as from heroin, are also "strung out" ("Glorie went through a few changes: pretending we were just visitors who were strung out over her.")[23] With "having your nose open," compare such conventional slang phrases as "to be led by the nose" and "to leave yourself wide open." To be without money is to be "dead" (I'm dead, brother. I need a dime to get some Lipton"),[24] or "busted," alongside the more conventional "broke." If you are arrested, you are also busted. Nonactivity on the street corner is "laying dead,"[25] besides the more conventional "hanging." Lack of personal freedom to move around is also implied by the term used to denote a nine-to-five job—a "slave"—whereas "gig," derived from jazz usage, would be used to denote a job that one enjoys (though it is also used without that connotation). Note "gig": "possible from *gigue,* a lively dance form of Italian origin . . . (cf. English counterpart *jig*): from Old French giguer."[26]

While the evidence generally supports the thesis, it is not without exception. "Laid out," which is derived from its use in funeral parlors to describe the procedure whereby the deceased person is displayed during the wake (clearly a static term), is used in the idiom to describe someone who is well dressed. Being well dressed is elsewhere expressed kinetically ("pressed"), and since the term refers to a favored norm I would assume it would continue to have favorable connotation in usage. I do not consider here that the term might be used mockingly to describe someone who is over-dressed, as I do not feel "over-dressed" has any meaning in black street culture—i.e., if your clothes are in style, being dressed in the extreme (which is denigrating according to conventional standards) is the favored norm there.

Other terms, such as "jam" and "set," which do not as conveniently fit the above thesis, require some discussion. It seems to me possible to argue that "jam" and "set" have meanings in conventional usage that exert a static quality, as in "traffic jam" and "set in his ways," i.e., rigid. Of course, in conventional usage "jam" can also suggest a spreading quality (as the counterpart of jelly), as well as exerting a kinetic quality in the expression "to jam through a proposal." Likewise, "set" in conventional usage can exert any number of different qualities depending on how it is used.

In black English, "jam" has been used to mean: (1) to play a musical instrument freely, (2) to dance, (3) to engage in sexual intercourse;

[22] Brown, *Manchild,* p. 158.
[23] King, "The Game," p. 20.
[24] Ibid., p. 22.
[25] Horton, "Time and Cool People," p. 6; Gold, *Jazz Lexicon,* p. 183.
[26] Gold, *Jazz Lexicon,* p. 123.

or, as a noun, to refer to (4) records, or (5) a party. In all of its uses it refers to activities or objects which have prestigious value within black culture. In its use as a verb it clearly embodies a kinetic quality. In all its uses it has favorable connotation.

What I have to show here, it seems to me, is that the conventional uses of "jam" and "set" in those expressions where they exert a static quality are *without* influence on the uses of "jam" and "set" in black idiom. There are two ways to do this: one is to cite the *etymology* of the terms in black English (i.e., the original terms in conventional English from which the terms in black usage derive); the other is to show that, under the influence of the *usage* of the terms in black English, which evokes on the psychic level of the black speaker (for "jam": a kinetic quality plus favorable connotation, and for "set": a "place where favorable things happen" plus favorable connotation), this would direct speakers *away* from the conventional usage of "jam" and "set" where they exert a static quality. This is a valid corollary to my original thesis which said that the kinetic or static quality of words in conventional usage influences the connotation of those words in black usage. In fact, it establishes a kinetic and static quality as a determining force which we now measure more conveniently by reversing the direction. With our test we measure whether the kinetic quality associated with "jam" and "set" in black English influences the black speaker's choice of *conventional* uses of the term.

The etymology of "jam," according to Gold,[27] shows that the model in conventional English was the food term, which, like "jelly" and "barbecue," was "one of several . . . given a sexual meaning and then associated with jazz by Negro jazzmen." All of its present uses in black English can be explained as being derived from the jazz route.

The etymology of the first two meanings of "set" given above, again according to Gold,[28] derive ultimately from the conventional English model *"set of pieces* played by musicians followed by a rest." The second meaning of "set," as a party, is a semantic extension of the first meaning. Two conventional English models for the third meaning of "set" in black English as "the organized center of street life" might be the track starter's command: "On your mark, get set, go!" as well as the expression "movie set," suggested by one of my students—or perhaps TV set! The first source promotes the notion of readiness ("Hanging on the set with the boys is the major way of passing time and waiting until some necessary or desirable action occurs"),[29] and the second source provides the notion of the "place where the action is happen-

[27] Ibid., p. 161.
[28] Ibid., p. 270.
[29] Horton, "Time and Cool People," p. 8.

ing" ("I seen 'em come down on the set last night, shootin' shotguns."[30]

While the etymology clearly disassociates the uses of "jam" and "set" in black English from those expressions in conventional English which exert a static quality, we must remember that the etymology of a word only identifies the association between conventional and black English at the time when the term is *introduced* into black idiom. After that, the processes of diffusion are at work which take into account not only what the actual model of the term was, but what people *think* it was (folk etymology!), and norms and activities which have contributed not only to the *currency* of the term, but also to its semantic extensions. I will discuss the process of diffusion below.

With respect to the present black usage of "jam" and "set," we wondered whether black speakers of the idiom would avoid those uses in conventional English which exert a static quality. We might then attribute the influence, if significant, to those elements: etymology, folk etymology, and prestigious cultural activities and norms which affect usage in black English. For example, we asked fifteen black speakers of the idiom to give conventional uses of "jam" and "set." Three of the fifteen used expressions which I would regard as exerting a static or restrictive force: "a jammed door" and "in a jam." All fifteen *avoided* using "set" in a conventional expression where it exerts a static force. Further testing of this kind, especially when comparing results with choices made by nonspeakers of the idiom, might reveal differences between black and white psychological processes affecting usage.

So far we have established a correlation between a kinetic and static quality in words and the respective favorable and unfavorable connotations associated with them in black usage. In so doing, we have made some reference to processes of diffusion which are at work to produce this correlation and which warrant further discussion.

It is clear that any kinetic or static force which influences the speaker in the words he selects from conventional English as well as from black English operates on an unconscious level. Because these qualities exert pressure on the meaning of the word, we can, after Bloomfield, consider them sememes. Because they also covert, they might appropriately be called *cryptosememes* (Whorf called them *cryptotypes*). Cryptosememes are important because they exert pressure in usage and over a period of time can change the original meaning of the word and permit the creation of other expressions. To take an example from conventional English, the Old English term for "bread" was *hlāf,* Modern English *loaf.* At some point in the history of the word the cryptosememe "molded mass" became the central meaning of that word, compelling speakers

[30] Conot, *Rivers of Blood,* p. 360.

to eventually say "loaf of bread" but also permitting the creation of such expressions as "meatloaf."

That there are forces at work within a language which operate on the minds and habits of its speakers below their level of awareness is an established fact in both diachronic and synchronic linguistics. On the other hand, while we know that these forces are at work at some unconscious level, we also are aware that they do not endure indefinitely. They have limited viability. The forces behind sound change operate for a period of time and then abate; likewise with the analogic forces operating within the grammar. This is also true of sememic forces operating within the lexicon.

Finally, we must recognize that cryptosememes may evolve out of a selective process that ultimately derives from values and attitudes of the community. The cryptosememes *kinetic quality* and *static quality* were created in black English by virtue of an unconscious process of selection from conventional English and perpetuation with favorable connotation within black idiom, which ultimately derives and continues to receive sustenance from an attitude in the community that values movement.

I will briefly discuss this process with respect to three terms in black usage: "hip," "boot," and "broom."

In black English, a person who is "hip" is generally aware, knowledgeable, resourceful, and skillful ("able to swing on any scene").[31] Etymologically, it comes from the expression "to have one's hip boots on" as a preparation and protection for wading through deep water ("So when you hear the words 'I'm hip' or 'I'm booted' it's said to let you know they have no fear or trouble or that they understand what's shaking [happening]").[32] I suggest that to this usage of "hip" was linked the kinetic cryptosememe from the role the hip plays in dancing, where it can be viewed as a synechdoche for the body and the locus of movement. Another way of saying this is that when a person uses "hip," it evokes on some psychic level a feeling that not only derives from the term "to have one's hip boots on" but from the movement of the hip in a highly prestigious and popular cultural activity. A question to ask would be: Would "hip" have as much currency in usage or as favored a connotation if dancing were *not* a particularly common and prestigious activity among the group? ("All that hip movement . . . . It's got new names but you know they were doing that at the Savoy Ballroom in Harlem when I was 17 . . . Harlem was doing the Twist 30 years ago and didn't know it.")[33] Eldridge Cleaver, in *Soul on Ice* feels that, when white people began doing the Twist, it was their first attempt to recap-

[31] Gold, *Jazz Lexicon,* p. 146.
[32] Ibid.
[33] Killer Joe Piro, quoted in Keil, *Urban Blues,* p. 46.

ture their bodies. Perhaps to become "hip," in the fullest black sense of the term, you have to use your hip.

"Boot," often pronounced "boo," derives etymologically, according to Gold, from the same expression as "hip," as cited above. It can mean being knowledgeable, aware, etc., as in the expression, "I'm booted." In addition the term is often used as a nickname by blacks, and as a term which, like "blood," "brother," or "splib," refers to blacks in general. I suggest that here, as with "hip," "boot" evokes a feeling of movement because it is a synechdoche for foot or leg, and, by extension, walking and running; the currency of the term and its favorable connotation are thereby sustained by the kinetic cryptosememe as well as by the original source expression, "having one's hip boots on." This convergence also conveniently fits the street notion that one becomes hip or booted (i.e., knows what's happening) by moving around. Interestingly, there is an apparently new derogatory connotation associated with "boot" to designate the "Uncle Tom"–type Negro. Folk etymology may explain the reason for this. Many blacks feel that "boot" derives from "bootblack." In this usage the negative image of Tomism is evoked: that of shining whitey's shoes. This image would more than counterbalance the positive force generated by the kinetic cryptosememe.

"Broom," meaning "fast getaway" ("I don't have a car so I think I'll broom"), is an onomatopoeic term probably deriving from "vroom" as used in the comic strip. The folk-etymological process by which vroom becomes broom I suggest was reinforced by the kinetic cryptosememe *sweeping sensation* associated with the conventional use of a broom, as well as *flying* from *"witch's broom."* Note that the original cryptosememe of *noise* of "vroom," as with "bop" and "bang," is replaced by the cryptosememe of *actual* or *potential but realizable movement*.

Other cryptosememes in black English which ultimately derive from favorable community attitudes are *control,* as manifested by such expressions as "getting oneself together," "taking care of business," "tightening your game," "playing it cool"; *contest,* as in "whupping your game," "mounting," "scoring," "rapping"; *forthrightness,* as in "telling it like it is," "getting basic," "getting down to the nitty-gritty," "funky," "soulful," etc. The above terms and expressions reflect themes that are demonstrably linked to the value system of the people who use them.

170

■ The African element in American English

DAVID DALBY

David Dalby is Reader in West African Languages at the School of Oriental and African Studies at the University of London and chairman of the Centre of African Studies in London. He is the author of *Black through White: Patterns of Communication in Africa and the New World,* and of numerous articles on Africa, African languages, and black English. Founding editor of *African Language Review,* he is also editor of *Language and History in Africa.*

This article provides us with an up-to-date documentation and account of the lexical impact that African languages have had on American English through the usage of Afro-Americans. As with the Sithole article, it provides us with an important general source for norms that exist within the black community and, as such, advances the argument that African cultures have had a much greater influence on the culture of Afro-Americans than was heretofore acknowledged. Finally, it suggests that further study and comparison of African and Afro-American cultures in other respects will yield still more correlations of the kind that Sithole and Dalby speak of here in the area of music and language—and thereby further strengthen the argument for African (as opposed to European or Euro-American) origination of various expressive aspects of black American culture as depicted throughout this volume.

When we examine the history of the English language, we need to examine the history of all the peoples who now speak it and who have contributed to its vocabulary and idiom. The mainstream of the language takes us back ultimately to the Germanic tribes who settled in England from the fifth century A.D., and whose language was greatly influenced by Norman French from the eleventh century. Modern English, as we now recognize it, began to crystallize around the fifteenth century, but almost immediately it ceased to be the exclusive property of the peoples of Britain. The language had reached West Africa by the sixteenth century and had begun its growth, in newly developed forms, as an important means of communication among peoples of African origin. The first West Africans known to have visited England in order to study the language did so in 1554,[1] ten years before the birth of Shakespeare and over half a century before the establishment of the English language in North America.

The multiplicity of West African languages encouraged the adoption

[1] See "The Voyages and Discoveries of William Towerson," in Richard Hakluyt, *The Principall Navigations, Voiages and Discoveries of the English Nation,* London, 1589 (reprinted 1965), p. 20.

of English—as well as Portuguese and French—as means of communication along the West African coast, but at the same time it led to the modification of the European languages to fit their new linguistic and cultural environment. Subsequently, just as forms of white English were carried to America by European settlers, so forms of black English were carried there by West African immigrants, thus providing American English with a dual heritage. The sad history of racial division in the New World, however, has prevented these two streams of English from fusing together completely, even after three and a half centuries of co-existence. It has also resulted in a failure, until very recently, to recognize much of the heritage of black English, including its wealth of independent vocabulary and idiom, or to give adequate acknowledgment to the contributions which it has made to the English language at large. The object of the present paper is to consider how this situation can best be rectified, with special reference to the tracing of African elements within modern forms of black American English and, through black American English, within the language as a whole. The general historical background has already been presented in a separate paper, covering patterns of black-white communication from the fifteenth century, when the Portuguese established themselves along the coast of West Africa, through to the twentieth, when black Americans established themselves in the inner cities of the United States.[2]

The failure to recognize the full contribution of African languages to black English, especially in its North American forms, and of black English to the English language at large, is to be attributed to three factors which still present an obstacle to scholarly research in this area. The first factor is the sheer multiplicity of African (particularly West African) languages, a situation which from the early arrival of Europeans on the African coast acted as a deterrent to an intimate knowledge of the languages by whites. Almost the whole burden of black-white communication during the last half millennium has fallen on the shoulders of black people and has been dependent on their own mastery of European languages. In tracing the origin of inter-European loan-words, or even of Oriental loan-words in European languages, we are able to deal with a relatively restricted number of well-documented languages. In tracing the origin of African or suspected African loan-words, however, we have to deal potentially with scores, if not hundreds, of different African languages, for only a minority of which any sort of comprehensive dictionary is available. The second factor, arising from the prejudices of slavery and post-slavery days, is the myth that black Americans lost virtually the whole of their linguistic and cultural heritage after

[2] David Dalby, *Black through White: Patterns of Communication in Africa and the New World* (Hans Wolff Memorial Lecture, 1969), African Studies Program, Indiana University, 1970.

their arrival in North America, and that divergences between black American and white American usages and customs are to be largely accounted for as divergences from a supposed white "norm," stimulated by the social circumstances of black Americans during and after the period of slavery. The third factor is the relative dearth of historical documentation on black English in all its forms, reflecting not only the traditional contempt with which so-called "nigger talk" has been held by many whites, and even by some blacks, but also the fact that the cultural heritage of black English, as of West African languages, is based on oral creativity and on transmission through the spoken (rather than written) word. White ignorance of black American language and linguistic culture has stemmed not only from traditional prejudice, but also from the fact that one of the main applications of black language has been to strengthen the in-group solidarity of black Americans to the specific exclusion of whites, and to deceive, confuse, and conceal information from white people in general. Hence it is that an in-group black expression will often be dropped from black speech—or changed in meaning— as soon as it becomes widely known among non-blacks. The use of such outmoded speech is aptly described by the black American phrase "talking dead," so that the first appearance in print of an originally black expression may not necessarily mark the time of its birth, but in a very real sense the time of its "death," perhaps after a long life in unrecorded black speech.

In investigating the African element in black American English, our first task must be to overcome the obstacle presented by these three unfavorable factors. First, our search for evidence among a multitude of African languages can be narrowed down in the initial stages by concentrating especially on those major West African languages which, for historical and geographical reasons, are most likely to have had an effect on the early development of black English, and which were certainly spoken by a large number of first-generation black Americans. These are *Wolof,* spoken between the Rivers Senegal and Gambia and the first black African language with which Europeans came into contact; *Mandingo* or *Manding* (including *Bambara*), spoken inland from the mouth of the River Gambia and, as the language of the ancient Mali empire, the most geographically extensive language in western West Africa; *Akan* (including *Fante* and *Ashanti*), spoken along and in the hinterland of the former Gold Coast; and *Hausa,* the most geographically extensive language in the interior of eastern West Africa, and spoken as a second language by speakers of many other smaller languages. (At a later stage, attention must be devoted also to a number of western Bantu languages, spoken much further south along the African coast but also represented among unwilling immigrants to the United States.) Second, we need to reconsider the whole question of African cultural and linguistic survivals in the United States. It is obvious that black Americans were prevented from maintaining in North America the large number of African cultural institutions and traditional customs which have survived in the Caribbean and in South America. It has been less obvious to outside observers, however, that black Americans have succeeded in preserving a high degree of their African "character" at the much deeper and more fundamental level of interpersonal relationships and expressive behavior. It is at this level that racial barriers which prevent the black American proletariat from assimilation into white American society have served also as cultural and linguistic barriers, enabling many African characteristics—including linguistic features—to be preserved behind an apparently American exterior. Third, we must not be tempted into concluding that, because a feature of black American language has not been documented until recent times, it must therefore be recent in origin. Some such features may well be modern, but where they closely resemble known African features it is more reasonable to postulate them as African survivals than to postulate that they were lost at an earlier date and then coincidentally re-created in modern times. Similarly, in examining the etymology of general Americanisms for which the origin is still uncertain, the possibility of a source in unrecorded black speech —and ultimately in African languages—should not be overlooked.

Until now, it has been generally assumed that the influence of African languages on the vocabulary of American English, and of the English language as a whole, did not go beyond a relatively small collection of direct loan-words, made up largely of specialized zoological, botanical, and culinary items, together with a few cultural terms. Examples of such loan-words are: *cooter* (turtle) from Mandingo; *pojo* or *poor joe* (heron) from Vai, a language closely related to Mandingo; *banana, yam,* and *benne* (sesame) from both Mandingo and Wolof; *cola,* hence also the second element in Coca-Cola, from Temne; *okra* from Akan and other West African languages; *pinder* (peanut), *goober* (peanut), and *gumbo* (okra or okra soup) from Western Bantu languages; *cush* (gruel) from Arabic, probably via Wolof; *mumbo-jumbo* from a corruption of the name of a Mandingo secret society; and *juju* (fetish, amulet) from Hausa and/or Mandingo.[3] Items of this kind are of considerable historical interest, not least for their confirmation of the relative importance of certain African languages. On the other hand, few of these words have specific relevance to modern black American English: in general, they have either been established for a long time in British as well as American English (*banana, yam* and *cola,* for example), or—at the other extreme—have had only a limited currency in parts of the American

[3] For a discussion of most of these examples, drawing heavily on the work of Lorenzo Dow Turner, see M. M. Mathews, *Some Sources of Southernisms* (University: University of Alabama Press, 1948).

South (*pojo, pinder,* and *cush*). Similarly, most items in the much wider range of African survivals discovered by Lorenzo D. Turner in the Gullah speech of the Sea Islands appear to be totally unknown to black Americans elsewhere in the United States.[4]

Faced with this evidence, one might be tempted to conclude that the majority of black Americans today retain no distinctive African element in their speech. Such a conclusion would be wrong.

As we have already observed, it is at the level of interpersonal relationships and expressive behavior that the black American proletariat has preserved a large part of its African character: it is in this area, therefore, that we should most expect the survival of African linguistic features. In searching for such features, we should realize that survivals from African languages are not necessarily restricted to direct loanwords. We need to look also for cases where there have been *convergences* between words introduced from African languages and words of similar sound already existing in English. The effect of such a process has been to extend or change the meaning of the English words in question, as is known to have happened also with the convergence of certain German and English words in the speech of European immigrants; cf. the transference of meaning from the German words *dumm* (stupid) and *frech* (impudent) to the English words *dumb* (speechless) and *fresh* (new, pure). Added impetus to this process, in the case of black American English, is provided by the fact that black Americans have always had a legitimate reason for concealing information from white people. The use of unfamiliar non-English words by slaves would have aroused suspicion (if not worse) among whites, whereas the use of English words with unconventional meanings (including meanings transferred from similar-sounding African words) will have served as a much more subtle code. In addition to such cases of convergence, we need also to look for so-called calques or loan-translations, in which African phrases and expressions were translated literally into English by speakers of West African languages and then retained in black speech with their original African meanings. A striking example is provided by the Southern expression "day-clean" for "dawn," now very rare in the United States but still current in certain Caribbean and West African forms of black English. This expression is modeled on constructions occurring in a number of West African languages, including Mandingo and Wolof, in which the day, or the surrounding countryside, is said to become clear or clean at dawn (in Mandingo, night is conceived of as being washed or laundered, leaving the land clean at dawn).

Black American English made its first powerful impact on the speech of non-blacks outside the American South during the early part of the

[4] Lorenzo D. Turner, *Africanisms in the Gullah Dialect* (Chicago: University of Chicago Press, 1949).

twentieth century, alongside the impact on Western music of jazz and other forms of black American music. The starting point for this linguistic and musical explosion, the effects of which have been accelerating since World War II, was of course New Orleans, the focal point for an area where African features of language and culture had been more easily preserved than in most other parts of North America (with the exception of the Sea Islands). Sugar plantations and levee construction on the lower Mississippi required larger gangs of black labor than did the cotton and tobacco plantations elsewhere, and the resulting larger social groupings among black Americans in that area better enabled them to resist the deprivation of their culture by southern whites. Since the beginning of the black cultural explosion and the subsequent migration of black Americans to the north and west, it is clear that black American English has been subjected to greater pressures and rates of change than during the previous more static period in the rural South; one of the reasons for this has already been mentioned, namely, the need for black Americans to remain linguistically "one jump ahead" of white Americans by changing and modifying items of their vocabulary as they become known to non-blacks. For this reason, it is important that special attention be devoted to items of black vocabulary known to have originated in the Deep South and to have become popularized through the impact of black American music.

The following alphabetical list of over eighty Americanisms has been compiled as an initial, tentative survey of the African influence on black American (and hence also on general American) speech. Further detailed research, although perhaps enabling us to revise some of these suggested etymologies, will almost certainly increase the overall total of traceable Africanisms in the American language. The present list excludes the specialized zoological, botanical, and culinary items recognized in the past as originating in Africa (see examples cited above), as well as excluding those African musical terms which appear to have entered the English language via South America and the Caribbean (*rumba, tango, samba,* and *conga*). If all these were included, the total number of Africanisms and probable Africanisms in the English language would be well over a hundred. Only a small proportion of the items listed below have been recognized previously as having an African source, and it is not therefore surprising that the origin of so many of them should have been regarded by American lexicographers as "obscure." Items which can be shown to have originated in black English are marked with a star (*) in the following list, or with a dagger (†) if they have remained largely restricted to the speech of black Americans. Items which are unmarked are assumed for present purposes to have originated in black English, but evidence is required to confirm this.

Over half the items listed below have been associated with black American music or with twentieth-century black American slang, and over half involve comparisons with *two* major West African languages, Mandingo and/or Wolof. This latter fact statistically reduces the possibility of purely fortuitous resemblances between American English and African languages, which would have been much greater had the resemblances been found to occur at random throughout a wide range of different African languages. That Mandingo and Wolof should prove to be the two most important languages as far as American English is concerned (as compared with the predominant influence of Akan on black Jamaican English,[5] for example) demonstrates that black Americans can indeed look toward a specific area of Africa for a major part of their cultural and linguistic heritage. The neighboring Mandingo and Wolof peoples of western West Africa share numerous cultural features, especially as far as their musical traditions are concerned, and there are reasons for believing that many of the roots of black American music are to be found in their area. It is true that Africans were brought to the United States from points all along the western coastline of Africa (sometimes via the Caribbean), but it has never been previously emphasized that up to 40 percent of first-generation black Americans were born in the extensive area of Mandingo cultural and linguistic influence, an area which—reflecting the vast extent of the Mali empire in precolonial times and the continuing cultural and economic power of the Mandingo—still embraces most of the whole western half of West Africa.[6] That a substantial proportion of forced African immigrants to the United States were able to speak Mandingo as a first or second language explains why Mandingo in particular made such an impact on black American speech. The parallel impact of Wolof, although a less geographically extensive language than Mandingo, reflects the fact that it is spoken on the stretch of African coastline nearest to the United States. There is reason to suspect that forced immigration from this area may have been higher than records suggest, especially at the very end of the slave trade just over a century ago. For slave ships endeavoring

[5] Cf. David Dalby, "African Survivals in the Language and Traditions of the Windward Maroons of Jamaica," *African Language Studies* 12 (1971).

[6] Philip D. Curtin, *The Atlantic Slave Trade* (Madison: University of Wisconsin Press, 1969), p. 157, estimates that about 46% of Africans transported to the North American mainland during the eighteenth century originated from the western half of West Africa (i.e., from the hinterlands of Senegambia, Sierra Leone, the "Windward Coast," and the Gold Coast). A large majority of these must therefore have come either from Mandingo-dominated areas, or from areas which were subject to some degree of Mandingo influence: see the map in David Dalby, "The Distribution and Nomenclature of the Manding Peoples and Their Language," published in Carleton T. Hodge, ed., *Papers on the Manding* (Bloomington: Indiana University Press). It should be noted that the Mandingo (or Manding) area of influence was even greater in the past than it is today, extending into what is now Ghana and reaching as far east as northern Nigeria.

to make secret runs from Africa to the southern states without detection and capture by antislavery patrols, the shortest and therefore safest route would have been from the Wolof- (and Mandingo-) speaking coastline and hinterland of Senegambia. It should also not be forgotten that the last Africans to arrive in America during this final period were still alive during the lifetimes of many readers of this paper.[7]

A tentative list of Africanisms and probable Africanisms in American English

†*bad* (esp. in the emphatic form *baad*), as used in the sense of "very good, extremely good"; similarly *mean,* as used in the sense of "satisfying, fine, attractive"; and *wicked,* as used in the sense of "excellent, capable." Cf. frequent use of negative terms (often pronounced emphatically) to describe positive extremes in African languages, e.g., Mandingo (Bambara) *a ka nyi ko-jugu,* "it's very good" (literally, "it is good badly"), or Mandingo (Gambia) *a nyinata jaw-ke,* "she is very beautiful" (lit. "she is beautiful wickedly"); similarly black West African English (Sierra Leone) *i gud baad,* "it's very good."

*bad-eye—"threatening, hateful glance." Cf. similar use of Mandingo *nyɛ-jugu,* "hateful glance" (lit. "bad eye"), and similar phrases in other West African languages.

*bad-mouth—"slander, abuse, gossip" (also as verb). Cf. similar use of Mandingo *da-jugu* and Hausa *mugum-baki,* "slander, abuse" (lit. "bad mouth" in both cases). Note also *fat-mouth.*

*bamboula (19th cent.)—"African drum, used in New Orleans"; hence (early 20th cent.) "vigorous style of dance, also in New Orleans" (or "drum," in early jazz use). Cf. Banyun *bombulaŋ,* and similar terms in other languages on the western coast of West Africa (recorded as *bambalo, bombalan,* etc., by European visitors to West Africa in the 16th and 17th centuries).

*banjo—"stringed musical instrument." Cf. Kimbundu *mbanza,* "stringed musical instrument" (whence also black Jamaican English *banja* and Brazilian Portuguese *banza*). Convergence with *bandore,* the name of a European stringed instrument.

*be with it—"to be in fashion." Cf. similiar use of Mandingo . . . *be a la* (lit. ". . . be with it, in it").

*big eye—"greedy." Cf. similar use of Ibo *anya uku,* "covetous, greedy"

---

[7] In the following list, a spelling orthography has been used for forms of black English spoken in the New World and Liberia, and a phonemic orthography for African languages and for forms of black English spoken in Sierra Leone and Cameroon.

(lit. "big eye"), and of black West African and Caribbean English *big yay/big eye.*[8]

†*bo,* an informal term of address to an equal. Cf. similar terms of address (among equals) in languages of the Sierra Leone region, e.g., Temme *bɔ* and Vai *bɔ* ("friend"); also in black West African and Caribbean English (in the forms *bo, bɔ* and *ba*).

*bogue, bogus—"fake, fraudulent" (the ending of the form *bogus* by analogy with *hocus-pocus?*). Cf. Hausa *boko, boko-boko,* "deceit, fraud"; hence also black West African English (Sierra Leone) *bogo-bogo* and Louisiana French *bogue,* "fake, fraudulent." Note also *phoney,* below.

bogus: see *bogue.*

*boogie(-woogie)—"fast blues music (eight beats to the bar)"; and *boog,* "to dance." Cf. Hausa *buga (bugi* before a noun object) and Mandingo *bugɔ,* "to beat," incl. "to beat drums"; also black West African English (Sierra Leone) *bogi(-bogi),* "to dance."

*bree, breigh—"girl, (young) woman." Cf. related terms in a number of West African languages, incl. Akan (ɔ)-*bere, -bre,* "female," Yoruba *obirî,* "woman, female," Temne (ɔ)-*bɛra,* "woman, female," Note also other terms for "girl, woman" below (*chick, mat, mouse, pharoah*), and see discussion under *mouse.*

brer, buh—"brother," as title before animal names in fables. Cf. similar use of Mandingo *kɔrɔ,* "(elder) brother," as title before animal names in fables.

buckaroo, bucker—"cowboy." See *buckra.*

*buckra—"white man," esp. "poor or mean white man" (now rare in U.S., but still current in black Jamaican English); hence also *buckaroo, bucker* ("cowboy"—convergence with Spanish *vaquero,* "cowboy"; used derisively by black cowboys?). Cf. Efik *mbakara,* "white man," and related forms in a number of languages of southeastern Nigeria and southern Cameroon.[9]

*bug[1]—"enthusiast," and *cat,* "man, fellow," esp. as final element in compounds, e.g., *jitter-bug* and *hep-cat.* Cf. Mandingo -*baga* and Wolof -*kat* (agentive suffixes), denoting person as final element in compounds, e.g., Mandingo *jitɔ-baga* and Wolof *hipi-kat* (see *jitter* and *hep,* below). Note also black West African English *baga,* "fellow"; convergence wtih English *bug/bugger* and *cat.*

bug[2]—"to bother, annoy." The same element is probably contained also in *humbug,* "to hoax, impose upon; hoax, imposition." Cf. Mandingo *baga,* "to offend, annoy, harm (someone)," and Wolof *bugal,* "to annoy, worry"; note also widespread black West African and Carib-

---

[8] Dr. J. L. Dillard has informed me that this term was rationalized by white Texans as "big I" (in the phrase "big I, little you").

[9] For a discussion of the etymology of *buckaroo,* see Julian Mason, *American Speech* 35 (1960): 51–55.

bean English *ambɔg, ambɔk,* "to annoy." These latter forms (together with American and British English *humbug,* first pronounced in 18th cent. with stress on second syllable) may reflect the nominal prefix *m-* in Wolof *mbúgal,* "hindrance, annoyance" (from *bugal,* see above).

bug[3]—"insect." Cf. Mandingo *baga-baga* and Susu *bɔg-bɔgi,* "termite, white ant"; also black West African English *bɔg-bɔg* (Sierra Leone) and *buga-bug* (Liberia), "termite," and black Jamaican English *bug-aboo,* "insect." This African term, recorded on the West African coast by European mariners from the 17th cent., appears to have converged with English *bug(aboo)* ("bogy"), thus stimulating its shift in meaning to "insect." Note that *bug* ("insect") is in more common use in the U.S. than in Britain.

*cat—"man, fellow." See *bug*[1].

*chick—"girl, young woman (esp. if hip, or attractive)"; also *chicken* "(attractive) young woman." Cf. Wolof *jigɛn,* "woman"; convergence with English *chick(en).* Note also *bree, mat, mouse,* and *pharoah,* and see discussion under *mouse.*

*cool—"calm, controlled, slow-tempo"; *hot*—"fast, energetic" (as applied esp. to music). Cf. similar application to music and dancing of Mandingo *suma* ("cool," hence also "slow") and *goni* ("hot," hence also "fast"), and of corresponding terms in other African languages.

*cuffy, cuffee, cuff—"black man" (also used as a greeting among the blacks of Charleston, S.C.). Cf. Akan *Kofi,* a common personal name (for any male born on a Friday).

*day-clean—"dawn" (now obsolete in U.S.?). Cf. similar West African phrases referring to dawn, e.g., Wolof *bɔr sɛt na,* "it has dawned" (lit. "day is clean") and Mandingo *dugu jɛra,* "it has dawned" (lit. "the country has become clean/clear"); also black West African and Caribbean English *do-klin/day-clean* and black Caribbean French *ju netye* (lit. "day cleaned").

*dig—"to understand," hence also "to appreciate, pay attention to." Cf. Wolof *deg, dega,* "to understand," hence also "to appreciate"; convergence with English *dig,* "to excavate."

†dinge—"black person"; *dingey,* "black child, person"; *dinkey* (Baltimore, now obsolete?), "black child." Cf. Mandingo *deŋ, diŋ,* "child, young person (younger than speaker)"; hence *deŋ-kɛ, diŋkɛ,* "male child, young man." Possible convergence with English *dingey,* "dark-colored."

dirt, in the sense of "earth" (as common in U.S., e.g., in *dirt road* or *dirt track*). Cf. Akan *dɔte,* "earth, soil"; whence widespread black West African and Caribbean English *dɔti/dirty,* "earth." Convergence with English *dirt(y)* in its original (and still principal British) sense of "filth(y)."

do one's thing—"to undertake one's favorite activity, or familiar role."
  Cf. similar use of Mandingo *ka a ʃen kɛ* (lit. "to do one's thing").

†*done,* as past completive marker (e.g., *he done go*). Cf. Wolof *dɔɔn* as
  past habitual marker and Mandingo *tun* as past completive marker;
  also black West African English *dɔn* as past completive marker. Convergence with English *done.*

†*fat-mouth*—"to talk excessively." Cf. Mandingo *da-ba,* "excessive talking" (lit. "big, fat mouth"). Note also *bad-mouth.*

ʃoo-ʃoo—"outsider, newcomer; one who does not belong or is not accepted; fool, worthless person." Cf. Akan *ʃoʃoro,* "new, fresh, strange,"
  hence -*ʃoʃoro,* "new person"; convergence with English *fool.* Cf. also
  black Jamaican English *ʃoo-ʃoo, ʃool-ʃool,* "credulous, easy to take
  advantage of, stupid."

ʃuzzy—"horse," in the two specialized senses of "range horse" and
  "sure bet at a horse race." Cf. Wolof *ʃas,* "horse" (*ʃas wi,* "the
  horse," *ʃas yi,* "the horses"); convergence with English *ʃuzz(y)-tail.*
  (Hence perhaps also *ʃuzz, ʃuzzy,* "policeman," from an earlier sense
  of "mounted policemen"?)

†*gam*—"to boast, show off." Cf. Hausa *gama,* "boastfulness, showing
  off."

goose—"to nudge someone in the anus." Cf. Wolof *kus,* "anus" (ultimately from Arabic?).

guy—"fellow, person," esp. as term of address, incl. pl. *you guys,* addressed even to a single man or woman. Cf. Wolof *gay,* pl. of *way,*
  "fellow, person," esp. as term of address. Convergence with English
  personal name *Guy.*

†*he*[1], as undifferentiated pronoun for "he" *or* "she" (now becoming increasingly rare in black American speech). Cf. undifferentiated third
  person sing. pronoun in most West African (and all Bantu) languages for either "he" or "she"; likewise in most forms of black West
  African and Caribbean English. Note the reverse African influence
  in the case of differentiation between second person sing. and pl.
  pronouns, see *you-uns* below.

†*he*[2], as undifferentiated pronoun for "his" (together with similar lack
  of differentiation in other pronouns, and lack of genitive *s* after
  nouns), e.g., *he hand,* "his hand." Cf. similar constructions in a number of West African languages, e.g., Mandingo *a bolo,* "his hand"
  (lit. "he hand").

†*hear,* in the sense of "to understand." Cf. similar application of verbs
  meaning "to hear" in West African languages, e.g., Mandingo *n ma
  a mɛn,* "I didn't understand" (lit. "I didn't hear it").

hep, hip—"well informed, alert, aware of what is going on"; hence
  hep-cat, "a well-informed person." Cf. Wolof *hepi, hipi,* "to open
  one's eyes, be aware of what is going on"; hence *hipi-kat,* "someone

with his eyes open, aware of what is going on." See *bug*,[1] *cat,* above.
honkie, hoggie—"white man" (but evidence required of usage before 1960's). Cf. Wolof *honq,* "red, pink," and frequent use of this color to describe white men in African languages (cf. also *pink,* "white man," and *red-neck,* "poor white farmer," in U.S.). Probable convergence with *hunkie,* "Hungarian, Eastern European immigrant."
hoodoo, voodoo—"witchcraft; to bewitch." Cf. Fon (Dahomey), *vodu, vodun,* "fetish" (into English via black French of New Orleans?).
humbug. See *bug.*[2]
Ibo, Ebo, in the phrase "stubborn as an Ibo"; from the name of the *Ibo* (or *Ebo*) people of eastern Nigeria, known in the former slave-states for their frequent refusal to accept captivity, seeking escape in suicide. Cf. the place-name *Ebo Landing* in the Sea Islands, commemorating the mass suicide by drowning of a group of Ibo.
jam (as in *jam session*)—"(to play) improvised or extemporized music, esp. in an informal gathering of jazz musicians, playing for their own entertainment." The same element may be contained also in *jamboree,* "noisy revel, celebration; a full hand of cards" (first recorded in the 1860's). Possible convergence between Mandingo and black West African English *jama* (from Arabic), "crowd, gathering," and Wolof *jaam,* "slave" (hence, in the U.S., a gathering of slaves or former slaves for their own entertainment?). Note also the related Wolof term *jaambuur,* "freeman, freed man" (hence, in the U.S., *jamboree* as a celebration by emancipated slaves?).
jamboree. See *jam.*
jazz, including the obsolete forms *jas* and *jasy.* The numerous applications of this term center around a basic verbal sense of "to speed up, excite, exaggerate, act in an unrestrained or extreme way" (including corresponding use as a noun, and in the adjectival form *jazzy*); hence applied to copulation, frenzied dancing, fast-tempo music, exaggerated talk, gaudy patterns and colors, excessive pleasure-seeking, etc. Cf. Mandingo *jasi,* "to become abnormal or out-of-character," either in the direction "to become diminished" or in the direction "to become exaggerated, excessive"; the term may be applied, for example, to exaggerated styles of dancing or music, excessive love-making, etc. Cf. also similar items in other West African languages, including Wolof *yees* (similar in meaning to Mandingo *jasi*) and Temne *yas,* "to be lively or energetic, to an extreme degree."[10]
jelly, jelly-roll—"virile man, who curries the sexual favors of women"; epithet applied to several black musicians, incl. *Jelly Roll* Morton (piano), *Jelly* Williams (bass), and *Jelly* Thompson (guitar). Cf.

[10] For a review of earlier discussion on this much-debated term, see Alan P. Merriam and Bradley H. Garner, "Jazz—the Word," *Ethnomusicology* 12, no. 3 (1968): 373–96.

Mandingo *jeli,* "minstrel" (often gaining popularity with women through his skill in the use of words and music); convergence with English *jelly* and *jelly-roll* (as items of food).[11]

jitter—"to tremble, shake"; hence *the jitters,* "nervousness, fear, cowardice," and *jitter-bug,* "excited swing addict who shakes and trembles in dancing." Cf. Mandingo *ji-tɔ,* "frightened, cowardly" (from *ji,* "to be afraid"); hence *jitɔ-baga,* "frightened, cowardly person." See *bug.*[1]

*jitter-bug. See *jitter.*

*jive—"misleading talk; to talk in a misleading or insincere way" (applied to sexual and musical activity, cf. semantic range of *jazz,* above). Cf. Wolof *jev, jew,* "to talk about someone in his absence, esp. in a disparaging way"; convergence with English *gibe, jibe,* "to sneer at, disparage."

*john—"an average man, esp. one who can be exploited, or easily taken in; a male lover, a prostitute's client." Cf. Mandingo *jɔŋ,* "slave, a person owned by someone else"; convergence with the personal name *John.* Note also the regular use of *John* in black American folklore as the name of the hero-slave who is frequently in conflict with *Massa* ("master"). The form *massa* provides a convenient convergence between English *master* and Mandingo *masa,* "chief." That Mandingo-speakers in the U.S. were conscious of this convergence is suggested by the fact that we have a cycle of black American tales, involving *John* versus *Massa,* corresponding to a similar genre of Mandingo tales in West Africa, involving *jɔŋ* (the slave) versus *masa* (the chief).

*kill—"to affect strongly" (as in "you kill me!"). Cf. similar use in a number of West African languages, including Mandingo and Wolof, of verbs meaning literally "to kill."

lam—"to go (or come); depart quickly, run away, escape." Cf. Ibo *a lam,* "I go, depart" (from *la,* "to go"). Convergence with English *lam,* "to beat."

*man, as term of address. Cf. similar use of Mandingo *cɛ,* "man."

*massa, See *John.*

†mat—"woman, wife." Cf. Hausa *mata* (or *mace*), "woman, wife." Note also *bree, chick, mouse,* and *pharoah,* and see discussion under *mouse.*

†mean. See *bad.*

mhm, m-m. See *uh-huh.*

†mojo—originally "magic spell, charm, amulet" (including "spell cast by spitting"): mainly used today in the sense of "something working

---

[11] I am indebted to Professor Charles S. Bird for drawing this item to my attention.

in one's favor," also "narcotics." Cf. *Fula moca,* "to cast a magic spell by spitting," hence *mocōre,* "magic spell, incantation (uttered while spitting)." Cf. Gullah *moco,* "witchcraft, magic" and probably also black Jamaican English *majoe, mojo,* "plant with renowned medicinal powers."

*mother, yo' mama, as term of severe abuse, or as term of jocular abuse between friends (incl. use in explicit insults, e.g., *mother-fucker*). Note similar but less frequent use of *father.* Cf. use of "your mother" (less frequently, "your father") as term of severe abuse, or as term of jocular abuse between friends, in many West African languages, incl. use in explicit insults, literally "mother-fucker," etc. (esp. in Wolof).

*mouse, in sense of "(attractive) girl, young woman; girl friend, wife." Cf. Mandingo *muso* and Vai *musu,* "woman, wife"; convergence with English *mouse.* Of the several terms for "woman" taken over into black American English from major West African languages (see also *bree, chick, mat,* and *pharaoh*), no less than three are listed together by Mencken[12] as jazz terms for "girl," although he had of course no realization of their African origin.

*ofay, also *oofay* and *fay,* and in the extended form *ofaginzy*—"white man." It has been suggested that *ofay* represents a rearrangement of the letters of the English word *foe* (Pig Latin), but from its form the word is more likely to be African in origin: *o-* occurs as a nominal/adjectival prefix in many West African languages, and a term for "white" beginning with *f-* also occurs widely (e.g., Bamum *fɛ,* Gola *fua,* Ndob *fowɛ,* etc.).

*okay[1]—"all right." Cf. widespread use in the languages of West Africa of *kay,* and similar forms, as a confirmatory marker, esp. after words meaning "yes," e.g., Wolof *waw kay, waw ke,* Mandingo, *õ-kɛ,* Dogon *ɔ-kay,* Djabo *o-ke,* Western Fula *'eeyi kay,* etc., all meaning "yes indeed"; cf. also Mandingo *o-kɛ,* "that's it, all right." The recorded use of *oh ki* in black Jamaican English in 1816 (indicating surprised affirmation) predates by over twenty years the popularization of *O.K.* in the white speech of New England, and the affirmative use of *kay/ki* in black speech in the U.S. is recorded from as early as 1776. Early attempts were made to explain *O.K.* as the initial letters of a misspelling of the English words *all correct* or as the French words *au quai* ("on the quayside"); subsequently, attempts have been made to derive the term from German, Greek, Scots English, Finnish, and Choctaw, but no consideration has

previously been given to the possibility of an origin in black speech.[13]

okay²—"after that," as link between sentences in a running narrative or discourse, serving to confirm the preceding sentence and to anticipate the following sentence. Cf. similar use of Mandingo *o-kɛ-leŋ*, "after that" (lit. "that being done"), and note widespread use of this syntactic construction in West African languages.

†*ol' Hannah*—"sun." Cf. Hausa *raanaa, laanaa*, "sun.'

**oobladee, oobladee-ooblada*—"forever," as exclamation of resignment to the eternity of life. Cf. similar use of black West African English (Sierra Leone) *abadi-abada*, derived via West African languages (e.g., Mandingo *abada*, Hausa *abadaa, abadaa-aabaadi*, "forever") from Arabic *abadan, abada l-abadin*, "forever."

†*pharaoh*—"girl, girlfriend" (blues term). Cf. Kanuri *fero* (with same pronunciation), "girl." Note also *bree, chick, mat*, and *mouse*, and see discussion under *mouse*.

phoney, foney—"false, sham, counterfeit, valueless." Cf. Mandingo *fāni, fōni*, "(to be) false, valueless; to tell a lie." Note also *bogue, bogus*.

*pin—"to stare (at), see." Cf. Temne and black West African English (Sierra Leone) *piŋ*, "staring," as an intensifying adverb after verbs denoting "to see"; also the related Temne verb *pind*, "to stare (at)." Convergence with English *pin*.

*pinto—"coffin" (South Carolina and Georgia). Cf. Temne (*a-*)*bentho*, "bier (for carrying corpse)."

poop—"to defecate, of a child." Cf. Wolof *pūp*, "to defecate, of a child." Convergence with similar forms in European languages (incl. Dutch).

**puntang, poontang*—"vagina, sexually attractive (black) woman; sexual intercourse." Cf. Limba *puntuŋ*, "vagina"; convergence with French *putain*, "prostitute."

*rap (descriptive of a variety of verbal techniques)—"to speak (to), greet; flirt (with), make a pass (at a girl); speak in a colorful way; tease, taunt; con, fool" (also as a noun). Cf. black West African English (Sierra Leone) *rap*, "to con, fool, get the better of (someone) in verbal play," indicating that the recently popularized black American usage of *rap* is in fact old. Convergence of English *rap* or *wrap* with an unidentified African item?

*rooty-toot—"old-fashioned music"; and *rootin-tootin*, "noisy, boisterous." Cf. Wolof *rutu-tuti*, "rapid drumming sound."

*sambo—"black man, male child." Cf. widespread West African per-

---

[13] See David Dalby, "O.K., A.O.K. and O Ke," New York *Times*, January 8, 1971, and "The Etymology of O.K.," *London Times*, January 14, 1971. For a review of earlier discussion on this term, see the several articles by Allen Walker Read in *American Speech* 38 and 39 (1963 and 1964).

sonal names: Wolof *Samb, Samba;* Mandingo *Sambu;* Hausa *Sambo.* The American story of Little Black Sambo appears to be a corruption of a West African folktale.

†*say, says* "that . . . ," introducing reported speech (as in "he tell him, says . . ."). Cf. similar use of items meaning literally "say" in numerous West African languages (e.g., Mandingo *ko* . . .) and in black West African and Caribbean English.

†*skin,* as in *give me some skin*—"shake my hand." Cf. use of similar phrases in West African languages when offering a handshake, e.g., Temne *bot mə-dɛr,* lit. "put skin," or Mandingo *i golo don m bolo,* lit. "put your skin in my hand."

tote—"to carry." Cf. similar forms in a number of western Bantu languages, incl. Kikongo *tota,* "to pick up," and Kimbundu *tuta,* "to carry, load"; also black West African English *tot* (Sierra Leone) and *tut* (Cameroon), "to carry."

**uh-huh, mhm*—"yes"; *uh-uh, m-m*—"no." Cf. widespread use throughout Africa of similar responses for "yes" and "no"; the scattered use of such forms occurs elsewhere in the world, esp. for "yes," but nowhere as regularly as in Africa, where in many languages they constitute the regular words for "yes" and "no." Note also the occurrence of intonational variants of these forms, to indicate differing intensities and situations of response, in both African languages and in black American English (as well as in black African and Caribbean English). The African origin of these items is confirmed by their much wider use in American than in British English, and in South African Dutch (Afrikaans) than in Netherlands Dutch.[14]

*uh-uh—"no." See *uh-huh.*

†*wicked.* See *bad.*

†*yacoo*—"white racist" (and also *Yacub,* described by Malcolm X as the "creator" of the white race).[15] Cf. use in West Africa of the name *Yacouba* (from Arabic *Yaᶜqūb,* "Jacob"), e.g., in Mandingo, as epithet for a bad but powerful chief.

†*yah* (emphatic concluding particle)—"indeed," often in an endearing tone, thus softening a statement or command. Cf. numerous conclud-

[14] In 1955, Raven I. McDavid, Jr., objected to a proposal by Elizabeth Uldall (University of Edinburgh) that the American negative *uh-uh* [ˀaˀa] might have an African source, *American Speech* 29 (1954): 232, and 30 (1955): 56. His grounds were (1) that Uldall had traced this item only to Idoma, a relatively small language of Nigeria (whereas it is, in fact, a pan-African feature) and (2) that it has a widespread distribution in the United States and has also been recorded—as a rare feature—in southern England (thus perpetuating the traditional view that black speakers can have had little or no influence on the mainstream of the English language, in spite of almost half a millennium of contact between English and the languages of West Africa). See Dalby, *Black through White,* pp. 19–20.

[15] See *The Autobiography of Malcolm X* (New York: Grove Press, 1966), p. 165.

ing particles in West African languages, including Grebo *ya,* after commands, and Temne *yo,* after statements or commands; also black West African and Caribbean English *ya,* after statements or commands.

†*yam*—"to eat." Cf. Wolof *nyam,* "to taste," Serer *nyam,* "to eat," and Fula *nyāma,* "to eat"; also black West African and Caribbean English *nyam,* "to eat."

you-all. See *you-uns.*

you-uns—"you (plural)," and similar use of *you-all.* The regular differentiation between second-person sing. and pl. pronouns in African languages undoubtedly played a part in the introduction of comparable differentiation in American English, esp. in the South Midland and South (perhaps also reinforced by the differentiated pronouns of French and Spanish). Cf. esp. Wolof *yow,* "you (sing.)," versus *yeen, yena,* "you (pl.)"; hence convergence with English *you* in the singular, and stimulation of *you + one* as a new second-person pl. form (with first-person *we-uns* by analogy). Cf. black West African and Caribbean English *yu,* "you (sing.)," versus *una, unu,* "you (pl.)" (Sierra Leone, Cameroon, Jamaica, etc.); Gullah *yu* versus *une;* and black Guyana English *you* versus *you-all.*

†zero copula, as in "he big" for "he is big," for example. Cf. similar constructions in many West African languages, e.g., Temne ɔ *bana,* "he is big (literally, "he big")."

*zombie—"ghost, raised corpse," hence "offbeat or mindless person." Cf. Kimbundu *nzumbi,* "ghost, phantom"; also black Haitian French *zombi* and black West African and Caribbean English *jombi* (Sierra Leone and Cameroon), *jumbi* (Guyana), *zombie* (Jamaica), etc.

The above list represents a first attempt to uncover an important "blind spot" in the recorded history of the American language. Ignorance of African languages, traditional prejudice against all things black, including black speech, and the dearth of historical records on early forms of black English have all contributed to the maintenance of this blind spot in linguistic scholarship. A great amount of research remains to be done to rectify the state of our knowledge in this field, and the evidence in this paper will need to be amended and expanded as further data come to light. A more comprehensive and fully documented study is in preparation, and the writer will be deeply indebted for any supplementary information or criticism, especially for evidence based on early printed or written records of American speech.[16]

[16] Constructive criticism will more than offset the inevitable emotional attacks on this line of research, which have already begun (e.g., *New York Times,* January 20, 1971). For valuable advice during the compilation of the present paper, I wish to express my gratitude to the editor of this volume, and to my friends Charles S. Bird, J. L. Dillard, Ian F. Hancock, Paul Oliver, Amadou Traoré, and A. K. Turay.

Expressive uses
of language

■ Stylin' outta the black pulpit

GRACE SIMS HOLT

For a Note on the Author, see p. 152.

"Long before there was a college degree in the race, there were great black preachers, there were great black saints, and there were great black churches. The man systematically killed your language, killed your culture, tried to kill your soul, tried to blot you out—but somewhere along the way he gave us Christianity, and gave it to us to enslave us. But it freed us—because we understood things about it, and we *made it work in ways for us that it never worked for him.*"

—Reverend Calvin Marshall,
Time, April 6, 1970, p. 71

Roots

The black church occupies a unique place in American society. It was born out of the necessity of immoral slave-holders attempting to justify their own conduct within the stringent mandates of Puritanism. The black church became the bastard child of white immorality, teaching the ultimate absurdity: the slave and the master both worshiping the identical benevolent God.

From the white slave-owner's perspective the early black church served a dual purpose. First, the slaves had to be made content with their status; this condition was partially accomplished by having blacks' thoughts directed toward attaining humanity upon entry into the pearly gates of heaven. Second, the master's devotion to his Christian God had to be satisfied to speed *his* entry into heaven. The blacks, denied access to other forms of institutional development, took the white man's religion and from within the black church developed routines and variations of form, substance, and ritual to satisfy black psychological needs.

A primary function of the church was to nourish and maintain the souls of black folk by equating them with the essence of humanness. Religion was molded into an adaptive mode of resistance to the dehumanizing oppression, degradation, and suffering of slavery. The black church developed as the institution which counteracted such forces by promoting self-worth and dignity, a viable identity, and by providing help in overcoming fear. It did this by using the power of the Holy

Spirit to transform black suffering and equate it with the suffering of Jesus. The religious aspect was always correlated with the common denominator of oppression. By enumerating perversions of the Christian ethic by white society in an emotional manner, the preacher hoped to alleviate the inhumane conditions under which blacks labored.

Similarity of problems (e.g., poverty, travail) was tied to release and redemption by the Lord. A slave seeking release from an overseer's whip could call on the Lord to help him and give him relief. This religious form of hallucination provided the basis of hope that allowed him to get through another week, when emotional release could again be provided.

White slave-owners perceived that the religion and the church served the function of containment and mollification. Religion undoubtedly served an important function as an outlet for frustration and for implanting the concept that no matter how tough things might be at present, in heaven everybody was going to enjoy the fruits of utopia. Yet it was also clear that the afterlife concept was intended to be sustaining rather than inviting (no sane people have been known to commit genocide or suicide to promote a quicker entry into heaven), and therefore much more had to be provided to make the slave reality bearable.

If the primary function of the church was to develop a will to survive, its ancillary functions were aimed at making survival endurable. It was through these secondary functions that the church became the matrix out of which black society was to be cohesive—by developing the social contacts necessary to provide intercourse between isolated plantations, by providing an outlet for musical and linguistic expression, and above all by concealing from the dominating eye of the master the activities of his slaves, regardless of their form or content. It was in this latter cast that a language code emerged to facilitate in-group communication and conceal black aspirations from the dominant white society. The black church thus also served the need to be devious in a white world.

Even today, a white person visiting a rural or ghetto church might find it difficult if not impossible to decipher or interpret the "code" talk of the preacher. What developed as a necessary mode of communication has become an integral part of the language system of blacks, though the necessity is not as great as it was in the beginning. This communication behavior is more prevalent in the nonreligious society of today's blacks, whose communication is specifically designed to baffle any white within hearing distance of the conversation. These codes are also used by blacks to say to one another that "I'm *really* a brother," and much satisfaction is gained from the fact that by using this device white society may be "put down" in the presence of whites, without their having the faintest notion that they are the objects of ridicule.

Rites, roles, and strategies

The service

The black church (if such diversity can be characterized as *a* church) has a ritual nearly as rigid and unvarying as that used by the Catholic and High Lutheran services. The service begins with the singing of hymns, some of which would be familiar to virtually all church-going whites, and some of which bear more relationship to African syncopation than to the solemn mass of the white church. The preacher usually begins his message in a low key, stating what the topic of the worship is to be. A moral virtue liberally borrowed from puritanism is common. A favorite theme is man's unworthiness to enter the kingdom of God. Then, like Beethoven building a masterpiece, the preacher begins the variations on the theme. The vices of man—cruelty, avarice, destructiveness, inhumanity, licentiousness, and sexual misconduct—flow from his mouth as easily as Catholic liturgy emanates from the pope. The congregation is warned of the consequences of practicing these vices and is authoritatively assured that the guilty ones cannot possibly enter the kingdom of God. The congregation gives verbal recognition by responding vigorously when these vices are paraded before their consciences. The more vividly worldly sins are painted, the more emotional are the responses.

The preacher relates his knowledge of local happenings to the sin context, exhorting his audience, which shares his local knowledge, to redeem themselves of their sins. The ritual begins with the preacher "stylin' out," which the audience eagerly awaits. ("Stylin' out" means he's going to perform certain acts, say certain things with flourish and finesse.) The virtuosity of the preacher is called to task, for he must get his message across (e.g., why one shouldn't "sin"), without offending the members of the congregation whose sins are being talked about. The preacher has to supplicate without alienating the "sinner." The preacher's beginning is slow-moving (funky) to get the audience physically involved. The preacher walks, body swaying from side to side, slightly bent, from one side of the pulpit to the other, or from one end of the platform to the other. He waits until he gets to one side, stands up straight, and makes a statement about sin. If a husband "ain't acting right," if he's running around with another woman, or gambling, and not bringing his money home to his wife and children, the preacher must "get on his case" with a strong use of melody and rhythm.

PREACHER: Husbands gettin' money and ain't comin' home wit it . . . Hunh?

AUDIENCE (*Usually female response here. Men will begin to fidget, shift arm positions, stare straight ahead, lean forward slightly, or lower the head)*: Yes? Let's go, alright now!

PREACHER: Gettin' Hogs (*Cadillacs*), booze, etc. Can I get a witness? Ya'll know what I mean?

AUDIENCE: You know it is. You got a witness. Oh yes! Yes, Jesus.

PREACHER: Dressin' it up when they children don't have shoes to wear and decent clothes.

AUDIENCE (*Females will react with anger and glee in responding*): Keep goin', go on, you tellin' it, Preach! Lord, yes!

PREACHER: Don't you think they got a *right* to what you earn?

AUDIENCE: Yeah, Preach, take yo time now, awright, awright now!

At this point the preacher walks to the other side of the pulpit or plat-form and makes another statement. He may at this point have a hand-kerchief in one hand and at intervals wipe his face as he builds the utterances in pitch, intensity, and volume. The white handkerchief signals the congregation that he's going to say something of importance and they'd better pay close attention. The spanking white handkerchief may be in the back pocket, tucked up a sleeve, folded and placed on the pulpit or in the Bible. The preacher reaches for it with a certain style, shakes it out with one flip of the wrist, and wipes the sweat from his brow or froth from his mouth.

PREACHER: Don't you think they got a *right* to —

AUDIENCE (*louder*): Yeah!

PREACHER: Don't you think they got a *right* to yo love? Y'all wit me?

AUDIENCE (*shouts*): Yeah! Eeesy! Awright now! Tell it, tell it right, Come on! He's on the road now. Preach!

The intensity and volume of audience response signals the preacher that he is getting across, that he's telling the truth, that the audience is enjoying what he says and appreciates how he says it. In this example the intimacy of the subject is tricky, and the preacher must maneuver the straying males into response if he is to be perceived as successful in his message. Thus, even though it is clear for whom the core of that message is intended (the preacher has "put the hurt on" the males), he must also "get on" the wives and effect a reconciliation as the climax of that message. Both males and females may be guilty of the same sin, and the message must be embroidered to include the role of the female. The next ritualistic step usually goes something like this:

PREACHER: Wives playin' round. Just about as bad as the husbands. . . . Hunh?

AUDIENCE (*male responses come strong and loud*): Tell the truth!

PREACHER: Talkin' bout I love you and not having no dinner ready when the man comes home from a hard day's work, and *he* got to wait. Let the church say A-men.

AUDIENCE: A-men! (*May be repeated several times with varying degrees of intensity.*)

The preacher then goes on to enumerate various "sins" of the wives to partially expiate the heavy male guilt, to indicate how the female contributes to the first sin, and to indicate a solution for both parties. The preacher talks about female sins with numerous variations on the theme, which leads into a charge of the woman's responsibilities.

PREACHER: To make the man do right—what would *God* have you do? Let the church answer A-men.

AUDIENCE: A-men.

PREACHER: To make the man do right you got to do yo part. Do I hear a witness?

AUDIENCE: Tell the truth! Tell it! Talk!

PREACHER: You got to get up early in the morning when your eyes still heavy and you limbs still weary.

AUDIENCE: Come on now. Tell it right. Tell it like it is.

PREACHER: You got to smile over tears, you got to make the man feel good like a *man*—when he's been kicked and tossed like a dog and a feather. You got to soothe his brow, tend his comfort, and *let him see* you love. You ain't got to talk 'bout yourself all the time.

AUDIENCE: Come on now!

PREACHER: And you got to smile—radiant, like the stars of heaven.

AUDIENCE: We hear ya; Go ahead! Go brother! I hear you.

PREACHER: You got to love . . . hunh? (*Meaning "Am I right," or "You ain't listening to me."*)

You got to persevere . . . hunh?

You got to give yo' all . . . hunh?

You got to be long suffering . . . hunh?

You got to *do* right!

The preacher has invoked the charge of forbearance, mutual responsibility, and hope for the future: "And things will be better by and by!" or "There'll be a new and brighter day." Then he must challenge the congregation to try to live up to the invocation.

"Will you do it? Will you *try?*" The preacher may quote scripture at this point in support of the anticipated effort, or he may break into a line of a moving song to accomplish the same purpose. Thus not only is the self-purification theme prevalent, but the strategies for self-purification or ridding oneself of sin and its temptations are also indicated. An aroused preacher and an emotional flock together make religious music, music never contemplated by John Calvin. What a white witness could never conceive is that the man who can never enter the kingdom of God is the *white* man. The flock understands this with crystal clarity, and it is this clarity which is the emotional furnace feeding the flames of fever, providing the orchestral accompaniment to this "Black Mass." How else could it be? The propertyless slave or black (take your choice) was incapable of being guilty of the sins of greed, avarice, gluttony, callousness, brutality, and hypocrisy. The emotion aroused was not so much *for* God as it was stimulated *by* a chronicle of the sins of The Man. It is in this manner that the sobriquet The Man became the synonym for "white" in black English. A white heaven was virtually abolished by definition since, also by definition, very few whites could meet the admission standards.

The verbal exchange between preacher and audience throughout the service is accompanied by a variety of counterpoint. When the preacher makes his charges of sin he may shout or whisper, point a finger, lean on the pulpit, pause, or look long and hard at the audience, letting the words sink in for effect. At this point, after a dead silence, some woman usually lets out a single piercing scream. The other women moan, groan, sway, wave fans, handkerchiefs, and hands at the preacher in total communion of the female wronged, while responding vocally. Men hang their heads lower in shame or raise them in determination to "do better." The preacher may use the pointed finger or hand at any time in the delivery to represent the feeling, which the black audience understands, to say the congregation *knows* that what he says is true, backed by the scripture. The white handkerchief, wiping the face, pausing to get a drink of water, and changing to a shaking voice all signal to the audience that the preacher is really going to get down and preach; the spirits of the audience lift. Attention, if wandering, is abruptly recaptured. Anticipation mounts for how and what the preacher will do next and is a signal to the audience to get ready to respond. The verbal responses may be accompanied by patting the feet several times in staccato fashion, one-foot stomps, hand-clapping, low moaning, and delighted laughter.

The preacher may roll his eyes heavenward, as though to invoke divine sanction; he may scowl, beat on the pulpit, or change facial expressions to pantomime the emotion he is talking about.

Ranging over a wide continuum of behavior, the preacher must constantly evaluate the feedback from the congregation and revise and create new, additional, or already frozen responses to that feedback in a continuing build-up to the climax of the sermon. At some point style becomes part of the substance, too, as the preacher combines past, present, and future in his sermon.

Because of the nature of the creation of black society, many congregations have a dual composition. Educated upper-class or middle-class blacks (I deny the existence of a bona fide black middle-class) and those of lesser intellectual attainments are integrated in the church structure, a common meeting-ground for all blacks. The minister inheriting such diversity will preach two sermons, one devoted to reason and intellect for his more affluent and sophisticated parishioners, appealing to reason and morals, a sermon more philosophical than religious in its focus. After getting warmed up with reason, he then proceeds to symbolically take off his frock (often physically doing so) and "gets with it," embrac-

ing all the myths, superstitions, and irrational assumptions of funda-
mentalist religion. Abe Jackson and Jesse Jackson, for example, use
black preaching style to bridge black class lines, to capitalize on a sense
of community by reminding the audience of past breaches, broken
promises, and access denied. *All* blacks are linked in a community of
historic suffering which allows the preacher to switch his image for dual
audiences. The preacher knows and capitalizes on the ability of black
intelligentsia to relate to and appreciate his ability to manipulate (perhaps momentarily) the real, though submerged, feelings of the audience
around black oppression.

The preacher

The role of the black preacher was defined and rooted in the very
circumstances that founded the existence of the black church. If, as
noted above, the slave-owners permitted the church to exist in order to
satisfy the Puritan-Protestant worldly mission to Christianize all members of the order of *Homo sapiens,* including subspecies, and were
psychologically shrewd enough to perceive, if not to understand, that
the primitive slave (at least that human facet of the beast) needed the
sustenance of his own kind to remain psychologically healthy enough
to do the master's work, then he also recognized his inability to accomplish these ends himself. This task was delegated to the black
preacher, who in reality was conceived by the master to be his agent in
the conspiracy to make the slave contented enough to work, to deter his
humanly murderous instincts toward the master, and to accept his miser-
able existence in the hope of living in streets of gold after death.
Lacking insight into the slave mentality, the slave-owner could not communicate with the slave directly or outline detailed instructions to the
agent-preacher. Given, therefore, this relative autonomy and broad discretion, and hidden from the eye of the owner, the preacher developed a
forum that was in fact a sanctuary, a platform and a captive audience,
which among other things was used to bring some cohesiveness into the
slave milieu. The historical fact that the black preacher became the only
leader permitted in black society has consequences that persist in today's
racial conflicts, the implications of which need to be dealt with in another paper. A moment's reflection by the reader now, however, will
note the lack of a truly national black leader who has not been a
preacher.

Stylin' out

Whatever other functions fell to the minister in the early black church,
it was clear that the most important one was to create the form of hallucination that would provide the basis of hope which would allow one to

endure another week, at which time emotional release could again be provided. It was in the capacity to arouse an emotional response that these ministers became true artists; none lacking this talent can survive in the black church. The rich, descriptive, allegorical phrases in black English are paraded before the congregation, and the response of the church is emotionally charged with sisters fainting, sweating, groaning, and simulating a mass orgasm. The service itself is as formal, rigid, and stylized as a Catholic mass, but unlike the mass—which is designed to be remote, mystical, solemn—the *raison d'etre* here is emotion. The frustrations of living the black life are vented in paying homage to the white God (more recently, black God). It was from such a tradition that such latter-day "Soul Jerkers" as the Reverend Clay Evans have come.

The "Soul Jerker" is renowned for his ability to move the congregation to shouting, whooping, hollering, and "falling out" (fainting) when he preaches. He is the most flamboyant preacher of all, with high style and a good, strong, singing voice. If he has a gravel voice, it is considered an additional asset.

The service usually begins with deacons or deaconesses singing old hymns reminiscent of slave dirges (I'm Gonna Wade in the Water" is one I distinctly remember from my childhood). The message of sorrow in lamentation and intonation resembles little of the formal liturgy of white churches. *A cappella* or accompanied by piano or organ, an assemblage of the church's official hierarchy begins the slow procession to the appointed places at the front of the church, just like slaves in chains. The emotional tone is set for cohesiveness and the ritual of expected response to an anticipated situation, act, and expression. After scripture and prayer the Soul Jerker swings very quickly into his liturgy. This type of ritual is so highly structured and familiar as a medium of emotional response that it doesn't take long for the congregation to begin "rejoicing." Joy, happiness, and ecstasy are actualized in shouting by the women. A woman will suddenly begin to get rigid: her head and face become trancelike, her arms and feet begin to move, her body twists and convolutes according to the way the Spirit moves. The woman may sit or stand upright where she is as she screams or shouts her joy. She may get up and move out in the aisles, feet moving in an ecstatic rhythm as she bends and sways, twists and moves her arms. She may shout all over the church. She is unhampered in her movements by the congregation. Members or ushers will often move to protect a member who is so carried away that she is in danger of hurting herself.

The male church member usually just sits there enjoying himself, watching the women get happy. Occasionally, a male may get carried away and shout—but usually he does not do so, for his masculinity may be questioned. He may react with tears, verbal responses, clenching the fist, patting the feet, rolling the eyes to look at a neighbor in agreement, nodding the head, or assisting a "fallen" female.

But the women, as the backbone of the church, are *expected* to react vigorously to the preacher. The more vigorous the reaction, the more a woman is moved by the Spirit. Some of the rejoicing is very reminiscent of African dances, especially when the shouting becomes frenzied. Many members may be rejoicing simultaneously. Those who do not shout rejoice in any of the ways previously discussed. Often, if the preacher is really good, the whole church is rejoicing and shouting, the preacher included; he urges the crowd on with praise and encouragement. During this time, if the Spirit moves, anyone may get up and testify to the power, joy, and release of the Holy Spirit. It's a way of praising the Lord in song, testimony, and dance. The love of God as a symbol of humanity gives those treated inhumanely a reason for being. The goodness of God, to be realized through man, is exemplified in "rejoicing" together. The preacher's ability to arouse an erotic response is an index of his success and vitality. The preacher evaluates his own power and becomes more aware of its usage and effect as he develops and polishes his personal style and delivery in manipulating the listeners. An example follows.

Preacher	Responses of congregation at various intervals
Early one morning!	Yeah!
	He's on the road now!
	Talk! Tell it!
Early one morning!	Come on now!
Early one morning!	Lord have mercy!
I walked through the valley—You	Preach it brother!
hear me? You hear what I said?	Yessih, Yessuh!
I said I've been through the valley.	
You followin' me?	A-men! Preach, preach!
Lord you know it's not right.	Tell the truth. Lord have mercy!
Look what they doin' to us *down* here.	
We know there's higher ground	Thas right!
and you said "come on up."	"Come on up!"
Come on up to higher ground.	"To higher ground."
You won't forsake us. There's a	Yes Lord!
brighter day ahead! You said—	Yes he said
You said you'd lift this burden	Lift this burden!
from my shoulders.	
We goin' to come on up to high	
ground.	Yes Lord! High ground—

The preacher indicates it's time to stop by signaling the choir to sing. He may also verbalize (e.g., "I'm go wrap up now!"). If, however, the audience is reluctant to stop the message, he will hear a shout, "Preach on! You got to tell it all!" "Go on and preach!" or "Keep on keepin' on!" The preacher may respond by continuing to preach a while longer before swinging into the next part of the ritual; or he may simply end the sermon anyway.

Asking for joiners (also called giving the call, extending fellowship, opening the doors of the church)

People in the congregation who are not members of that particular church or who have not "been saved by Jesus" are entreated to come and join the church. The preacher states the invitation as he steps down to the floor of the congregation, hands extended in welcome. "Jesus is waiting. Won't you come? He needs you. He will help you. Won't you come?" The deacons (and sometimes the church mother) stand in a semicircle, arms folded front or back. The preacher is free to move any-place within the semicircle to increase his effectiveness. Music provides a soft, enticing background. The preacher may continue to issue as many calls as he deems advisable. He has to be expert at reading the body cues of any sinners who may be tempted but are wavering and can't make the final big decision to plunge down the aisle. The congregation is watching these potential candidates and expects the preacher to turn on his most persuasive powers to get them into the fold. The preacher is allowed great verbal latitude and as much time as he thinks he needs to accomplish this task. Since this part of the ritual is not formalized, it presents the greatest challenge to his communicative virtuosity. If he fails, he is judged harshly. If he succeeds, he enhances his stature. If the congregation observes that no potential candidates exist at that time, the preacher's reputation is not damaged. The evangelist or revivalist, as the visiting preacher, is most skilled at getting sinners to join. He usually has a week of revival meetings with mighty sermons. He is ex-pected to provide highly intense emotional communion and release which result in bringing many sinners into the bosom of the church. When sinners are moved to come, from the efforts of the preacher and the prayerful urging of the congregation, they are asked to sit on the mourners' bench, and they are welcomed by handshakes all around. Official processing to the church roll, and duties to be assumed, occur at a later date.

When the invitation and joining are over, the whole audience joins in singing "Halleluyah, Tis Done" or some other favorite. The song is one of distilled joy that another soul is saved by the grace of God.

It is traditional to have prayer at this point. Numerous forms are available from a wide repertoire of prayers. The preacher chooses the prayer best suited to a given event in the ritualistic process; the deacon may also assume this responsibility.

The Reverend C. L. Franklin begins a prayer with: "Can I get somebody to pray with me right now—Great God!"

The Reverend R. B. Thurmond moans, followed by a hushed rendition of "Great God—" and finishes the prayer with a moan and, "And that will be enough."

Reverend Daniel Harris uses a more extensive prayer:

PREACHER (*moans*): Good God—a mighty (*Moans.*) One day the sun will refuse to shine. (*Moans* —————) Sooooon, soon one morning, soon-uh one morning, I said, soon-uh one morning death is a-comin'.

CONGREGATION: Come on Rev.!

PREACHER: Pray wit' me. Lord have mercy on me. O-o-o-h Lord, the chariot of God will swing low, the wheels of justice will turn.

CONGREGATION: Let the wheels turn.

PREACHER: Let the church say A-men, 'cause one day I was way down yonder by myself and I couldn't hear nobody pray.

(*Congregation moans and hums softly.*)

PREACHER: We need good church members to pray, and tell God how these dark clouds are hanging above our heads and how deep the valley is, and how high the mountain is. Tell God about the rough roads you got to walk. But thank God, the journey's started. A-men. Let the church say A-men.

CONGREGATION: A-men.

The money ritual (also called collecting the money, taking the collection, or passing the plate/basket)

Without missing a beat, the choir begins the offertory song. The preacher or head deacon extends the invitation to contribute while the people are still aroused. The preacher often preaches a short post-sermon about the beauty of having a church, a place to meet and enjoy oneself worshiping God. The preacher will take his glasses off (if he wears them), wipe his brow again, reach into his pocket to "put the first dollar in," come back down from the pulpit, and hand it to the church mother—*always* to the church mother. After the collection the church is blessed and dismissed until another Sunday.

Another device used is the "build-up" approach to finance. The build-up of the audience is designed to stimulate giving money to the church. The preacher, as Jesse Jackson illustrates, also calls on select people in the audience to "lead off the taking of the collection." Usually these leaders are financially better off than most or have some status or influence in the community. Put on the spot, they must "lead off" with a most generous contribution. The preacher cajoles the audience to continue giving generously as the congregation either parades down the aisles to the offertory table (a fast-disappearing practice) or the offertory baskets or plates are passed. A running stream of chatter and encouragement, even to the point of sometimes embarrassing a reluctant giver, is kept up by the preacher. Soft choir music usually accompanies this ritual. Every effort is expended to amass as much money for the church as possible. The congregation is highly appreciative of the pastor's remarks during this time. The offering is finally blessed with a short prayer.

The discussion up to this point has attempted to sketch the Baptist ritual and ceremony, with its call and response patterns reminiscent of African drum ceremonies, as an illustration of the matrix out of which black communication style has evolved. It is clear, for example, that the black ministerial figure (pastor, preacher, reverend, or leader) does not deliver a message *to* his audience; he involves the audience in the message. Expressive communication (emotion, feeling) is mandatory for both speaker and receiver. Both move without shame to the syncopation of movement, are sensitive to the shifting nuances, and call on the church for guidance whenever and wherever the spirit moves. The preaching style displays virtuosity in both effect and affect, using devices filled with emotion and a sense of the dramatic. From this communication cradle have come such Spellbinders (as opposed to Soul Jerkers) as Father Divine, Martin Luther King, Jr., Calvin Marshall, Adam Clayton Powell, Tom Skinner, Samuel Williams, Rabbi Divine, Jesse Jackson, Frank Sims, and Abe Jackson.

"Movin' out"—church communication styles in secular contexts

As has been shown above, how to deal with The Man, maintain black identity, and improve the conditions of existence for black people have long been functions of the church. To these functions a new and pressing one has been added: to aid in the acquisition of power to achieve economic goals.

In organizing black people around this objective, ministers like Tom Skinner of the east coast and Jesse Jackson of the midwest illustrate the use of manipulative, expressive, black modes in blending evangelistic fervor with pragmatic goals. Tom Skinner is especially appealing to the young when his evangelistic style compares David and Goliath with blacks and "whitey." He relates what David accomplished with what blacks can do when God is on their side. Skinner "hustles" his past gang-leader role to young ghetto blacks as proof of blacks' ability to play David and Goliath. "Hustling" in this context is the promotion of black pride, awareness, dignity, identity, and power.

Jesse Jackson uses his spellbinding abilities in the deliberate manipulation of symbols to change attitudes and beliefs. Jackson engenders awareness and hustles a sense of pride and power with "I Am Somebody." Being black requires an absolute commitment to an illusionary view of reality (that rats *don't* exist) with equal commitment to hope for the future (that rats *won't* exist). Jackson's "hustling time" clearly serves religious purposes, but it is a good deal more social and economic than religious. With an awareness of his power to verbally transfigure disillusionment and despair into powers of survival, Jackson shouts, "I Am Somebody" and black audiences respond, "I Am Somebody." Blacks know full well that when the rats stop biting they'll know they're somebody, but the power and magic of the word as antecedent for the action are so strong it is for the moment believed. In "true believing," blacks' actions are thereby influenced to help make the words reality. Claude Lewis reports from an Operation Breadbasket meeting in 1968 the following excerpts which illustrate Jackson's expert manipulation of black communicative patterns and functions.

"I am what I am and I am proud."
"We seek not the privilege to integrate, but rather the *power* to negotiate."
"Money is the next most righteous thing in the Kingdom other than subjects."
"David sought not a church but a kingdom. Go take the land, then make the decisions. I know my Father's house from the hog trough."

And while he preaches he asks for response:

"We black people ought to reappraise our relationship to American white people and redefine our relationship with our colored brothers elsewhere. . . . Can I get a witness?" And the entire congregation becomes his witness with a resounding "Yes brother" and "Tell it like it is."

He moves his audience, he excites them, he pushes them, he inspires and manipulates them.

"To have the symbols of freedom and no power is to be denied the substance of freedom."
"Now we deserve the job or an income."
"Stay on the case," a black woman shouted.
"Tell it like it is brother," an old black man yelled out.
"We've got to keep on pushing."
"I'm constantly reminded of Martin's favorite prayer that goes like this: 'Lord, we ain't what we ought to be, and we ain't what we want to be, we ain't what we gonna be, but thank God, we ain't what we was.'"

Crises within the black community are also frequently handled within a church or church-like setting. For example, recently in Chicago a South Side church was burned; its pastor, the Reverend Curtis Burrell, had declared war on Chicago street gangs. The Reverend Jesse Jackson was invited to preach the next Sunday's sermon. In order to ensure maximum attendance and participation in the creation of the event, he announced through the press that he was going to preach a "Dry Bones" sermon. The mention of "Dry Bones" was a signal to the black community that an overriding and urgent social issue was going to be discussed; since the "Dry Bones" sermon is a ritual within the black church—many variations of the sermon exist which have become quite formalized through time—interest and speculation was high over how Jackson would develop the sermon relative to the current social conflict.

Traditionally, the "Dry Bones" sermon has functioned as a unifying force within the black community; it was designed especially to bridge class lines and overcome divisive factionalism. Whatever structural and stylistic variations existed among preachers in their handling of the sermon, one theme has been invariant—namely, that conflicts within the black community arise out of the conditions under which black people are forced to live and that such conflicts produce divisions which aid and abet The Man in his efforts to keep black people down. Therefore, one of the chief goals of the preacher through the use of the "Dry Bones" sermon is to supplant inhuman white authority with religious black authority where white authority is declared unjust and un-Christian and the authority of the black church is declared the only just authority for black people. Listeners are inspired, impressed, and challenged to aspire to the loftier means and ends, to move from the "Dry Bones valley" of degradation and internal social conflict to the "garden humanity" of the mountain. Aware of this tradition, most Chicago blacks knew or antici-pated that Jackson would use the sermon to talk about the local conflict between blacks. The mere mention of "Dry Bones" produced maxi-mum attendance and participation that Sunday. (Since Burrell's church was burned, the service occurred in a makeshift, open, sidewalk church.)

What follows are some quotes from Jackson's sermon:

> *Who is it that* does not mind the people here burning up, destroying each other so they can get this property back? . . .
> *Who is it that* burns the houses, that the people are movin' out of, not puttin' people back in 'em, so they can use it for airport property?
> *Who is it wants* . . . Lake Meadows and Prairie Shores?
> *Repeated refrain:* God made the garden.
> Man made the valley.
> The valley just makes you tired.
> *You just get tired* of seein' the blue lights turn aroun'.
> *You get tired* of seein' people stand in line to use the bathroom.
> *You just get tired* of men being treated like boys.
> *You just get tired of* women being treated like girls.
> You just get tired, and wanna leave the valley. And

however you can get out you leave.
I get tired of *criticism*. But there's something within.
I get tired of *the lies*. But there's something within.
I get tired of *exploitation*. But there's something within.
I get tired of *oppression*. But there's something within.

As each successive line of the pattern is enumerated, the voice rises ever higher and becomes increasingly emphatic. The congregation usually responds with corresponding intensity after each line if the preacher is effective. When the audience does not respond, it signals the speaker that he is not moving the listeners. He may then try some other motivational device from his repertoire with more success.

See, if you just walkin' up and down the streets of the ghetto, you get frustrated talkin' bout the *effect* and you *never* get to the cause. *The effect is,* an illiterate and semi-literate people. *The effect is,* babies dying. *The effect is,* fathers fighting sons, *and* mothers fighting daughters, *and* confusion in the household *and,* burning the church *and,* glorifying the corner. . . .

The communication devices illustrated function in Operation Breadbasket meetings, a semi-religious context. Jesse Jackson is the speaker.

Man making money *can be crude,* but his making nuff money to send his child to college.
Man *can be crude,* but if he's makin' enough money, he can get a house.
Can be crude, if he's makin' nuff money, he can get a car. Can fly an airplane, can go to the doctor, does not have to be on welfare.

Wherever you're listening, pull out a quarter and a dime. Twenty-five-cent piece and a dime. Y'all too. *Quarter and a dime.* I'm not really a teacher, but I can if I have to. Necessity is the mother of invention I told y'all. All the "war on poverty" people up there pullin' out these—I didn't say a ten dollar bill or a $25.00 bill, I say *a quarter money and a dime.*

We are in Chicago a little better than 25% of the population. That what this quarter is. We live on less than 10% of the land. Follow me now! Now what you must do is to try to *fit the quarter on the dime.*
AUDIENCE: Tell it! Right on Jesse!
JESSE: Try to fit it. Figure out how you can do it. One a ya'll smart nough to figure it out just when I'm telling it. You got a position on how you *put the quarter on the dime?* Hear what I said? You can't stick all black folks up on top of each other. You got to *fit on it.* I didn't say stick it on the dime. (AUDIENCE: *Right!*) That's what the———are trying to do. They're tryin' to *stick us on the dime.* Now turn it over so you can look at the dime. These people that are on the dime *live* in the ghetto. . . . It ain't no accident that 30,000 people per square mile live in the black community, and 3,000 per square mile live in the white community. Which means that in the white community you got more land than people,

and the premium is on the people and not on the land. And in a black community you got more people than property and therefore the premium is on the property and not on the man. In the white community you defend white folks. In the black community you defend property. No accident. Listen!!

AUDIENCE: Awright!

JESSE: Listen!

AUDIENCE: Awright!

JESSE: Think about the *people who can't get on the dime.*

Besides the use of other stylistic devices already mentioned, note how Jackson makes effective use of *repetition* as a communication device, which serves to emphasize and drive home to the congregation an important point. By means of repetition, Jackson ensures that the cruciality of *what* he is saying is not lost in the emotionalism of the audience. Black speakers generally are keenly aware of the need to offset any emotionalism that might interfere with information processing. For example, at another Operation Breadbasket meeting, on introducing another speaker, Jackson prepares his audience to receive and relate to a different tempo and rhythm from that of the preacher: "Brothers and sisters, I want you to greet warmly at this time, not a preacher. You won't hear no—them things me and Bob and Calvin and Ed 'n' 'em go through where we start dippin' and goin' on, cause Holy Ghost a start us movin'. Information be makin' him stand still, so you got to *hear* him. Just be hearing what's on his mind."

In summary, communication in the black church is highly dependent on the style and skill of the preacher interacting with the affective responses of involved audiences. This "turn-on" ability in terms of communication style is a cohesive force incorporating a large body of blacks. Black preaching style mixes moralism and idealism with pragmatism, promotes institutionalized authority, bridges generations, and relies on and extends the general effect that is basic to the black experience.

■ Street talk

H. RAP BROWN

H. Rap Brown is well known as a former head of SNCC and for his overall involvement in the black civil rights struggle. Author of *Die Nigger Die!* (from which the present selection was taken), Brown describes what "growing up black" was for him and many other blacks in the streets of Baton Rouge, Louisiana, and around the country, and what survival meant there in the street context and within the context of the larger society.

This selection from Brown's autobiography demonstrates not only his own considerable verbal expertise in "talk-ing that talk," an ability for which he was aptly nicknamed "Rap" by his peers, but also the general high esteem with which verbal skill and play is regarded in black culture, an expertise which the cultural norms serve to promote and develop among its members. Brown's extraordinary verbal ability is not unique, but representative of the varying degrees and types of oral expertise to be found within black culture at all levels, from street corner, to podium, to pulpit.

The street is where young bloods get their education. I learned how to talk in the street, not from reading about Dick and Jane going to the zoo and all that simple shit. The teacher would test our vocabulary each week, but we knew the vocabularly we needed. They'd give us arithmetic to exercise our minds. Hell, we exercised our minds by playing the dozens.

> I fucked your mama
> Till she went blind.
> Her breath smells bad,
> But she sure can grind.

> I fucked your mama
> For a solid hour.
> Baby came out
> Screaming, Black Power.

> Elephant and the Baboon
> Learning to screw.
> Baby came out looking
> Like Spiro Agnew.

And the teacher expected me to sit up in class and study poetry after I could run down shit like that. If anybody needed to study poetry, she needed to study mine. We played the dozens for recreation, like white folks play Scrabble.

In many ways, though, the dozens is a mean game because what you try to do is totally destroy somebody else with words. It's that whole competition thing again, fighting each other. There'd be sometimes forty or fifty dudes standing around and the winner was determined by the way they responded to what was said. If you fell all over each other laughing, then you knew you'd scored. It was a bad scene for the dude that was getting humiliated. I seldom was. That's why they call me Rap, 'cause I could rap. (The name stuck because Ed would always say, "That my nigger Rap," "Rap my nigger.") But for dudes who couldn't, it was like they were humiliated because they were born black and then they turned around and got humiliated by their own people, which was really all they had left. But that's the way it is. Those that feel most humiliated humiliate others. The real aim of the dozens was to get a dude so mad that he'd cry or get mad enough to fight. You'd say shit like, "Man, tell your mama to stop coming around my house all the time. I'm tired of fucking her and I think you should know that it ain't no accident you look like me." And it could go on for hours sometimes. Some of the best dozens players were girls.

Signifying is more humane. Instead of coming down on somebody's mother, you come down on them. But before you can signify, you got to be able to rap. A session would start maybe by a brother saying, "Man, before you mess with me you'd rather run rabbits, eat shit and bark at the moon." Then, if he was talking to me, I'd tell him:

> Man, you must don't know who I am.
> I'm sweet peeter jeeter the womb beater
> The baby maker the cradle shaker
> The deerslayer the buckbinder the women finder
> Known from the Gold Coast to the rocky shores of Maine
> Rap is my name and love is my game.
> I'm the bed tucker the cock plucker the motherfucker
> The milkshaker the record breaker the population maker
> The gun-slinger the baby bringer
> The hum-dinger the pussy ringer
> The man with the terrible middle finger.
> The hard hitter the bullshitter the poly-nussy getter
> The beast from the East the Judge the sludge
> The women's pet the men's fret and the punks' pin-up boy.
> They call me Rap the dicker the ass kicker
> The cherry picker the city slicker the titty licker
> And I ain't giving up nothing but bubble gum and hard times and I'm
>   fresh out of bubble gum.
> I'm giving up wooden nickels 'cause I know they won't spend
> And I got a pocketful of splinter change.
> I'm a member of the bathtub club: I'm seeing a whole lot of ass but I
>   ain't taking no shit.
> I'm the man who walked the water and tied the whale's tail in a knot

Taught the little fishes how to swim
Crossed the burning sands and shook the devil's hand
Rode round the world on the back of a snail carrying a sack saying AIR
  MAIL.
Walked 49 miles of barbwire and used a Cobra snake for a necktie
And got a brand new house on the roadside made from a cracker's hide,
Got a brand new chimney setting on top made from the cracker's skull
Took a hammer and nail and built the world and calls it "THE BUCKET OF
  BLOOD."
Yes, I'm hemp the demp the women's pimp
Women fight for my delight.
I'm a bad motherfucker. Rap the rip-saw the devil's brother 'n law.
I roam the world I'm known to wander and this .45 is where I get my
  thunder.
I'm the only man in the world who knows why white milk makes yellow
  butter.
I know where the lights go when you cut the switch off.
I might not be the best in the world, but I'm in the top two and my
  brother's getting old.
And ain't nothing bad 'bout you but your breath.

Now, if the brother couldn't come back behind that, I usually cut
him some slack (depending on time, place, and his attitude). We learned
what the white folks call verbal skills. We learned how to throw them
words together. America, however, has black folk in a serious game
of the dozens. (The dirty muthafucka.) Signifying allowed you a choice
—you could either make a cat feel good or bad. If you had just destroyed someone or if they were just down already, signifying could
help them over. Signifying was also a way of expressing your own
feelings:

Man, I can't win for losing.
If it wasn't for bad luck, I wouldn't have no luck at all.
I been having buzzard luck
Can't kill nothing and won't nothing die
I'm living on the welfare and things is stormy
They borrowing their shit from the Salvation Army
But things bound to get better 'cause they can't get no worse
I'm just like the blind man, standing by a broken window
I don't feel no pain.
But it's your world
You the man I pay rent to
If I had your hands I'd give 'way both my arms.
Cause I could do without them
I'm the man but you the main man
I read the books you write
You set the pace in the race I run

Why, you always in good form
You got more foam than Alka Seltzer . . .

Signifying at its best can be heard when brothers are exchanging tales. I used to hang out in the bars just to hear the old men "talking shit." By the time I was nine, I could talk Shine and the Titanic, Signifying Monkey, three different ways, and Piss-Pot-Peet, for two hours without stopping.

Sometimes I wonder why I even bothered to go to school. Practically everything I know I learned on the corner.

■ Shoe-shine on 63rd

JAMES MARYLAND

James Maryland is presently a district manager trainee within the Dodge sales division of the Chrysler Corporation after serving as an administrative advisor in their manpower training program. Prior to that he was program director of the Old Town Chicago Boys Club and "Outpost" director for Youth Action under the general auspices of the YMCA, positions obtained after several years working the streets as an extension worker for the Chicago Youth Development Project and as a youth worker for the Chicago Boys Club. This experience brought him into intimate contact with black youth who were members of gangs, giving him more firsthand knowledge of the streets to add to that which he had already acquired while growing up in the Woodlawn area of Chicago's South Side. A master's degree candidate at Northeastern Illinois University's Center for Inner City Studies, the author's special research interest is in youth gang activity, especially in those social conditions which have contributed to increasing the violent behavior among black teen gangs in low-income areas over the past several years.

Maryland's contributions to this volume, as exemplified by his own piece and the example of "sigging" that Kochman uses in his article on black speech behavior, demonstrate a writer's ability to capture the full sense and effect of a scene in which he participated or to which he was witness. This ability allows the reader to derive secondhand much of the richness and flavor of the expressive language and life style of black American culture.

The following verbal play is indicative of the type that might be found in any of a number of shine parlors, taverns, barber shops, pool rooms, and alley garages or street corners where the signifiers can be found congregating each day. The setting of this verbal contest is Chicago's Woodlawn Community, but the verbal play described herein could occur in any black community.

Apart from style, a major difference between the verbal contest recorded in this paper and some more common ones (like the stories of the Signifying Monkey, Stackolee, the Titanic) is the absence of levity. The comments here were made either in deadly earnest, or as a matter of fact. The absence of good-natured joking which normally accompanies verbal play accentuated the tensions that existed at this time (November, 1968) as a result of the newly developed sense of pride and consciousness in the black community.

To oversimplify the characteristics of this new verbal play and contest would be to state that the verbal play here sought to probe the "blackness" of a brother or sister.

The major characters in this verbal contest are Sweet Red (a successful pimp) and the Reverend Black Power (a former pimp who spent five years in the penitentiary for the sale and use of narcotics, who is now a confirmed, self-styled, Black Power minister). Specifically, this verbal contest took place in Woodlawn in an enclosed shoe-shine stand on Sixty-third Street.

One afternoon at Little Bob's shoe-shine stand (a location frequented by a variety of players, hustlers, pimps, gangsters, and even some legitimate businessmen), the regulars milled around signifying and rapping to each other while they passed the time waiting for something to happen. Little Bob stood at the cash register ringing up shine fees, while Sweet Red waited patiently for Little Bob to return to the stand and begin to work on his shoes.

Sweet Red was a well known six-trey (Sixty-third Street) pimp who was always "clean" (neatly dressed) and known to keep a large roll of twenty-dollar bills on him. In addition Red was known to be "swinging" (pushing narcotics). This didn't matter to the cats that hung around the stand, or in the community. They seemed to care only about how shrewd, cool, and successful Red was—a cat who would "turn them on" whenever they were in need. They seemed to take pride in the fact that they had seen Red graduate from white port wine to C.C. (Canadian Club) and now to Grant's Scotch; from a used T-Bird to a new Eldorado Cadillac. Red had grown out of wash pants and levis to Oleg Cassini imported mohair suits, Prince Ferrari shirts and ties. Red's gator shoes always glittered with a professional diamond-like shine. His visit to the stand was as much a front as were his manicured nails, diamond rings on each hand, and neatly processed hair. While Red rapped to Little Bob and the others, his white girl friend Tessie waited impatiently in Red's white Hog (Cadillac) which was parked in front of the stand.

Bob moved over from Bill's shoes to begin work on Red's shoes, popping his rag and maintaining a constant flow of slick talk on nothing in particular as he worked at the shine stand. Finally he tapped the end of Red's shoe, indicating that he had finished the shine. Red stepped down from his seat and handed Bob five dollars for the shine as Black Power approached the stand.

Black Power still retained his former pimp attitudes about clothes. His daily attire consisted of the following: black spit-shined combat boots, black silk and mohair slacks neatly bloused at the top of each boot, black turtleneck shirt, Afro beads around his neck, and a white satin formal cape around his shoulders. In his hand he carried a long cypress-root staff. Black Power was bearded and wore his hair au naturel; both beard and hair were neatly trimmed, and on some occasions he sported a black beret. The sight of a handsome black man standing well over six feet tall and dressed as Black Power was never failed to create a reaction in all who saw him; the nature of that attitude depended upon their relationship with or knowledge of him.

As Black Power drew closer to the shoe-shine stand, the conversation at the stand began humming in anticipation. Sweet Red's face registered an uneasy and uncomfortable expression. It was obvious that Red wanted to "split" (leave) before Black Power arrived, but that wouldn't have contributed to Red's front—for every one knew he didn't dig Black Power, nor did Black Power dig him.

Black Power entered the stand, greeted the men with the symbolic sign of bent wrist, tightened fist, and vertically extended arm. (Some blacks feel this gesture originated in prisons, where black prisoners could greet each other only in silence and therefore devised the gesture to communicate with the other black men without speaking). The men at the stand returned Black Power's greeting with the same gesture.

Pretty Black, another well-known pimp on both Forty-seventh and Sixty-third Streets, sat on the stand waiting to get his shoes shined and observed the change in Sweet Red as Black Power entered. Pretty Black was dressed in the same fashion as was Red, drove a "Deuce and a quarter" (Electra 225 Buick) and was popular among the ladies, pawn-brokers, police, and small-time criminals, especially the "young gang-bangers" (teenage gang members).

Black Power began to deliver one of his "messages" (soapbox ser-mons) after replying to the greeting of the "players" (audience partici-pants in the verbal play) located at the stand, when Pretty Black interrupted him.

"Wait a minute Rev. Black Power," said Pretty Black, grinning, "we all know you around here and know how you're always trying to bring the word to us black brothers; but what do you think of a pimp ass nigger running around here with the devil herself, Miss Ann?"

The crowd started nudging each other, indicating that the signifying was about to go down.

Black Power replied, "P.B., you are very intelligent to observe the very things I preach against doing. The mother running round with that white devil ought to be offed [assaulted and/or killed]."

"Damn, Rev., that's some real cruel shit, suggesting a sweet man [pimp] be iced," replied Pretty Black, grinning and checking the crowd to be sure everyone was hip to the happenings.

Red was attempting to ignore the conversation, but he knew he couldn't leave now. The rules of the game did not permit Red to leave with the balance of power in Black Power's favor.

Pretty Black continued his rap. "Brother Black Power's out here try-ing to free us brothers and sisters and some jive motherfucker is out here fouling his game." Pretty Black was using Black Power to try to build up his own image at the expense of Red's.

The crowd began to laugh and react to the scene, waiting to see how it came down.

"Why don't you simple sonofabitches stop fucking with my man Red," stated Slim (a former policeman and current pimp), "y'all see he ain't messing with you cats; the man's got business to tend to."

"Who said anything about Sweet Blood [Sweet Blood being synonymous with Sweet Red] running around here with Ann?" asked Freeze, a Sixty-third Street salesman and moonlighting pimp.

Big Al added fuel to the contest by laughing and shouting, "Somebody gonna snatch y'alls asses out of place for signifying."

Black Power began to speak again after digging the comments being made, gearing his message to the conversation. He began, "The bottom rail would have been on top long ago, if it weren't for these white devils and she-devil lovers. These here she-devils ain't nothing but trouble and these tack-head niggers are at 'em like a hound dog in Mississippi on nigger shit."

"Rev. is sho' in his new thing, brothers," stated Pretty Black.

"New thing my ass, motherfuckers! Black Power is always been like this, talking slick and talking shit. I 'member when his mama got off the train from Mississippi with this boy. Shit, he was just knee high to a duck; he was preaching the truth then, and still is," replied Cotton (a Sixty-third Street wino).

The crowd roared with laughter after hearing Cotton's comments.

"Damn Cotton is the biggest liar on the trey," laughed Seed, Cotton's wine-drinking buddy (Cotton/Seed).

Red saw the change in conversation as an opportune time to leave without losing face. Red moved toward the door, saying, "I'm going to step now, and make this little run."

However, Pretty Black wasn't ready to let Red ease out of the confrontation between Red and Black Power which he was trying to bring about. He therefore asked loudly, "Running to what, and from Black Power?"

"Man, motherfuck you and Black Ass Power," retorted Red, as he stopped with annoyance before reaching the door.

The crowd whooped and hollered with laughter, for they knew the signifying was really on.

"Pity a poor fool, brothers, for he knoweth not what's happening. He's a lost sheep in a pasture of white bullshit," commented Black Power.

Red angrily shouted, "Lost my ass, nigger! What about all that shit you've been pulling with them damn white hippie bitches? You going around here with that damn white collar turned backwards talking shit about you being somebody's savior from the East! You ain't shit! Some of these young *real* black brothers ought to beat that holy shit outa you!"

The tempo of the signifying had grown stronger and stronger; the crowd made fewer and fewer comments, not sure of whether or not the two participants were still signifying or were "for real." This withdrawal of comment by the crowd also keeps the verbal contest from being sparked into a fight by a nonparticipant.

Following Red's outburst, Black Power looked out the window and spotted three bearded black men wearing dashikis (African shirts) walking toward the stand. He pointed to them and stated, "What I ought to do is call them young brothers over here to investigate these white whore-hungry niggers."

Red's face became uneasy, and his hands trembled as he attempted to light his cigarette. The other players noticed this and joined in at this point.

"Don't be nervous, nigger, ain't nobody going to turn you in," stated Pretty Black.

Slick chimed in seriously with, "You ought to get that grey broad off the trey, Red."

Pretty Black saw that Red was nervous and frightened and tried to ease Red's tension by directing the play at Cotton who, as a wino, was less likely to have been involved and could therefore be expected to be less tense. He said, "Damn Cotton, wake up and turn your head the other way, cause your funky breath smells like rat piss."

Black Power, also hip to the direction and tone of the verbal contest, tried to minimize the tension and said, "Don't be scared son, I come to save you and not to condemn you nigger. I've been commissioned to help niggers like you."

"The only help you can give me," stated Red, "is to buy my smokes, and rent my ladies!"

Hearing this, Cotton jumped and howled, "Say it Sweet Blood, rap that shit baby! Rap it!"

Pretty Black then grinned and stated, "Now that ain't hip, Blood, telling a preacher that kind of shit."

Black Power jumped back in, saying, "Don't worry baby, before this devil-lover leaves here, that lye in his hair is either gonna eat the sickness outta this nigger's head or eat up his damn brains."

"Oooowhee! The preacher's talking shit now," stated Slick.

It was obvious that the anger and tension were diminishing by the laughter and facial expressions of the players.

"Say, Rev., tell them 'bout the little white lady that called you all of the Black M.F.'s and S.O.B.'s at Big Joe's party last Christmas," commented Red, assured now that he and Black Power were only signifying and working the game on each other with their raps.

"Yeah Brother! That happened to me," commented Black Power, as he seemed to be amused by the mental picture of the scene recalled. "That happened then, but it don't happen no more!"

Before anyone could get on Black Power's "case," a volley of shots was fired very close to the shoe-shine stand. Then several young boys ran past the stand into the alley. Shortly after that, a police car sped into the alley in pursuit of the boys. The excitement of this shooting ended the mood, and the verbal play ceased. The players all started heading for the door, stating, "Peace," "Later," "Hat time," "I'm in the wind," etc. All gave the Black Power sign as they left, including Red.

The signifying and rapping were over until the next set of players arrived.

■ Joking: the training of the man of words in talking broad

ROGER D. ABRAHAMS

Roger D. Abrahams is director of the African and Afro-American Research Institute and professor of English and anthropology at the University of Texas. Author of *Deep Down in the Jungle: Negro Narrative Folklore from the Streets of Philadelphia, Positively Black,* and other books, monographs, articles, and reviews, he is presently editing a book with Rudolph Troike entitled *Language, Culture, and Education.* Primarily a folklorist and ethnographer, Abrahams's collection of toasts, boasts, and jokes from an urban black Philadelphia community long represented the only actual (uncensored) version of black American verbal play in publication. It was viewed as one of those rare pieces that was not primarily concerned with catering to white middle-class norms or sensibilities, but rather to a set of criteria that acknowledged and appreciated the existence of

a much broader aesthetic, one that included black vernacular expression as well.

Extending his collection of language and lore of Afro-Americans from the urban areas of Philadelphia and Texas to the Caribbean, Abrahams's present article represents one of a series from that area and here serves to illustrate further the pervasiveness of expressive language as a cultural phenomenon throughout Afro-America. Focusing on the training of the man-of-words in talking broad (in contrast to talking sweet), Abrahams draws upon the *speech event*—the speech context as well as the speech itself—to evolve a conception of the various "rules" which create the performance aesthetic held and shared by the speaker and his audience.

I

One of the great enigmas about Afro-Americans in the United States and the West Indies is, why has there been no widespread use of standard English as the primary code of discourse? The usual (and stereotypical) explanations turning on attributions of a social pathology or a genetic incapacity to perform in certain ways are totally unacceptable to anyone who has lived in an Afro-American community. There are too many instances in which members of such groups have both learned and constantly performed certain of the more complex dimensions of this "standard" code. There is therefore no inability to *learn* the standard language—only a continuing social resistance to its *use* in everyday discourse among a great majority of the peasantry in the West Indies and the rural South, and among the lower classes in urban areas. In its place remains some form of Afro-American Creole or a dialect form somewhere between Creole and standard English.

The enigma is simply one of many problems which have arisen because our model of acculturation insists that European practices be culturally dominant, since other things Western are. Because of this, and because of our stereotypic mentality which assumes that anything culturally different evidences a lack of social order, we have ignored the abundant evidence which shows that Afro-Americans operate in terms of a highly ordered, predictable discourse system—one which is, in many crucial regards, different from that of whites.

One dimension of this system is the procedure of contending or dueling with words. Verbal contests are a major means by which black men communicate with and entertain each other. But one must understand the demands of such a speaking community to fathom the contest orientation's place of importance.

One of the dominant features of life style in most Afro-American communities is the continuing reliance on oral expression. This means that there is still a good deal of social value placed on verbal abilities; these can often be best exhibited in a contest fashion, contests which are waged in Creole or street language rather than in standard English. Discussing the role of such verbal abilities in one Washington ghetto neighborhood, Ulf Hannerz recently noted:

> The skill of talking well and easily is widely appreciated among ghetto men; although it is hardly itself a sign of masculinity, it can be very helpful in realizing one's wishes. "Rapping," persuasive speech, can be used to manipulate others to one's own advantage. Besides, talking well is useful in cutting losses as well as in making gains. By "jiving" and "shucking," ghetto concepts with the partial denotation of warding off punishment or retribution through tall stories, feigned innocence, demeaning talk about one-self, or other misleading statements, a man may avoid the undesirable consequences of his own misdemeanors. . . . However, all prestige accrued from being a good talker does not have to do with the strictly utilitarian aspect. A man with good stories well told and with a quick repartee in arguments is certain to be appreciated for his entertainment value, and those men who can talk about the high and mighty, people and places, and the state of the world, may stake claims to a reputation of being "heavy upstairs."[1]

The ability to contend effectively with words, then, is a social skill and is highly valued as such. Furthermore, it seems significant, in light of the black language enigma, that these contests reinstate talk (or, as most West Indians refer to it, bad, broken, broad talk) as a high art. One might hypothesize that the ongoing importance and usefulness of such practices may contribute to the retention of Creolized speech patterns as the major code for in-group black interpretations and entertain-

---

[1] Ulf Hannerz, *Soulside* (New York: Columbia University Press, 1969), pp. 84–85.

ments. This argument seems even more pausible as one investigates the crucial place which certain of these verbal contests, like "playing the dozens" (mother-rhyming), takes in the socialization process of young men in widely scattered black communities.

The importance of these skills in actively contending are amply testified to by those who have grown up in the ghetto environment in the United States: Malcolm X, Dick Gregory, Claude Brown, Jr., and most recently H. Rap Brown. Brown says of the whole language "problem":

> I learned how to talk in the street, not from reading about Dick and Jane going to the zoo. . . . The teacher would test our vocabulary each week, but we knew the vocabulary we needed. They'd give us arithmetic to exercise our minds. Hell, we exercised our minds by playing the dozens. . . . We played the dozens for recreation, like white folks play Scrabble. . . . Though, the dozens is a mean game because what you try to do is totally destroy somebody else with words. . . . Signifying is more humane. Instead of coming down on somebody's mother, you come down on them. But, before you can signify you got to be able to rap.[2]

Playing the dozens, as Brown explains here, is just one of a number of verbal-contest traditions which ghetto boys learn and use as the basis of their entertainments. However, this kind of joking activity is not unique to ghetto blacks. The practice of mother-rhyming has also been observed in various other Afro-American communities as well as in a number of groups in Africa, including the Yoruba,[3] Efik,[4] Dogon,[5] and some Bantu tribes. Peter Rigby, for instance, notes among the Bantu Wagogo, "The abuse between age-mates is of the strongest kind. . . . Grandparents . . . may be freely included in the verbal banter, as well as references to each other's 'parents' particularly 'mothers'. . . . Completely free conversation, which therefore includes references to sexual matters, is characteristic of relations between age-mates."[6] Philip Mayer similarly reports among the Gusii that "the true measure of the unique unrestraint of pals and the climax of their intimacy is to exchange pornographic references to the other's mother and particularly to impute that he would be prepared for incestuous relations with her."[7]

[2] H. Rap Brown, *Die Nigger Die* (New York: Dial Press, 1969), pp. 25–27, and in this volume.

[3] Personal communication, Robert Farris Thompson.

[4] Donald Simmons, "Possible West African Sources for the American Negro Dozens," *Journal of American Folklore* 75 (1962): 339–340.

[5] This kind of joking is reported by Genevieve Calame-Griaule, *Ethnologie et langage: La Parole chez les dogon* (Paris, 1965), as carried on between the Dogon and their neighbors, the Bozo. Cf. Sister Peter Marie Hogan, "Some Functions of Speech among the Dogon of West Africa," unpublished paper.

[6] Peter Rigby, "Joking Relationships, Kin Categories and Clanship among the Gogo," *Africa* 38 (1968): 150. See also Dominique Zahan, *La Dialectique du verbe chez les bambara* (Paris: Mouton, 1963), pp. 73–77.

[7] "The Joking of Pals in Gusii Age-Sets," *African Studies* 10 (1941): 31–32.

These reports are almost unique because they make a reference to content features as a part of the process of joking. There has been a good deal of discussion concerning the social form and functions of the joking relationships in various African groups. But these discussions (other than those noted above) focus primarily on who can joke with whom, not how and why they joke. Thus it is difficult to tell how widespread such mother-rhyming is and what alternatives there are in joking situations in Africa. We do know that such specially licensed behavior is very widespread on that continent, and that it plays an important part in the informal verbal traditions there.

In the New World, such play is one aspect of a special kind of aggressive joking activity calling for verbal quickness and wit. This highly aggressive joking domain is known by a number of names like "rapping" or "signifying" in the United States, while the British West Indians term it "giving rag," "making mock," and "giving fatigue."[8] These joking domains, whether in Africa or the New World, are always described in terms of the giving of license because of special relationships or festive occasions. Joking, in this way, is related to the entire scandal-piece tradition and the various practices of clowning or playing the fool. These scandalizing practices are equally widespread and important in African and Afro-American communities. One can infer from the range of practices and their importance in community life that, when mother-rhyming is practiced by adolescents, it is part of the training procedure for adult performances. To comprehend this, however, it is necessary to quickly review the types of verbal techniques important in Afro-American communities, and to describe actual rhyming traditions from some West Indian Afro-American communities.

II

Peasant and lower-class communities in the West Indies and the United States share this attitude toward effective use of words. The range of this verbal repertory includes the ability to joke aggressively (in some groups this includes riddling), to "make war" with words by insult and scandal-pieces, to tell Anansi stories (any kind of folktales), and to make speeches and toasts appropriate to ceremonial occasions. Community status is designated in the British West Indies by making a man of words

[8] Cf. Roger. D. Abrahams and Richard Bauman, "Sense and Nonsense on St. Vincent: Performance and Behavior in a West Indian Peasantry," *American Anthropologist,* forthcoming; Thomas Kochman, "Toward an Ethnography of Black American Speech Behavior," in *Afro-American Anthropology: Contemporary Perspectives,* ed. Norman E. Whitten, Jr., and John F. Szwed (New York: The Free Press, 1970), pp. 145–62, and in this volume; Roger D. Abrahams, "Rapping and Capping: Black Speech as Art," in *Black Americans,* ed. John F. Szwed (New York: Basic Books, 1970); Roger D. Abrahams, *Positively Black* (Englewood Cliffs, N.J.: Prentice-Hall, 1970).

the chairman at a wake or tea meeting or service of song, the toast-master at weddings and other fêtes. Few, of course, achieve such distinction.

There tends to be some distinction between two kinds of artful word use: one emphasizes joking and license, and the other centers on decorum and formality. The former emphasizes bringing the vernacular Creole into stylized use, in the form of wit, repartee, and directed slander. The latter is a demonstration of the speaker's abilities in standard English, but strictly on the elaborate oratorical level. From this distinction two types of men of words have been posited: the "broad talker" who, using license, brings Creole into stylized form, and the "sweet talker" who emphasizes eloquence and manners through the use of formal standard English.

Artful broad talk may occur at any time, most commonly in public places; it is not considered appropriate in the yard or the house.[9] This is almost certainly because it involves foolishness or nonsense behavior which is regarded as a frontal assault on family values. Therefore it occurs on the streets and at places where the men congregate apart from the women. As a rule, only on special occasions like Carnival or tea meeting is this type of performance carried on in front of women; on such occasions women may involve themselves in the by-play, especially if they are masking in any way. Further, on such occasions there may be a confrontation between such broad-talking performances and ones which call for *sweet* speech-making. In such a case the community is dramatically presenting the widest range of their performance styles.[10]

Both types of speaking are not only useful for individuals seeking special performance status within the community; they also fit into the system of social control. The speech-making is an overt articulation of the ideals of the community. The sweet talker achieves his position of moral authority by not only invoking these ideals but by further embodying them in a formal rhetoric. The broad talker, on the other hand, achieves license to joke because he commonly focuses on behavior of others which is in gross violation of these ideals. His scandalizing therefore acts as something of a moral check on community activities.

But the broad talker does a good deal more than this, especially on ceremonial occasions. He is licensed to play the fool or the clown, and as such he may enact behaviors which are regarded as improper on any other occasion. By playing the fool or by describing the antics of the trickster Anansi, the broad talker therefore enacts something of an anti-

---

[9] The social, linguistic, and ceremonial dimensions of the yard-road distinction are described more fully in my "Social Uses of Space in an Afro-American Community," to be published in the Proceedings of the Conference on Traditional African Architecture.

[10] See my "Patterns of Performance in the British West Indies" in *Afro-American Anthropology: Contemporary Perspectives*, pp. 163–79.

ritual for the community, producing a needed sense of classless liminality, serving as a steam valve for antisocial community impulse. Furthermore, by giving him this power, the community provides itself with a set of persons who will bring a sense of liminality upon the entire participating group, under special circumstances (like Carnival or Christmas revels) permitting everyone to forget themselves and to enter into the licentious occasion. The importance of this lapsing of the social order for its eventual reorganization is crucial to an understanding not only of the festival but also of such licentious ceremonies as wakes.

For both kinds of verbal performers there is, of course, a training procedure which has been evolved by the community. These differ in their particulars from one Afro-American enclave to another, but some general comments can be made of them. Throughout the British West Indies (and to a certain extent in the United States) there is an identification of talking sweet with family occasions, especially ceremonial rites of passage. Certainly talking sweet embodies values which focus on the family as the modal institution in which proper "responsible" behavior is to be learned and carried out. But there is also a feeling that parents or grandparents should be responsible for a child learning how to talk sweet. Therefore, if neither parent knows speeches to teach the child for those occasions in which such talking is necessary, they will send the child to someone in the community who is an expert in such matters, paying that person in some way if there is no close kinship involved. This person will either train the child orally or, more commonly, will write out a lesson which the child will memorize. When the lesson is learned, the child will return, recite the piece, and receive help on his delivery.[11]

Learning to artfully talk broad, however, would not be developed within the family. In fact, there is an identification of dramatic and stylized broad talk with values which run counter to those of the family and which are associated with public life at the crossroads, rum shops, and markets. Artfully talking broad, therefore, is a technique developed apart from the yard and the family environment, as a function of the friendship system on which masculine identity relies. As such, there is a certain degree of antagonism which develops between the values implicit in talking broad and those of the family, because friendships take one (especially the young man) away from the yard. This antagonism is complex and often ambivalent, because friendship values in their most

[11] For another type of apprenticeship in "sweet" performance, see my "Speech Mas' on Tobago," in *Tire Shrinker to Dragster,* ed. Wilson M. Hudson (Austin: Publications of the Texas Folklore Society, no. 34), pp. 125–44. A formalized procedure of speech learning is recorded in "The Training of the Man of Words in Talking Sweet," unpublished manuscript.

important expressions develop from those of the family, especially in the positive valuation and practices of sharing and trust. In a sense, the sharing dimension of friendship actually creates an area of potential conflict because there is just so much to be shared and families and friends are therefore vying for what they regard as their due. But the deepest distrust which family people have of friendships arises because drinking is carried on between friends, and this often means a breakdown of decorum (rum is called "the nonsense-maker" on St. Vincent) and the possibility of any number of assaults on family values.

Nevertheless, even the strongest of family people acknowledge, openly or by implication, that both friendship and license are important for the continuing vitality of the group. This is why such value is placed on "keeping company" and why social pressure is often brought on the shy (West Indian "selfish") person and the loner (West Indian "garden man"), who are distrusted because of their lack of sociability. Often "selfish" is equated with "gettin' on ignorant" and means an inability to take a joke and reply in kind. A joking capacity is therefore one of the key behavioral manifestations of group membership extending beyond the family and the yard. The young, especially the young men, are expected to get out of the yard and the garden and to develop friends, both as a means of broadening the network of people upon whom they can rely in times of need and as a technique for creating some kind of interlock within the community by which the problems which arise within the family may be taken care of.

The most important of these problems are related to the antagonisms arising from the distribution of power and responsibility within the family. Whether the family is headed by a male or a female, peasant West Indian groups find themselves confronted with the problem of maintaining an age-based hierarchy and forcing the young into observing continuing respect for elders. This naturally creates problems with those seeking autonomy—problems which are greatly increased when working opportunities outside the family exist which may provide employment for the young. Whether or not these wage-earning positions exist, there is a strong feeling of shared needs and experiences among male age-mates in these peasant communities, a sharing which results in a mutual and supportive friendship arrangements in the face of the common problems. Since the focus of these problems is on the social institution which most constrains them—the family—there is a tendency toward channeling their performance energies into antifamily forms. In these societies, as discussed above, there already exists a licensed role (or roles) which provides a model of performance for these motives. Consequently, there are a number of traditional broad-talk verbal activities, joking forms which are appropriate to the age-mate relationship,

which serve both as a training ground for future "nonsense" performances and as a device by which friendship can be demonstrated and
the problem focused upon and dispelled. Thus, as in many groups,
joking is an index to the type and closeness of a relationship.

In such situations, learning to be verbally adept is part of the process
of maturation. For the adult performer, the man of words provides a
model of ongoing masculine abilities, especially in a contentious and
economically marginal world. Consequently, there is in the practice of
the rhyming insult found through this culture area an element of masculine role-playing which is one facet of an informal initiation procedure. It is, at the same time, a technique by which young men may voice
their peer-group identification, and in so doing achieve license within
that segment of the community to try out their talents. Just such an
orientation toward this age-mate joking practice has been exhibited by
a number of those commenting on similar practices in Africa, but most
pointedly in Ayoub and Barnett's discussion of "sounding" practices
among whites in the United States: "Sounding, especially Mother-
Sounding, demonstrates the second place given to the mother-son bond
in comparison to the primary place assigned the clique and defines the
in-group's boundaries. . . ."[12] But such verbal practices do much more,
for they permit a trying-on of mature roles in the safety of peer-group
confines while arming the boys with weapons useful in adult life. It
seems useful therefore to compare these word-play practices with those
carried on by adults, especially those of the age-grade immediately
above them.

III

The relationship between adolescent and adult practices is clear in most
cases because of the different subjects and formulas used to channel
joking aggressiveness. Thus, in the West Indian community in Panama,
the most common subject of adolescent rhyming shares adult joking's
concern with attributing homosexuality to the other (a focus probably
borrowed from Latin American neighbors), while reference to the
other's mother except to start a fight is prohibited for the most part.

On the other hand, rhyming in Plymouth, Tobago, a fishing community, permits this focus on the maternal figure but severely restricts the
practice—a focus which is shared with the numerous songs, ring-play,
and verbal routines in Tobagonian Bongo (wake), as performed by
adults in the community. A few of the most common wake dance-songs
are given to indicate the intensity and licentious playfulness of this
focus:

[12] Millicent R. Ayoub and Stephen A. Barnett, "Ritualized Verbal Insult in
White School Culture," *Journal of American Folklore* 78 (1965): 343.

An' de bull take 'e pizzle an' he make his mama whistle,
De bull, de bull, de bull jump 'e mama.[13]
And de bull jump Elita[14] in a open savannah.
De bull, de bull, de bull in de Savannah.

An' de bull, de bull, de bull jumped 'e mother.
De bull, de bull, de bull jump 'e mama.

An' de bull take a whistle and everybody whistle,
De bull, de bull, de bull jump 'e mama.

An' de bull down Carrerra with some peas and cassava,
De bull, de bull, de bull in de savannah.

An' de bull jumped 'e mama and he bring forth a heifer,
De bull, de bull, de bull jump 'e mama.

An' de bull jump 'e sister in a open savannah,
De bull, de bull, de bull jump 'e sister.

An' de bull in de savannah, he make your sister partner,
De bull, de bull, de bull in de savannah.

An' de bull take de pizzle an' 'e make your sister whistle,
De bull, de bull, de bull jump 'e mama.

(*ad-lib*)

Rover dover, roll body over,
Pam palam, knock 'em palam.
T'row way me breakfast an' gi' me de moon-a
Pam palam, knock 'em palam.

A little, little woman carry a big, big moon-a
Pam palam, knock 'em palam.
A big fat woman carry a small, small moon-a
Pam palam, knock 'em palam.

Them small, small woman, bottle neck moon-a,
Pam palam, knock 'em palam.
Them big, big, woman got a small, small moon-a
Pam palam, knock 'em palam.

Dem bottle neck moon got lard at the corner,
Pam palam, knock 'em palam.
Big fat woman serve like a sugar,
Pam palam, knock 'em palam.

But the small, small woman hard like a rock stone,
Pam palam, knock 'em palam.

[13] The refrain is sung with many variations by the group. I give here only the ones that come out most clearly on the tape.
[14] Any girl's name will do, preferably that of someone's mother or sister outside the dance, used to pick up their attention.

T'row way me breakfast and gi' me de moon-a,
Pam palam, knock 'em palam.

If you t'ink man lie you can ask Contractor [a locally famous woman's man]
Pam palam, knock 'em palam.
If you t'ink is a lie, you can ask a Gardiner [another man in the crowd, *not* known for his prowess].

This fascination with incest, female genitalia, and the acceptance element of the feminine principle is exhibited in a number of other ways during Bongo. One example which stands out in my memory was a fifteen-minute exercise in metaphor in which a woman's sexual parts were compared to a water well, the major point being the pleasures attendant upon digging and finding water.

The practice of adolescent rhyming is more easily understood in light of these adult performance pieces. For purposes of comparison on the content level, I report here one ritual argument which I heard in November, 1965, in a group of six male age-mates, all ages fourteen and fifteen. Each rhyme was punctuated with punching motions and foot-shiftings. Each rhyme was followed by hilarity and a fight to see who would give the next, so that the underlying impersonality of the invective was even more pronounced than if only two were trading insults. (This may have occurred because of my presence and the fact that I was recording their contest with a promise of playing it back. They indicated that this often happened when first assailants ran out of ready rhymes.)

1. Ten pound iron, ten pound steel.
   Your mother' vagina is like a steering wheel.
2. I put your mother to back o' train.
   When she come back she porky strain.
3. Christmas comes but once a year.
   I fuck your mother in a rocking chair.
4. Ten crapaud [inedible frogs] was in a pan;
   The bigger one was your mother' man.
5. If aeroplane was not flying in the air,
   Your mother' cyat wouldn't get no hair.
6. If snake was not crawlin' on the ground [pronounced *grung*]
   Your mother' cyat would not get no tongue.
7. Beep bop, what is that?
   A tractor falling a tree in your mother' cyat.
8. Beep bop, what is that?
   Thunder roll in your mother' cyat.
9. Tee-lee-lee tee-lee-lee, what is that?
   A tractor stick in your mother' cyat.
10. Voo, voo, what is that?
    A blue fly worrying your mother' cyat.

11. Your mother fucking an old pan,
    and bring fort' Dan.
12. A for apple, B for bat.
    Your mother' cyat like alphabet.
13. Me and your mother in a pork barrel,
    And every word a give she porky quarrel [i.e., made noise].
14. Me and your mother was digging potato.
    Spy under she and saw Little Tobago.
15. Sixty second, one minute,
    Sixty minute, one hour.
    Twenty-four hour, one day,
    I fucked your mother on Courland Bay [Plymouth's main beach].
16. A little boy with a cocky suit
    Fuck your mother for a bowl of soup.
17. Me and your mother was rolling roti [a curry dish introduced by East
    Indians];
    I drop the roti and take she porky.
18. I put your mother on a electric wire,
    And every word I give she, porky send fire.
19. I put your mother on a bay leaf,
    And every word I give she was a baby free.
20. I eat the meat and I t'row away the bone.
    Your mother' cat like a saxophone.
21. Forty degrees, the greasy the pole.
    That was the depth of your mother' porky hole.
22. Three hundred and sixty-six days, one leap year.
    I fucked your mother in a rocking chair.
23. Me and your mother was two friend.
    I fucked your mother and bring forth Glen [the name of one of the
    boys].
24. I fucked your mother on a telephone wire,
    and every jerk was a blaze of fire.
25. Me and your mother was cooking rice,
    And she kill she cat and frighten Chris' [she burnt her vagina and
    hollered].
26. Up into a cherry tree,
    Who should come but little me.
    I held the trunk with both my hand'
    And I fuck your mother in a frying pan.
27. Ding dong bell
    Pussy in the well.
    Your mother' pussy like a conk shell.

The rhymes, however, cannot be fully understood only in terms of
content features. Rhyming is just one of many contest performances
which until recently were very common in Tobagonian festivities, especially Carnival. In another forum I have described one of these tradi-

tions, "Speech Mas'," and attempted to explain why it has begun to disappear.[15]

In the past there have been two types of performances which have been fostered by the community (in line with practices throughout Trinidad and Tobago): performances by the group as a whole or by individuals within the group, and performances by individuals addressed to the group, generally while engaged in competition with other individuals. The primary occasions for these are at Bongo wakes, Carnival, and on St. Peter's Day (June 29), which is a special event for Plymouth; other times are christenings, Emancipation Day, and Christmas. All of these occasions present opportunities for both types of performances. Carnival, for instance, commonly calls for the town to get together for some costume mas', a group enterprise in which a theme of decoration is agreed upon and many dress themselves in line with the theme. Then, on Carnival Tuesday, the entire mas' along with the local steel band goes to Scarborough to "jump up" together—to show off, in a sense, their community solidarity and strength. A great deal of time and money is expended on this enterprise—so much so that in a bad fishing season such as 1965–66 they didn't have the resources or spirit to put together a mas'.

In the past, Carnival has also offered an opportunity for the individual performer to have his day. There were a number of traditional ways in which the individual could dress and perform in competition with other such performers. One of these was the "Caiso Mas'" (the ancestor of calypso) groups led by a "chantwell," a man gifted not only in writing songs but in extemporizing on any given subject. Another such competition was "Speech Mas'," which involved the composition of boasting and deprecatory speeches of inflated rhetoric and pungent invective. A further activity of this sort was the well-known *kalinda* stick-fight dance.

Recently in Plymouth these competitive exercises are being rejected by the younger members of the community and are dying. The young men still admire the good competitors, but not enough to emulate them. The one remaining chantwell in Plymouth no longer performs at Carnival, and the one Speech Mas' performer comes from another community and must go to still another village to find others to form a troupe. It is difficult to understand why this is happening, but one possible explanation is that such competitive expression is no longer as highly valued as the more cooperative performance or the fully solo activity which takes the calypsonian off the street and places him on a stage.

This retreat from competitive expression is seen in the need for excuses and explanations which is felt by competitive performers. They

[15] Abrahams, "Speech Mas' on Tobago," in *Tire Shrinker to Dragster*, pp. 125–44.

self-consciously insist that they are involved in a harmless game of words, though the contests of the speeches, songs, and stick fights are totally aggressive and destructive in tendency. As one Plymouth member of the Speech Mas', Duncan "Bootsbrush" Osmond, observes:

> Speeching is only a play, man. You does have some who doesn't play it that way though. Now like that Speech Band, they coming up and you have your band at the square [in Scarborough, capital of Tobago]. . . . They cannot pass the road without they don't answer [your challenge] . . . you will make an arrangement with them now for you to say two or three speech to each man. And then when you finish you will all shake hand and pass. Say, "Shake hand and pass." If a man want to fight, you say, "Man, go on and pass and go if you come to fight."

The same rationale has been used in rhyming sessions among adolescents. Those who play today insist that a nonviolence pact must be made before beginning: "We make an agreement that we can rhyme on your mother. Then we start. I say, 'Go and rhyme.' He might say, 'O.K.' or something like that. Then he first will start. The person who first to ask to rhyme, he won't give a rhyme first in case they break the arrangement."[16]

Yet the idea is clearly not to play but to hurt as much as possible, to "come back with a hurtful one to make more vex; something like when two persons cursing." The rationale of play arises because the value of this invective contest has been challenged and is to an extent undermined. This defensiveness of the contest seems to be a recent phenomenon, judging by the reminiscences of men in Plymouth.

Whether this development is an indication that rhyming will go the same way as Speech Band and Caiso Mas' is unclear. More important is to understand that this self-conscious reaction does not mean a rejection of all the licentious and joking traditions that surround these practices. Rhyming is just one technique of exhibiting verbal wit and directing it toward persons outside one's own peer group. There are numerous other such traditions, and some of these provide the primary entertainment forms and themes for adolescents. Most important in this regard are a series of short legendary jokes and songs about local happenings, especially ogre-fool figures. These compositions are very much in the scandal-piece tradition, for they focus on activity regarded as foolish and inappropriate. Any kind of action which elicits laughter because it is a disruption of the expectations of the group may become the subject of such scandal-pieces among the boys. For instance, when a local boy, Egbert, found a ring in the road, he wore it on his penis and made an exhibition himself. His father then compounded the indiscre-

[16] From a recorded interview with Daniel Dumas, 15, Plymouth, Tobago, March, 1966, who also aided me in gathering the rhyme texts.

tion by giving him a public beating for it, and so the boy sang this song:

> Egbert, he busting [he was so happy]
> An' he t'ought he get a ring,
> But Uncle Darnell
> Pitch 'e big wood on him.

Another such song sung by the young is not only a scandal-piece but involves many of the same motives as rhyming. It is a formulaic composition into which can be fit the names of any couple who have recently been caught at illicit love-making. Then, however, this song sometimes is performed as a rhyming boast in which the singer becomes the fornicator.

> People, if I hear de fix
> Charlie eat up Miss Vaughnie' chicks
> People, if I hear de fix
> Charlie eat up Miss Vaughnie' chicks.
> Den I [or 'e] gi' she one
> She started to run.
> When I gi' she two
> She buckle she shoe.
> When I gi' she three
> She cut down tree.
> When I gi' she four
> She break down door.
> When I gi' she five
> Now I started to drive.
> When I gi' she six
> She break up sticks.
> When I gi' she seven
> She t'ink she was in heaven.
> When I gi' she eight
> She lay down 'traight.
> And I gi' she nine
> She started to whine.
> When I gi' she ten
> Den my cock ben'.

As with rhyming, these stories are similar in content and focus to some of the song games performed at Bongo by adults. In the case of the Bongo pieces, however, it is assumed that everyone knows the story and therefore there are many little details given, but not the narrative part of the story. Here, for instance, is the saga of Jean-Louis from Lescoteau [lə-ki-to] who made a determined pass at a young girl who promptly ran away and was said to bawl out this song:

> You know Mr. Jean-Louis
> Tim bam.
> Come out a Lescoteau

Tim bam.
You know wha' he hold me for?
Tim bam.
You know Mr. Jean-Louis
Tim bam.
He hold me for pom-pom soir,
Tim bam.
He hold me for pom-pom soir,
Tim bam.
He know me a very long
Tim bam.
You never hear a trus' before,
Tim bam.
Well you know Mr. Jean-Louis
Tim bam.
He come up from Lescoteau,
Tim bam.
He born in Tobago,
Tim bam.
He ain' never call me yet.
              (*ad lib*)

Rhyming on Tobago, then, is one of a number of traditional devices by which adolescents group themselves on an age-grade basis and learn how to perform while joking upon their shared problems and perspectives. Though one of these problems certainly is in defining their masculinity—and this is attempted, in part, by the combination of boast and taunt in rhyming—this fascinated focus on female symbols is not the only means they have of asserting this generational unity and independence from the constrictions of the extended family. License is given them to focus on the generational split as well as the sexual one, and to impute that older members of the community are as improperly schooled in social ways as they are accused of being—that "rudeness" is a vice not just characteristic of young men.

IV

On Nevis, in the British Leeward Islands, *rhyming* is also practiced, for many of the same reasons. But here the boys rely almost entirely upon the scandal-piece tradition, or they use the closely related techniques of the taunt. As on Tobago, the focus of their joking is on the feminine and on older people, but the rhymes never use the strategy of impersonality in order to make their point. Rather, the rhymes are directed at individuals, usually making reference to the names of those present. These are primarily formulaic rhymes in which virtually any name may be inserted. There are two exceptions: those which simply make fun of a class of outsiders—young girls, older men—or those which make specific reference to an item of gossip. Here is a series of rhymes as performed by a group of fourteen- and fifteen-year-old Nevisian males during the summer of 1962. The idea, as it was explained, was usually to attack some close relation or friend of one boy, to which he might or might not make a bantering reply. Once the rhyming begins, there is apparently license for any rhyme to be performed, whether it happens to be directed at someone's familiars or not. Thus, later in the series, there are a few rhymes which are scandal-pieces on people who live elsewhere.

> Just for sake of a box of matches,
> Rose can't put in common patches.
>> [Rose, the sister of one of the boys, doesn't even
>> know how to sew, something which all girls would
>> learn.]

> Just for the sake of a banana,
> Jim knocked Sam from corner to corner.

> Twenty boobies on a rock
> Sonny catch them by the flock.
> Bobs put them in the pot
> And Mirie eat them piping hot.
>> [The idea of eating boobies is ridiculous; the rhyme
>> also makes fun, on occasion, of a boy and girl who
>> are courting.]

> The sweetest pumpkin ever born
> Mirie turn some [mix and fry] in the corn;
> The pumpkin was so sweet
> It knocked out three of Audrey's front teeth.

> I went to Dolly' house last night
> To tell you the truth I didn't sleep all right.
> I got up in the night to make my pee,
> I found bug all over biting me.
> Bug is a t'ing don't have any respect
> It walks from my chin to the back of my neck.
> I bawl, I bawl,
> For the dogs, fleas and all.

> I went down to Booby Island [small rocky island between Nevis
>>   and St. Kitts]
> I never went to stay.
> I rest my hand on Dinah[17]
> And Dinah went away.

---

[17] Any girl's name may fit here; sometimes the name of someone's mother is given here, but more often the name of a neighbor girl or sister or girlfriend of one of the others. The humor resides most in simply mentioning someone's name in a scandalous context.

Just for the sake of a root of cassava,
That's why some of those young girls don't know their
    pickny' [baby's] father.

Young bee meck honey,
Old bee meck comb.
Those young girls get their bellies
Because they won't stay home.

I went up the lane,
I met the parson kissing Jane.
He gave me a shilling not to tell,
An' that's why me suit fit me so well.

When I was young and in my prime,
I used to jump around those young girls no less and a time
Now I am old and feeble,
They call me "Dry Sugar Weeble" [weevil].

Just for the sake of Mr. Kelly's bell
That's why Halstead and Berdicere kisses so well.
    [Mr. Kelly was a teacher at a local school. The
    other two were "friending."]

Raccoon was a curious man,
He never walked till dark.
The only thing could disturb his heart
Is when he hear old bringle dog bark.
    [Raccoon was a "selfish" man who lived alone, had never
    a wife, and who was constantly chasing dogs.]

Penny ha' penny woman
Sit down on a pistol.
Pistol leggo boom boom
Knock off Miss Wallace hairy poom poom.

Miss Pemberton has a landing [porch, balcony]
The landing work with spring.
The wind blow her petticoat
And then you see her magazine [genitalia].

Miss Budgeon has a pepper tree,
Jennifer hang she panty dey;
When the pepper tree begin to bear
It burn off all of Jennifer' pussy hair.
    [Any mother and daughter may be inserted here, but
    especially those who have recently been observed fighting.]

The longer I live, the more I hear.
Bullwiss bite off Rose Pig ear.
    [They were brother and sister; biting ears is a common
    practice in fights.]

When Mr. Clark falls asleep
George Baker run with the sheep
[A court case the previous year].

As in Tobago, there is a great similarity between these adolescent rhymes and adult entertainments here, both in content and form. In fact, there are a number of the same rhymes which are to be found both among adolescents and adults, though in the case of the latter, they are only used as part of the licentious clowning performances found (at least until recently) in certain Christmas sports and tea meetings. In their adult uses, the rhymes are commonly associated with songs in some way, either as introduction or as providing the text. There are a number of different Christmas troupes who perform ribald and scandalous inventions, each involving a portrayal in broad comic terms of some power figure. Politicians, kings and queens, preachers and schoolteachers, landlords and overseers—none are spared. One of these groups, performing what is called Nigger Business, takes a piece of scandal which has come to their notice; they reenact it, while also performing a song with veiled references to the socially disapproved doings. This group first plays in the yard of the miscreants, to see if they can exact a bribe; but even if they are able to, there is no guarantee that the show will not be given in other yards as well.

Groups like Saguas or Buzzards or Schoolchildren do not have such a unity to their performance; rather, they have a series of comic routines which comment on human nature or on recent noteworthy events heard through gossip. It is this type of group which most performs rhymes and songs closely related to those of the adolescent boys.

The idea of the Sagua group, for instance, is for a group to dress up in broadly rendered cutaways and other formal wear and to go from yard to yard alternating songs and dances with rhymed speeches. These rhymes are often close to those of adolescents, only they are performed with a great deal more liberty and are more often pointed to an item of scandal. Here are some of the songs and speeches performed by a group of Saguas from the community of Brown Hill.

> *Sung:*
> Monday morning, break a day,
> When the old folks got me goin'.
> Saturday night when the sun goes down
> All those young girls are mine.
> (*Repeat ad-lib.*)
>
> *Spoken:*
> Here we are, the higher classes,
> Of all the pie asses,

Straight from Missy Wallace, Limited and Company
[a clothing store in St. Kitts].

Spoken:
I've done got me business organized and planned.
Dis year when de next boat land [i.e., gets wrecked, as
    happened recently]
Luther got 'e paddle ready,
Charles Ward got he saw.
Shorty got 'e pickaxe,
And me, Steel, got me clawhammer
[naming members of the community].

Spoken:
One Monday morning, I went up the lane.
I met the parson fixing a Jane.
He shove me a six pence, told me not to tell.
That's why me sagua coat fit me so well.

Sung:
Dollars again, dollars again,
I put me hands on dollars again. . . .
(*Repeat ad-lib*)

Spoken:
Out of the hollow tree I came,
Calabash is my name.
So long me got me long hungry gut full,
Calabash still remain.

Spoken:
Hark, hark, the dogs do bark,
Beggars are coming to town.
Some give them white bread
Some give them brown.
But I just give them a big cut-ass
And send them out of town.

Spoken:
By golly, you that man Mr. Clifton from Churchground?
He motor bike gi'en him one fall, land him 'pon ground.
So when get up he say, "That won't be all.
I goin' to collect sufficient money and buy Mr. Abbott'
    Vauxhall."

Similar alternations of speeches, including rhymes and songs, occur
in a number of other licentious Christmas sports, such as the following routines from Schoolchildren. Here the antisocial content is more
pointed.

The setting is a Sunday school, and the butts of the major part of the
jokes are specific local Sunday school teachers who are here scored for

their pomposity and their mock erudition. The characters are dressed up as scholars, with black robe and mortar board, and they invariably carry a very large book which they can hardly handle but to which they constantly refer with great mock solemnity. The other characters are dressed as little children or, in the case of Robin, in motley. (He is the one who scares all of the bystanders as the group goes from yard to yard—and thus stands in the same position as the Devil does in many other groups, or Father Christmas in the St. George Play).[18] These scenes can go in any sequence, and are more or less ad-libbed. Between each scene, the fife and drum group play and everyone dances, including members of the audience. Robin tries to scare some of the children.

ROBIN: Now here we are, Robin speaking. Yeah!
Christmas come but once a year, yeah heh!
When 'e come, it bring good cheer (I'm glad, you know),
All what I see happnin' this year
Is the minister dem a breed off all de young girls dat come in here.
(*Music and dancing.*)
WARD: I'm Godfrey Ward speaking, but I would not like to anything before the captain reaching, which is Samuel Daniel.
(*Music and dancing.*)
WARD: Hello!
DANIEL: Hello, man.
WARD: A book here.
DANIEL: I ready to meet you [i.e., to contest to see who knows the Bible better].
WARD: To your exclusion.
DANIEL: Damned confusion.
(*Music and dancing.*)
WARD: Madam, come inside here.
BRADSHAW (*man dressed as woman*): Inside?
WARD: Inside. All you all time out to make confusion [mispronunciation of confession].
BRADSHAW (*acting seductive*): Fix me good.
WARD: Is all right?
BRADSHAW: Sure.
WARD: Dat right? (*He goes up next to her.*)
BRADSHAW: Is me, Miss Bradshaw [Bradshaw is the name of the then labor leader, now head of government in St. Kitts].
(*Music and dancing.*)
DANIEL: Well, den, I want fifty thousand men take up a me book of a dictionary. Well yes, fifty thousand men to lif' de book of the dictionary. Tha's right. So now I look [leafing through book] from the fif' to de six of June, never too late and never too soon, from six o'clock in

18 For a reporting, see my "A St. George Mumming in the British West Indies," *Folklore* 79 (1968): 176–201.

the afternoon. Blessed assurance after three. One, two, three.

Song (*to the tune of hymn "This Is My Story, This is My Song"*):

Send them a pasha [pasture], dey wouldn't go.
Take up my cat whip and leggo one blow.
Well dem dey reverse back, dey wouldn't go.
Dem dey reverse back, well-a chooga pooh-pooh
  [Let them have it with whip, acted out, scaring children in audience].
Going on a mountain, no walk with no bread.
I going to use potato, dasheen and tania head [types of taro root]
Worser me boy we, de dasheen dems sprout.
I wouldn't buy no tania head to scratch out me mout'
  [tanias, unless cooked properly, will scratch].

DANIEL: Now look in the back of the hymnbook for them, boy.
Four-nine-nine.

ALL: Four-nine-nine.

DANIEL: Last verse, "We Going on Mountain" after three; One, two, three.

(*Repeat "Going on the Mountain"*)

. . . .

WARD: Boys, open your hymn book. Four-nine-two.

ALL: Four-nine-two.

WARD: Las' time I speakin' to you; not again. I hope everyt'ing will come true. You heard me? De las' time we sang a proper program:

My sister had a penny pork [a penny's worth of pork, but also the slang for female genitalia].
She bind them wid a twine.
She po'k 'em in a doving pot [cook pot]
An' make my water shine. [The pun here is on pot water, which will shine with fat when pork is put into it, and semen, which is referred to as water.]

The basis of the joking humor here is on presenting nonsense as if it were sense, of putting together dialogue and song in a continuous fashion but without the usual logic which determines continuities. Thus the laughter is directed at the nonsensical aspects of these characters. But this is just one dimension of the occasion's license, for the high are made low, and the virtuous revealed as lecherous and dishonest charlatans. The conventions of this kind of humor turn on presenting discontinuities, and this is the most common technique of the songs and rhymes. Laughter arises because of the introduction of the unexpected, though in this setting such introductions are really expected (even if their content is not known in advance). The mock hymn and the rhymes all rely upon the disruption of expectations derived from the usual uses of these specific items (the hymn, the "Christmas comes but once a year" rhyme) to elicit laughter and to add to the irreverent tone. In such a setting, however, the minute such a device is introduced into the performance, an expectation of disruption arises on the part of the audience. This is also true of the adolescent rhymes, which trade both on such humorous conventions and their expectations, and the discontinuities associated with openly attacking others in the protected and licensed confines of palship groupings.

Significantly, the focus of the nonsense is on the symbols of the "sensible" world: the school and the church. The use of broad talk to confound talking sweet is thus all the more pointed, for nothing represents family-based ideals more fully than teacher and preacher, their books, and their variety of oratorical speech. In these mock speeches, then, especially in schoolchildren, we witness a direct (but licensed) confrontation between family ideals and friendship values in which the latter, for the moment, win the day.

V

The importance of license is that it permits a restructuring of the world in terms of whatever logic asserts itself. That is, there is a recognized community order of things, actions, and especially interactions. This order has a deeply felt sense of logic to it, simply because it is ordered and provides comfort and control to those who share in this world view. But everyone at some time feels contradictions or tensions arising from within or without the system. One way of handling this shared problem is for the community to get together ceremonially and reenact or recite in its most basic terms the condition and the genesis of the world's order. Another way is to provide license to members of the community to impose a new sense of order to the world, an order which is so different from that of the everyday that it produces laughter through manipulating discontinuities and contrasts. Masking is, of course, one of the most extreme examples of this effect, because it permits an overturning of the usual social order and the imposition of new status and power arrangements based upon assumed roles.

Joking is, in many ways, like masking because of its reorganization of the social order on the basis of different logics. But joking often establishes continuities on only a verbal level, through the use of puns and other non sequitur juxtapositions. This is essentially what produces the response to children and adolescent rhymes on both Nevis and Tobago. Further, in both traditions, the potentially disruptive implications of the non sequitur and anti-taboo arguments are rendered harmless by insisting that what is transpiring is only play (and verbal play at that), and that there has been a tying together of the most discontinuous things by means of the most elementary restricted verbal formulas.

This perspective is an extension of Freud's thesis that wit exists as an arbitrary order which permits a freeing of otherwise restrained motives. Or, as Mary Douglas expressed it recently,

> A joke is a play upon form. It brings into relation disparate elements in such a way that one accepted pattern is challenged by the appearance of another which in some way was hidden in the first . . . any recognizable joke falls into this joke pattern which needs two elements, the juxtaposition of a control against that which is being controlled, this juxtaposition of being such that the latter triumphs . . . a successful subversion of one form by another completes or ends the joke for it changes the balance of power. . . . The joke merely affords opportunity for realizing that an accepted pattern has no necessity. Its excitement lies in the suggestion that any particular ordering of experience may be arbitrary and subjective. It is frivolous in that it produces no real alternative, only an exhilarating sense of freedom from form in general.[19]

There is no joking, then, unless there is an order which can be overturned or at least challenged by the establishment of new continuities and relationships. But simply because a joke relies upon this previous social order indicates that it acts in response to certain pressures already existing within that order, tensions which are shared by the group who participate in the joking.

Joking thus helps give the community the feeling that such situations are under control. But looking at joking from a performance-centered perspective, the joke seizes on such subjects because they already have tremendous attention-potential due to their residence in the crucial areas. From this point of view, joking induces a high affect participative response on the part of all involved, because joking generally embodies a potential embarrassment—but in such a context of social and verbal control that relief rather than embarrassment occurs. Laughter arises in response to the failure of expectations in a patterned situation, but joking occurs only when there has been an assent already given to articulating this failure, this abrogation of the usual. Joking capitalizes on the release of energies attendant on embarrassments, but it provides a useful channel for these energies by supplying a special social relationship and a conventional verbal form. Joking uses embarrassments and other social dislocations, but it puts the disruptions in a controlled form.

Social anthropologists argue that joking is essentially akin to anti-ritual, since ritual underlines and reenacts social order and cosmology, while joking and clowning challenge this for the purpose of channeling off anti-social tendencies. However, E. R. Leach has suggested that there is an intimate structural relation between rite and anti-rite masking, simply speaking in regard to their occurrence: "They are in practice

---

[19] Mary Douglas, "The Social Control of Cognition: Some Factors in Joke Perception," *Man* (1968): 365.

closely associated. A rite which starts with a formality (e.g., a wedding) is likely to end in masquerade; a rite which starts with masquerade (e.g., New Year's Eve, Carnival) is likely to end in formality."[20]

Further, as Victor Turner has effectively argued, it is necessary to achieve a "liminal" state for the formal ritual to be effective.[21] This seems equally true of anti-rituals. Liminality is the acceptance, by the group and especially by the participants, of a sense of community in which social distinctions are rejected in favor of a classless state commonly symbolized by the assumption of symbolic garb and mien of the lowest social creatures. Costuming during festivals of this sort often jokes in the same way, bringing together unusual combinations of materials and colors; this is, in fact, the original meaning of "motley." Joking is similar in almost every sense, given its antisocial thrust and its totally participative strategy in which the joking group coheres on an egalitarian basis.

Joking arises, at least among adolescents, as a ritualistic type of behavior in which hierarchical order is challenged, and something like liminality occurs in which it becomes possible (in fact necessary) to assert a new order on an age-grade basis. Thus the conventions of joking are crucial not only because they provide a sense of artificial ordering (of words) in the face of disorder (of concepts or themes), but because the conventions are regarded as the insignia of the age group and their performance is therefore a statement of group solidarity in the face of those who must be considered the common enemy, the actors of hierarchically established roles within the community. This means that such jokes can be looked to as indications of where the adolescent group sees constraint asserting itself socially. But it does not mean that these jokes focus on *all,* or even on the most important, of these problems. As I have tried to show, adolescents on Tobago and Nevis are given the cues to what subjects may be discussed licentiously in the content of the songs and rhymes and stories which arise during adult ceremonies of license. Looked on in this way, the declaration of groupness and independence from the social hierarchy is a very limited one, for the independent community move, seen in terms of the modal life-history of group members, is also a preparation for adult activities. This is especially evident in communities like those on Nevis and Tobago in which the verbal abilities learned by pursuing these joking forms can provide a means of proclaiming the social norms of the community in the face of disruption, while at the same time one develops the verbal abilities by which he may achieve status in young adult life.

[20] E. R. Leach, *Rethinking Anthropology* (London: Athlone Press, 1961), pp. 135–36.
[21] Victor Turner, *The Ritual Process* (Chicago: Aldine, 1969).

The success of this system depends on the casting off of these age-mate ways after a certain period, and the using of these talents for the entertainment of the entire community. On many of the West Indian islands, however, there are indications that to do so would be an act of incorporation into an extended-family system which the young are not willing to go through. Because of the occasional availability of wage-earning employment on the island, or the possibility of emigration to places where such jobs are to be found, there has been a weakening of the hold which the family may exert on the young. Consequently, this kind of grouping on an age-grade basis tends to continue, leading to the older community members' feeling that the system is falling apart, a situation which they consequently attribute to the constant rudeness on the part of the young. Essentially this indictment must be read not as a rejection of youthful license, which is part of the system, but as a charge that the young do not understand the proper occasions on which license is permitted. Joking, it would seem, has spilled over from the joking relationship into other performances and communications, and this must be read by those who have lived with the system as a social disruption.

The elaboration of this kind of rude joking behavior, further, is paralleled to a certain degree with some loss of respect for other parts of the speaking repertoire—specifically, the ceremonial "sweet" speech-making. Significantly, this kind of ceremony generally discusses overtly the most important features of household values in which the aged (and the ancestors) are given great respect. Thus, in a sense, this gravitation is away from an acceptance of the English language system and is part of a drift away from an age-based and hierarchical, extended-family structure. This is not to argue that this is the only explanation of why broad-talk Creole has persisted, in spite of the obvious opportunities for employment and mobility accruing to those who learn standard English. It is simply to urge that we must more fully understand the relationship between speech acts and events, the varieties used by different segments of the community and the social order which are articulated through the interactions among and between these segments. In the British West Indies and the United States we are witnessing a virtual takeover of crucial areas of discourse by the young and the rude. They are utilizing their licentious performance techniques now in interactions that are outside the peer group, and they are finding it an extremely useful aggressive device. Unless we understand the process by which this joking is learned and what purpose it fulfills in the learning group, we cannot hope to comprehend some of the most important social forces intruding themselves on the consciousness of the middle-class world. To bring about this understanding we will have to recognize that our embarrassments arising from this aggressive behavior are not the creation of people operating without any system of manners, but are rather the results of conscious verbal manipulations—and creative ones at that.[22]

[22] The University of Texas Research Institute, the John Simon Guggenheim Foundation, and the National Institute of Mental Health MH-15706-01 ("Stereotype and Prejudice Maintenance") all helped enable me to gather data for this article.

■ Toward an ethnography of black American speech behavior

THOMAS KOCHMAN

For a Note on the Author, see p. 160.

In the black idiom of Chicago and elsewhere, there are several words that refer to talking: "rapping," "shucking," "jiving," "running it down," "gripping," "copping a plea," "signifying," and "sounding." Led by the assumption that these terms, as used by the speakers, referred to different kinds of verbal behavior, this writer has attempted to discover which features of form, style, and function distinguish one type of talk from the other. In this pursuit, I would hope to be able to identify the variable threads of the communication situation—speaker, setting and audience—and how they influence the use of language within the social context of the black community. I also expect that some light would be shed on the black perspective behind a speech event, on those orientating values and attitudes of the speaker that cause him to behave or perform in one way as opposed to another.

The guidelines and descriptive framework for the type of approach used here have been articulated most ably by Hymes in his introduction to *The Ethnography of Communication,* from which I quote:

> In short, "ethnography of communication" implies two characteristics that an adequate approach to the problems of language which engage anthropologists must have. Firstly, such an approach cannot simply take results from linguistics, psychology, sociology, ethnology, as given, and seek to correlate them, however partially useful such work is. It must call attention to the need for fresh kinds of data, to the need to investigate directly the use of language in contexts of situation so as to discern patterns proper to speech activity, patterns which escape separate studies of grammar, of personality, of religion, of kinship and the like, each abstracting from the patterning of speech activity as such into some other frame of reference. Secondly, such an approach cannot take linguistic form, a given code, or speech itself, as frame of reference. It must take as context a community, investigating its communicative habits as a whole, so that any given use of channel and code takes its place as but part of the resources upon which the members of the community draw.
>
> It is not that linguistics does not have a vital role. Well analyzed linguistic materials are indispensable, and the logic of linguistic methodology

is a principal influence in the ethnographic perspective of the approach. It is rather that it is not linguistics, but ethnography—not language, but communication—which must provide the frame of reference within which the place of language in culture and society is to be described.[1]

The following description and analysis is developed from information supplied mainly by blacks living within the inner city of Chicago. Their knowledge of the above terms, their ability to recognize and categorize the language behavior of others (e.g., "Man, stop shucking!"), and on occasion to give examples themselves, established them as reliable informants. Although a general attempt has been made here to illustrate the different types of language behavior from field sources, I have had, on occasion, to rely on published material to provide better examples, such as the writings of Malcolm X, Robert Conot, Iceberg Slim, and others. Each example cited from these authors, however, is regarded as authentic by my informants. In my own attempts at classification and analysis I have sought confirmation from the same group.

"Rapping," while used synonymously to mean ordinary conversation, is distinctively a fluent and lively way of talking which is always characterized by a high degree of personal style. To one's peer group, rapping may be descriptive of narration, a colorful rundown of some past event. A recorded example of this type of rap follows, an answer from a Chicago gang member to a youth worker who asked how his group became organized.

> Now I'm goin tell you how the jive really started. I'm goin tell you how the club got this big. 'Bout 1956 there used to be a time when the Jackson Park show was open and the Stony show was open. Sixty-six street, Jeff, Gene, all of 'em, little bitty dudes, little bitty. . . . Gene wasn't with 'em then. Gene was cribbin [living] over here. Jeff, all of 'em, real little bitty dudes, you dig? All of us were little.
>
> Sixty-six [the gang on Sixty-sixth Street], they wouldn't allow us in the Jackson Park show. That was when the parky [?] was headin it. Everybody say, If we want to go to the show, we go! One day, who was it? Carl Robinson. He went up to the show . . . and Jeff fired on him. He came back and all this was swelled up 'bout yay big, you know. He come back over to the hood [neighborhood]. He told [name unclear] and them dudes went up there. That was when mostly all the main Sixty-six boys was over here like Bett Riley. All of 'em was over here. People that quit gang-bangin [fighting, especially as a group], Marvell Gates, people like that.
>
> They went on up there, John, Roy and Skeeter went in there. And they start humbuggin [fighting] in there. That's how it all started. Sixty-six found out they couldn't beat us, at *that* time. They couldn't *whup*

[1] John J. Gumperz and Dell Hymes, eds., *The Ethnography of Communication,* special publication of *American Anthropologist* 66, no. 6, pt. 2, pp. 2ff.

seven-0 [70]. Am I right Leroy? You was cribbin over here then. Am I right? We were dynamite! Used to be a time, you ain't have a passport, Man, you couldn't walk through here. And if didn't nobody know you it was worse than that. . . .

Rapping to a woman is a colorful way of "asking for some pussy." "One needs to throw a lively rap when he is 'putting the make' on a broad."[2]

According to one informant the woman is usually someone he had seen or just met, who looks good, and who might be willing to have sexual intercourse with him. My informant remarked that the term would not be descriptive of talk between a couple "who have had a relationship over any length of time." Rapping, then, is used by the speaker at the beginning of a relationship to create a favorable impression and be persuasive at the same time. The man who has the reputation for excelling at this is the "pimp," or "mack man." Both terms describe a person of considerable status in the street hierarchy, who, by his lively and persuasive rapping ("macking" is also used in this context), has acquired a stable of girls to hustle for him and give him money. For most street men and many teenagers he is the model whom they try to emulate. Thus, within the community you have a pimp walk, pimp-style boots and clothes, and perhaps most of all "pimp talk." A colorful literary example of a telephone rap (which one of my informants regards as extreme, but agrees that it illustrates the language, style, and technique of rapping) is set forth in Iceberg Slim's *Pimp: The Story of My Life*. Blood is rapping to an ex-whore named Christine in an effort to trap her into his stable.

Now try to control yourself baby. I'm the tall stud with the dreamy bedroom eyes across the hall in four-twenty. I'm the guy with the pretty towel wrapped around his sexy hips. I got the same hips on now that you x-rayed. Remember that hump of sugar your peepers feasted on?

She said, "Maybe, but you shouldn't call me. I don't want an incident. What do you want? A lady doesn't accept phone calls from strangers."

I said, "A million dollars and a trip to the moon with a bored, trapped, beautiful bitch, you dig? I'm no stranger. I've been popping the elastic in your panties since you saw me in the hall. . . ."[3]

Field examples of this kind of rapping were difficult to obtain, primarily because talk of this nature generally occurs in private, and when occurring in public places such as parties and taverns, it is carried on in an undertone. However, the first line of a rap, which might be regarded as introductory, is often overheard. What follows are several such lines

[2] John Horton, "Time and Cool People," *Trans-action*, April, 1967, and in this volume.

[3] Iceberg Slim, *Pimp: The Story of My Life* (Los Angeles: Holloway House, 1969), p. 179.

collected by two of my students in and around the South Side and West Side of Chicago:

> "Say pretty, I kin tell you need lovin' by the way you wiggle your ass when you walk—and I'm jus' the guy what' kin put out yo' fire."
> "Let me rock you mamma, I kin satisfy your soul."
> "Say, baby, give me the key to your pad. I want to play with your cat."
> "Baby, you're fine enough to make me spend my rent money."
> "Baby, I sho' dig your mellow action."

Rapping between men and women often is competitive and leads to a lively repartee, with the woman becoming as adept as the man. An example follows:

> A man coming from the bathroom forgot to zip his pants. An unescorted party of women kept watching him and laughing among themselves. The man's friends hip [inform] him to what's going on. He approaches one woman—"Hey baby, did you see that big black Cadillac with the full tires ready to roll in action just for you?" She answers— "No mother-fucker, but I saw a little gray Volkswagen with two flat tires."
> Everybody laughs. His rap was *capped* [excelled, topped].

When "whupping the game" on a "trick" or "lame" (trying to get goods or services from someone who looks like he can be swindled), rapping is often descriptive of the highly stylized verbal part of the maneuver. In well-established con games the verbal component is carefully prepared and used with great skill in directing the course of the transaction. An excellent illustration of this kind of rap came from an adept hustler who was playing the "murphy" game on a white trick. The maneuvers in the murphy game are designed to get the trick to give his money to the hustler, who in this instance poses as a "steerer" (one who directs or steers customers to a brothel), to keep the whore from stealing it. The hustler then skips with the money.

> Look Buddy, I know a fabulous house not more than two blocks away. Brother you ain't never seen more beautiful, freakier broads than are in that house. One of them, the prettiest one, can do more with a swipe than a monkey can with a banana. She's like a rubber doll; she can take a hundred positions.
> At this point the sucker is wild to get to this place of pure joy. He entreats the con player to take him there, not just direct him to it.
> The "murphy" player will prat him [pretend rejection] to enhance his desire. He will say, "Man, don't be offended, but Aunt Kate that runs the house don't have nothing but high-class white men coming to her place. . . . you know, doctors, lawyers, big-shot politicians. You look like a clean-cut white man, but you ain't in that league are you?"[4]

4 Ibid., p. 38.

After a few more exchanges of the murphy dialogue, "the mark is separated from his scratch."

An analysis of rapping indicates a number of things. For instance, it is revealing that one raps *to* rather than *with* a person, supporting the impression that rapping is to be regarded more as a performance than a verbal exchange. As with other performances, rapping projects the personality, physical appearance, and style of the performer. In each of the examples given above, in greater or lesser degree, the intrusive "I" of the speaker was instrumental in contributing to the total impression of the rap.

The relative degree of the personality-style component of rapping is generally highest when asking for some pussy (Rapping 2) and lower when whupping the game on someone (Rapping 3) or running something down (Rapping 1). In each instance, however, the personality style component is higher than any other in producing the total effect on the listener.

In asking for some pussy, for example, where personality and style might be projected through nonverbal means (stance, clothing, walking, looking), one can speak of a "silent rap" where the woman is won without the use of words, or rather, with the words being implied that would generally accompany the nonverbal components.

As a lively way of running it down the verbal element consists of two parts: the personality-style component and the information component. Someone *reading* my example of the gang member's narration might get the impression that the information component would be more influential in directing the audience response—that the youth worker would say, "So that's how the gang got so big," in which case he would be responding to the information component, instead of saying "Man, that gang member is *bad* [strong, brave]," in which instance he would be responding to the personality-style component of the rap. However, if the reader could *listen* to the gang member on tape or could have been present (*watching-listening*) when the gang member spoke, he likely would have reacted more to the personality-style component, as my informants did.

Supporting this hypothesis is the fact that in attendance with the youth worker were members of the gang who *already knew* how the gang got started (e.g., "Am I right, Leroy? You was cribbin over there then"), and for whom the information component by itself would have little interest. Their attention was held by the *way* the information was presented—i.e., directed toward the personality-style component.

The verbal element in whupping the game on someone, in the above illustration, was an integral part of an overall deception in which the information component and the personality-style component were skillfully manipulated to control the trick's response. But again, greater weight must be given to the personality-style component. In the murphy game, for example, it was this element which got the trick to *trust* the hustler and to leave his money with him for "safekeeping."

The function of rapping in each of the forms discussed above is *expressive*. By this I mean that the speaker raps to project his personality onto the scene or to evoke a generally favorable response from another person or group. In addition, when rapping is used to ask for some pussy (Rapping 2) or to whup the game on someone (Rapping 3), its function is *directive*. By this I mean that rapping here becomes the instrument used to manipulate and control people to get them to give up or do something. The difference between rapping to a "fox" (pretty girl) for the purpose of getting inside her pants and rapping to a "lame" to get something from him is operational rather than functional. The latter rap contains a concealed motivation, whereas the former does not. A statement made by one of my high school informants illustrates this distinction: "If I wanted something from a guy I would try to *trick* him out of it. If I wanted something from a girl I would try to *talk* her out of it [emphasis mine]."

"Shucking," "shucking it," "shucking and jiving," "S-ing and J-ing," or just "jiving," are terms that refer to one form of language behavior practiced by the black when interacting with The Man (the white man, the Establishment, or *any* authority figure), and to another form of language behavior practiced by blacks when interacting with each other on the peer-group level.

When referring to the black's dealings with the white man and the power structure, the above terms are descriptive of the talk and accompanying physical movements of the black that are appropriate to some momentary guise, posture, or facade.

Originally in the South, and later in the North, the black learned that American society had assigned him a restrictive role and status. Among whites his behavior had to conform to this imposed station, and he was constantly reminded to "keep his place." He learned that before white people it was not acceptable to show feelings of indignation, frustration, discontent, pride, ambition, or desire; that real feelings had to be concealed behind a mask of innocence, ignorance, childishness, obedience, humility and deference. The terms used by the black to describe the role he played before white folks in the South was "tomming" or "jeffing." Failure to accommodate the white Southerner in this respect was almost certain to invite psychological and often physical brutality. The following description by black psychiatrist Alvin F. Poussaint is typical and revealing:

> Once last year as I was leaving my office in Jackson, Miss., with my Negro secretary, a white policeman yelled, "Hey, boy! Come here!"

Somewhat bothered, I retorted: "I'm no boy!" He then rushed at me, inflamed and stood towering over me, snorting "What d'ja say, boy?" Quickly he frisked me and demanded "What's your name, boy?" Frightened, I replied, "Dr. Poussaint, I'm a physician." He angrily chuckled and hissed, "What's your first name, boy?" When I hesitated he assumed a threatening stance and clenched his fists. As my heart palpitated, I muttered in profound humiliation, "Alvin."

He continued his psychological brutality, bellowing, "Alvin, the next time I call you, you come right away, you hear? You hear?" I hesitated. "You hear me, boy?" My voice trembling with helplessness, but *following my instincts of self-preservation,* I murmured, "Yes, sir." *Now fully satisfied that I had performed and acquiesced to my "boy" status,* he dismissed me with, "Now boy, go on and get out of here or next time we'll take you for a little ride down to the station house!"

In northern cities the black encountered authority figures equivalent to the southern "crackers": policemen, judges, probation officers, truant officers, teachers, and "Mr. Charlies" (bosses), and he soon learned that the way to get by and avoid difficulty was to shuck. Thus, he learned to accommodate The Man, to use the total orchestration of speech, intonation, gesture, and facial expression to produce whatever appearance would be acceptable. It was a technique and ability that was developed from fear, a respect for power, and a will to survive. This type of accommodation is exemplified by the "Yes sir, Mr. Charlie," or "Anything you say, Mr. Charlie," "Uncle Tom"–type Negro of the North. The language and behavior of accommodation were the prototype out of which other slightly modified forms of shucking evolved.

Through accommodation, many blacks became adept at concealing and controlling their emotions and at assuming a variety of postures. They became competent actors in the process. Many developed a keen perception of what affected, motivated, appeased, or satisfied the authority figures with whom they came into contact. What became an accomplished and effective coping mechanism for many blacks to "stay out of trouble" became for others a useful artifice for avoiding arrest or "getting out of trouble" when apprehended. Shucking it with a judge, for example, would be to feign repentance in the hope of receiving a lighter or suspended sentence; with a probation officer, to give the impression of being serious and responsible so that if you violate probation, you would not be sent back to jail. Robert Conot reports an example of the latter in his book: "Joe was found guilty of possession of narcotics. But he did an excellent job of shucking it with the probation officer." The probation officer interceded for Joe with the judge as

[5] Alvin F. Poussaint, "A Negro Psychiatrist Explains the Negro Psyche," *New York Times,* August 20, 1967, sec. 6, pp. 52ff.

follows: "His own attitude toward the present offense appears to be serious and responsible and it is believed that the defendant is an excellent subject for probation."[6]

The cartoon by Cal Barker illustrates this point nicely. (It appeared originally in the *Chicago Defender*.)

"Alright, alright! So what if I did sing a couple stanzas of Dixie and cut a few buck and wing steps back there. It saved the both of us from going to jail for vagrancy. The trouble with you is that you don't know how to differentiate between tomming and progressive maneuvering!"

Some field illustrations of shucking to get out of trouble after having been caught come from some seventh-grade children from an inner-city school in Chicago. The children were asked to "talk their way out of"

[6] Robert Conot, *Rivers of Blood, Years of Darkness* (New York: Bantam, 1967), p. 333.

a troublesome situation. Examples of the situation and their impromptu responses follow:

> *Situation:* You're cursing at this old man and your mother comes walking down the stairs. She hears you. Response to "talk your way out of this": "I'd tell her that I was studying a scene in school for a play."
>
> *Situation:* What if you were in a store and were stealing something and the manager caught you? Responses: "I would tell him that I was used to putting things in my pocket and then going to pay for them and show the cashier."
>
> "I'd tell him that some of my friends was outside and they wanted some candy so I was goin to put it in my pocket to see if it would fit before I bought it."
>
> "I would start stuttering. Then I would say, 'Oh, Oh, I forgot. Here the money is.'"
>
> *Situation:* What do you do when you ditch school and you go to the beach and a truant officer walks up and says, "Are you having fun?" and you say, "Yeah," and you don't know he is a truant officer and then he says, "I'm a truant officer, what are you doing out of school?" Responses: "I'd tell him that I had been expelled from school, that I wasn't supposed to go back to school for seven days."
>
> "I'd tell him that I had to go to the doctor to get a checkup and that my mother said I might as well stay out of school the whole day and so I came over here."
>
> *Situation:* You're at the beach and they've got posted signs all over the beach and floating on the water and you go past the swimming mark and the sign says "Don't go past the mark!" How do you talk your way out of this to the lifeguard? Responses: "I'd tell him that I was having so much fun in the water that I didn't pay attention to the sign."
>
> "I'd say that I was swimming under water and when I came back up I was behind the sign."

One literary and one field example of shucking to avoid arrest follow. The literary example of shucking comes from Iceberg Slim's autobiography. Iceberg, a pimp, shucks before "two red-faced Swede rollers [detectives]" who catch him in a motel room with his whore. My italics identifies which elements of the passage constitute the shuck.

> I put my shaking hands into the pajama pockets. . . . *I hoped I was keeping the fear out of my face. I gave them a wide toothy smile.* They came in and stood in the middle of the room. Their eyes were racing about the room. Stacy was open mouthed in the bed.
>
> I said, *"Yes gentlemen what can I do for you?"* Lanky said, "We wanta see your I.D."
>
> I went to the closet and got the phony John Cato Frederickson I.D. I put it in his palm. I felt cold sweat running down my back. They looked at it, then looked at each other.
>
> Lanky said, "You are in violation of the law. You signed the motel

register improperly. Why didn't you sign your full name? What are you trying to hide? What are you doing here in town? It says here you're a dancer. We don't have a club in town that books entertainers."

I said, *"Officers, my professional name is Johnny Cato. I've got nothing to hide. My full name had always been too long for the marquees. I've fallen into the habit of using the shorter version. My legs went out last year. I don't dance anymore. My wife and I decided to go into business. We are making a tour of this part of the country. We think that in your town we've found the ideal site for a southern fried chicken shack. My wife has a secret recipe that should make us rich here."*[7]

The following example from the field was related to me by one of my colleagues. One black gang member was coming down the stairway from the club room with seven guns on him and encountered some policemen coming up the same stairs. If they stopped and frisked him, he and others would have been arrested. A paraphrase of his shuck follows: "Man, I gotta get away from up there. There's gonna be some trouble and I don't want no part of it." This shuck worked on the minds of the policemen. It anticipated their questions as to why he was leaving the club room, and why he would be in a hurry. He also gave *them* a reason for wanting to get up to the room fast.

It ought to be mentioned at this point that there was not uniform agreement among my informants in characterizing the above examples as shucking. One informant used shucking only in the sense in which it is used among the black peer group—viz., bull-shitting—and characterized the above examples as "jiving" or "whupping game." Others, however, identified the above examples as shucking and reserved "jiving" and "whupping game" for more offensive maneuvers. In fact, one of the apparent criterial features of shucking is that the posture of the black when interacting with members of the establishment be a *defensive* one. Some of my informants, for example, regarded the example of a domestic who changed into older clothing than she could afford before going to work in a white household as shucking, provided that she was doing it to keep her job. On the other hand, if she did the same thing to get a raise in pay, they regarded the example as whupping the game. Since the same guise and set of maneuvers are brought into play in working on the mind and feeling of the domestic's boss, the difference would seem to be whether the reason behind the pose were to protect oneself or to gain some advantage. Since this distinction is not always so clearly drawn, opinions are often divided. The following example is clearly ambiguous in this respect. Frederick Douglass, in telling of how he taught himself to read, would challenge a white boy with whom he was playing by saying that he could write as well as the white boy, whereupon he would write down all the letters he knew.

[7] Slim, *Pimp,* p. 294.

The white boy would then write down more letters than Douglass did. In this way, Douglass eventually learned all the letters of the alphabet.[8] Some of my informants regarded the example as whupping game. Others regarded it as shucking. The former were perhaps focusing on the maneuver rather than the language used. The latter may have felt that any maneuvers designed to learn to read were justifiably defensive. One of my informants said Douglass was "shucking *in order to* whup the game." This latter response seems to be the most revealing. Just as one can rap to whup the game on someone, so one can shuck or jive for the same purpose—i.e., assume a guise or posture or perform some action in a certain way that is designed to work on someone's mind to get him to give up something. The following examples from Malcolm X illustrate the use of *shucking* and *jiving* in this context, though *jive* is the term used. Today, *whupping game* might also be the term used to describe the operation. "Whites who came at night got a better reception; the several Harlem nightclubs they patronized were geared to entertain and *jive* [flatter, cajole] the night white crowd to get their money."[9]

The maneuvers involved here are clearly designed to obtain some benefit or advantage.

> Freddy got on the stand and went to work on his own shoes. Brush, liquid polish, brush, paste wax, shine rag, lacquer sole dressing . . . step by step, Freddie showed me what to do.
>
> "But you got to get a whole lot faster. You can't waste time!" Freddie showed me how fast on my own shoes. Then because business was tapering off, he had time to give me a demonstration of how to make the shine rag pop like a firecracker. "Dig the action?" he asked. He did it in slow motion. I got down and tried it on his shoes. I had the principle of it. "Just got to do it faster," Freddie said. *"It's a jive noise, that's all. Cats tip better, they figure you're knocking yourself out!"*[10]

I was involved in a field example in which an eight-year-old boy whupped the game on me as follows:

> My colleague and I were sitting in a room listening to a tape. The door to the room was open and outside was a soda machine. Two boys came up in the elevator, stopped at the soda machine, and then came into the room and asked: "Do you have a dime for two nickels?" Presumably, the soda machine would not accept nickels. I took out the change in my pocket, found a dime and gave it to the boy for two nickels. After accepting the dime, he looked at the change in my hand and asked, "Can I have two cents? I need carfare to get home." I gave him the two cents.

[8] Frederick Douglass, *Narrative of the Life of an American Slave* (New York: New American Library, 1968), p. 57.

[9] Malcolm X, *Autobiography* (New York: Grove Press, 1965), p. 87.

[10] Ibid., p. 48. Italics mine.

At first I assumed the verbal component of the maneuver was the rather weak, transparently false reason for wanting the two cents. Actually, as was pointed out to me later, the maneuver began with the first question, which was designed to get me to show my money. He could then ask me for something that he knew I had, making my refusal more difficult. He apparently felt that the reason need not be more than plausible because the amount he wanted was small. Were the amount larger, he would no doubt have elaborated on the verbal element of the game. The form of the verbal element could be directed toward rapping or shucking and jiving. If he were to rap, the eight-year-old might say, "Man, you know a cat needs to have a little bread to keep the girls in line." Were he to shuck and jive he might make the reason for needing the money more compelling: look hungry, or something similar.

The function of shucking and jiving as it refers to transactions involving confrontation between blacks and The Man is both expressive and directive. It is language behavior designed to work on the mind and emotions of the authority figure to get him to feel a certain way or give up something that will be to the other's advantage. When viewed in its entirety, shucking must be regarded as a performance. Words and gestures become the instruments for promoting a certain image or posture. In the absence of words, shucking would be descriptive of the *actions* which constitute the deception, as in the above example from Malcolm X, where the movement of the shine rag in creating the "jive noise" was the deceptive element. Similarly, in another example, a seventh-grade boy recognized the value of stuttering before saying, "Oh, I forgot. Here the money is," knowing that stuttering would be an invaluable aid in presenting a picture of innocent intent. Iceberg showed a "toothy smile" which said to the detective, "I'm glad to see you," and "Would I be glad to see you if I had something to hide?" When the maneuvers seem to be defensive, most of my informants regarded the language behavior as shucking. When the maneuvers were offensive, my informants tended to regard the behavior as whupping the game. The difference in perception is culturally significant.

Also significant is the fact that the first form of shucking which I have described above, which developed out of accommodation, is becoming less frequently used today by many blacks as a result of a newfound self-assertiveness and pride, challenging the system "that is so brutally and unstintingly suppressive of self-assertion."[11] The willingness on the part of many blacks to accept the psychological and physical brutality and general social consequences of not "keeping one's place" is indicative of the changing self-concept of the black man. Ironically, the

11 Poussaint, "Negro Psychiatrist," p. 52.

shocked reaction of the white power structure to the present militancy of the black is partly due to the fact that the black has been so successful at "putting whitey on" via shucking in the past—i.e., compelling a belief in whatever posture the black chose to assume. The extent to which this attitude has penetrated the black community can be seen from a conversation I recently had with a shoe-shine attendant at O'Hare airport in Chicago.

I was having my shoes shined and the black attendant was using a polishing machine instead of the rag that was generally used in the past. I asked whether the machine made his work any easier. He did not answer me until about ten seconds had passed and then responded in a loud voice that he "never had a job that was easy, that he would give me one hundred dollars for any *easy* job I could offer him, that the machine made his job 'faster' but not 'easier.' " I was startled at the response because it was so unexpected, and I realized that here was a new "breed of cat" who was not going to shuck for a big tip or ingratiate himself with "whitey" anymore. A few years ago his response would have been different.

The contrast between this shoe-shine scene and the one illustrated earlier from Malcolm X's autobiography, when "shucking whitey" was the common practice, is striking.

"Shucking," "jiving," "shucking and jiving," or "S-ing and J-ing," when referring to language behavior practiced by blacks when interacting with one another on the peer-group level, is descriptive of the talk and gestures that are appropriate to "putting someone on" by creating a false impression, conveying false information, and the like. The terms seem to cover a range from simply telling a lie, to bull-shitting, to subtly playing with someone's mind. An important difference between this form of shucking and that described earlier is that the same talk and gestures that are deceptive to The Man are often transparent to those members of one's own group who are able practitioners at shucking themselves. As Robert Conot has pointed out, "The Negro who often fools the white officer by 'shucking it' is much less likely to be successful with another Negro. . . ."[12] Also, S-ing and J-ing within the group often has play overtones in which the person being put on is aware of the attempts being made and goes along with it for the enjoyment of it or in appreciation of the style involved. An example from Iceberg Slim illustrates this latter point:

> He said, "Ain't you the little shit ball I chased outta the Roost?"
> I said, "Yeah, I'm one and the same. I want to beg your pardon for making you salty [angry] that night. Maybe I coulda gotten a pass if I had told you I'm your pal's nephew.

---

[12] Conot, *Rivers of Blood*, p. 161.

I ain't got no sense, Mr. Jones. I took after my idiot father."[13]

Mr. Jones, perceiving Iceberg's shuck, says,

> "Top, this punk ain't hopeless. He's silly as a bitch grinning all the time, but dig how he butters the con to keep his balls outta the fire."

Other citations showing the use of "shucking" and "jiving" to mean simply "lying" follow:

> It was a *jive* [false] tip but there were a lot of cats up there on humbles [framed up charges].[14]
> How would you like to have half a "G" [$500] in your slide [pocket]? I said, "All right, give me the poison and take me to the baby." He said, "I ain't *shucking* [lying]. It's creampuff work."[15]

"Running it down" is the term used by ghetto-dwellers when they intend to communicate information in the form of an explanation, narrative, giving advice, and the like. The information component in the field example cited under Rapping 1 would constitute the run down. In the following literary example, Sweet Mac is "running this Edith broad down" to his friends

> Edith is the "saved" broad who can't marry out of her religion . . . or do anything else out of her religion for that matter, especially what I wanted her to do. A bogue religion, man! So dig, for the last couple weeks I been quoting the Good Book and all that stuff to her; telling her I am now saved myself, you dig.[16]

The following citation from Claude Brown uses the term with the additional sense of giving advice: "If I saw him [Claude's brother] hanging out with cats I knew were weak, who might be using drugs sooner or later, I'd *run it down* to him."[17]

Iceberg Slim (1967:79) asks a bartender regarding a prospective whore: "Sugar, *run her down* to me. Is the bitch qualified? Is she a whore? Does she have a man?"[18]

It seems clear that running it down has basically an informative function, telling somebody something that he doesn't already know.

"Gripping" is of fairly recent vintage, used by black high school students in Chicago to refer to the talk and facial expression that accompanies a *partial* loss of face or self-possession, or displaying of fear. Its appearance alongside "copping a plea," which refers to a total loss of

[13] Slim, *Pimp*, p. 162.
[14] Claude Brown, *Manchild in the Promised Land* (New York: Macmillan, 1965), p. 142.
[15] Slim, *Pimp*, p. 68. Italics mine.
[16] Woodie King, Jr., "The Game," *Liberator*, August, 1965, and in this volume.
[17] Brown, *Manchild*, p. 390. Italics mine.
[18] Slim, *Pimp*, p. 79. Italics mine.

face, in which one begs one's adversary for mercy, is a significant new perception. Linking it with the street code which acclaims the ability to "look tough and inviolate, fearless, secure, 'cool,' "[19] suggests that even the slightest weakening of this posture will be held up to ridicule and contempt. There are always contemptuous overtones attached to the use of the term when applied to others' behavior. One is tempted to link it further with the degree of violence and level of toughness that is required to survive on the street. The intensity of both seems to be increasing. As one of my informants noted, "Today, you're *lucky* if you end up in the hospital [i.e., are not killed]."

Both "gripping" and "copping a plea" refer to behavior that stems from fear and a respect for superior power. An example of gripping comes from the record *Street and Gangland Rhythms.*[20] Lennie meets Calvin and asks him what happened to his lip. Calvin tells Lennie that a boy named Pierre hit him for copying off him in school. Lennie, pretending to be Calvin's brother, goes to confront Pierre. Their dialogue follows:

> LENNIE: Hey you! What you hit my little brother for?
> PIERRE: Did he tell you what happen man?
> LENNIE: Yeah, he told me what happen.
> PIERRE: But you . . . but you . . . but you should tell your people to teach him to go to school, man. (*pause*) I . . . I know . . . I know I didn't have a right to hit him.

Pierre, anticipating a fight with Lennie if he continued to justify his hitting of Calvin, tried to avoid it by gripping with the last line.

"Copping a plea" originally meant "to plead guilty to a lesser charge to save the state the cost of a trial"[21] (with the hope of receiving a lesser or suspended sentence), but is now generally used to mean "to beg, plead for mercy," as in, "Please cop, don't hit me. I give."[22] This change of meaning can be seen from its use by Piri Thomas in *Down These Mean Streets:* "The night before my hearing, I decided to make a prayer. It had to be on my knees, cause if I was gonna *cop a plea* to God, I couldn't play it cheap."[23] For the original meaning, Thomas uses "deal for a lower plea": "I was three or four months in the Tombs, waiting for a trial, going to court, waiting for adjournments, trying to *deal for a lower plea,* and what not."[24]

---

[19] Horton, "Time and Cool People," p. 11.
[20] *Street and Gangland Rhythms,* Band 4, "Dumb Boy."
[21] Harold Wentworth and Stuart Berg Flexner, *Dictionary of American Slang* (New York: Crowell, 1960), p. 123.
[22] *Street and Gangland Rhythms,* Band 1, "Gang Fight."
[23] Piri Thomas, *Down These Mean Streets* (New York: Knopf, 1967), p. 316. Italics mine.
[24] Ibid., p. 245. Italics mine.

The function of gripping and copping a plea is obviously expressive. One evinces noticeable feelings of fear and insecurity which result in a loss of status among one's peers. At the same time one may arouse feelings of contempt in one's adversary.

An interesting point to consider with respect to copping a plea is whether the superficial features of the form may be borrowed to mitigate one's punishment, in which case it would have the same directive function as shucking, and would be used to arouse feelings of pity, mercy, and the like. The question whether one can arouse such feelings among one's street peers by copping a plea is unclear. In the example cited above from the record *Street and Gangland Rhythms,* which records the improvisations of eleven- and twelve-year-old boys, one of the boys convincingly *acts out* the form of language behavior, which was identified by all my informants as copping a plea with the police officer: "Please cop, don't hit me. I give." In this example it was clearly an artifice with a directive function; here we have the familiar dynamic opposition of black vs. authority figure discussed under shucking.

"Signifying" is the term used to describe the language behavior that, as Abrahams has defined it, attempts to "imply, goad, beg, boast by indirect verbal or gestural means."[25] In Chicago it is also used as a synonym to describe a form of language behavior which is more generally known as "sounding" elsewhere and will be discussed under the latter heading below.

Some excellent examples of signifying as well as of other forms of language behavior discussed above come from the well-known "toast" (narrative form), "The Signifying Monkey and the Lion," which was collected by Abrahams from black street-corner bards in Philadelphia. In the above toast the monkey is trying to get the lion involved in a fight with the elephant:

> Now the lion came through the jungle one peaceful day,
> When the signifying monkey stopped him, and that is what he started to say:
> He said, "Mr. Lion," he said, "A bad-assed motherfucker down your way,"
> He said, "Yeah! The way he talks about your folks is a certain shame.
> "I've even heard him curse when he mentioned your grandmother's name."
> The lion's tail shot back like a forty-four
> When he went down that jungle in all uproar.

Thus the monkey has goaded the lion into a fight with the elephant by signifying, indicating that the elephant has been "sounding on" (in-

[25] Roger D. Abrahams, *Deep Down in the Jungle* (Hatboro, Pa.: Folklore Associates, 1964), p. 267.
[26] Ibid., p. 150ff.

sulting) the lion. When the lion comes back, thoroughly beaten up, the monkey again signifies by making fun of the lion:

> . . . a lion came back through the jungle more dead than alive,
> When the monkey started some more of that signifying jive.
> He said, "Damn, Mr. Lion, you went through here yesterday, the jungle rung.
> "Now you come back today, damn near hung."

The monkey, of course, is delivering this taunt from a safe distance away on the limb of a tree when his foot slips and he falls to the ground, at which point

> Like a bolt of lightning, a stripe of white heat,
> The lion was on the monkey with all four feet.

In desperation the monkey quickly resorts to copping a plea:

> The monkey looked up with a tear in his eyes.
> He said, "Please, Mr. Lion, I apologize."

His plea, however, fails to move the lion to any show of pity or mercy so the monkey tries another verbal ruse—shucking:

> He said, "You lemme get my head out of the sand
> Ass out of the grass, I'll fight you like a natural man."

In this he is more successful as

> The lion jumped back and squared for a fight.
> The motherfucking monkey jumped clear out of sight.

A safe distance away again, the monkey returns to signifying:

> He said, "Yeah, you had me down, you had me at last.
> But you left me free, now you can still kiss my ass."

The above example illustrates the methods of provocation, goading, and taunting as artfully practiced by the signifier. Interestingly, when the *function* of signifying is *directive,* the *tactic* which is employed is one of *indirection*—i.e., the signifier reports or repeats what someone else has said about the listener; the "report" is couched in plausible language designed to compel belief and arouse feelings of anger and hostility. There is also the implication that if the listener fails to do anything about it—what has to be "done" is usually quite clear—his status will be seriously compromised. Thus the lion is compelled to vindicate the honor of his family by fighting or else leave the impression that he is afraid, and that he is not "king of the jungle." When used to direct action, signifying is like shucking in also being deceptive and subtle in approach and depending for success on the naïveté or gullibility of the person being put on.

When the function of signifying is only expressive (i.e., to arouse feelings of embarrassment, shame, frustration, or futility, for the purpose of diminishing someone's status, but without directive implication), the tactic employed is direct in the form of a taunt, as in the above example where the monkey is making fun of the lion. Signifying frequently occurs when things are dull and someone wishes to generate some excitement and interest within the group. This is shown in another version of the above toast:

> There hadn't been no disturbin in the jungle for quite a bit,
> For up jumped the monkey in the tree one day and laughed, "I guess I'll start some shit."

"Sounding" is the term which is today most widely known for the game of verbal insult known in the past as "playing the dozens," "the dirty dozens," or just "the dozens." Other current names for the game have regional distribution: "signifying" or "sigging" (Chicago), "joning" (Washington, D.C.), "screaming" (Harrisburg), and so on. In Chicago, the term "sounding" would describe the initial remarks which are designed to sound out the other person to see whether he will play the game. The verbal insult is also subdivided, the term "signifying" applying to insults which are hurled directly at the person and the "dozens" applying to insults hurled at your opponent's family, especially the mother.

Sounding is often catalyzed by signifying remarks referred to earlier, such as "Are you going to let him say that about your mama?" in order to spur on an exchange between two (or more) other members of the group. It is begun on a relatively low key and built up by means of verbal exchanges.

Abrahams describes the game:

> One insults a member of another's family; others in the group make disapproving sounds to spur on the coming exchange. The one who has been insulted feels at this point that he must reply with a slur on the protagonist's family which is clever enough to defend his honor (and therefore that of his family). This, of course, leads the other (once again, more due to pressure from the crowd than actual insult) to make further jabs. This can proceed until everyone is bored with the whole affair, until one hits the other (fairly rare), or until some other subject comes up that interrupts the proceedings (the usual state of affairs).[27]

McCormick describes the dozens as a verbal contest

> in which the players strive to bury one another with vituperation. In the play, the opponent's mother is especially slandered . . . then, in turn

[27] Roger D. Abrahams, "Playing the Dozens," *Journal of American Folklore* 75 (1962): 209–10.

fathers are identified as queer and syphilitic. Sisters are whores, brothers are defective, cousins are "funny" and the opponent is himself diseased.[28]

An example of the game collected by one of my students goes as follows:

> *Frank looked up and saw Leroy enter the Outpost. Leroy walked past the room where Quinton, Nap, Pretty Black, Cunny, Richard, Haywood, Bull, and Reese sat playing cards. As Leroy neared the T.V. room, Frank shouted to him.*
>
> FRANK: Hey, Leroy, your mama—calling you man.
>
> *Leroy turned and walked toward the room where the sound came from. He stood in the door and looked at Frank.*
>
> LEROY: Look motherfuckers, I don't play that shit.
>
> FRANK (*signifying*): Man, I told you cats 'bout that mama jive (*as if he were concerned about how Leroy felt*).
>
> LEROY: That's all right Frank; you don't have to tell those funky motherfuckers nothing; I'll fuck me up somebody yet.
>
> *Frank's face lit up as if he were ready to burst his side laughing. Cunny became pissed at Leroy.*
>
> CUNNY: Leroy, you stupid bastard, you let Frank make a fool of you. *He* said that 'bout your mama.
>
> PRETTY BLACK: Aw, fat ass head, Cunny shut up.
>
> CUNNY: Ain't that some shit. This black slick head motor flicker got nerve 'nough to call somebody fathead. Boy, you so black, you sweat super Permalube Oil.

This eased the tension of the group as they burst into loud laughter.

> PRETTY BLACK: What'chu laughing 'bout Nap, with your funky mouth smelling like dog shit.

Even Leroy laughed at this.

> NAP: Your mama motherfucker.
>
> PRETTY BLACK: Your funky mama too.
>
> NAP, *strongly:* It takes twelve barrels of water to make a steamboat run; it takes an elephant's dick to make your Grandmammy come; she been elephant fucked, camel fucked and hit side the head with your Grandpappy's nuts.
>
> REESE: Goddor damn; go on and rap motherfucker.

Reese began slapping each boy in his hand, giving his approval of Nap's comment. Pretty Black, in an effort not to be outdone but directing his verbal play elsewhere, stated:

> PRETTY BLACK: Reese, what you laughing 'bout? You so square you shit bricked shit.

[28] Mack McCormick, *The Dirty Dozens: The Unexpurgated Folksongs of Men,* Arhoolie record album, 1960.

FRANK: Whoooowee!

REESE (*sounded back*): Square huh, what about your nappy ass hair before it was stewed; that shit was so bad till, when you went to bed at night, it would leave your head and go on the corner and meddle.

The boys slapped each other in the hand and cracked up.

PRETTY BLACK: On the streets meddling, bet Dinky didn't offer me no pussy and I turned it down.

FRANK: Reese scared of pussy.

PRETTY BLACK: Hell yeah; the greasy mother rather fuck old, ugly, funky cock Sue Willie than get a piece of ass from a decent broad.

FRANK: Goddor damn! Not Sue Willie.

PRETTY BLACK: Yeah ol' meat beating Reese rather screw that cross-eyed, clapsy bitch, who when she cry, tears drip down her ass.

HAYWOOD: Don't be so mean, Black.

REESE: Aw shut up, you half-white bastard.

FRANK: Wait man, Haywood ain't gonna hear much more of that half-white shit; he's a brother too.

REESE: Brother, my black ass; that white ass landlord gotta be this motherfucker's paw.

CUNNY: Man, you better stop foolin with Haywood; he's turning red.

HAYWOOD: Fuck yall (*as he withdrew from the "sig" game*).

FRANK: Yeah, fuck yall; let's go to the stick hall.

The above example of sounding is an excellent illustration of the game as played by fifteen-, sixteen-, and seventeen-year-old Negro boys, some of whom have already acquired the verbal skill which for them is often the basis for having a high "rep." Abrahams observed that "the ability with words is as highly valued as physical strength."[29] In the sense that the status of one of the participants in the game is diminished if he has to resort to fighting to answer a verbal attack, verbal ability may be even more highly regarded than physical ability. However, age within the peer group may be a factor in determining the relative value placed on verbal vis-à-vis physical ability.

Nevertheless, the relatively high value placed on verbal ability must be clear to most black boys at an early age in their cognitive development. Abrahams is probably correct in linking sounding to the taunt which is learned and practiced as a child and is part of signifying, which has its origins in childlike behavior.[30] The taunts of the Signifying Monkey, illustrated above, are good examples of this.

Most boys begin their activity in sounding by compiling a repertoire of one-liners. When the game is played among this age group, the one who has the greatest number of such remarks wins. Here are some

[29] Abrahams, *Deep Down*, p. 62.
[30] Ibid., p. 53.

examples of one-liners collected from fifth- and sixth-grade black boys in Chicago:

> Yo mama is so bowlegged, she looks like the bite out of a donut.
> You mama sent her picture to the lonely hearts club, and they sent it back and said, "We ain't that lonely!"
> Your family is so poor the rats and roaches eat lunch out.
> Your house is so small the roaches walk single file.
> I walked in your house and your family was running around the table. I said, "Why you doin that?" Your mama say, "First one drops, we eat."

Real proficiency in the game comes to only a small percentage of those who play it, as might be expected. These players have the special skill in being able to turn what their opponents have said and attack them with it. Thus, when someone indifferently said "Fuck you" to Concho, his retort was immediate and devastating: "Man, you haven't even kissed me yet."

The best talkers from this group often become the successful street-corner, barber shop, and pool hall storytellers who deliver the long, rhymed, witty narrative stories called "toasts." A portion of the toast "The Signifying Monkey and the Lion" was given above. However, it has also produced entertainers, such as Dick Gregory and Redd Foxx, who are virtuosos at repartee, and preachers whose verbal power has been traditionally esteemed.

The function of the dozens or sounding is invariably self-assertive. The speaker borrows status from his opponent through an exercise of verbal power. The opponent feels compelled to regain his status by sounding back on the speaker or some other member of the group whom he regards as more vulnerable. The social interaction of the group at the Outpost, for example, demonstrated less an extended verbal barrage between two people than a "pecking order." Frank sounds on Leroy; Cunny signifies on Leroy; Pretty Black sounds on Cunny; Cunny sounds back on Pretty Black who (losing) turns on Nap; Nap sounds (winning) back on Pretty Black; Pretty Black finally borrows back his status by sounding on Reese. Reese sounds back on Pretty Black but gets the worst of the exchange and so borrows back his status from Haywood. Cunny also sounds on Haywood. Haywood defaults. Perhaps by being half-white, Haywood feels himself to be the most vulnerable.

The presence of a group seems to be especially important in controlling the game. First of all, one does not play with just anyone, since the subject matter is concerned with things that in reality one is quite sensitive about. It is precisely *because* Pretty Black has a "black slick head" that he is vulnerable to Cunny's barb, especially now when the Afro-American natural hairstyle is in vogue. It is precisely *because* Reese's girlfriend *is* ugly that he is vulnerable to Pretty Black's jibe that Reese can't get a "piece of ass from a decent broad." It is *because* the living conditions are so poor and intolerable that they can be used as subject matter for sounding. Without the control of the group, sounding will frequently lead to a fight. This was illustrated by a tragic epilogue concerning Haywood; when Haywood was being sounded on by his best friend in the presence of two girls (other members of the group were absent), he refused to tolerate it. He went home, got a rifle, came back, and shot and killed his friend. In the classroom from about the fourth grade on, fights among black boys invariably are caused by someone sounding on the other person's mother.

Significantly, the subject matter of sounding is changing with the changing self-concept of the black regarding to those physical traits that are characteristically Negro, and which in the past were vulnerable points in the black psyche: blackness and "nappy" hair.

They still occur, as in the above example from the Outpost, and the change in the above illustration is notably more by what has been added than subtracted—viz., the attack on black *slick* hair and half-white color. With regard to the latter, however, it ought to be said that, for many blacks, blackness was always highly esteemed; it might be more accurate to regard the present sentiment of the black community toward skin color as reflecting a shifted attitude for only a *portion* of the black community. This suggests that sounding on someone's light skin color is not new. Nevertheless, one can regard the previously favorable attitude toward light skin color and "good hair" as the prevailing one. "Other things being equal, the more closely a woman approached her white counterpart, the more attractive she was considered to be, by both men and women alike. 'Good hair' (hair that is long and soft) and light skin were the chief criteria."[31] Also, children's rhymes which before Black Power were

If you like black
Keep your black ass back

and

If you like white
You're all right

have respectively changed to

If you like black
You have a Cadillac

and

[31] Elliot Liebow, *Tally's Corner* (Boston: Little, Brown, 1966), p. 138, and in this volume.

If you like white
You're looking for a fight.

Both Abrahams and McCormick link the dozens to the overall psychosocial growth of the black male. McCormick has stated that a "single round of a dozen or so exchanges frees more pent-up aggressions than will a dose of sodium pentothal." The fact that one permits a kind of abuse within the rules of the game and within the confines of the group which would otherwise not be tolerated is filled with psychological importance, and this aspect is fully discussed by Abrahams. It also seems important, however, to view its function from the perspective of the nonparticipating members of the group. Its function for them may be directive: i.e., they incite and prod individual members of the group to combat for the purpose of energizing the elements, of simply relieving the boredom of just "hanging around" and the malaise of living in a static and restrictive environment. One of my informants remarked that he and other members of the group used to feed insults to one member to hurl back at another if they felt that the contest was too uneven, "to keep the game going." In my above illustration from the Outpost, for example, Frank seemed to be the precipitating agent as well as chorus for what was going on and Bull did not directly participate at all. For them the dozens may have had the social function of "having a little fun," or, as Loubee said to Josh, of just "passing the time."[32]

A summary analysis of the different forms of language behavior which have been discussed permit the following generalizations.

The prestige norms which influence black speech behavior are those which have been successful in manipulating and controlling people and situations. The function of all forms of language behavior discussed above, with the exception of "running it down," was either expressive or expressive-directive. Specifically, this means that language was used to project personality, assert oneself, or arouse emotion, frequently with the additional purpose of getting the person to give up or do something which will be of some benefit to the speaker. Only "running it down" has as its primary function to communicate information—and often here, too, the personality and style of the speaker in the form of rapping is projected along with the information.

The purpose for which language is used suggests that the speaker views the social situations into which he moves as essentially agonistic, by which I mean that he sees his environment as consisting of a series of transactions which require that he be continually ready to take advantage of a person or situation or defend himself against being victimized. He has absorbed what Horton has called "street rationality."[33] As one

[32] Earl Shorris, *Ofay* (New York: Dell, 1966).
[33] Horton, "Time and Cool People," p. 8.

of Horton's respondents put it: "The good hustler . . . conditions his mind and must never put his guard down too far, to relax, or he'll be taken."

I have carefully avoided, throughout this paper, delimiting the group within the black community of whom the language behavior and perspective of their environment is characteristic. While I have no doubt that it is true of those who are generally called "street people," I am not certain of the extent to which it is also true of a much larger portion of the black community, especially the male segment. My informants consisted of street people, high school students, and blacks who by their occupation as community and youth workers possess what has been described as a "sharp sense of the streets." Yet it is difficult to find a black male in the community who has *not* witnessed or participated in the dozens or heard of signifying, or rapping, or shucking and jiving, at some time while he was growing up. It would be equally difficult to imagine a high school student in a Chicago inner-city school not being touched by what is generally regarded as street culture in some way.

In conclusion, by blending style and verbal power, through "rapping," "sounding," and "running it down," the black in the ghetto establishes his personality; through "shucking," "gripping," and "copping a plea" he shows his respect for power; through "jiving" and "signifying" he stirs up excitement. With all of the above, he hopes to manipulate and control people and situations to give himself a winning edge.

■ Rules for ritual insults

WILLIAM LABOV

William Labov is professor of linguistics and psychology at the University of Pennsylvania. A graduate of Harvard College and Columbia University, he has authored *The Social Stratification of English in New York City* and a number of books and articles dealing with the structure and evolution of language within the speech community. While teaching in the linguistics department at Columbia University, he directed a study of the nonstandard language of the black community in Harlem and other inner-city areas from 1965 to 1968; from that effort came several books and reports dealing with the relation of linguistic and cultural differences to educational problems. The present article is a product of this investigation, focusing essentially on the use of ritual insult, a specific black cultural form of language known as "sounding" or "playing the dozens," within a teenage peer group in Harlem. In attempting to answer the question, "What kinds of insults lead to a fight, and which do not?" Labov has identified, in effect, some of the underlying cultural propositions that regulate verbal and action behavior among the members of this group. This information is not only theoretically significant in developing a grammar of discourse; it is also useful in helping us to more thoroughly know and understand the communicative behavior of black Americans. In great demand as a guest lecturer, Labov also serves as a member of the executive committee of the Linguistic Society of America and on the sociolinguistics committee of the Social Science Research Council.

Linguists have not made very much progress in the study of discourse; by and large, they are still confined by the boundaries of the sentence. If discourse analysis is not a virgin field, it is at least technically so in that no serious penetration of the fundamental areas has yet been made. There is of course a well-known publication by Harris entitled *Discourse Analysis Reprints,* but it is concerned with rearrangements of sentence structure which are not related to the general questions to be raised here.[1] Although there are linguists who are beginning to make contributions to the study of discourse—Gunter, Grimes, Stennes, and

[1] The definition of discourse analysis with which Zelig Harris begins his *Discourse Analysis Reprints* (The Hague: Mouton, 1963) shows no relation to the problems to be raised in this paper, nor to any other theoretical problems which I have been able to discover. For Harris, "discourse analysis is a method of seeking in any connected discrete linear material . . . some global structure characteristic of the whole discourse. . . ." This global structure is "a pattern of occurrence . . . of segments of the discourse relative to each other." Harris points out that this is the only type of structure that can be investigated "without bringing into account other types of data, such as relations of meanings throughout the discourse." This pursuit therefore forms part of Harris's previous interest in analyzing the phonology and grammar of a language without reference to meaning.

others—it is somewhat startling for linguists to discover that the major steps have been taken by sociologists. Sacks and Schegloff have isolated a number of fundamental problems and made some progress toward solution: the selection of speakers, the identification of persons and places, and the isolation of that social competence which allows members of a society to engage in talk. The influence of their work on my own paper will be apparent in the focus on sequencing in ritual insults, and on the social knowledge required for their interpretation.

Linguists should be able to contribute their skill and practice in formalization to this study. It would not be too much to say that the concepts of invariance and rule-governed behavior are more fully developed in linguistics than in any other field of social study. Yet there may be such a thing as premature formalization, which Garfinckel, Goffman, Sacks, and Schegloff are anxious to avoid: the categorical model of linguistic behavior may indeed lead linguists to set up paradigms of discrete features, mutually defined by their oppositions, for fields where only open sets are to be found in reality. But formalization is a fruitful procedure even when it is wrong: it sharpens our questions, and promotes the search for answers.

Some general principles of discourse analysis

The first and most important step in the formalization of discourse analysis is to distinguish *WHAT IS SAID* from *WHAT IS DONE*. There are a few sentence types from a grammatical viewpoint (principally *statements, questions,* and *imperatives*), and these must be related by discourse rules to the much larger set of actions done with words. It is commonplace to use these terms interchangeably with the names of certain actions: *assertions, requests for information,* and *commands,* respectively. But there is no such simple one-to-one relationship: it is easy to demonstrate, for example, that requests for information can be made with statements, questions, or imperatives:

I would like to know your name.
What is your name?
Tell me your name!

Furthermore, there are a great many other actions which are done with words and which must be related by rule to the utterance: refusals, challenges, retreats, insults, promises, threats, etc. The rules which connect what is said to the actions being performed with words are complex; the major task of discourse analysis is to analyze them, and thus to show that one sentence follows another in a coherent way. If we hear the dialogue:

A: Are you going to work tomorrow?
B: I'm on jury duty.

we know intuitively that we are listening to coherent discourse. Yet there is no formal basis in sentence grammar to explicate our reaction to this well-formed sequence. A *statement* follows a *question;* the question is a *request for information;* but in what way does the statement form an *answer* to that request? Some fear that linguists will never be able to answer such questions, because one would have to enter into our grammars every known relation between persons and objects— in this case, that people on jury duty are not able to work.[2] However, the form of discourse rules is independent of such detail. In answering A's request for information Q-S_1 with a superficially unrelated statement S_2, B is in fact asserting that there is a proposition known to both A and B that connects this with S_1. When A hears B say "I'm on jury duty," he searches for the proposition which B is asserting; in this case, he locates, "If someone is on jury duty, he cannot go to work." B's answer is then heard as "I'm not going to go to work tomorrow."

The rule of discourse which we can then formulate will read as follows: *If A makes a request for information Q-S_1, and B makes a statement S_2 in response which cannot be expanded by rules of ellipsis to the form X S_1 Y, then S_2 is heard as an assertion that there exists a proposition P known to both A and B:*

$$\text{If } S_2, \text{ then (E) } S_1$$

where (E) is an existential operator, and from this proposition there is inferred an answer to A's request: (E) S_1.

This is a rule of interpretation which relates what is said (S_2) to what is done (the assertion of P and the answer to Q-S_1). Note that there is no direct connection between the two utterances Q-S_1 and S_2, and it would be fruitless to search for one.

The overall relation of discourse rules to utterances shows several levels of abstraction. Consider a conversation of the following superficial form:

A: Are you going to work tomorrow? (U_1)
B: I'm on jury duty. (U_2)

[2] It was an unpublished draft by Bever and Ross on "Underlying Structures in Discourse?" (mimeo, 1966) which put the issue most directly. In order to show coherence in a discourse such as "Everyone should read the Bible. Deuteronomy is one of the greatest books of the world," Bever and Ross thought that it would be necessary to include in the grammar that Deuteronomy is one of the books of the Bible, and that discourse analysis therefore lay outside linguistics. The rules of discourse developed here are not subject to this problem; they would typically show that some such relation is being asserted by the sequence itself, as listeners unfamiliar with the Bible would infer without difficulty.

A: Couldn't you get out of it? (U_3)
B: We tried everything. (U_4)

To understand the connections between these four utterances, they must be expanded to a scheme such as the following: Speaker A begins with

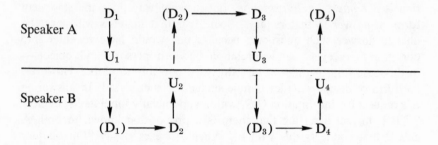

the intention of performing the action D_1; by a production rule, he does so with the utterances U_1. Speaker B uses the inverse interpretation rule to interpret U_1 as A's action D_1, and then applies a sequencing rule to decide his response D_2. He then codes D_2 into the utterance U_2 by a production rule, and Speaker A interprets this—in this case, by the rule cited which tells him that the statement *I'm on jury duty* is a response to D_1 to be interpreted as "I'm not going to work because I'm on jury duty." The other sequences follow in the same manner.

There are two types of discourse rules here: rules of interpretation UD (with their inverse rules of production DU), and sequencing rules DD which connect actions. There are of course other rules which connect actions at higher levels of abstraction. The diagram may actually show such structures as where D_5, D_6, and D_7 may be considered exchanges, encounters, inquiries, or even challenges and defenses depending on the larger context of interaction and higher-level rules.

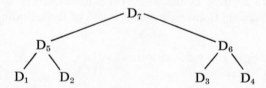

Any statement S_2 will not do in these sequences. If B had replied, "De Gaulle just lost the election," A could reasonably complain, "What has that to do with your going to work tomorrow?" The rule tells A to search for a proposition P which will make the connection: if he fails to find it, he will reject B's response. But the operation of the rule is invariant. A *must* inspect S_2 as a possible element in a proposition *if S_2 then (E) S_1*, before he can react. Failure to locate such a proposition

may reflect a real incompetence; younger members of a social group
may not be able to find the proposition being asserted. Thus Linus
knocks at Violet's front door and says:

LINUS: Do you want to play with me, Violet?
VIOLET: You're younger than me (*shuts the door*).
LINUS: (*puzzled*): She didn't answer my question.[3]

The unstated proposition being asserted here by Violet is presumed to
be part of the communal *shared knowledge,* but it has not in fact reached
Linus yet. This concept of shared knowledge is an essential element in
discourse analysis; to illustrate its importance further, we may consider
examples in which statements are heard as *requests for confirmation.*
The following exchanges are taken from a therapeutic interview.[4]

THERAPIST: Oh, so she *told* you.
PATIENT: Yes.
THERAPIST: She didn't say for *you* . . .
PATIENT: No.
THERAPIST: And it never occurred to her to prepare dinner.
PATIENT: No.
THERAPIST: But she does go to the store.
PATIENT: Yes.

These four instances are typical of a great many examples, where the
first utterance is a statement and the second is "yes" or "no." It seems
that a statement is functioning as equivalent to a yes-no question—that
is, a *request for information.* These statements have the same compelling
force as requests made in question form; we frequently see that the patient is not allowed to continue until a yes or no is given.

A great many speakers habitually use statements to ask for confirmation. How is it that we regularly and reliably recognize these as
requests, and not as assertions? There is a simple and invariant rule of
discourse involved here; it depends upon the concept of shared knowledge, which I will introduce into the rules by classifying all reported
events as A-events, B-events, or AB-events. Given any two-party conversation, there exists an understanding that there are events which A
knows about, but B does not; events which B knows about, but A
does not; and events which are known to both. We can then state simply
the rules of interpretation: *If A makes a statement about a B-event, it
is heard as a request for confirmation.* If A makes a statement about an
A-event ("I'm sleepy"), it is not heard as such a request. But if he

[3] Charles M. Schulz, *Peanuts à Vendre* (J. Dupuis, Marcinelle-Charleroi-Bel-
gíque, 1968), p. 64. I happen to have seen this in a French translation, but I am
sure that the English original reflects many parallel cases in real life.
[4] From current studies of therapeutic interviews being carried out by David
Fanshel of the Columbia School of Social Work and myself.

270 Rappin' and stylin' out

utters a statement about a B event ("You were up late last night"), it is heard as requesting a confirmation, "Is it true that. . . ."[5]

In addition to these concepts of shared and unshared knowledge, there are other elements of discourse which are based on sociological concepts: notions of role, rights, duties, and obligations associated with social rules. Now consider the following exchange from a narrative of the patient, Rhoda, in the therapeutic sessions cited above.

RHODA: Well, when are you planning to come home?
RHODA'S MOTHER: Oh, why-y?

In the face of such a sequence, it is common to say that "a question is answered with a question." But questions do not answer questions, any more than statements do. *Answers* are given to *requests;* they may occasionally take the form of questions. Closer examination of this sequence shows that Rhoda's question is a *request* for action, not information, and her mother's question is a *refusal* of that request. But what are the rules which allow us to make this interpretation?

A parallel case can be observed in the following extract from one of our group sessions with the Jets.[6] The speakers involved here are Stanley, the president of the Jets, and Rel, a Puerto Rican member who is also one of the officers (prime minister). At one point Rel called for quiet:

REL: Shut up please!
STANLEY: . . . 'ey, you tellin' *me?*
REL: Yes. Your mother's a duck.

Rel's first remark—an imperative—is clearly a command or *request for action.* Stanley's response is formally a *question,* but it is certainly not a *request for information;* again, we intuitively recognize that Stanley is refusing,[7] but by what regular rule of interpretation do we recognize this? The general form of the answer may be outlined as follows. The underlying rules for *requests* for action appear to have this form: *A requests B to do X for the purpose Y under conditions Z.* For this

---

[5] There are cases where A makes a statement about an AB-event which require an answer; but these seem to be equivalent to rhetorical questions which are not requests for information, and should probably be covered by a different rule.

[6] An adolescent club in South Central Harlem, composed of a number of peer groups of Negro boys thirteen to seventeen years old, one of the main sources of data for the study of nonstandard Negro English as reported in Labov et al., Cooperative Research Report 3288 (see footnote 9). This particular session was the subject of considerable study; it was recorded on videotape as well as on multiple audio tracks.

[7] At a higher level of analysis, this is a challenge to Rel (see Labov et al., Cooperative Research Report 3288, sec. 4.2.4.). However, the rules presented here are aimed at the lowest level of abstraction, closest to the linguistic material.

to be heard as a valid command, it is necessary for the following additional preconditions to hold. *B must believe that A believes that:*

X needs to be done;
B has the ability to do X;
B has the obligation to do X;
A has the right to tell B to do X.

There are many ways to perform this request, and many ways of aggravating or mitigating the force of the command. One device involves making statements or asking questions which refer to any of the four preconditions. The same mechanism can be used to refuse the request. In both of the examples just given, B refuses by asking a question concerning the relation of A, B, and X which is heard as a question about (and a challenge to) the fourth precondition.

These brief illustrations from current work on discourse analysis show that the form of discourse rules is independent of the particular propositions being asserted, challenged, or denied. These rules have to do with invariant relations between the linguistic units and actions intended or interpreted. Discourse rules also contain references to unstated assumptions about social relations, some of which we are only beginning to work out. These involve the concepts of shared or social knowledge, the roles of speaker, addressee, and audiences, their rights and obligations, and other constraints which have not appeared before in the array of linguistic primitives. Some linguists who are currently analyzing the deep structure of sentences have come to realize that one must posit elaborate presuppositions to explain syntactic data, but they have not yet attempted to incorporate such presuppositions into their formal rules.

The questions we have posed so far have been based upon examples relatively transparent to our intuitive sense of what was being done (especially when larger sections of the text are taken into account). But in the last example, Rel's closing remark is not at all clear in this sense. Why did Rel tell Stanley that his mother was a duck? Does this have any cognitive meaning, and if so, what rules of interpretation are operating? Rel's remark performed some kind of work, because Stanley then retired from his threatening posture, and he apparently considered the incident closed. Stanley regularly insists on his status as president of the Jets; he never backs down from a challenge or backs away from a fight. There are a number of times in this group session when sequences such as these led to fights—semi-serious, but nonetheless real. If Rel had just said, "Yes," there would certainly have been some punches traded. But his last remark was accepted as appropriate, coherent discourse, establishing some kind of closure to the incident. To those outside this subculture, Rel's utterance, and the action intended, are as opaque as the previous examples were transparent. Those who have some knowledge of urban ghetto culture will recognize Rel's "Your mother's a duck" as a ritual insult, and they will connect it with the institution of "the dozens," "sounding" or "signifying." "Sounding" is a well-organized speech event which occurs with great frequency in the verbal interaction of Negro adolescents we have studied, and it occupies long stretches of their time. This speech event is worth describing as part of the general program of "the ethnography of speaking" outlined by Hymes.[8] Here we have an opportunity to go further; we hope to establish the fundamental rules which govern this sounding, and to use this investigation to achieve some deeper understanding of discourse analysis. If the rules for sounding are appropriate and well constructed, it should be possible to throw light on the particular problem cited here: Why does Stanley retire when Rel says to him, "Your mother's a duck"?

Studies on nonstandard Negro English

For the past four years, we have been engaged in a study of the nonstandard English of Negro speakers in urban ghetto areas, principally in South Central Harlem.[9] Our purpose was two-fold: (1) to examine the differences in structure between nonstandard Negro English and the standard English of the classroom, and (2) to examine the differences in the use of language in these two subcultures—to understand the speech events and standards of verbal skill which governed language in the vernacular culture. Our study of ritual insults is drawn from this second part of our work.

Although we used a variety of means of studying and recording speech, including surveys of adult speakers, our basic approach was through long-term interaction with adolescent peer groups. We first made contact with the group through our participant observer, John Lewis, who was located in the area. Several leading members were

[8] Dell Hymes, "The Ethnography of Speaking," in *Anthropology and Human Behavior* (Washington: Anthropological Society of Washington, 1962), pp. 13–53. Reprinted in H. Joshua Fishman, ed., *Readings in the Sociology of Language* (The Hague: Mouton, 1968).

[9] This work is described in detail in Cooperative Research Report 3288 (William Labov et al., *A Study of the Non-Standard English of Negro and Puerto Rican Speakers in New York City* [Washington, D.C.: Office of Education, 1969]). This research, carried out from 1965 to 1968, was supported by the U.S. Office of Education. I am indebted to Paul Cohen, Clarence Robins, John Lewis, and Benji Wald for their assistance in this study, and particularly to Benji Wald for suggestions incorporated into the present version of the analysis of sounding. Much of the following material on sounding is adapted from Section 4.2.3. of CRP 3288, vol. 2.

interviewed individually, and a number of trips and group sessions were held in which the members were recorded in spontaneous interaction with each other. Most of the important material for grammatical analysis was recorded at group sessions, where each person was recorded on an individual track. We also obtained a great deal of valuable material on sounding from recordings made en route in a microbus, where it is difficult to say at all times who has said what. Both kinds of data will be used in the analysis to follow. We finally interviewed all members of each group in individual sessions, so that we can compare individual and group speech styles for the preadolescent Thunderbirds and Aces, and the adolescent Jets, Cobras, and Oscar Brothers, as well as for the comparable white groups from Inwood. All of the data on sounding, however, are drawn from group sessions where members were talking to each other.

The following pages present a large body of information about this speech event. There should be very little difficulty in understanding the literal meaning of the sounds as English sentences: the grammar used (nonstandard Negro English, NNE) presents no particular difficulty to most Americans; the vocabulary is not especially hip or esoteric; the trade names and personalities mentioned are part of the general American scene. But the activity itself is not well known: the point of the whole proceeding will escape many readers. The ways in which sounds are delivered, and the evaluation of them by the group, follow a well-established ritual pattern which reflects many assumptions and much social knowledge not shared by members of other subcultures. To understand the significance of sounds, and the function of this activity for members of the vernacular NNE culture, it will be necessary to write explicit rules of discourse for producing, interpreting, and answering sounds. In our original investigation of sounding, we were much concerned with the syntactic structures involved. Much of this material is preserved here, since it adds considerable depth to our understanding of the abstract operations involved.

Terms for the speech event

A great variety of terms describe this activity: "the dozens," "sounding," and "signifying" are three of the most common. The activity itself is remarkably similar throughout the various Negro communities, both in the form and content of the insults themselves and in the rules of verbal interaction which operate. In this section we will refer to the institution by the most common term in Harlem—"sounding."

Sounding, or playing the dozens, has been described briefly in a number of other sources, particularly Dollard and Abrahams. Koch-

274   *Rappin' and stylin' out*

man has dealt with sounding in Chicago in his general treatment of speech events in the Negro community.[10]

The oldest terms for the game of exchanging ritualized insults is "the dozens." Various possibilities for the origin of this term are given by Abrahams, but none is very persuasive. One speaks of "the dozens," "playing the dozens," or "putting someone in the dozens."[11] The term "sounding" is by far the most common in New York, and is reported as the favored term in Philadelphia by Abrahams. "Woofing" is common in Philadelphia and elsewhere, "joning" in Washington, "signifying" in Chicago, "screaming" in Harrisburg, and, on the West Coast, such general terms as "cutting," "capping," or "chopping." The great number of terms available suggests that there will be inevitably some specialization and shift of meaning in a particular area. Kochman suggests that "sounding" is used in Chicago for the initial exchanges, "signifying" for personal insults, and "the dozens" for insults on relatives. In New York, "the dozens" seems to be even more specialized, referring to rhymed couplets of the form:

I don't play the dozens, the dozens ain't my game
But the way I fucked your mama is a god damn shame.

But "playing the dozens" also refers to any ritualized insult directed against a relative. "Sounding" is also used to include such insults, and includes personal insults of a simpler form. Somebody can "sound on" somebody else by referring to a ritualized attribute of that person.

It seems to be the case everywhere that the superordinate terms which describe a verbal activity are quite variable and take on a wide range of meanings, while the verbal behavior itself does not change very much from place to place. People talk much more than they talk about talk, and as a result there is more agreement in the activity than in the ways of describing it. A member of the NNE subculture may have idiosyncratic notions about the general terms for sounding and the dozens without realizing it. He can be an expert on sounds and be quite untrustworthy on sounding.

The shape of sounds

As noted above, some of the most elaborate and traditional sounds are dozens in the form of rhymed couplets. A typical opening dozen is cited above. Another favorite opening is:

[10] John Dollard, "The Dozens: The Dialect of Insult," *American Imago* I (1939):3–24; Roger D. Abrahams, "Playing the Dozens," *Journal of American Folklore* 75 (1962):209–18. See also the Kochman ethnography article in this volume.
[11] Abrahams, "Playing the Dozens," p. 209.

I hate to talk about your mother, she's a good old soul
She got a ten-ton pussy and a rubber asshole.

Both of these initiating dozens have "disclaiming" or retiring first lines, with second lines which contradict them. They are in this sense typical of the usage of young adults, who often back away from the dozens, saying "I don't play that game," or quoting the proverb, "I laugh, joke and smoke, but I don't play." There is a general impression that sounding is gradually moving down in the age range—it is now primarily an adolescent and preadolescent activity, not practiced as much by young men twenty to thirty years old; but we have no exact information to support this notion. The rhymed dozens were used by adolescents in New York City twenty years ago. In any case, most young adolescents do not know many of the older rhymed dozens, and are very much impressed by them. To show the general style, we can cite a few others which have impressed the Jets and Cobras (and are not included in the twenty examples given by Abrahams):

I fucked your mother on top of the piano
When she came out she was singin' the Star Spangled Banner.

Fucked your mother in the ear,
And when I came out she said "Buy me a beer."

The couplet which had the greatest effect was probably

Iron is iron, and steel don't rust,
But your momma got a pussy like a Greyhound bus.

The winner in a contest of this sort is the man with the largest store of couplets on hand, the best memory, and perhaps the best delivery. But there is no question of improvisation, or creativity when playing, or judgment in fitting one sound into another. These couplets can follow each other in any succession; one is as appropriate as another. The originators certainly show great skill, and C. Robins remembers long hours spent by his group in the 1940's trying to invent new rhymes, but no one is expected to manufacture them in the heat of the contest. The Jets know a few rhymed dozens, such as "Fucked his mother on a red-hot heater/ I missed her cunt 'n' burned my peter," but most of the traditional rhymes are no longer well known. One must be quite careful in using the rhymed dozens with younger boys; if they cannot top them, they feel beaten from the start, and the verbal flow is choked off. To initiate sounding in a single interview, or a group session, we used instead such primitive sequences as: What would you say if someone said to you, "Your momma drink pee?" The answer is well known to most peer-group members: "Your father eat shit." This standard reply allows the exchange to begin along conventional lines, with room for elaboration and invention.

For our present purposes, the basic formulas can be described in terms of the types of syntactic structures, especially with an eye to the mode of sentence-embedding. I will draw most of the examples from two extended sounding sessions in which sounds were *used* rather than simply *quoted*. One was on a return trip from an outing with the Jets. Thirteen members were crowded on a single microbus; 180 sounds were deciphered from the recordings made in a thirty-five-minute ride. The other was a group session with five Thunderbirds in which Boot, Money, David, and Roger sounded against each other at great length. For these sixty sounds, the record is a complete and exact identification of every utterance possible.

There are of course many other sessions where sounds are cited or used: included in the examples given below are some from a trip with the Cobras in the microbus, where thirty-five sounds were deciphered from one short section of a recording.

Your mother is (like) . . .

Perhaps the simplest of all sounds is the comparison or identification of the mother with something old, ugly, or bizarre: a simple equative predication. The Jets use great numbers of such simple sounds:

> Your mother look like Flipper . . . like *Hoppity* Hooper. . . . Your mother's a Milk Dud . . . a Holloway Black Cow . . . a rubber dick . . . They say your mother was a Gravy Train. . . . Your mother's a bookworm . . . a ass, period. . . . Your mother James Bond. . . . Your mother Pussy Galore.

The Cobras use a number of sounds of this type:

> Your mamma's a weight-lifter . . . a butcher . . . a peanut man . . . a iceman . . . a Boston-Indian. Your mother look like Crooked-Mile Hank! . . . like that piece called King Kong! . . . Quahab's mother look like who did it and don't want to do it no more!

Note that the mass media and commercial culture provide a rich body of images. Such sounds were particularly appropriate on the Jet outing because every odd or old person that passed on the way would be a stimulus for another sound.

> Your mother look that taxi driver. . . . Your mother a applejack-eater . . . a flea-bag . . . the abominable snowman. . . . Your mother is Phil D. Basket (calypso accent). . . . Your mother's a diesel . . . a taxicab driver.

Another passerby sets off a train of simple identifications at the very end of the Jet outing:

—There go Willie mother right there.
—Your mother *is* a lizard.
—Your mother smell like a roach.
—Your mother name is Benedict Arnold.

One passing lady is the focus of a whole series of sounds. One can sound on someone simply by saying, "There go your mother."

—Hey-ey! (*whistle*) That's your mother over there!
—I know that lady.
—That's your mother.
—Hell, look the way that lady walk.
—. . . she sick in the head.
—Walk like she got a lizard-neck.

Your mother got . . .

Equally simple, from a syntactic point of view, is the series of sounds with the form *Your mother got so and so*. The Thunderbirds use long sequences of this type.

BOOT: Your mother got a putty chest.
BOOT: Your mother got hair growin' out her dunkie hole.
ROGER: Your mother got a .45 in her left titty.
MONEY: Your mother got a 45 degree titty.
BOOT: Your mother got titties behind her neck.

The first statement here is not a sound: it simply provides the base on which the sound is built, in this case the verb "got." The Jets use simple sounds of this sort as well.

—You got the nerve to talk.
—Your mother got funky drawers.
—Your mother got braces between her legs.

Again,

—Your mother got boobies that shake . . . hangdown lips . . .
—Bell mother got a old beat-up boot.
—Her mother got a face like a rubber ass . . .
—Junior got a face like a clown . . .

From an adolescent Chicago group: "Your momma got three titties: chocolate milk, white milk, and one half-and-half."

The Cobras show the same style; note that "wear" does as well as "got" where clothes are concerned:

—Your mother got on sneakers!
—Your mother wear high-heeled sneakers to church!

—Your mother wear a jock-strap.
—Your mother got polka-dot drawers!
—Your mother wear the seat of her drawers on the top of her head!

The Cobras sounds on clothes gradually drift away from the basic sounding pattern to a more complex structure that plays on the names of New York department stores:

—Your momma got shit on . . .
—Bra's mother bought her clothes from Ohrbach's—all front and no back!
—You get your shit from Bob Hope—Bob give it to you and you hope they fit!
—You got your suit from Woolworth! All wool but it ain't worth shit!
—You get your shoes from Buster Brown—brown on the top and all busted on the bottom!

Note that one of the Jets or Cobras can appear as the subject of a sound, though the majority are directed against someone's mother. In some ways, sounds of the *X got* . . . type are more complex when directed against a member, possibly because the comparisons are not as ritualized. Some of these are original and/or complex similes:

—He got a head like a water-hydrant, and sit . . .
—He got a head like a water-pump . . . a mailbox . . . like the front of a bus.
—You got a nose like a car fender!

The Thunderbirds say:

BOOT: Money got a head like a tornado mixed with a horse.
MONEY: You got a head of a motor.

Your mother so _____ she _____.

More complex comparisons are done with a quantifier, an adjective, and an embedded sentence of the type (b) or other predication.

DAVID: Your mother so old she got spider webs under her arms.
BOOT: Your mother so old she can stretch her head and lick out her ass.

Such sounds can be made freely against a member of the group.

ROGER: Hey Davy, you so fat you could slide down the razor blade without gettin' cut. . . . an' he so thin that he can dodge rain drops.

These are traditional "fat" and "thin" similes; they take on a particular value here because David *is* fat (a ritualized attribute for him). Boot continues with ritual sounds along these lines:

Boot: Eh eh, your mother's so skinny she could split through a needle's eye.

Boot: Your mother's so skinny, about that skinny, she can get in a Cheerioat and say, "Hula hoop, hula hoop!"

This last variant is one step more complex, with two clauses subordinated and two commercial products conjoined into one rhetorical figure. The same simile appears with a different breakfast cereal in a Jet sound (Stanley's):

—Your mother so skinny, she do the hula hoop in a Applejack.

Other Jet similes are somewhat more advanced than the T-Bird ones.

—Bell grandmother so-so-so-ugly, her rag is showin'.
—Bell mother was so small, she bust her lip on the curve.
—Your mother so white she hafta use Mighty White.
—Your mother so skinny, she ice-skate on a razor blade.
    . . . so skinny she can read under the doorknob . . .
    . . . so low she c'play Chinese handball on a curve.
    . . . so low, got to look down to look up.
    . . . so ugly, she got stinkin' with a glass of water.
    . . . so black, she sweat chocolate.
    . . . so black that she hafta steal to get her clothes.
    . . . so black that she has to suck my dick to get home.

Sometimes these similes have clauses subordinated within them: "Your mother is so _____ that when she _____ you can _____." To get all of this into one proposition is sometimes difficult in the heat of the moment.

—Your mother's so small, you play hide-and-go-seek, y'all c'slip under a penny.

Here the conjunction "when" is omitted (not uncommon in the speech of children), but the "y'all" seems out of place, and it could not be too unfair to say that this syntax is just beyond the range of performance available to the speaker. Boot of the Thunderbirds can handle constructions of this complexity, but he is the only one who can. The following sound of Boot is even more complex, since the "when" clause conjoins two other clauses:

Boot: His mother was so dirty, when she get the rag take a bath, the water went back down the drain.

Here the only flaw in the surface structure is perhaps the absence of "and" before "take a bath." The underlying structure of this sentence might be shown as:

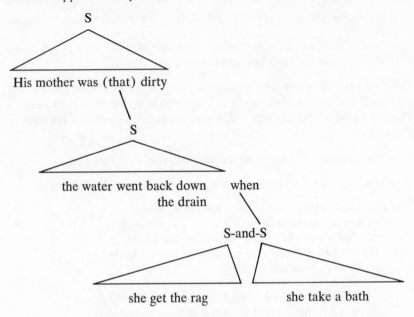

The structure of the sound makes it necessary to foreground the "when" clauses, so that the action which makes the insult can be last rather than ending with a condition. This means that two clauses interpose between the quantifier and the predication "went down"—a type of left-hand embedding in the surface which is indeed rare in colloquial speech. Boot uses a similar construction without the initial "so" clause in the following sound, which again is well beyond the syntactic competence of most members:

> Boot: Your mother, when she got to work and she had—those, you know—open-toe shoes, well, her stockings reach her—be sweeping the ground.

Notice that the following sound is much simpler, since the main point is made by a subordinated clause which can therefore appear in a final position:

> Boot: His mother go to work without any drawers on, so that she could get a good breeze.

Some of the Jets can use constructions as complex as those of Boot just given. The most complex syntax occurs in sounds of the type *Your X has Y* with attributive quantifiers dominating several sentences.

> —Who father wear raggedy drawers?
> —Yeh, the ones with so many holes in them when-a-you walk, they whistle?

This sound is received with immediate enthusiasm.

—Oh shi-it! When you walk they whistle! Oh shit!
—Tha's all he got left'. . . . He never buys but one pair o' drawers.

And shortly afterward, this sound models another of the same form:

JR.: Ronald got so many holes in his socks, when he walks them shoes hum!
—Them shoes say MMMM!

Again, it may be helpful to show some of the abstract structure which underlies sounds of this complexity:

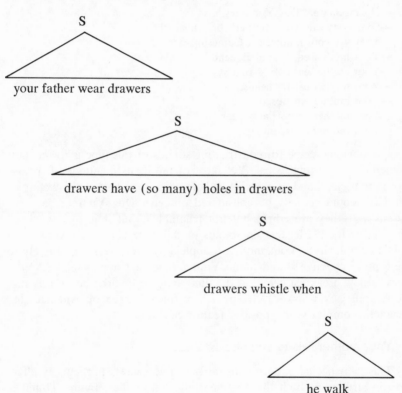

The comparative node "so many" is contained in a relative clause, and it dominates in turn a sentence which dominates a time clause. It cannot be accidental that all of these complex structures are positively evaluated by the group. We can argue that only an idea of exceptional merit would justify the originator's effort of using such syntax, and that the evaluation refers to the idea; or we can argue that the complexity of the structure itself is impressive for the listener.

Your mother eat _____.

We now return to a different type of sound which does not involve similes or metaphors, but portrays direct action with simple verbs. The power of these sounds seems to reside in the incongruity or absurdity of the elements juxtaposed—which may be only another way of saying that we do not really understand them.

> BOOT: I heard your mother eat Rice Krispies without any milk.
> ROGER: Eat 'em raw!
> BOOT: Money eat shit without puttin' any cornflakes on.

The Jets use such constructions freely as well.

> —His mother eat Dog Yummies.
> —Somebody said your mother's breath smell funny.
> —They say your mother eat Gainesburgers.
> —Your mother eat fried dick heads.
> —Your mother eat coke-a-roaches.
> —Your mother eat rat heads.
> —Your mother eat Bosco.
> —Your mother a applejack-eater.
> —Your mother eat scumbag.

The obvious recipe for constructing sounds of this type is to mention something disgusting to eat. Yet most of the items mentioned here are not in that class, and as we will see below less than half of the examples we have could actually be considered obscene. Dog Yummies are not disgusting (they are edible but not palatable), but it is plainly "low" to eat dog food. Elegance in sounds of this type can also involve syntactic complexity: "Your mother a applejack eater" seems intuitively to be a more effective sound than "Your mother eat applejack." (Applejack, a new breakfast cereal at the time, may be favored because it suggests applejack whiskey). If so, it is a further piece of evidence that syntactic complexity is a positive feature of sounds.

Your mother raised you on _____.

This is a specific pattern with fairly simple syntax, particularly effective in striking at both the opponent and his mother. In the Thunderbirds' session, a series of such sounds was initiated by one of the investigators.

> WL: Your mother raised you on ugly milk.
> BOOT: Your mother raised you on raw corn.
> DAVID: Your mother raised you with big lips.
> BOOT: Your mother gave you milk out a cave.
> BOOT: Your mother gave you milk out her ass.
> . . . When you just born, she say "Take a shot."

I went to your house . . .

A very numerous and important series of sounds are directed against the household and the state of poverty that exists there. Some of these are complex rhymes, quite parallel to the rhymed dozens:

> BOOT: I went to your house to ask for a piece of cheese
> The rat jumped up and say "Heggies, please."

"Heggies" is the claiming word parallel to "dibbs," "halfsies," "allies," "checks," etc., which was standard in New York some twenty years ago. Today "heggies" is a minor variant, though it is still recognized, having given way to "thumbs up."

Most sounds of this type are in prose. Many are directed at the strong position of rats and roaches in the household. They may take the form of anecdotes disguised as true stories.

> BOOT: Hey! I went up Money house and I walked in Money house, I say, I wanted to sit down, and then, you know a roach jumped up and said, "Sorry, this seat is taken."
> ROGER: I went in David house, I saw the roaches walkin' round in combat boots.

Several sounds from a session with the Aces may be quoted here, in which the members noted where they had learned various sounds.

> TONY: A boy named Richard learned me this one: When I came across your house, a rat gave me a jay-walkin' ticket.
> RENARD: When I came to your house, seven roaches jumped me and one search me.
> TED: And I made this one up: I was come in your house; I got hit on the back of my head with a Yoohoo bottle.

Ted's original sound seems weak; it leans upon the humor of specifying a Yoohoo bottle but does not connect with one of the major topics of sounding. One such topic is the bathroom, or lack of one, a strong point to sound on:

> BOOT: I went to your house and ask your mother, could I go to the bathroom. She said "The submarine jus' lef'."
> ROGER: I went to his house—I wanted to go to the bathroom, and her mother—his mother gave me a pitchfork and a flashlight.
> ROGER: I ringed his bell and the toilet stool flushed.

Remarks about someone's house and how poor it is are apt to become quite personal, as we will see below. The Jets did not produce many of the "I went in X's house . . ." sounds, but the following occurred in quick succession:

> —I went in Junior house 'n' sat in a chair that caved in.
> —You's a damn liar, 'n' you was eatin' in my house, right?

—I went to Bell's house 'n' a Chinese roach said, "Come and git it."
—I brought my uncle—I brought my uncle up Junior house—I didn't
trust *them* guys.

The tendency to take "house" sounds personally shows up in the second
line of this series. As we will see below, the charge, "You was eatin' in
my house" returns the accusation of hunger against the originator, and
this can have a solid basis in real life.

Other anecdotal forms

There are many other anecdotal sounds which do not fall into a single
mold. Some are quite long and include the kind of extra detail which
can give the illusion, at the outset, that an actual story is being told.
From the Jets' session we find:

—I ran over Park Avenue—you know, I was ridin' on my bike—and-uh-I
seen somebody fightin'; I said lemme get on this now. I ran up there and
Bell and his mother, fallin' all over: I was there first x x x gettin' it—
gettin' that Welfare food x x

The incoherent sections are filled with slurping noises which are an important part of such food sounds—indicating that those involved were
so desperately hungry and so uncivilized that they behaved like animals.
One can also deliver an anecdote with the same theme as the rhymed
dozens quoted above:

—Boah. I'm not gonna say who it was, boah. But I fucked somebody's
mother on this bridge one night, Whooh! That shit was so good, she
jumped overboard in the river.

There are any number of miscellaneous sounds that can be disguised as
pseudo-anecdotes.

ROGER: One day, Money's mother's ass was stuck up and she called
Roto-Rooter.

On the other hand, there are anecdotes which take the form of rhymes:

BOOT: I went down south to buy a piece of butter
I saw yo' mother layin' in the gutter.
I took a piece of glass and stuck it up her ass
I never saw a motherfucker run so fas'.

Such narratives typically use the simplest type of syntax, with minimal
subjects and preterit verb heads. The anecdotal type of sound appears
to be most effective when it is delivered with hesitations and false starts,
rather than with the smooth delivery of the other types of sounds. The
technique is therefore closely associated with certain types of narrative

styles in which the point is delayed to the final clause, where the evaluation is fused with result and coda, as in a joke.[12] It is generally true that all sounds have this structure: the evaluative point must be at the very end.

Portraits

Just as narrative calls for simple syntax, sounds which present elaborate portraits demand syntactic complexity. The most common are those which place someone's mother on the street as a whore.

—Willie mother stink; she be over here on 128 St. between Seventh 'n' Eighth, waving her white handkerchief: (*falsetto*) "C'mon, baby, only a nickel."

—Hey Willie mother be up there, standin' the corner, be pullin' up her-her dress, be runnin' her ass over 'n' see those skinny, little legs.

Absurd and bizarre forms

The formal typology of sounds presented so far actually covers the great majority of sounds used. But there are a number of striking examples which are not part of any obvious pattern, sounds which locate some profoundly absurd or memorable point by a mechanism not easy to analyze. There is the darkly poetic sound used by Eddie of the Cobras:

—Your mother play dice with the midnight mice.

Rhyme also plays an essential part in this uncommon sound:

—Ricky got shot with his own fart [fat].

We might also cite the following exchange:

—Your mother take a swim in the gutter.
—Your mother live in a garbage can.
—Least I don't live on 1122 Boogie Woogie Avenue, two garbage cans to the right.

The attraction of trade names like Right Guard or Applejack may be largely based on their bizarre and whimsical character. Any kind of unfeminine or outlandish behavior on the part of one's mother can be charged:

—Willie mother make a livin' playin' basketball.
—I saw Tommy mother wearin' high-heel sneakers to church.

[12] William Labov and Joshua Waletsky, "Narrative Analysis," in *Essays on the Verbal and Visual Arts,* Proceedings of the American Ethnological Society (Seattle: University of Washington Press, 1967), pp. 12–44.

Response forms: puns and metaphors

Sounds are usually answered by other sounds, and the ways in which they follow each other will be discussed below. But there is one formal feature of a sound which is essentially made for responses: "At least my mother ain't . . ." Although these forms cannot be used to initiate sounding, several can succeed each other, as in these sequences from the Aces' session:

—At least I don't wear bubblegum drawers.
—At least his drawers ain't bubblegum, it's not sticky like yours.
—At least my mother don't work in the sewer.
—At least my mother don't live in the water-crack, like yours.

There is a series of traditional responses of this form which incorporates complex puns. Abrahams cites a dozen from South Philadelphia, including five common in Harlem. Perhaps the best known is:

—At least my mother ain't no railroad track, laid all over the country.

Such forms frequently occur as simple similes, such as

—Your mother's like a police station—dicks going in and out all the time.

Although puns such as these seem to have been part of the original dozens tradition, they are no longer common among adolescents in Harlem. They seem to have been adopted by white groups in the city, where they are quite well known. When our white interviewers used some of these in sounding sessions, they were admired, but they did not initiate a series of other sounds, as in the case of "Your mamma drink pee" or "Your mother raised you on ugly milk."

This presentation of the "shape" of sounds has also given the reader some idea of the range of topics which are sounded on. Our own exploratory interviews in other parts of the country show that this scheme applies quite well to other cities and other Negro communities. Kochman and his students have provided descriptions of the Chicago patterns which are very similar to those of Harlem.[13] O. C. Wortham in San Francisco has collected a large body of preadolescent sounds, many of which might have been quoted directly from the Thunderbirds, Jets, or Cobras: "Your mama got a cast on her right titty"; "Your mama wears a jocky strap"; "Your mother wears holy drawers"; "Ricky's mama eat shit"; "Your mother named Mike"; "Your mother wears tennis shoes to work"; "He say his mama plays Batman"; "Hey, it's so cold in your house the roaches walk around with fur coats on"; "Man I done busted

[13] See Kochman ethnography article, in this volume.

you so low, you can walk up under that piece of paper with a top hat on."

Ritual insults among white peer groups

While some elements of the dozens and other Negro ritual insults have appeared among white peer groups in the urban centers, the typical forms used among whites are quite different from those of Negroes. The personal experience of two of our own investigators (Paul Cohen and Benji Wald), drawn from different areas of New York, shows firm agreement on ritual insults. Whereas the NNE practice of sounding ranges over a wide variety of forms and topics which are combined with great flexibility, the white forms are essentially a limited set of routines. Two of the most common begin with "Eat shit":

A: Eat shit.
B: What should I do with the bones?
A: Build a cage for your mother.
B: At least I got one.
A: She *is* the least.

A: Eat shit.
B: Hop on the spoon.
A: Move over.
B: I can't, your mother's already there.

These are indeed ritual and impersonal insults, directed in part against the opponent's mother. But the sequencing occurs in a fixed form, and there is little room for individual choice. These are essentially "snappy answers" which show how knowledgeable rather than how competent the speaker is. It is the aptness of the rejoinder which is looked for:

A: Kiss my ass.
B: Move your nose.

A: Fuck you.
B: Yeh, that would be the best one you ever had.

A: You motherfucker.
B: Your mother told.

A: Got a match?
B: My ass against your face.

These are trick responses. The first speaker may say something aggressive (but not particularly clever) or he may be tricked into a routine such as:

A: How tall are you?
B: Five foot seven.
A: I didn't think shit piled that high.

The white groups also use a certain number of comparisons of the "You are so *X* that *Y*" type: "You're so full of shit your eyes are brown." Furthermore, there are similes directed against one's mother that overlap those cited (p. 278): "Your mother so low she could play handball on a curve . . . walk under a pregnant cockroach without stooping."

The white material is limited in content as well as form and quantity. Shit is the most common topic, and in general the insults are based on taboo words rather than taboo activities. One does not find the proliferation of odd and bizarre elements and the wide range of choice characteristic of the NNE forms. Furthermore, this activity does not occupy any considerable time for the white groups—in a word, it is not a speech event for white groups in the sense that sounding is a speech event for the Negro groups.

There is some evidence that southern whites (e.g., Mississippi Delta area) show the same range of ritual insults as northern whites, and that the rich development of sounding described here is indeed a characteristic of the Negro speech community.

Attributes and persons sounded on

A review of the content of the sounds given above (pp. 276–86) will show that a wide but fairly well-defined range of attributes is sounded on. A mother (grandmother, etc.) may be cited for her age, weight (fat or skinny), ugliness, blackness, smell, the food she eats, the clothes she wears, her poverty, and of course her sexual activity. As far as persons are concerned, sounding is always thought of as talking about someone's mother. But other relatives are also mentioned—as part of the search for variety in switching, or for their particular attributes. In order of importance, one can list the opponent's relatives as: mother, father, uncle, grandmother, aunt. As far as number of sounds is concerned, the opponent himself might be included as second-most important to his mother, but proverbially sounds are thought of as primarily against relatives.

One of the long epic poems of the NNE community ("toasts"), called "Signifying Monkey," gives us some insight into the ordering of relatives. Signifying Monkey stirs up trouble ("signifies") by telling the lion that the elephant had sounded on him:

"Mr. Lion, Mr. Lion, there's a big burly motherfucker comin' your way,
Talks shit about you from day to day."

The monkey successively reports that the elephant had talked about the lion's sister, brother, father and mother, wife and grandmother.

The monkey said, "Wait a minute, Mr. Lion," said, "That ain't all,"

He said, "Your grandmother," said, "she was a lady playin' in the old
  backyard,"
Said, "evertime he seen her, made his dick get on the hard."

Even more relatives are brought in, which brings the monkey to the
inevitable conclusion:

He said, "Yeah he talked about your aunt, your uncle and your cousins,
Right then and there I knew the bad motherfucker was playin' the
dozens."

What is said about someone's mother's age, weight, or clothes can be
a general or traditional insult, or it can be local and particular. The
presence of commercial tradenames in the sounds is very striking:
Bosco, Applejack, Wonder Bread, Dog Yummies, Gainesburgers, Gravy
Train, as well as the names of the popular figures in the mass media:
James Bond, Pussy Galore, Flipper. The street culture is highly local,
and local humor is a very large part of sounds. As noted before, one of
the best ways to start a loud discussion is to associate someone with a
local character who is an "ultra-rich" source of humor. Trade names
have this local character—and part of the effect is the superimposing
of this over-specific label on the general, impersonal figure of "your
mother" (as in "Your mother look like Flipper"). Local humor is omnipresent and overpowering in every peer group—it is difficult to explain
in any case, but its importance cannot be ignored.

The odd or whimsical use of particular names can be illustrated by
a sequence that occurred when John Lewis left the microbus at an
early stop. As a parting shot, he leaned back in the window and
shouted genially "Faggots! Mother-fuckers!" This set up a chain of responses including a simple "Your mother!" from Rel, "You razor
blade bastard!" from someone else, and finally an anonymous "Winnie
the Pooh!"

Obscenity does not play as large a part as one would expect from
the character of the original dozens. Many sounds *are* obscene in the
full sense of the word. The speaker uses as many "bad" words and
images as possible—that is, words subject to taboo and moral repri-
mand in adult middle-class society. The originator will search for
images that would be considered as disgusting as possible: "Your
mother eat fried dick-heads." With long familiarity the vividness of this
image disappears, and one might say that it is *not* disgusting or obscene
to the sounders. But the meaning of the sound and the activity would
be entirely lost without reference to these middle-class norms. Many
sounds are "good" because they are "bad"—because the speakers know
that they would arouse disgust and revulsion among those committed to
the "good" standards of middle-class society. Like the toasts, sounds

derive their meaning from the opposition between two major sets of values: *their* way of being "good" and *our* way of being "bad."

The rhymed dozens are all uniformly sexual in character; they aim at the sexual degradation of the object sounded on. But the body of sounds cited above depart widely from this model: less than half of them could be considered obscene, in any sense. At one point in the Jet session, there is a sequence of three sounds concerning fried dick-heads. This is immediately followed by

—Your mother eat rat heads.
—Your mother eat Bosco.
—Your mother look that taxi driver.
—Your mother stinks.
—Hey Willie got on a talkin' hat.
—Your mother a applejack-eater.
—Willie got on a talkin' hat.
—So, Bell, your mother stink like a bear.
—Willie mother . . . she walk like a penguin.

This sequence of nine remarks contains no sexual references; the strongest word is *stink*. Many sounds depend upon the whimsical juxtaposition of a variety of images, upon original and unpredictable humor which is for the moment quite beyond our analysis. But it can be noted that the content has departed very far from the original model of uniform sexual insult.

Only someone very unfamiliar with the NNE subculture could think that the current generation is "nicer" and less concerned with sex than previous generations. The cry of "Winnie the Pooh!" does not mean that the Jets are absorbing refined, middle-class wit and culture. Its significance can only be understood by a deeper study of the nature of this ritual activity.

Evaluation of sounds

One of the most important differences between sounding and other speech events is that most sounds are evaluated overtly and immediately by the audience. In well-structured situations, like the Thunderbird sounding session, this is true of every sound. In wilder sessions with a great many participants, like the Jet session in the microbus, a certain number of sounds will follow each other rapidly without each one being evaluated.

The primary mark of positive evaluation is laughter. We can rate the effectiveness of a sound in a group session by the number of members of the audience who laugh. In the Thunderbird session, there were five members; if one sounded against the other successfully, the other three would laugh; a less successful sound showed only one laugh, or none.

The value of having a separate recording track for each speaker is very great indeed.

A really successful sound will be evaluated by overt comments: In the Jet session, the most common forms are: "Oh!" "Oh shit!" "God damn!" or "Oh Lord!" By far the most common is "Oh shit!" The intonation is important: when approval is to be signaled, the vowel of each word is quite long, with a high, sustained, initial pitch and a slow-falling pitch contour. The same words can be used to express negative reaction or disgust, but then the pitch is low and sustained. The implication of the positive exclamations is, "That is too much," or "That leaves me helpless."

Another even more forceful mode of approving sounds is to repeat the striking part of the sound oneself—in the Jet session, for example:

> JOHN L.: Who father wear raggedy drawers?
> WILLIE: Yeh the ones with so many holes in them when-a-you walk they whistle?
> REL: Oh . . . shi-it! When you walk they whistle! Oh shit!

Negative reactions to sounds are common and equally overt. The most frequent is phony: "Tha's phony!" "Phony shit!" But sounds are also disapproved as corny, weak, or lame. Stanley, the president of the Jets, elaborates his negative comments quite freely:

> JUNIOR: Aww, Nigger Bell, you smell like B. O. Plenty.
> BELL: Aww, nigger, you look like—you look like Jimmy Durante's grandfather.
> STAN: Aw, tha's phony [bullshit] . . . Eh, you woke me up with that phony one, man. . . .
> BELL: Junior look like Howdy Doody.
> STAN: That's phony too, Bell. Daag, boah! . . . Tonight ain't your night, Bell.

At another point, Stanley denounces a sound with a more complicated technique: "Don't tell 'im those phony jokes, they're so phony, you *got* to laugh."

The difference between these negative terms is not clear. For our present purposes, we may consider them equivalent, although they are probably used in slightly different ways by different speakers. The Cobras do not use the same negative terms as the Jets. They will say "Sh—you fake—take that shit outa here!" or most often, "That ain't where it's at."

These evaluative remarks are ways of responding to the overall effect of a sound. There is also considerable explicit discussion of sounds themselves. In the case of a traditional sound, like a rhymed dozen, one can object to an imperfect rendition. For example, Stevie answers one of our versions with "Tha's wrong! You said it wrong! Mistake!" Members are also very clear on who the best sounders are. Among the Thunderbirds, it is generally recognized that "Boot one of the best sounders . . . he's one of the best sounders of all." This very reputation will interfere with the chances of getting other members to initiate sounding —they know in advance that they will be outdone. In general, sounding is an activity very much in the forefront of social consciousness: members talk a great deal about it, try to make up new sounds themselves, and talk about each other's success. Sounding practices are open to intuitive inspection. It is possible to ask a good sounder, "What would you say if somebody said to you . . ." and he will be glad to construct an answer. Members will also make meta-comments on the course of a sounding session ("Now he's sounding on you, Money!!") or announce their intentions, as Roger does: "Aw, tha's all right. Now I'm gonna sound on you pitiful."

Furthermore, members take very sharp notice of the end result of a sounding contest, as noted below. In a sounding session, everything is public—nothing significant happens without drawing comment. The rules and patterning of this particular speech event are therefore open for our inspection.

The activity of sounding

We can distinguish two very different uses of sounds: (1) ritual sounding, and (2) applied sounding. The quotations given above are taken from sounding sessions which are examples of the first: rituals in which the sounding is done for its own sake. Applied sounding involves the use of sounds for particular purposes in the midst of other verbal encounters, and it follows a very different set of rules. We will consider ritual sounding first, beginning with the general rules which apply, and then looking at the operation of these rules in the two sessions which have been cited.

There are three participants in this speech event: antagonist A, antagonist B, and the audience. A sounds against B; the audience evaluates; B sounds against A; his sound is evaluated. The general structure is then more complex than most ABABAB exchanges: it is

A-1 e B-1 e A-2 e B-2 e . . .

A-1 almost always contains a reference to B's mother. B-1 should be based on A-1; to the extent that it is an original or well-delivered transformation of A-1, B may be said to have won. A-2 may be an entirely new sound. But if A-2 is a further transformation of B-1, it is usually evaluated even more highly. Whereas we may say that A-2 "tops" B-1 if it is intrinsically better, A may be said to "get" B most often if A-2 is a variant or clearly related to B-1. This is what is meant by "topping"

B—the exchange is held open. A skillful sounder can hold an exchange of variants open beyond the point where it would normally be considered ended by conventional estimates. The series may be terminated when one antagonist clearly wins over the other. Thus in that part of the Thunderbirds' session following Ricky's collapse, Boot clearly beats Money. The exchange starts with Boot's long story of how Money was tricked into thinking that a jar of urine was ice tea, and he drank it. Money objects, rather incoherently: "I know you love thuh—ice tea. I know you love to pee—i—ice cream tea." Boot then begins sounding:

A-1 BOOT: His mother go to work without any draws on so that she c'd get a good breeze.

B-1 MONEY: Your mother go, your mother go work without any, anything on, just go neked.

e DAVID: That's a lie.

In the first exchange, Money clearly fails, as evidenced by his hesitation; he simply exaggerates Boot's well-constructed and witty sound without the corresponding wit. David's comment is negative—particularly in that it takes Money's sound to be a factual claim.

A-2 BOOT: Your mother, when she got to work and she had—you know th- toe shoes, well her stockings reach her be—sweeping the ground.

e RICKY *laughs.*

e ROGER: Ho lawd! (*Laughs.*)

Boot's A-2 is stretching the limits of the syntax available to him, and he has considerable difficulty in getting it out. It is clearly an extension of A-1 and B-1, of the form "Your mother go to work with . . ." But instead of the conventional wit of A-1, or the reduced variant of B-1, A-2 enters the field of the unconventional and absurd. Boot scores two strong responses from Ricky and Roger.

Money cannot build further on the syntactic model, but he does attempt to respond to the theme of holes in shoes. There is no audience response.

B-2 MONEY: Your mother have holes—potatoes in her shoes.

Since Boot has won this exchange, he now begins a new sequence:

A-3 BOOT: Your mother got a putty chest [*laugh*].

B-3 MONEY: Arrgh! Aww—you wish you had a putty chest, right?

Money responds, but he does not sound. Boot continues with another sound of the "got" type; now, however, the pattern is complicated as Roger joins in, sounding specifically against Money. This is a second stage which occurs when one antagonist is clearly losing ground: he becomes the object of group sounding.

A-4   BOOT: Your mother got hair growing out her dunkee hole.
C-4 ⎰ ROGER: Money your mother got a 45 in her left titty.
      ⎱ MONEY: Awwww!
e   RICKY *laughs.*

Money now responds to Roger's sound with a variant which strikes us
as a very able one.

B-4   MONEY: Your mother got a 45° titty.

Now it is Roger who answers Money, and gets a strong response. Boot
then adds a sound which is rather incoherent and gets no response.

C-5   ROGER: Your mother got baptised in a whiskey bottle.
e   ⎰ MONEY *laughs.*
e   ⎨ RICKY *laughs.*
e   ⎱ DAVID *laughs.*
A-5   BOOT: Your mother sail the seven seas in a sardine can. (*Laughs.*)

The situation has become unclear. Sounding is defined for members as
one person sounding upon another, but three are involved. Money's
laughter indicates that he thinks Roger's sound is not against him, but
against Boot. David now explicitly says that the antagonists are Boot
and Roger, but Roger denies this; he is still sounding against Money.
Boot adds a further dig which recognizes that Roger's *him* means Money,
not Boot.

   DAVID: Now you and Roger sounding. (*Laughs.*)
 ⎰ ROGER: I'm sounding on him.
 ⎱ BOOT: That half of a motor. (*Laughs.*)

Given the sanction of a group attack against Money, David now begins
his own. But Money turns to us suddenly and says, "Can we sing now?"
(The formal recording of singing was one of the purposes of the session.) Money's question is interpreted as a transparent attempt to escape, and a storm of abuse descends on his head from the leaders of
the group. He is forced to acknowledge his defeat explicitly.

D-6 ⎰ DAVID: Everytime Money looks at the moon, everytime—
     ⎨ MONEY: Could we sing now?
     ⎨ BOOT *laughs.*
     ⎱ ROGER *laughs.*
     ⎰ DAVID: Money look at moon, he say "Ooo, look at the moon-
     ⎨ shine"—
     ⎨ ROGER: He changing the subject!
     ⎱ RICKY: Aww! Tryin' to change thuh -ih -subject!
      ROGER: What's the matter, you feeling all right, or you want some
      more sounding?
      MONEY: Uh-uh.

The sounding session goes on, with Money saying nothing. When he speaks up later on, Ricky says, "Hey Money, you better keep quiet, if you don't want 'em soundin' bad on you." It should be quite clear that there are winners and losers in sounding sessions.

The speech event we call sounding is not isolated from other forms of verbal interaction; it can merge with them or become transformed into a series of personal insults. When ritual insult changes into personal insult, the difference between the two becomes quite clear. We take as an instance the beginning of the sounding session with the Thunderbirds. To save space, evaluative reactions to each sound will be put in brackets after it.

In this session, we can observe the difficulty that members have in distinguishing between hypothetical and actual sounding. "What would you say if . . ." is quickly transformed into actual sounding. The series was initiated by an effort of C. Robins to get Money to sound.

> CR (*to* MONEY): What would you say if Boot said "Your father look like Funjie!"? (ROGER: "O Lord, oh Money . . . oh ho . . . Funjie . . . ooo!" ROGER, BOOT, RICKY, DAVID: *laugh.*)
> MONEY: Hunh?
> CR: That's like Funjie's your father. (ROGER: Ohh! BOOT, RICKY: *laugh.*)
> BOOT: He's sounding on you, Money!
> CR: No, no, if *Boot* said it. . . .

At this point, other staff members join in and try to make it clear that we are only asking what Money would say *if*. Money tries to answer, but Boot takes over with the support of the rest of the group. Our efforts to push Money to the fore do not succeed.

> DAVID: Boot one of the best sounders.
> MONEY: I say, uh-uhm-
> BOOT: Now if you said that to me . . .
> CR: No no no no, you sound him, tell him, say that . . .
> MONEY: He's one of the best sounders of all.
> CR, WL: Money sounds good too.
> BOOT: Now if he said that to me, know what I'd say? I'd say—

Boot is irrepressible. Money's failure to sound well in the face of Boot's dominant position is precisely the same phenomenon that W. F. Whyte observed in Doc's corner gang.[14] Followers did not bowl as well against the leader of the group as they could by themselves. In other situations we have seen Money sound very well.

> B-1 BOOT: I'd say, "His father got four lips."

[14] William F. Whyte, *Street Corner Society: The Social Structure of an Italian Slum* (Chicago: University of Chicago Press, 1955).

296 *Rappin' and stylin' out*

A-2 MONEY: I'd say, "Your mother got four lips." (BOOT: "That ain't nothin'." CR: "What does that mean?")

Boot's sound hits on the familiar topic of thick lips, part of the self-derogatory pattern of NNE (cf. Jets: "Your father got lips like a— Oldsmobile"). Money's hypothetical A-2 is the weakest kind of switch: substitution of one relative for another, and it is properly and immediately derogated. Money has failed again. The part of second antagonist is now taken up by David, a small, fat boy who is continually being pushed aside by Boot and is the constant butt of jokes. On the other hand, he has a great deal of courage and, unlike others in the group, he never gives up in the struggle to establish his position and never allows Boot to dominate the situation entirely. In the following sounding session, Boot applies his verbal skill with ruthless force to crush David, but David's verbal resources are greater than one would have predicted.

A-3 DAVID: So your . . . So then I say, "Your father got brick teeth."
B-3 BOOT: Aw your father got teeth growing out his behind! (MONEY, RICKY, ROGER *laugh.*)

Boot's response is a clear example of a winning effort. He takes David's hypothetical A-3 and adds to it elements of absurdity and obscenity that obtain positive evaluation from all three members of the audience. Note that Boot's sound is no longer hypothetical: it is the first "real sound" of the series. David attempts to top this by staying with the "behind" theme, but he fails to get a coherent thought out. He is not fluent in this area, at least in the face of Boot's ability.

A-4 DAVID: Yeah, your father, y- got, your father grow, uh, uh, grow hair from, from between his, y'know. (MONEY *laughs.*)
B-4 BOOT: Your father got calluses growin' up through his ass, and comin' through his mouth. (BOOT, MONEY, *and* RICKY *laugh.*)

Boot builds further on the original model and crushes David with a display of virtuosity that leaves him with nothing to say. Boot is not willing to leave it there; like many a good sounder, he can seize his advantage by piling one sound on another. He switches abruptly to:

B-4' BOOT: Your father look like a grown pig. (BOOT, MONEY, *and* RICKY *laugh.*)
A-5 DAVID: Least my—at least my father don't be up there talking uh-uh-uh-uh-uh-uh!

The fact that this is a personal insult and not a ritual insult is shown by the fact that Boot answers it. Since ritual insults are not intended as factual statements, the allegations of sounds are not denied. But Boot vigorously responds to David's taunt. Roger's comment acknowledges that Boot has been hit.

BOOT: Uh-so my father talks stutter talk what it mean? (ROGER: He talk the same way a little bit.)

Now Boot responds to David's insult with a comparable one, which is related to A-5 in exactly the way that one sound is related to another. Boot's father stutters; David's father is old and has gray hair—a simple fact, but Boot makes a great deal of it.

A-6 BOOT: At least my father ain't got a gray head! His father got a big bald spot with a gray head right down there, and one long string . . .

David is hurt, and he too feels it necessary to deny the personal insult. But Boot doesn't stop; he picks up the point of "one long string" and grinds it in over and over, to the amusement of Roger and Money.

⎰ DAVID: Because he' old, he's old, that's why! He's old, that's why! . . .
⎱ BOOT: . . . and one long string, that covers his whole head, one long string, about that high, covers his whole head. (ROGER: Ho Lord, one string! MONEY, BOOT *laugh*.)

Boot brings tears to David's eyes. Boot's sidekick Money does not mind, but Ricky objects.

DAVID: You lyin' Boo! . . . You know 'cause he old, tha's why!
RICKY: Aw man, cut it out.

Boot has won the day, but he has no sense of restraint. He now returns to ritual sounding: his next insults are not intended as allegations of fact, but David continues to take them as personal.

What follows now is no longer the controlled counterpoint of sounding, of the form A e B e, but an excited argument, in which both parties are in strident overlap most of the time. It is mostly David against Boot now; Boot's insults do not draw much response from the others, and one can sense the group support ebbing from him.

B-7 BOOT: Your father look like this—with his butt coming out, and he go (*slurp*) he look like . . .
DAVID: You a liar!
B-8 BOOT: You know one time I came over his house, I saw some slop in the garbage, you know, and then, and I left it there, and David say, David say (*slurp, chomp, chomp, chomp*). [MONEY *laughs*.]

David is ready to take up any weapon at hand. He seizes upon the poverty theme, and a personal charge that hits home. It takes some time for David to be heard; finally Boot stops his chomping effect to issue a vigorous (but ineffective) denial.

A-9 DAVID: So! and you always come over my house and say, yeah, Boot always come over my house and say, Boot always comin over my house to eat. He aks for food, and Ohhh lawww . . .

BOOT: I don't come over your house—I don't come nuttin! I only come over your house on school days and from now on I do.

David senses his advantage and pursues it.

DAVID: . . . and when we go swimmin', we go, you aks for food, and ever ti—and you come over my house—

Boot can no longer deny the factual truth of David's charge, but he tries to mitigate the facts—foolishly, perhaps, because David is ready with a crushing response.

BOOT: Yeah, I only be playin', I only be playin'!
DAVID: *Yeah, but you sure be eatin'!*

Not every story ends with the underdog showing as well as David. David's momentary success is all the more striking because Boot is without doubt in verbal control of the group. As we have seen, Boot continues his triumphant progress sounding against others, in no way daunted by this reversal. In these extracts, we have the full weight of evidence for the important point that Boot is the *verbal leader* of the Thunderbirds—that he excels at all the verbal skills of the NNE sub-culture. It is not only that Boot has a larger store of sounds at his disposal and can draw upon them more readily; his syntax is also more complex, and he can deliver sounds that no one else can. All of the more complex examples from the Thunderbirds cited above are those of Boot.

The rules for ritual sounding

In the presentation of sounding so far, we have seen that this speech event has a well-articulated structure. These rules can be broken; it is possible to hurl personal insults, and it is possible to join in a mass attack on one person. But there is always a cost in stepping out of the expected pattern—in the kind of uncontrolled and angry response which occurs, or in the confusion as to who is doing what to who.

As we examine these examples of sounding, the fundamental opposition between ritual insults and personal insults emerges. The appropriate responses are quite different: a personal insult is answered by a denial, excuse, or mitigation, whereas a sound or ritual insult is answered by another sound. Sounds are then necessarily chained into longer sequences, since a sound and its response are essentially the same kind of thing, and a response calls for a further response. The complexity of sounding is actually the result of this comparatively simple structure, so that our semantic diagram of sounding might be reduced to:

$$S_1 \quad e \quad S_2 \quad e \quad S_3 \quad e \quad . . .$$

On the other hand, personal insults produce dyads of interaction: insult (I) and denial or excuse (D). We observe a chain in this last exchange between Boot and David:

$$I_A \quad D_B \quad I_B \quad D_A \quad I_A \quad D_B \quad \ldots$$

but there is no inherent, structural reason for chaining as in the case of sounds. These are DD sequencing rules in the scheme outlined on page 268.

There is an invariant rule operating here which is not subject to violation. What is normal and automatic for a personal insult is unthinkable with sounds. We have the exchanges A: *You come over to my house and ask for something to eat.* B: *I do not!* and A: *Your father got gray hair and one long string . . .* B: *That's cause he's old, that's why!* But we do not have such exchanges as A: *You momma drink pee.* B: *That's a lie!* Instead, the response is, *Your father eat shit.* If this was merely a semicategorical rule, we would expect joking responses with denials and deliberate misinterpretations of the sounds, parallel to those we sometimes hear with requests: *Would you mind opening the window? No. Can you give me the time? Yes.* Since responses to sounds are so automatic and deep seated, we must presuppose a well-formed competence on the part of members to distinguish ritual insults from personal insults. On the face of it, it does not seem easy to make this distinction. It is a question, among other things, of how serious the antagonist is: Does he want to start a fight? Does he mean it? Are people going to believe this is true? What is the internal competence which allows Boot to recognize David's personal insult immediately, and to respond with a denial? How can the Jets sound on each other for hours without anyone being insulted?

To answer this question, it is necessary to specify more precisely the structure of sounds. The superficial taxonomy given above (pp. 276–86) merely charts the differences in the syntactic forms of sounds as they are uttered. If sounds are heard as one kind of utterance, there must be a uniform mode of interpretation which shows all of these forms as derived from a single underlying structure. We propose that this structure is:

$$T(B) \quad \text{is} \quad \text{so} \quad X \quad \text{that} \quad P$$

where T is the target of the sound, X is the attribute of T which is focused on, and P is a proposition that is coupled with the attribute by the quantifier "so . . . that" to express the degree to which T has X. The target $T(B)$ is normally B's mother or other relative. (It may seem as if there are more complex targets such as "Your mother's clothes" or "Your mother's face," but these may best be seen as derived from constructions such as "Your mother is so ugly that her face. . . .") The attribute X is drawn from the range of features or topics outlined above: age, weight, clothes, etc. It is limited to a specifically *pejorative* value: *age* is specifically *old, weight* is *skinny* or *fat, clothing* is *ragged* or *dirty, appearance* is *ugly* or *dirty, sexual behavior* is *loose* or *immoral; smell* is *stink, wealth* is *poor, food* is *poor* or *disgusting.* The proposition P may have a wide variety of forms, although there are lower-level sequencing rules and standards of excellence that govern its form. Thus we have a typical sound, *Your mother* [T(B)] *so old* [X,] *she fart dust* [P].

It will be observed that there are a great many sounds with simpler forms than this, and some that are more complex. We might consider that the simpler forms such as "Your mother the abominable snowman" are derived from a full form $T(B)$ *is so X that P* by rules of deletion parallel to syntactic rules for ellipsis. However, it seems more plausible to write discourse rules for making sounds indirectly, parallel to the rules for making commands or requests. One can make commands by statements which mention only the conditions or preconditions for such commands. Thus someone can request a glass of water by stating that he is thirsty. A sound may be made by simply stating the proposition P. The deletion of $T(A)$ *is so X that* . . . is recoverable in the interpretation of the listener, who has the competence to know what attribute is being sounded on. For example, "Your mother look like Flipper" must be understood as "Your mother is so ugly that she looks like Flipper," whereas "Your mother name the Black Boy" will be interpreted as "Your mother is so black that she is named 'Black Boy.'" "Your father got teeth growing out his ass" is one of many sounds that must refer to an attribute odd, crazy, or perhaps most literally, fucked up.

Of the simpler forms listed above (pp. 276–82), the only types which offer serious difficulty in this interpretation are the equative forms. The type, *Your mother the abominable snowman,* can be understood as either "Your mother is so ugly that she looks like the abominable snowman" or ". . . that she is named the abominable snowman." If one takes a more mystical approach—that the speaker is asserting "Your mother is in fact the abominable snowman"—this is equivalent to saying that the insult is directed against the opponent himself, rather than his (ritual) mother. If we hold the notion that the sound is intended to insult or degrade the opponent's mother, rather than to claim he has an altogether different mother, then the interpretation of "like" and "is named" are called for.

Sounds of the "Your mother eat . . ." type are usually interpreted as referring to the attribute "poor" (or "hungry," whch may be subsumed under "poor"). Thus "Your mother eat corn flakes without any milk" may be understood as "Your mother is so hungry that she eats cornflakes without any milk!" or as "Your mother is so poor that she has to eat cornflakes without any milk."

On the other hand, the following sequence of sounds must be given a different interpretation:

—His mother eat Dog Yummies . . .
—Somebody said your mother's breath smell funny.
—They say your mother eat Gainesburgers.
—They say your mother was a Gravy Train.

These are plainly based on the traditional mode of insulting someone's mother by calling her a dog. The direct insults "Your mother's a bitch . . . a dog . . . You're a son of a bitch" do not have any weight in sounding today. But the existence of this model makes it plain that the underlying interpretation is not "Your mother is like a dog" or "Your mother is named Dog" but rather "Your mother is a dog." On the other hand, Boot's sound "Your father looks like a grown pig" is not equivalent to saying "Your father is a pig . . . a swine"; rather, it must be taken to mean, "Your father is so fat that he looks like a grown pig."

The type "Your mother raised you on ugly milk" is unique in this series, because it must be interpreted as a sound directly against the opponent: *"You* are so ugly that your mother [must have] raised you on ugly milk." But we might add that the mother is also being insulted here, so that the sound adds, in effect; "and it's your mother's fault!"

The more complex sounds such as the anecdotal "I went to B's house . . ." type must be taken as directed against the whole family: "B's family is so poor that . . ." On the other hand, complex comparisons such as "Your father drawers have so many holes in them that when he walk they whistle" can be interpreted as "Your father's drawers are so ragged that . . ." or as one step further, "Your father is so ragged that his drawers have so many holes in them that when he walks they whistle."

There are, of course, a certain number of miscellaneous sounds which are difficult to interpret in any scheme: "Your mother play dice with the midnight mice" is in many ways ambiguous.

It is clear that the formal definition given does not include the rhymed dozens, which have the underlying structure "I fucked your mother so much that . . ." A number of other sounds, such as "I took your mother," are based upon the model in which the sounder asserts that he sexually insulted or degraded the opponent's mother. This model must be added as an alternative mode of sounding to the one outlined above. But the great majority of sounds used by the Jets, Cobras, and Thunderbirds fit the $T(B)$ *is so X that P* model. We must presuppose that members have the competence to make such interpretations if we are to explain their behavior.

The capacity to interpret sounds perfectly depends on the ability to locate the underlying negative adjective X when only the proposition P remains. What does it mean to say "Your mother eat Bosco!" It requires native competence to decide if this is a sound against your mother's blackness (Bosco is a chocolate product; cf. "Your mother so black she sweat chocolate"); or her poverty (cf. "Your mother eat corn flakes without any milk"); or her decency (cf. "Your mother eat scumbag").

We can now write rules for sounding that will account for the interpretation of a sound and selection of an appropriate response to it. The following rule (1) begins with the listener B's position, as he hears what is said and interprets it to decide what has to be done: a rule of interpretation UD in the scheme given on page 268.

> (1) If A makes an utterance S in the presence of B and an audience C, which includes reference to a target related to B, T(B), in a proposition P, and
>
> (a) B believes that A believes that P is not true and
> (b) B believes that A believes that B knows that P is not true . . .
> then S is a *sound,* heard as *T(B) is so X that P* where X is a pejorative attribute, and A is said to have *sounded on* B.

This rule can (and must) be abbreviated by identifying conditions (a) and (b) as conditions for shared or social knowledge. These are only the first of an infinite series of recursive conditions which represent the fact that there is shared knowledge between A and B that P is not true. In the terminology of discourse analysis now being developed, an A-event is one known to be known only to A [in A's biography] and a B-event is one known to be known only to B, whereas an AB-event is one known to be known to both. We may summarize conditions (a) and (b) as *it is an AB event that P is not true.*

The audience C is an essential ingredient here. It is true that one person *can* sound against another without a third person being present, but the presupposition that this is public behavior can easily be heard in the verbal style. Sounds are not uttered in a direct, face-to-face conversational mode. The voice is raised and projected, as if to reach an audience. In a two-person sounding situation, the antagonists treat each other as representing the audience.

Note that rule (1) does not require the attribute X to be explicitly mentioned. On the other hand, the proposition P must be present. We rarely hear sounds of the form T(B) is (Q)X where Q is a simple quantifier, and it is doubtful if they are to be classified as sounds. "Your mother is very fat," Your father is real black" are not heard as sounds. Indeed, we can explain the nondeletability of P as we return to the question of the conditions for recognizing sounds as opposed to personal insults. The rule (1) is designed to answer the original question: how does B recognize a ritual insult? First, he recognizes an appropriate target. Second, he recognizes the *sounding situation:* a remark is made by A in a loud voice designed to be heard by the audience C. Third, he judges the proposition P to be appropriate to a ritual insult in that everyone present plainly knows that it is not true. The Jets' mothers do not look like Flipper or Howdy Doody; they are not the abominable snowman; they do not eat Dog Yummies or fried dick-heads. Furthermore, it is a matter of human competence to know that everyone knows that these propositions are not true. On the other hand, the attributes X may justly be attributed to one's mother: she may very well be fat, or skinny, or ugly, or black, or poor, or old, if the propositional insult "Your family is poor!" is not a ritual insult, but a personal one. We have noted that Boot's stepfather does stutter; David's father is old and has gray hair—and all the Thunderbirds know this.

Outsiders would of course be able to recognize ritual propositions P. But without the shared knowledge of members as to whose family was poor, which family was poorest, and which mother was blackest, the outsider could not as readily recognize a personal insult. He would have to suspend judgment. The group does not share all knowledge equally, and sounding is not confined within a single peer group or hang-out group. Therefore sounds must be recognized as ritual insults in themselves, without presupposing any specific knowledge of the sounder's family. For this reason, the propositions P tend to become more and more bizarre and unlikely. "Your mother so low she c' play Chinese handball on a curve [curb]" is a safe sound. Nobody is that low. On the other hand, there is something dangerously personal in "Your mother look like *his* father, boy; 'n' you know how *he* look, boy." There are other cases, some noted below, where weak sounds can be interpreted as personal insults; they are then denied, and conflict follows. But if one reviews the sounds quoted above, it will be immediately obvious in almost every case that the propositions P are known to be untrue.

The same argument applies to the rhymed dozens. Among young adults, to say "I fucked your mother" is not to say something obviously untrue. But it is obviously untrue that "I fucked your mother from tree to tree/Your father said, 'Now fuck me!' " The situation can become difficult in some neighborhoods. In the Puerto Rican barrio of East 111th Street, it is a common sound to say "Your mother's on Fifth Avenue!"—meaning that she is a prostitute. To the question, "What about the kids whose mothers *are* on Fifth Avenue?" members reply, "They don't say much."

The danger of sounds being misinterpreted as personal remarks cannot be overstated. One real incident is worth citing.[15] A group of musicians were returning to New York on a bus, and they started sounding on the wife of one member of the band who lived in Detroit: "Jumps into the hay with the ice man," and so on. When they got to the hotel, they noticed he was missing. Later they found out that he went back to Detroit, and he did find his wife in bed with someone. A short while later he committed suicide.

There is no need to compile a great many such incidents to demonstrate the danger of ritual sounding which is not obviously untrue. In dealing with strangers, it is considerably harder to say what is a safe sound, and there are any number of taboos which can be broken with serious results. Generally speaking, extended ritual sounding is an in-group process, and when sounding occurs across group lines, it is often intended to provoke a fight. One such case has been documented by Swett.[16] A musician named Young Beartracks killed another young man known as Chicago Eddie outside a poolroom in East Palo Alto. In the court testimony, it was said that there had been an argument between the two preceding the shooting. Swett, who knew the situation quite well, points out that they were engaged in the dozens, and that there was considerable tension already present between the two: Eddie was a member of an urban gang, and Young Beartracks a recent member of a rural gang. The role of the dozens in this situation was plainly relevant to the shooting that followed—actually a case of verbal aggression by Eddie against Young Beartracks—but the judge and jury did not understand this point:

> The first witness for the prosecution, the poolroom attendant and a member of the urban gang, did state in cross-examination that "Eddie put him (Young Beartracks) in the dozens," but the effort of the defense counsel to procure a clarification of the term "dozens" was objected to by the prosecution on the grounds that the witness had not qualified as an expert in semantics.[17]

First it is worth noting that P *can* be deleted if X is also missing; we then have "Your mother!" This is a very common sound; as cited above,

JOHN LEWIS: Faggots!! Motherfuckers!!
REL: Your mother!

[15] While this incident is necessarily anonymous, it was reported to me through close associates who are related to some of those involved.
[16] Daniel Swett, "Cross-Cultural Communications in the Courtroom: Applied Linguistics in a Murder Trial" (San Francisco: San Francisco State College, 1966), mimeographed.
[17] Ibid. I am indebted to Daniel Swett of San Francisco State College for further data on this incident; he was directly acquainted with some of the principals in this affair.

Here of course there is unrecoverable deletion—that is, there is no X or P that can be reconstructed. We can interpret "Your mother" as signaling either a generalized insult, or as referring to the intention to sound on someone. It may also be used in public places as an elliptical form where behavior is not as free as normal. I observed the following sequence used by two ten-year-olds entering a delicatessen:

—Your mother!
—Your father!
—Your uncle!

We can now give rule (2) for responding to a sound.

(2) If A has sounded on B, B sounds on A by asserting a new proposition P′ which includes reference to a target related to A, T(A), and such that it is an AB-event that P′ is untrue. P′ may be embedded in a sentence as a quantification of a pejorative attribute X′ of T(A).

This is a DU production rule in the scheme outlined on page 268. It also contains reference, in the first clause, to the DD sequencing rule which may be stated independently as

(3) The response to a sound is a sound.

We have thus filled out the original paradigm for discourse analysis which may be shown as

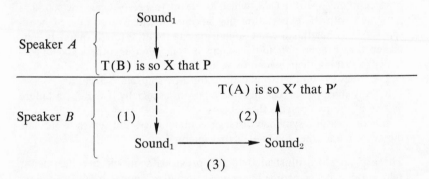

There is an interesting condition here on P′ which is, *If X′/X, then P′/P.* In other words, if A says, "Your mother so old she fart dust," B cannot say "Your mother so skinny she fart dust," or "Your mother so black she fart dust." But if X′ = X, then it is possible P′ = P, if the target *T* is shifted, although this is the weakest kind of response. Among young children who do not sound well, one will hear such sequences as:

—Your mother got funky drawers.
—Your father got funky drawers.

But one does not hear as an answer, *"Your* mother got funky drawers," for this would be equivalent to a denial of the sound. We can now see why denial of ritual sounds is impossible: to deny a sound is to admit that it is *not* a matter of general knowledge that it is obviously untrue, just as to excuse or mitigate the sound is to admit it as factually true.

The description of P as being obviously untrue—that its untruth is an AB event—is equivalent to deciding that the sounder is not "serious." This decision must be made in any conversational exchange —whether it is a matter of commands, requests, assertions, or sounds— and it is the first act of interpretation which the listener must make. As Harvey Sacks has pointed out,[18] there are important consequences of this decision: if the speaker is judged serious, a suitable response must be constructed to fit the situation. If the speaker is joking, then all that is usually required is a laugh—no matter what was said by the first speaker. In the case of sounding, the judgment is made that the speaker is not serious—the insult is a ritual one—but the answer will be governed to a certain extent by the nature of the proposition P. Excellence in sounding, and the winning of the contest, will depend upon the relation of P′ to P. The following more general formulation of the interactional structure of sounding is based upon the suggestions of Erving Goffman in response to an earlier presentation of this analysis. Goffman's framework isolates four basic properties of *ritual* sounding, as opposed to other types of insult behavior:

1. A sound opens a *field,* which is meant to be sustained. A sound is presented with the expectation that another sound will be offered in response, and that this second sound may be built formally upon it. The player who presents an initial sound is thus offering others the opportunity to display their ingenuity at his expense.

2. Besides the initial two players, a third-person role is necessary.

3. Any third person can become a player, especially if there is a failure by one of the two players then engaged.

4. Considerable symbolic distance is maintained and serves to insulate the event from other kinds of verbal interaction.

These properties, illustrated in the previous sections, are the means by which the process of insult becomes socialized and adapted for play. They may eventually be formalized in higher-level rules of verbal interaction. In the following discussion, we will see in greater detail how the first principle operates in ritual sounding.

Sequencing in the content of sounds

The rules given in the subsection above are all that are needed to generate a series of sounds between two antagonists. There are further

---

[18] Harvey Sacks, Lecture notes (Los Angeles: University of California, 1967), mimeographed.

complications involved when a third person enters the exchange, and when a number of members join in sounding on one antagonist who is falling behind. But sequencing is much more than the fact that speakers take turns and succeed each other; sequencing involves the substance of sounds which succeed each other—how one sound is built on another, and how a series of sounds is brought to a conclusion. Above all, we are concerned with the standards of excellence in sounding—what makes one person a better sounder than another, and how the group evaluates the performance of an individual. This topic will provide us with the best insight into the factors which control the use of language in the street culture. In settings far removed from the classroom, under standards of performance that are alien to those of the school, peer-group members develop a high level of competence in syntax, semantics, and rhetoric. One part of this competence was seen in the toasts developed by adults. In this discussion of sounding, we will observe the creative use of language by adolescents. We will consider first simple sequences of the type AB, where B builds on A's sound to achieve a greater level of complexity, and may be judged in some sense to have surpassed it.

The extensive selections from the Thunderbirds' session show a number of such AB sequences. We cite:

DAVID: Your father got brick teeth.
BOOT: Your father got teeth growin' out his behind.

Note that both sounds feature the same attribute (odd or misshapen appearance) and the same target, relative to the speaker. Boot also preserves the same surface form: that is, in neither sound does the *T is so X that* . . . sentence appear. We do not in fact find sequences of the form:

A: Your father got brick teeth.
B: Your father got such long teeth that they growin' out his behind.

We also note that the most superficial syntax of the proposition P is preserved: "Your father got . . ." Finally, Boot builds his sound on the same specific notion of misshapen teeth that David introduced. But Boot does not limit himself to mere exaggeration, such as "Your father got teeth a mile long." Instead, he adds a new theme which combines anal interest with absurdity. We will not attempt to explore here the question of how "original" Boot's effort is. Most sounds are repetitions or recombinations of elements that have been used before. But it should be clear that sheer memory will not do the trick here, as it will with rhymed dozens. The reply must be appropriate, well formed; it must build upon the specific model offered. It was observed before that Boot clearly won this round, judging by the response of the audience.

Turning to the Jet session, we find that the targets usually shift more rapidly, since more than two members are involved and there is more overt play to the audience. The sequence AB is illustrated by many examples such as:

A: Bell grandmother so-so-so ugly, her rag is showin'.
B: Bell grandmother got so many wrinkles in her face, when they walk down the street, her mother would say, "Wrinkles and ruffles."

In the second sound, the attributes of age and ugliness overlap. The proposition is embedded in a more complex way in the *T is so X* clause; the embedded P combines three sentences as against the one sentence of the A model, and again shows the left-hand embedding which is so rare in colloquial speech. The underlying structure of this sentence is certainly as complex as any we have seen:

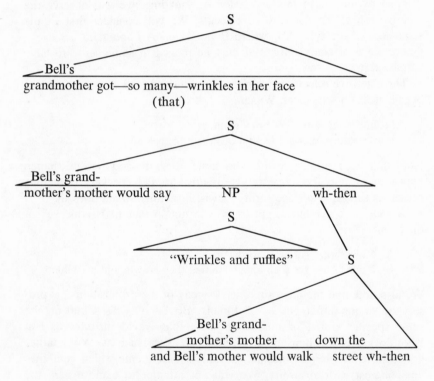

Most of the sequences in the Jet session are more complex than this, but throughout we see the general pattern that B builds on A. We do not find sequences which reverse this order—in which the same target and attribute are preserved, but in which the proposition P is simpler —as would be the case, for example, if B and A were reversed above.

In the Cobras' sounding, we get many long sequences of comparable structure until someone arrives with a more complex form which ends the series:

—Your momma's a peanut man!
—Your momma's a ice man!
—Your momma's a fire man!
—Your momma's a truck driver!
—Your father sell cracker-jacks!
—Your mother *look* like a cracker-jack!

The last sound in this series cannot be topped, and the sounding goes off in a completely different direction: "Your father named Theodore . . ." Here is another example of Cobras building on each other:

—Your mother got on sneakers!
—Your mother wear high-heeled sneakers to church!
—Your mother wear high-heeled sneakers to come out and play on the basketball court!

The complication which B adds is often a semantic one—an additional pejorative attribute is inserted, as in the following:

A: Your mother name Black—Black Boy.
B: Your mother name the Black Bruiser.

The attribute given to the target is now not only blackness, but also masculinity or lack of femininity (as in "Your mother James Bond.")

When a sound becomes too ordinary—too possible—we can then observe a sudden switch in the pattern of response to that appropriate for a personal insult. This can happen by accident when a sound is particularly weak. For example, in the Jet session:

A: I went in Junior house 'n' sat in a chair that caved in.
B: You's a damn liar; 'n' you was eatin' in my house, right?

This is the only instance in the Jet sounding session where a statement is denied, and it is plainly due to the fact that the proposition P is not appropriate for a ritual insult. Its untruth is not at all a matter of general knowledge—it is quite possible that a chair in somebody's house would cave in, and that the chair in Junior's house *did* cave in. It is interesting that Junior takes the same line that David took in countering Boot's personal insult. First Junior denies the charge; second, he hits back with another proposition that is again a personal (not a ritual) statement: "You came over to my house to eat [since there was no food in your own], and so what right have you to complain?" Of course, the second part implicitly contradicts the first—if no chair caved in, how does Junior know what occasion is being talked about? Just as Boot was forced to concede the truth of David's point, so Junior here is plainly speaking of an actual event. There is no immediate response to contradict Junior's last remark. Instead, the theme of sounding is continued, based on A as a first element in the series.

> B: I went to Bell's house 'n' a Chinese roach said, "Come and git it."
> A: I brought my uncle—I brought my uncle up Junior house: I didn't trust *them* guys.

Triads

There are many triads in the Jet session, where *B* tops *A* and a third person adds a sound against *B*. This third sound often has a different target, attribute, and/or form of proposition: it is shorter and more pointed, acting as a coda which terminates the series.

> A: Your mother got funky drawers.
> B: Your mother got braces between her legs.
> C: Looks like your mother did it 'n' ran.

> A: Bell mother got a old beat-up boot.
> B: Her mother got a face like a rubber ass.
> C: Junior got a face like a clown.

In both of these cases, the final sound is contributed with authority by Bell, a senior member of the 100's group. In the second triad, it is Bell who is sounded against by A, and again by B, and Bell who answers as C. A short, firmly delivered sound of this sort, with heavy stress on the last monosyllable, seems to close off debate effectively. After the first two members of a series, the closing element provided by a third person will usually show formal simplification. Thus we have:

> A: Your mother eat coke-a-roaches.
> B: Your mother eat fried dick-heads.
> A: Your mother suck fried dick-heads.
> C: His mother eat *cold* dick-heads.

The theme here from the beginning is "so hungry that she eats . . .."; the sounder is engaged in a search for something as disgusting to eat as he can find. B certainly tops A in this respect; note the complex noun phrase with an embedded participle. But A does not lose: he keeps the series open, capitalizing on the sexual element introduced by B. A's reply does not depend upon syntactic complication. In simply changing the verb, he introduces semantic complexity by introducing the implicit attribute of sexual immorality. *Sex* takes a higher place on the implicit agenda of relevant topics than *hunger* or *poverty,* so that we now have to read the sound as "Your mother is so hot that . . .." Thus A's reply achieves semantic change with a minimum of formal change. The third man achieves closure by returning to the original verb and shortening the form with a much simpler noun phrase. The absurdity of C's sound is based upon the assertion that the substitute of cold for hot food can be relevant at this stage in the search for disgusting attributes. This is a very low-ranking item on the agenda of relevance which governs discourse. It is a common source of humor to make such a sudden, incongruous claim to reverse the order of relevance.

We have seen that one way to achieve excellence in sounding is to develop complex comparisons with a high degree of left-hand embedding which suspends the final proposition. Another is to learn to close off sequences with short sounds which abruptly change the prevailing form. The third (and perhaps the subtlest) method has been illustrated here —bringing about striking semantic shifts with minimal changes of form: a "minimax" solution. This is best illustrated by the following sequence at the very beginning of the Jet session.

> JOHN L: I'll take you to the last man.
> JUNIOR: I'll take your mother.
> REL: I took your mother.

The initial remark of John Lewis is not a sound; he is simply "louding," or "granning." Junior's counter is a sound of the dozens model. The introduction of the target "your mother" also introduces the sexual meaning of "take," so that ambiguity is achieved with a minimum formal change. Rel's final addition seems to us an even more adept example of semantic shift with a minimal effort. By changing from the challenge of the future form to the simple assertion of the past tense, Rel resolves the ambiguity in favor of the sexual meaning. (The semantic machinery operating here is not obvious, but the effect is.) As a third element in the series, Rel's sound also fits the pattern of a short, decisive closure.

There are other forms of sounding which use the same targets and attributes, but very different formal structure. For example, questions are not common as sounds, but the following series begins with two:

> A: Hey didn't I see . . . shit on your mother bed?
> B: A shot gun . . .
> C: Did you see me under your mother bed when your father came in?
> D: No I saw your uncle.
> C: Oh my uncle was there too.

This whole series is positively evaluated by the group with great enthusiasm. But we will not explore the formal side of sounding further in this discussion.

Applied sounding

So far, we have been considering the speech event called "sounding" as the principal focus of verbal activity. But sounding also occurs as an element in other kinds of interaction. Members with great verbal "presence of mind" are able to use sounds at critical moments to channel the direction of personal interaction in a direction that favors them. We may call such a use of ritual insults "applied sounding." It will be immediately apparent that applied sounds do not follow the rules set forth for ritual sounding—they are embedded in other rule sequences and other higher-level structures of verbal interaction. But rule (1) for interpreting utterances as sounds will apply. Of the four more general properties of the ritual sounding situation, set forth on page 306 above, only the fourth property is preserved: that symbolic distance is obligatory. But this property will prove essential to the analysis, and ultimately to the solution of the initial problem posed in this paper.

First it must be understood that verbal interaction among the Jets requires great verbal "presence of mind." Sounding is only one of the many ways of putting someone down. For example, the sounding session in the microbus cited above was initiated when Junior called out, "Hey what's your name! When a we goin' on the next one, K.C.?" This was out of line in two respects. First, in using "What's your name" with someone whose name was as well known as his own; by adding "K.C." (the usual term of address for John Lewis), the insult was only compounded. Second, this remark was out of line in that there had been no promise of a second outing, and Junior was showing extreme hubris in demanding it. John Lewis turned around and replied without hesitation: "Next time you give me some pussy!" There was considerable uproar at this—it was evident to one and all that Junior had been put down decisively.

John Lewis's remark is one of a large class of ritual insults which impute homosexuality to the antagonist by indirection. Here it catches Junior in a double bind. If he wants to refute the ritual charge of homosexuality, then he has to interpret Lewis's reply as meaning "Never!" But that is his decision—John Lewis has neatly left it up to him. If Lewis had said, "You're not going!" he would have been faced with a roar of injured innocence and fierce denunciation: "You cheap bastard!" etc. He has sidestepped the problem and put Junior down decisively: "Got you Junior—got you that time!"

Among the Jets, Rel is one of the most skilled at using sounds in this way. At one point in the Jets' session, thirteen-year-old Stevie was trying to push his way into a fight developing between Larry and Rel by warning Larry, "He gon' getchyou with 'is legs . . . he got legs—he got leg like—lik—" Larry gave Stevie no more than a withering look, but Rel said: "Aah, your *mother* got legs on 'er *nose!*" This sound crushed Stevie, and he made no effort to reenter the higher-status group for some time. Rel's sound was as apt and crushing as Stevie's effort was bumbling and ineffective. Note, however, that Stevie is ordinarily a verbal leader of his own age-group—another instance of the dominance of power relations over verbal skill.

We are now in a position to return to the original problem posed by Rel's sound, "Your mother's a duck." How is this a coherent response to Stanley's challenge? A closer examination of the context will help. First of all, we can note that when Rel first called for quiet, he was talking to the group as a whole, especially the younger, lower-status members at the other end of the table.

REL: Shut up, please!

It was a deliberate, half-serious decision on Stanley's part to interpret Rel's request for action as being directed at *him*. As president, it was quite in order for him to challenge Rel's right to tell *him* to be quiet.

STANLEY: . . . 'ey, you tellin' *me?*

Stanley put his elbow on the middle of the table, and stretched out his long forearm toward Rel. His emphasis on *me* indicated that he was choosing to take this request personally. At this point, neither Rel nor Stanley could retreat.

REL: Yes.
STANLEY: Come a li'l closer.

Now Rel applied a simple sound against Stanley:

REL: Your mother's a duck. Get outa here.
STANLEY: Come a li'l closer an' say—
REL: Your mother's a duck.

At this point, Stanley withdrew his arm, looked around, and became involved with someone else. Our understanding of why Stanley retreated is based on the definition of a sound as a ritual insult—one that is obviously not true. Though Stanley chooses to say, "I take this personally," Rel puts him down by redefining the situation as a ritual one. Informally, the message is "What are you carrying on for? This is just a game we're playing, and you know it—unless your mother *is* a duck." If Stanley insisted on taking the situation seriously, then he would be saying that it *could* be true—his mother could be a duck.

The logic of Rel's sound is the same as that of John Lewis's reply to Junior. The skill of the sounder leaves the ultimate decision up to the challenger: if he insists on taking the matter personally, the fight will go on, but he has already condemned himself and will find it very hard to regain his lost ground.

Thus the answer to the original problem we posed lies in the concept of a ritual event as one which is formulated without regard to the persons named. Sounds are directed at targets very close to the opponent (or at himself), but by social convention it is accepted that they do not denote attributes which persons actually possess: in Goffman's formulation, symbolic distance maintained serves to insulate this exchange from further consequences. The rules given above for sounding, and the development of sounds in a bizarre and whimsical direction, all have the effect of preserving this ritual status. As we have seen, the ritual convention can break down with younger speakers or in strange situations —and the dangers of such a collapse of ritual safeguards are very great. Rituals are sanctuaries; in ritual we are freed from personal responsibility for the acts we are engaged in. Thus when someone makes a request for action in other subcultures, and he is challenged on the fourth pre-condition ("What right have you to tell me that?"), his reply may follow the same strategy:

"It's not my idea—I just have to get the work done."
"I'm just doing my job."
"I didn't pick on you—somebody has to do it."

Any of these moves to depersonalize the situation may succeed in removing the dangers of a face-to-face confrontation and defiance of authority. Ritual insults are used in the same way to manage challenges within the peer group. An understanding of ritual behavior is an important element in constructing the general theory of discourse, and this analysis of sounding is submitted with that end in view.

■ Signifying, loud-talking and marking

CLAUDIA MITCHELL-KERNAN

Claudia Mitchell-Kernan is assistant professor of anthropology in the department of social relations and anthropology at Harvard University. A graduate of Indiana University and the University of California at Berkeley, she was also the recipient of several grants and fellowships that enabled her to conduct and publish research in the study of child language acquisition and of language behavior in urban communities. The present selection was taken from her doctoral dissertation, *Language Behavior in a Black Urban Community,* now published in its entirety as Monograph (#2) of the Language Behavior Research Laboratory, University of California, Berkeley; it is a product of research done in a black community in California in the late 1960's.

This selection expands significantly the knowledge of black folk speech categories that presently comprises the literature on the subject. It also focuses on the extent to which black people are aware of and appreciate the expressive and manipulative aspects of verbal behavior practiced within the community. By including samples of verbal behavior from female and mixed adult groups in her investigation, the author has significantly enlarged the conceptual category of "signifying" advanced by Abrahams, Kochman, and Labov which evolved from their work with male teen and adult groups; as such, it complements nicely the Kochman and Labov discussions presented in this volume, as well as allowing the reader to see the progressive development in the area.

Signifying—introduction

A number of individuals interested in black verbal behavior have devoted attention to the way of talking which is known in many black communities as "signifying." Signifying can be a tactic employed in verbal dueling which is engaged in as an end in itself; it is signifying in this context which has been the subject of most previous analysis. Signifying, however, also refers to a way of encoding messages or meanings which involves, in most cases, an element of indirection. This kind of signifying might best be viewed as an alternative message form, selected for its artistic merit, and may occur embedded in a variety of discourse. Such signifying is not focal to the linguistic interaction in the sense that it does not define the entire speech event. While the primacy of either of these uses of the term is difficult to establish, the latter deserves attention due to its neglect in the literature.

According to Abrahams, signifying

> can mean any number of things; in the case of the toast, "The Signifying Monkey and the Lion," it certainly refers to the monkey's ability to talk with great innuendo, to carp, cajole, needle and lie. It can mean in other

instances the propensity to talk around a subject, never quite coming to the point. It can mean "making fun" of a person or situation. Also it can denote speaking with the hands and eyes, and in this respect encompasses a whole complex of expressions and gestures. Thus, it is signifying to make fun of the police by parodying his motions behind his back, it is signifying to ask for a piece of cake by saying, "My brother needs a piece of that cake." It is, in other words, many facets of the smartalecky attitude.[1]

While the present researcher never obtained consensus from informants in their definition of signifying, most informants felt that some element of indirection was criterial to signifying; many would label the parodying of the policeman's motions "marking" and the request for cake "shucking," in the examples above.

Kochman differentiates two forms of signifying and classifies them in terms of their functions:

> When the function of signifying is *directive* the *tactic* employed is indirection, i.e., the signifier reports or repeats what someone else has said about the listener; the "report" is couched in plausible language designed to compel belief and arouse feelings of anger and hostility. There is also the implication that if the listener fails to do anything about it—what has to be done is usually quite clear—his status will be seriously compromised. . . . When the function of signifying is to arouse feelings of embarrassment, shame, frustration, or futility, to diminish someone's status, the tactic employed is direct in the form of a taunt.[2]

Informants in the present sample referred to the direct taunts which Kochman suggests are the formal features of signifying when its function is to arouse emotions in the absence of directive intent as "sounding" or "woofing." Differences in usage may in part reflect regional variation. More important, however, they may correspond to internal social-structural differentiation, particularly of sex and age. Verbal dueling receives its greatest elaboration among young males, and the routines of dueling are commonly highly stylized. As a consequence, we may expect to find that usage differs in this context in contrast to other speech events where signifying may be employed. One informant suggested that only when direct insults were attributed to a third party could they be considered signifying. When I was a child in the Chicago area, my age group treated signifying and sounding as contrasting tactics. Signifying at that time was a fairly standard tactic which was employed in sounding (as a verbal insult game). That is, the speech event sounding could involve either direct insults (sounds) or indirect insults

[1] Roger D. Abrahams, *Deep Down in the Jungle* (Hatboro, Pa.: Folklore Associates), p. 54, n. 8.

[2] Thomas Kochman, " 'Rapping' in the Black Ghetto," *Trans-action*, February, 1969, pp. 26–34.

(signifying), but they were mutually exclusive tactics. Closely related was the activity of playing the dozens, which then involved broadening the target of the insults to include derogatory remarks about the family of the addressee, particularly his mother. In playing the dozens, one could either sound on the addressee's ancestors or signify about them. Sounding and playing the dozens categorically involve verbal insult; signifying does not. It may be that what these folk categories have in common has obscured what are felt by many to be crucial differences and, moreover, functions which are more diverse than have been assumed.

The standard English concept of signifying seems etymologically related to the use of this term within the black community. An audience, for example, may be advised to signify "yes" by standing or to signify its disapproval or permissive education by saying "aye." It is also possible to say that an individual signified his poverty by wearing rags. In the first instance we explicitly state the relationship between the meaning and the act, informing the audience that in this context the action or word will be an adequate and acceptable means of expressing approval. In the second instance the relationship between rags and poverty is implicit and stems from conventional associations. It is in this latter sense that standard English usage and black usage have most in common.

The black concept of signifying incorporates essentially a folk notion that dictionary entries for words are not always sufficient for interpreting meanings or messages, or that meaning goes beyond such interpretations. Complimentary remarks may be delivered in a left-handed fashion. A particular utterance may be an insult in one context and not another. What pretends to be informative may intend to be persuasive. The hearer is thus constrained to attend to all potential meaning-carrying symbolic systems in speech events—the total universe of discourse. The context embeddedness of meaning is attested to by both our reliance on the given context and, most important, by our inclination to construct additional context from our background knowledge of the world. Facial expressions and tone of voice serve to orient us to one kind of interpretation rather than another. Situational context helps us to narrow meaning. Personal background knowledge about the speaker points us in different directions. Expectations based on role or status criteria enter into the sorting process. In fact, we seem to process all manner of information against a background of assumptions and expectations.

More formal features of signifying

Labeling a particular utterance "signifying" involves the recognition and attribution of some implicit content or function which is potentially obscured by the surface content or function. The obscurity may lie in the relative difficulty it poses for interpreting (1) the meaning or message the speaker is adjudged as intending to convey; (2) the addressee—the person or persons to whom the message is directed; (3) the goal orientation or intent of the speaker. A precondition for the application of "signifying" to some speech act is the assumption that the meaning decoded was consciously and purposely formulated at the encoding stage. In reference to function the same condition must hold.

Some examples of signifying with accompanying explanations

The present section will be devoted to the presentation of a series of examples of speech acts which are labeled signifying in the community in question. The examples will be followed by interpretations which are intended to clarify the messages and meanings which are being conveyed in each case.

> (1) *The interlocutors here are Barbara (an informant), Mary (one of her friends), and the researcher. The conversation takes place in Barbara's home; the episode begins as I am about to leave.*
>
> BARBARA: What are you going to do Saturday? Will you be over here?
>
> R: I don't know.
>
> BARBARA: Well, if you're not going to be doing anything, come by. I'm going to cook some chitlins. (*rather jokingly*) Or are you one of those Negroes who don't eat chitlins?
>
> MARY: (*Interjecting indignantly*): That's all I hear lately—soul food, soul food. If you say you don't eat it you get accused of being saditty [affected, considering oneself superior]. (*matter of factly*) Well, I ate enough black-eyed peas and neckbones during the depression that I can't get too excited over it. I eat prime rib and T-bone because I like to, not because I'm trying to be white. (*sincerely*) Negroes are constantly trying to find some way to discriminate against each other. If they could once get it in their heads that we are all in this together maybe we could get somewhere in this battle against the man. (*Mary leaves.*)
>
> BARBARA: Well, I wasn't signifying at her, but like I always say, if the shoe fits, wear it.

While the manifest topic of Barbara's question was food, Mary's response indicates that this is not a conversation about the relative merits of having one thing or another for dinner. Briefly, Barbara was, in the metaphors of the culture, implying that Mary and/or I were assimilationists.

First of all, let us deal with the message itself, which is somewhat analogous to an allegory in that the significance or meaning of the words must be derived from known symbolic values. An outsider or nonmember (perhaps not at this date) might find it difficult to grasp the significance of eating chitlins or not eating chitlins. Barbara's "one of those Negroes that" places the hearer in a category of persons which, in turn, suggests that the members of that category may share other features (in this case, negatively evaluated ones) and indicates something more significant than mere dietary preference.

Chitlins are considered a delicacy by many black people, and eating chitlins is often viewed as a traditional dietary habit of black people. Changes in such habits are viewed as gratuitous aping of whites and are considered to imply derogation of these customs. The same sort of sentiment often attaches to other behaviors, such as changes in church affiliation of upward-mobile blacks. Thus not eating or liking chitlins may be indicative of assimilationist attitudes, which in turn imply a rejection of one's black brothers and sisters. It is perhaps no longer necessary to mention that assimilation is a far from neutral term, intraculturally. Blacks have traditionally shown ambivalence toward the abandonment of ethnic heritage. Many strong attitudes attached to certain kinds of cultural behavior seem to reflect a fear of cultural extermination.

It is not clear at the outset to whom the accusation of being an assimilationist was aimed. Ostensibly, Barbara addressed her remarks to me. Yet Mary seems to indicate that she felt herself to be the real addressee in this instance. The signifier may employ the tactic of obscuring his addressee as part of his strategy. In the following case the remark is, on the surface, directed toward no one in particular.

(2) "I saw a woman the other day in a pair of stretch pants, she must have weighed 300 pounds. If she knew how she looked she would burn those things."

Such a remark may have particular significance to the 235-pound member of the audience who is frequently seen about town in stretch pants. She is likely to interpret this remark as directed at her, with the intent of providing her with the information that she looks singularly unattractive so attired.

The technique is fairly straightforward; the speaker simply selects a topic which is selectively relevant to his audience. A speaker who has a captive audience (such as a minister) may be accused of signifying by virtue of his text being too timely and selectively apropos to segments of his audience.

It might be proposed that Mary intervened in the hope of rescuing me from a dilemma by asserting the absence of any necessary relationships between dietary habits and assimilationist attitudes. However, Barbara's further remarks lend credence to the original hypothesis and suggest that Mary was correct in thinking that she was the target of the insinuation.

BARBARA: I guess she was saying all that for your benefit. At least, I hope she wasn't trying to fool me. If she weren't so worried about keeping up with her saditty friends, she would eat less T-bone steak and buy some shoes for her kids once in a while.

Although Mary never explicitly accuses Barbara of signifying, her response seems tantamount to such an accusation, as is evidenced by Barbara's denial. Mary's indignation registers quite accurately the spirit in which some signifying is taken. This brings us to another feature of signifying: the message often carries some negative import for the addressee. Mary's response deserves note; her retaliation also involves signifying. While talking about obstacles to brotherhood, she intimates that behavior such as that engaged in by Barbara is typical of artificially induced sources of schism which are in essence superficial in their focus—and which, in turn, might be viewed as a comment on the character of the individual who introduces divisiveness on such trivial grounds.

Barbara insulted Mary, her motive perhaps being to injure her feelings or lower her self-esteem. An informant asked to interpret this interchange went further in imputing motives by suggesting possible reasons for Barbara's behavior; he said that the answer was buried in the past. Perhaps Barbara was repaying Mary for some insult of the past—settling a score, as it were. He suggested that Barbara's goal was to raise her own self-esteem by asserting superiority of a sort over Mary. Moreover, he said that this kind of interchange was probably symptomatic of the relationship between the two women and that one could expect to find them jockeying for position on any number of issues. "Barbara was trying to *rank* Mary," to put her down by typing her. This individual seemed to be defining the function of signifying as the establishment of dominance in this case.

Terry Southern narrates an excellent example of this allegorical kind of signifying message-form in the anthology *Red Dirt Marijuana*. Here we find two brothers signifying at each other in an altercation leading to a razor duel in which both men are killed. One of the brothers, C.K., tells the following story:

(3) C.K.: There was these two boys from Fort Worth, they was over Paris, France, and with the Army, and they was standin' on the corner without much in partic'lar to do when a couple of *o-fay* chicks come strollin' by, you know what I mean, a couple of nice French gals—and they was very nice indeed with the exception that one of them appeared to be considerable *older* than the other one, like she might be the great grandmother of the other one or somethin' like that, you see. So these boys was diggin' these chicks and one of them say: "Man, let's make a move, I believe we do awright there!" And the other one say: "Well, now, similar thought occurred to me as well, but . . . er . . . uh . . .

how is we goin decide who takes the grandmother? I don't want no old bitch like that!" So the other one say: "How we decide? Why man, I goin take the grandmother! I the one see these chicks first, and I gets to take my choice!" So the other one say: "Well, now you talking! You gets the grandmother, and I gets the young one—that's fine! But tell me this, boy, —how comes you wants the old lady, instead of the fine young gal?" So the other one say, "Why don't you know? Ain't you with it? She been *white* . . . LON-GER!"

   BIG NAIL: You ain't change much, is you boy?

This story was not told for its pure entertainment value. C.K.'s message to Big Nail was that the fellow who preferred the grandmother was his allegorical counterpart. This alleged social type is the target of some ethnic humor and has been explored particularly by Cleaver in *Soul on Ice*. Such an allegation would be considered a deep insult by many.

The preceding messages are indirect not because they are cryptic (i.e., difficult to decode), but because they somehow force the hearer to take additional steps. To understand the significance of not eating chitlins or a yen for a grandmotherly white woman, one must voyage to the social world and discover the characteristics of these social types and cultural values and attitudes toward them.

The indirect message may take any number of forms, however, as in the following example.

   (4) *The relevant background information lacking in this interchange is that the husband is a member of the class of individuals who do not wear suits to work.*

   WIFE: Where are you going?
   HUSBAND: I'm going to work.
   WIFE: [You're wearing] a suit, tie and white shirt? You didn't tell me you got a promotion.

The wife, in this case, is examining the truth value of her husband's assertion (A) "I'm going to work" by stating the obvious truth that (B) he is wearing a suit. Implicit is the inappropriateness of this dress as measured against shared background knowledge. In order to account for this discrepancy, she advances the hypothesis (C) that he has received a promotion and is now a member of the class of people who wear suits to work. (B) is obviously true, and if (C) is not true then (A) must also be false. Having no reason to suspect that (C) is true, she is signifying that he is *not* going to work; moreover, he is lying about his destination.

Now the wife could have chosen a more straightforward way of finding an acceptable reason for her husband's unusual attire. She might have asked, for example, "Why are you wearing a suit?" And he could have pleaded some unusual circumstances. Her choice to entrap him suggests that she was not really seeking information but more than likely already had some answers in mind. While it seems reasonable to conclude that an accusation of lying is implicit in the interchange, and one would guess that the wife's intent is equally apparent to the husband, this accusation is never made explicit. This brings us to some latent advantages of indirect messages, especially those with negative import for the receiver. Such messages, because of their form—they contain both explicit and implicit content—structure interpretation in such a way that the parties have the option of avoiding a real confrontation.[3] Alternately, they provoke confrontations without at the same time unequivocally exposing the speaker's intent. The advantage in either case is for the speaker, because it gives him control of the situation at the receiver's expense. The speaker, because of the purposeful ambiguity of his original remark, reserves the right to subsequently insist on the harmless interpretation rather than the provocative one. When the situation is such that there is no ambiguity in determining the addressee, the addressee faces the possibility that, if he attempts to confront the speaker, the latter will deny the message or intent imputed, leaving him in the embarrassing predicament of appearing contentious.

Picture the secretary who has become uneasy about the tendency of her knee to come in contact with the hand of her middle-aged boss. She finally decides to confront him and indignantly informs him that she is not that kind of girl. He responds by feigning hurt innocence, "How could you accuse me of such a thing?" If his innocence is genuine, her misconstrual of the significance of these occasions of body contact possibly comments on her character more than his. She has no way of being certain, and she feels foolish. Now a secretary skilled in the art of signifying could have avoided the possibility of "having the tables turned" by saying, "Oh, excuse me, Mr. Smith, I didn't mean to get my knee in your way." He would have surely understood her message if he were guilty, and a confrontation would have been avoided. If he were innocent, the remark would have probably been of no consequence.

When there is some ambiguity with reference to the addressee, as in the first example, the hearer must expose himself as the target before the confrontation can take place. The speaker still has the option of retreating and the opportunity (while feigning innocence) to jibe, "Well, if the shoe fits, wear it."

The individual who has a well-known reputation for this kind of signifying is felt to be sly and, sometimes, not man or woman enough to come out and say what he/she means.

Signifying does not, however, always have negative valuations attached to it; it is clearly thought of as a kind of art—a clever way of

---

[3] Cf. Roger Brown, *Words and Things* (Glencoe, Ill.: The Free Press, 1958), for a similar discussion.

conveying messages. In fact, it does not lose its artistic merit even when it is malicious. It takes some skill to construct messages with multi-level meanings, and it sometimes takes equal expertise to unravel the puzzle presented in all of its many implications. Just as in certain circles the clever punster derives satisfaction and is rewarded by his hearers for constructing a multi-sided pun, the signifier is also rewarded for his cleverness.

The next example was reported by an informant to illustrate the absence of negative import as a criterial feature of signifying.

(5) *After I had my little boy, I swore I was not having any more babies. I thought four kids was a nice-sized family. But it didn't turn out that way. I was a little bit disgusted and didn't tell anybody when I discovered I was pregnant. My sister came over one day; I had started to show by that time.*

ROCHELLE: Girl, you sure do need to join the Metrecal for lunch bunch.

GRACE: (*noncommitally*) Yea, I guess I am putting on a little weight.

ROCHELLE: Now look here, girl, we both standing here soaking wet and you still trying to tell me it ain't raining.

Grace found the incident highly amusing. She reports the incident to illustrate Rochelle's clever use of words, the latter's intent being simply to let her know in a humorous way that she was aware of her pregnancy. "She was teasing—being funny." Such messages may include content which might be construed as mildly insulting, except that they are treated by the interlocutors as joking behavior.

(6) What a lovely coat; they sure don't make coats like that anymore. (*Glossed: Your coat is out of style.*)

(7) You must be going to the Ritz this afternoon. (*Glossed: You're looking tacky.*)

(8) *The following interchange took place in a public park. Three young men in their early twenties sat down with the researcher, one of whom initiated a conversation in this way:*

I: Mama, you sho is fine.

R: That ain't no way to talk to your mother.

(*Laughter.*)

I: You married?

R: Um hm.

I: Is your husband married?

(*Laughter.*)

R: Very.

(*The conversation continues with the same young man doing most of the talking. He questions me about what I am doing and I tell him about my research project. After a couple of minutes of discussing "rapping," I returns to his original style.*)

I: Baby, you a real scholar. I can tell you want to learn. Now if you'll just cooperate a li'l bit, I'll show you what a good teacher I am. But first we got to get into my area of expertise.

R: I may be wrong but seems to me we already in your area of expertise.

(*Laughter.*)

I: You ain't so bad yourself, girl. I ain't heard you stutter yet. You a li'l fixated on your subject though. I want to help a sweet thang like you all I can. I figure all that book learning you got must mean you been neglecting other areas of your education.

II: Talk that talk! (*Gloss: Olé!*)

R: Why don't you let me point out where I can best use your help.

I: Are you sure you in the best position to know?

(*Laughter.*)

I: I'mo leave you alone, girl. Ask me what you want to know. Tempus fugit, baby.

(*Laughter.*)

The folk label for the kind of talking engaged in by I is "rapping," defined by Kochman as "a fluent and lively way of talking characterized by a high degree of personal style," which may be used when its function is referential or directive—to get something from someone or get someone to do something. The interchange is laced with innuendo—signifying because it alludes to and implies things which are never made explicit.

The utterance which initiated the conversation was intended from all indications as a compliment and was accepted as such. The manner in which it was framed is rather stylized and jocularly effusive; it makes the speaker's remarks less bold and presumptuous and is permissive of a response which can acknowledge the compliment in a similar and jokingly impersonal fashion. The most salient purpose of the compliment was to initiate a conversation with a strange woman. The response served to indicate to the speaker that he was free to continue. Probably any response (or none at all) would not have terminated his attempt to engage the hearer, but the present one signaled to the speaker that it was appropriate to continue in his original style. The factor of the audience is crucial, because it obliges the speaker to continue attempting to engage the addressee once he has begun. The speaker at all points has a surface addressee, but the linguistic and nonlinguistic responses of the other two young men indicate that they are very aware of being integral participants in this interchange. The question "Is your husband married?" is meant to suggest to the hearer, who seeks to turn down the speaker's advance by pleading marital ties, that such bonds should not be treated as inhibitory except when one's husband has by his behavior shown similar inhibition.

The speaker adjusts his rap to appeal to the scholarly leanings of his addressee, who responds by suggesting that he is presently engaging in his area of virtuosity. I responds to this left-handed compliment by pointing out that the researcher is engaging in this same kind of speech behavior and is apparently an experienced player of the game—"I ain't heard you stutter yet"—as evidenced by her unfaltering responses. At the same time he notes the narrowness of the speaker's interests and states the evidence leading him to the conclusion that there must be gaps in her knowledge. He benevolently offers his aid. His maneuvers are offensive and calculated to produce defensive responses. His repeated offers of aid are intended ironically. A member of the audience interjects, "Talk that talk!" This phrase is frequently used to signal approval of some speaker's virtuosity in using language skillfully and colorfully, language which is appropriate and effective to the social context. The content of the message is highly directive, but the speaker indicates by many paralinguistic cues (particularly a highly stylized leer) that he does not expect to be taken seriously; he is parodying a tête à tête and not attempting to engage the hearer in anything other than conversation. He is merely demonstrating his ability to use persuasive language. He is playing a game, and he expects his addressee and audience to recognize it as such. He signals that the game is over by saying, "I'mo leave you alone" and redirecting the conversation. The juxtaposition of the lexical items, which typically are not paired, is meant to evoke more humor by the dissonant note it strikes.

Another tactic of the signifier is to allude to something which somehow has humor value or negative import for the hearer in a casual fashion—information-dropping.

(9) Thelma, these kids look more and more like their fathers every day. (*Signifying about the fact that the children do not all have the same father.*)

(10) What time is it? (*May in certain contexts be taken to mean, "It's time for you to go." It will be said that the person was signifying that it's time to go home.*)

(11) Who was that fox [pretty girl] I saw you with last night? Sure wish you'd introduce me to her. (*Signifying: I saw you with a woman who was not your wife. If said in the presence of the addressee's wife, this kind of signifying is felt to have a highly malicious intent, because it drops information which is likely to involve negative consequences for the addressee.*)

(12) I: Man, when you gon pay me my five dollars?

II: Soon as I get it.

I (*To audience*): Anybody want to buy a five-dollar nigger? I got one to sell.

II: Man, if I gave you your five dollars, you wouldn't have nothing to signify about.

I: Nigger, long as you don't change, I'll always have me a subject.

Signifying as a form of verbal art

Not all attempts at signifying are as artful as those illustrated above. That these attempts are poor art rather than nonart is clear from comments with which some of them are met. For example, needless and extreme circumlocution is considered poor art. In this connection, Labov has similar comments about sounding.[4] He cites peer-group members as reacting to some sounds with such metalinguistic responses as "That's phony," and "That's lame." Signifying may be met with similar critical remarks. Such failures, incidentally, are as interesting as the successes, for they provide clues as to the rules by violating one or more of them, while at the same time meeting other criteria.

One of the defining characteristics of signifying is its indirect intent or metaphorical reference. This indirection appears to be almost purely stylistic. It may sometimes have the function of being euphemistic or diplomatic, but its art characteristics remain in the forefront even in such cases. Without the element of indirection, a speech act would not be considered signifying.

Indirection means here that the correct semantic (referential) interpretation or signification of the utterance cannot be arrived at by a consideration of the dictionary meaning of the lexical items involved and the syntactic rules for their combination alone. The apparent significance of the message differs from its real significance. The apparent meaning of the sentence "signifies" its actual meaning.

Meaning conveyed is not apparent meaning. Apparent meaning serves as a key which directs hearers to some shared knowledge, attitudes, and values or signals that reference must be processed metaphorically. The words spoken may actually refer to this shared knowledge by contradicting it or by giving what is known to be an impossible explanation of some obvious fact. The indirection, then, depends for its decoding upon shared knowledge of the participants, and this shared knowledge operates on two levels.

It must be employed, first of all, by the participants in a speech act in the recognition that signifying is occurring and that the dictionary-syntactical meaning of the utterance is to be ignored. Second, this shared

---

[4] William Labov et al., *A Study of the Nonstandard English of Negro and Puerto Rican Speakers in New York City,* Cooperative Research Project #3288, vol. 2; see also Labov article in this volume, pp. 290–91.

knowledge must be employed in the reinterpretation of the utterance. A speaker's artistic talent is judged upon the cleverness used in directing the attention of the hearer and audience to this shared knowledge.

Topic may have something to do with the artistic merit of an act of signifying. Although practically any topic may be signified about, some topics are more likely to make the overall act of signifying more appreciated. Sex is one such topic. For example, an individual offering an explanation for a friend's recent grade-slump quipped, "He can't forget what happened to him underneath the apple tree," implying that the young man was preoccupied with sex at this point in his life and that the preoccupation stemmed from the relative novelty of the experience. A topic which is suggested by ongoing conversation is appreciated more than one which is peripheral. Finally, an act of signifying which tops a preceding one, in a verbal dueling sense, is especially appreciated.

Kochman cites such an example in the context of a discussion of rapping: "A man coming from the bathroom forgot to zip his pants. An unescorted party of women kept watching him and laughing among themselves. The man's friends hip [inform] him to what's going on. He approaches one woman—'Hey, baby, did you see that big Cadillac with the full tires, ready to roll in action just for you?' She answers, 'No, mother-fucker, but I saw a little gray Volkswagen with two flat tires.' "[5]

Verbal dueling is clearly occurring; the first act of signifying is an indirect and humorous way of referring to shared knowledge—the women have been laughing at the man's predicament. It is indirect in that it doesn't mention what is obviously being referred to. The speaker has cleverly capitalized on a potentially embarrassing situation by taking the offensive and at the same time displaying his verbal skill. He emphasizes the sexual aspect of the situation with a metaphor that implies power and class. He is, however, as Kochman says, "capped." The woman wins the verbal duel by replying with an act of signifying which builds on the previous one. The reply is indirect, sexual, and appropriate to the situation. In addition, it employs the same kind of metaphor and is, therefore, very effective.

The use of "mother-fucker" is a rather common term of address in such acts of verbal dueling. The term "nigger" is also common in such contexts. For example: "Nigger, it was a monkey one time wasn't satisfied till his ass was grass," and "Nigger, I'm gon be like white on rice on your ass."

These two examples are illustrative of a number of points of good signifying. Both depend on a good deal of shared cultural knowledge for their correct semantic interpretation. It is the intricacy of the allusion to shared knowledge that makes for the success of these speech acts.

[5] Kochman, " 'Rapping,' " p. 27, and in this volume.

The first refers to the toast, "The Signifying Monkey." The monkey signified at the lion until he got himself in trouble. A knowledge of this toast is necessary for an interpretation of the message. "Until his ass was grass" can only be understood in the light of its common use in the speech of members of the culture—meaning, until he was beaten up—occurring in such forms as "His ass was grass and I was the lawn-mower." What this example means is something like: You have been signifying at me and like the monkey, you are treading on dangerously thin ice. If you don't stop, I am likely to become angry and beat you!

"Nigger, I'm gon be like white on rice on your ass," is doubly clever. A common way of threatening to beat someone is to say, "I'm gonna be all over your ass." And how is white on rice? All over it. Metaphors such as these may lose their effectiveness over time due to over-use. They lose value as clever wit.

The use of "nigger" in these examples is of interest. It is often coupled with the use of code features which are farthest removed from standard English. That is, the code utilizes many linguistic markers which differentiate black speech from standard English or white speech. More such markers than might ordinarily appear in the language of the speaker are frequently used. Interestingly, the use of "nigger" with other black English markers has the effect of "smiling when you say that." The use of standard English with "nigger," in the words of an informant, is "the wrong tone of voice" and may be taken as abusive.

It would seem that the use of these terms and this style of language serve the same function. They both serve to emphasize that black English is being used, and that what is being engaged in is a black speech act. This serves a function other than simply emphasizing group solidarity; it signals to the hearer that this is an instance of black verbal art and should be interpreted in terms of the subcultural rules for interpreting such speech acts.

Such features serve to define the style being used, indicating its tone and describing the setting and participants as being appropriate to the use of such an artistic style. Further, such features indicate that it should be recognized that a verbal duel is occurring and that what is said is meant in a joking, perhaps also threatening, manner. A slight switch in code may carry implications for other components in the speech act. Because verbal dueling treads a fine line between play and real aggression, it is a kind of linguistic activity which requires strict adherence to socio-linguistic rules. To correctly decode the message, a hearer must be finely tuned to values which he observes in relation to all other components of the speech act. To do so he must rely on his conscious or unconscious knowledge of the sociolinguistic rules attached to this usage. Meaning, often assumed by linguists to be signaled entirely through code features, is actually dependent upon a consideration of other components of a speech act.[6] A remark taken in the spirit of verbal dueling may, for example, be interpreted as insult by virtue of what on the surface seems to be merely a minor change in personnel or a minor change in topic. Crucially, paralinguistic features must be made to appropriately conform to the rules. Change in posture, speech rate, tone of voice, facial expression, etc., may signal a change in meaning. The audience must also be sensitive to these cues. A change in meaning may signal that members of the audience must shift their responses and that metalinguistic comments may no longer be appropriate.

It is this focus in black culture—the necessity of applying sociolinguistic rules, in addition to the frequent appeal to shared background knowledge for correct semantic interpretation—that accounts for some of the unique character and flavor of black speech. There is an elaboration of the ability to carefully and skillfully manipulate other components of the speech act in relation to code to signal meaning, rather than using poor syntactic and lexical elaboration.[7]

Loud-talking

The term "loud-talking" is applied to a speaker's utterance which by virtue of its volume permits hearers other than the addressee, and is objectionable because of this. Loud-talking requires an audience and can only occur in a situation where there are potential hearers other than the interlocutors. It may take the form of a statement, question, or imperative, or a response to any of these, and may be delivered at low, normal, or high volume, requiring only overhearing.

What to say, what not to say, and what should be said privately are decisions commonly made on the basis of the semantic content of the message; one is expected to exhibit sensitivity and an awareness of the appropriate in this regard. The loud-talker breaches norms of discretion; his strategy is to use the factor of audience to achieve some desired effect on his addressee. Loud-talking often has the effect of unequivocally signaling the intent of the speaker from the perspective of the addressee. That is to say, it assures that intent will be imputed beyond the surface function of the utterance, which might be to seek information, make a request, make an observation, or furnish a reply to any of these.

The presence of an audience (overhearers) may act as a deciding factor in the addressee's interpretation of whether, for example, some utterance is an expression of compassion and sympathy or a "catty"

[6] John J. Gumperz, "Linguistic and Social Interaction in Two Communities," John J. Gumperz and Dell Hymes, eds., in *The Ethnography of Communication,* special publication of *American Anthropologist* 66, no. 6, pt. 2, p. 196.
[7] Ibid.

330 Rappin' and stylin' out

remark. "I'm sorry to hear that you and Bill are separated" may be taken in the former spirit when the addressee is the only potential hearer, but when an audience is present, such a remark may be felt to be mean and malicious. It is as if the audience factor causes the addressee to reject the harmless interpretation of intent while, at the same time, rendering more opprobrious the real intent because it intensifies its effect. Loud-talking serves as a key to the interpretation of ends.

An accusation of loud-talking carries the implication that the speaker (loud-talker) has, by his remarks, trod on some taboo area. It may be taboo solely due to the presence of an audience, or it may be reproachable under any circumstances—in which case the audience factor compounds the effrontery. The remark is tactless because it divulges some information the addressee does not wish to have made public or comments in some negative way about the speaker or his private affairs, causing him discomfort and embarrassment.

Except in the context of joking behavior, it is defined as a hostile and aggressive speech act which violates social conventions where shared expectations are taken for granted. Thus, when it occurs, it is assumed to be deliberate and with malice aforethought. When an individual has been the victim of loud-talking, his aggravation derives from, and is intensified by, the fact that he has been made vulnerable through exposure. The fact that the remark has functioned to expose in some way serves to define it as offending and, in addition, magnifies the offense. Although its effect may be shattering on the addressee, this tactic frequently serves to insure some form of retaliation as a face-saving device, no matter how passive and noninterfering the audience.

Whispered communications often signal to an addressee that the speaker does not wish to be overheard. When an addressee permits his response to be overheard, making it possible for those present to infer the content of the remark which the speaker has signaled should be kept private, he is loud-talking his interlocutor. Such a response may occur not as a provocation but as a sanction to censure the original remark, which perhaps has been felt to be impertinent. When an audience hears a huffy "I don't know" or an indignant "None of your business," it is usually clear that some offense (prying, in this case) has been committed and is being censured. Such a sanction carries the further implication that the transgression was so great as to require no diplomacy, creating an aura of justified indignation.

In a classroom situation, a student upon completing an assignment had begun reading a novel when he noticed that a neighbor had turned his paper over and was copying his answers. He turned to the young lady and at a volume sufficiently loud to enable all those present to overhear said, "What are you doing, girl?" The young lady retorted angrily, "You didn't have to loud-talk me," attempting to imply that he too had violated a norm. The circumstances were such that the speaker could have avoided both having his work copied and exposing the transgressor with a minimum of effort. It was, therefore, apparent that his desire to censure and expose his addressee at least equaled his desire to protect his work. The result was that everyone in the class got a laugh at the young lady's expense.

Loud-talking may be used, for example, when an individual is the focus of undesired attention. If polite and discreet requests to cease the annoyance have been ineffectual, the victim may resort to a retort or reply which will not only make known to all present that he is being pestered, but also the issue involved.

An informant reported that, after having been the repeated focus of the unwanted and offensive attention of a middle-aged man, she no longer felt any necessity to be polite and responded to an advance in a voice audible to others present, saying, "Mr. Williams, you are old enough to be my father. You ought to be ashamed of yourself." This served not only to communicate to the audience (which had probably perceived Mr. Williams's intent) that he was being unsuccessful, but to make his effrontery public, which assured an end to the annoyance.

To loud-talk is to assume an antagonistic posture toward the addressee. When it is used to censure, it reveals not only that the loud-talker has been aggrieved in some way; it also indicates, by virtue of making the delict public, that the speaker is not concerned about the possibility of permanently antagonizing his addressee. It is therefore revealing of the speaker's attitude toward the addressee. Although such a breach is not irreversible, one would not ordinarily loud-talk an individual one liked. Whether it occurs as a provocation or a sanction, it frequently serves to sever friendly relations if they were held theretofore.

When a speaker uses the presence of an audience to add persuasive pressure, it may also be said that he is loud-talking. This may occur when a speaker is trying to direct an addressee to do something that he is not disposed to doing, but the reasonableness of the request, for example, may put the hearer in a somewhat bad light if he refuses. The factor of audience adds persuasive pressure because it compounds the loss of face engendered by the refusal.

Loud-talking may occur in a context to expose the failure of the addressee to fulfill some obligation. A young man of seventeen years recounted an event where this form of loud-talking generated a violent confrontation in which he shot a peer, leading to his subsequent detention for several years. Although he does not describe his initiation of the encounter as loud-talking, it appears that his addressee did just that. Larry reported that he had loaned several dollars to a young man whom he did not know well at the request of a mutual friend. On the occasion that he next saw the fellow, several months later, he requested repayment. There was a rather large audience present, including several young girls who were accompanying the debtor. Larry apparently made no attempt to be circumspect, saying, "When you gon give me my money, man?" This accusation of being beholden in the context served to raise Larry's status at the expense of loss of face on his addressee's part. Larry notes that at this point the fellow began loud-talking him, "showing off for a bunch of girls." The response elicited was a stream of verbal abuse and epithets causing loss of face for our protagonist and, unfortunately, escalating the conflict. The alleged debtor made a gesture toward his pocket; Larry reacted by drawing a pistol and shooting him twice. Altercations between males are not uncommon when an individual has been made to lose face via loud-talking, although the former may be atypical in its degree of physical violence.

Labov mentions the term "louding" in the context of verbal interaction between teenagers, describing it as a style where loud comments are made by a speaker about or to some individual in order to exert social pressure on the subject. This use seems very much related to the one described here.

An accusation of loud-talking symbolizes that some norm of social interaction has been violated, a norm relating to discretion which must be observed with regard to the content of messages. The boundaries with regard to what is permissible and what is taboo vary according to the social situation, topic, participants, and characteristics of the group. The addressee may, depending on the interplay of these components, define the speech act as rude, in poor taste, or (in the extreme) real provocation. The kinds of sanctions which are likely to be employed relate also to the factors of the speech event. Except in the context of joking, a teenage boy may feel that the loss of face resulting from loud-talking requires physical engagement, if he can find no suitable verbal response. An adult might respond to loud-talking with a retort in kind or merely with a cold rebuff.

A speech act may be defined as both signifying and loud-talking (see Example 12 in the section on signifying) if the audience is being used to achieve an end. When some norm operates to exclude signifying or loud-talking, a simple accusation of engaging in these behaviors may be sufficient censure for the individual violating the norm and, to some degree, puts the offending party in a position of losing face.

Marking

A common black narrative tactic in the folktale genre and in accounts of actual events is the individuation of character through the use of direct quotation. When a narrator, in addition to reproducing the words of individual actors, affects the voice and mannerisms of the speaker, he is using the style referred to as "marking."[8] "Marking" is essentially a mode of characterization. The marker attempts to report not only what was said, but the way it was said, in order to offer implicit comment on the speaker's background, personality, or intent. Rather than introducing personality or character traits in some summary form, such information is conveyed by reproducing or sometimes inserting aspects of speech ranging from phonological features to particular content which carry expressive value. The above dictionary-entry meaning in the message of the marker is signaled and revealed by his reproduction of such things as phonological or grammatical peculiarities, his preservation of mispronounced words or provincial idioms, dialectal pronunciation, and, most particularly, paralinguistic mimicry.

The marker's choice to reproduce such features may reflect only his desire to characterize the speaker. It frequently signifies, however, that the characterization itself is relevant for further processing the meaning of the speaker's words. If, for example, some expressive feature has been taken as a symbol of the speaker's membership in a particular group, his credibility may come into question on these grounds alone.

The marker attempts to replay a scene for his hearers. He may seek to give the implications of the speaker's remarks, to indicate whether the emotions and affect displayed by the speaker were genuine or feigned— in short, to give his audience the full benefit of all the information he was able to process by virtue of expressive or context cues imparted by the speaker. His performance may be more in the nature of parody and caricature than true imitation. But the features selected to overplay are those which are associated with membership in some class. His ability to get his message across, in fact, relies on folk notions of the covariance of linguistic and nonlinguistic categories, combined, of course, with whatever special skills he possesses for creating imagery.

The kind of context most likely to elicit marking is one in which the marker assumes his hearers are sufficiently like himself to be able to interpret this metaphoric communication. Since there is, more likely than not, something unflattering about the characterization, and the element of ridicule is so salient, the relationship between a marker and his audience is likely to be one of familiarity and intimacy and mutual positive effect.

An informant quoted a neighbor to give me an appreciation of her dislike for the woman. She quoted the following comment from Pearl in a style carefully articulated in order to depict her as "putting on the dog," parodying gestures which gave the impression that Pearl is preposturously affected: "You know my family owns their own home and I'm just living here temporarily because it is more beneficial to collect

---

[8] Clearly related to "mocking."

the rent from my own home and rent a less expensive apartment." "That's the kind of person she is," my informant added, feeling no need for further explanation. This is, incidentally, a caricature of a social type which is frequently the object of scorn and derision. This quote was delivered at a pitch considerably higher than was usual for the informant, and the words were enunciated carefully so as to avoid loss of sounds and elision characteristics of fluid speech. What was implied was not that the phonological patterns mimicked are to be associated with affectation in a one-one relationship, but that they symbolize affectation here. The marker was essentially giving implicit recognition to the fact that major disturbances in fluency are indices of "monitored" speech. The presence of the features are grounds for the inference that the speaker is engaged in impression management, which is contextually inappropriate. Individuals who are characterized as "trying to talk proper" are frequently marked in a tone of voice which is rather falsetto.

A marker wishing to convey a particular impression of a speaker may choose to deliver a quotation in a style which is felt to best suit what he feels lies underneath impression management or what is obscured by the speaker's effective manipulation of language. In the following example, the marker departs radically from the style of the speaker for purposes of disambiguation. The individuals here, with the exception of S_1, had recently attended the convention of a large corporation and had been part of a group which had been meeting prior to the convention to develop some strategy for putting pressure on the corporation to hire more blacks in executive positions. They had planned to bring the matter up in a general meeting of delegates, but before they had an opportunity to do so a black company man spoke before the entire body. S_2 said, "After he spoke our whole strategy was undermined, there was no way to get around his impact on the whites."

S_1: What did he say?

S_2 (*drawling*): He said, "Ah'm so-o-o happy to be here today. First of all, ah want to thank all you good white folks for creatin so many opportunities for us niggers and ya'll can be sho that as soon as we can git ourselves qualified we gon be filin our applications. Ya'll done what we been waiting for a long time. Ya'll done give a colored man a good job with the company."

S_1: Did he really say that?

S_3: Um hm, yes he said it. Girl, where have you been? (*Put down by intimating S_1 was being literal.*)

S_1: Yeah, I understand, but what did he really say?

S_4: He said, "This is a moment of great personal pride for me. My very presence here is a tribute to the civil rights movement. We now have ample evidence of the good faith of the company and we must now begin to prepare ourselves to handle more responsible positions. This is a major step forward on the part of the company. The next step is up to us." In other words, he said just what S_2 said he said. He sold us out by accepting that kind of tokenism.

S_2 attempted to characterize the speaker as an Uncle Tom by using exaggerated, stereotyped southern speech coupled with content that was compromising and denigrating. It would certainly be an overstatement to conclude that southern regional speech is taken by anyone as a sign of being an "Uncle Tom," but there is a historical association with the model of this stereotype being southern.

The characterization of individuals according to the way they speak is of course not peculiar to black people, although the implicit association of particular ways of speaking with specific social types may be more elaborated than elsewhere.

The parodying of southern regional black speech may sometimes serve as a device for characterizing a speaker as uneducated or unintelligent, and sometimes it is used to underscore the guilelessness of the speaker.

The marker encodes his subjective reactions to the speaker and is concerned with the *expressive* function of speech more than with its *referential* function.

Because marking relies on linguistic expression for the communication of messages, it is revealing of attitudes and values relating to language. It frequently conveys many subtleties and can be a significant source of information about conscious and unconscious attitudes toward language. An individual, on occasion, may mark a non-black using exaggerated black English, with emphasis clearly on communicating that the subject was uneducated and used nonstandard usages. Perhaps more than anything, marking exhibits a finely tuned linguistic awareness in some areas and a good deal of verbal virtuosity in being able to reproduce aspects of speech which are useful in this kind of metaphorical communication.

■ Black poetry—where it's at

CAROLYN RODGERS

Carolyn Rodgers is a native Chicagoan and a Roosevelt University graduate. Her published works include *Paper Soul* and *Songs of a Blackbird,* as well as several other articles and poems which have appeared in journals and anthologies. The present article appeared originally in *Negro Digest* in September, 1969. It is perhaps the most comprehensive typology of black linguistic expression that has been advanced to date and, as such, complements nicely the cultural categories delineated and analyzed by Kochman, Labov, and Mitchell-Kernan in their analyses of black speech events elsewhere in this volume. It also demonstrates the richness and variety of black folk speech and how the *oral vernacular* culture can readily be extended to provide the basis for an equally rich and unique *literary* expression, as exemplified by Rodgers with her own and others' poems.

In the last few years, we have seen a significant increase in the amount of black poetry being published. We have also seen a change in style and subject matter. At this point, it is possible to see distinctions in the various types of poetry being written. That is to say, all black poets don't write the same *kind* of poetry, or all black poems ain't the same kind. They differ. Just as white poems differ, and just as white poems come in sonnets, ballads, or whatever.

I have attempted to place all black poetry in several broad categories, all of which have variations on the main form. Very few poems are all one type or another. It is possible and probable that a poem will be three or four different types of poetry at one time. That is, a signifying poem will be a *teachin', spaced, pyramid* poem. Here are the main headings:

1. *signifying*
    a. open
    b. sly
    c. with or about
2. *teachin'/rappin'*
3. *covers-off*
    a. rundown
    b. hipto
    c. digup
    d. coatpull
4. *spaced* (spiritual)

   a. mindblower (fantasy)
   b. coolout
5. *bein'* (self/reflective)
   a. upinself
   b. uptight
   c. dealin'/swingin'
6. *love*
   a. skin
   b. space (spiritual)
   c. cosmic (ancestral)
7. *shoutin'* (angry/cathartic)
   a. badmouth
   b. facetoface (warning/confrontation)
   c. two-faced (irony)
8. *jazz*
   a. riffin'
   b. cosmic ('Trane)
   c. grounded (Lewis)
9. *du-wah*
   a. dittybop
   b. bebop
10. *pyramid* (getting us together/building/nationhood)

Some of these categories are self-explanatory and familiar. Most poems, as previously stated, fall into more than one category which, to my way of thinking, attests to the flexibility of black writers. Unconsciously, I think, poets fall into their bag—or bags—and it is no discredit to a writer if he chooses to deal with only one form—or two, or three. . . . However, a black writer will be classifiable in at least *one* of these categories, although it is conceivable to me that black writers are creative enough to uncover forms which are yet to be acknowledged. We will know if the writing is black.

Briefly, I am going to give examples of several of the headings, and then devote a large amount of discussion to signifying poetry since it has reached an exciting unprecedented level of sophistication in the written word.

The *teachin'* poem is a poem which seeks to define and give direction to black people. The two examples chosen and quoted in part here are Ronda Davis's "Towards a Black Aesthetic" and Barbara Mahone's "What Color Is Black."

> if tomorrow's black poetry will
> not EXPLAIN what is
> but BE it
> then pens will be electric with feeling

igniting
and the paper shall become the poet
and the poets shall be earth-clouds . . .
　　　　　　　　　—Ronda Davis

and Mahone:

Black is the color of
my little brother's mind,
the grey streaks
in my mother's hair.
Black is the color of
my yellow cousin's smile,
the scars upon my neighbor's wrinkled face . . .

The *covers-off, rundown, hipto, digup or coatpull* are basically the same type of poem, so the terms can be used interchangeably. There are many, many examples of this kind of poem today. For example, Cleveland Webber's poem (from his recently released book of poetry, *Africa Africa Africa*) "In America"—

the people are in all the areas
we occupy little parts of air,
telling little lies, taking little trips,
at least 5 days a week . . .
. . . ghetto streets get empty while the pig is
internalized in a suffering too old to be.

or Don L. Lee's poem on "Nigerian Unity"—

little niggers
killing
little niggers
the weak against the weak
the ugly against the ugly . . .

These poets hip you to something, pull the covers off of something, or run it down to you, or ask you to just dig it—your coat is being pulled.

The *spaced* poem is very beautiful, and many black poets, after writing a lot of *signifying, coversoff* or *shoutin'* poems, find an inner calm and, inherent in that, a mystical and positive way of looking at the black man's relationship to the universe. Ameer Baraka (LeRoi Jones) has a poem called "Black People: This Is Our Destiny," and I quote from it here:

. . . we go to meet the realization of makers knowing who we are . . .
knowing how to live, and what life is . . .
. . . we must spin through in our seven adventures in the endlessness of
all existing feeling, all existing forms of life, the gasses, the plants, the
ghosts minerals the spirits the souls the light in the stillness where the

storm the glow the nothing in God is complete except there is nothing to be incomplete the pulse and change of rhythm, blown flight to be anything at all . . . vibration holy nuance beating against itself, a rhythm a playing re-understood now by one of the 1st race the primitives the first men who evolve again to civilize the world . . .

The *spaced* poem returns to the spiritual wisdom of our Egyptian/ African forefathers. Returns to the natural laws, the natural state of man before subhuman massacres. Spaced poems say that our ancestors are in the air and will communicate with us. As is the case in Jones' "No Matter, No Matter, the World Is the World"—

> A broke dead genius
> moved on to dust
> will touch you one night . . .
> . . . and the stacked dust of a gone brother will
> hunch you
> some father you needed who left you . . .

We speak of the vibrations, positive and negative, and we believe again in what we have never truly denied; the power of Nommo, Ju-Ju, and the collective force of the positive spirits, moving in time with the universe. In our poetry, we sing of Sun-Ra and Coltrane, and their life-motion which is sound. The new black poets believe that we are the seventh dimension (as the seventh sun/son). They further believe in the overall importance of the astrological signs of people (the writer is Sagittarius—#5). The dream is to utilize our beginning to conceptualize and direct a black end that is as beautiful as our beginning.

The *mindblower* poem may seem similar to the *spaced* poem, but the two are not to be confused. There are basic differences. *Mindblower* poems seek to expand our minds, to break the chains that strangle them, so that we can begin to imagine alternatives for black people. They seek to ridicule and mutilate that which may have formerly been esteemed. Often these poems predict an awful or glorious future and are gorier than the *spaced* poem. Sometimes the awful predictions are for black people; oftener, for subhumans.

Larry Neal, in his book, *Black Boogaloo,* in an untitled poem says:

> We gathered in the open place
> Piled their symbols one on top of the other,
> Their flags and their death books; took their holidays rolled
> their platitudes into nice burnable heaps,
> Gathered and piled this stuff from the stink
> pots of the earth which they have made so.
> In the distance their cities burn . . .
>   We piled their histories skyward with destruction
> acknowledgement to our ancestors and gods,

    then we light it.
      Singing.

By contrast is Jewel Latimore's "Folk Fable"—

    . . . but the niggas wadn't hip & wadn't hipped
    until they was copped.
    too.
    to work in the mines on the moon
    . . . & the ships has promises had names
    that all the niggas knew names
    like JESUS & HEAVEN & FREEDOM
    to take the niggas to a new world . . .
    . . . & when they was shipped to the moon
    mainland sold
    to companies who
    was bidden
    while the chasemanhattan bank
    supervised the auctions . . .

Or Ebon's poem, "The Statue of Liberty Has Her Back to Harlem"
(two other alternate titles excluded)—

    I saw them bayonet
    her spine
    and pin her 16th birthday
    to a cross
    where it hung.
    dank and slimey
    it hung,
    like stagnant death
    in shallow pools.
    vomiting blood
    on poets
    and mothers
    and flower children . . .

Surely, he was talking about "them," and he is a master of the gory.

    Every poet has written a *bein'* poem. In fact, most poets start off writing them. Just writing about the way they be, they friends be, they lovers be, the world be. . . .

    An example presented here is one of my own, from my *Songs of A Blackbird*—

    it's me
    bathed and ashy
    smellin down with
               (revlons aquamarine)
    me with my hair black
    and nappy good and rough

as the ground
me sitting in my panties
. . . it's me in the sky
where pharoah and coltrane playing
. . . and it's me screammmmmmmming into the box
and the box is screammmmmmmming back
. . . in kulu se & karma . . .

And all praise is due Allah; we are now getting more, more and more
love poems from/about black men and women. Such is this fragile jewel
of Barbara Mahone's. The poem, "With Your Permission," combines
skin and *space* (spiritual) aspects, as they should be—

smooth surfaces are easy
. . . i would rather deal with
what moves you
explore the fire and texture
of your soul
with your permission
i would chart a course
across your skin
and travel all day
all night

And one black warrior, William Wandick, writes spears of honey:

my eyes took your slender fingers & dreamed on them,
they thinned imagination to a queen called sheba/nefertiti
deeming you royalness/making a fetish of your hand . . .

And there are love poems for all black people, such as Ronda Davis's
poem about the "Wine Dipped Woman." And we need more. And
more. More . . .

The *shoutin'* poem is perhaps at this time the most familiar to us all.
For a while, it seemed to be the only kind of poem being written. It
usually tells the subhuman off. Or offs him with word bullets. An example of the *facetoface poem,* which is an aspect of the *shoutin'* type,
is one written by Sonia Sanchez in her hard-hitting book of poetry,
Homecoming—

git the word out
now to the man/boy
taking a holiday
from murder tell him
we hip to his shit and that
the next time he kills one
of our
blk/princes
some of his faggots

> gonna die
>> a stone/cold/death.
>>> yeah.

The last category with which I will deal briefly is the *two-faced* poem. As kids, we used to call people two-faced if they grinned in our faces and talked about us behind our backs. In poetry, this concept takes on similar, but broader, meanings. For example, I will use my poem, "You Name It"—

> I will write about things that are universal!
> So that hundreds, maybe even thousands of
> years from now, White critics and readers
> will say of me, Here is a good Black writer,
> who wrote about truth and universal topics.
> I will write about people who eat,
>> as it was in the beginning
> I will write about people who sleep,
>> is now
> I will write about people who fuck,
>> and ever shall
> I will write about babies being born,
>> world without end
> I will write about Black people
> re-po-sses-sing this earth,
>> ah-men.

I would hope that everyone who reads the poem catches the two-facededness (irony) implicit in the theme.

Signifying poetry holds a special fascination for me, probably because I could not/cannot signify and have always admired those who can. From a literary point of view, it is an exciting aspect of today's poetry. I know, and you know, that we have always signified. On the corners, in the poolrooms, the playgrounds, anywhere and everywhere we have had the opportunity. We "sig" with somebody, about somebody, and if we can't be open about it, we "sig" on the sly! Langston Hughes's character, Simple, signified: with his landlady, his partners, his girl-friend, everybody. And Richard Wright deals it in *Black Boy*. However, to my knowledge, no *group* of black writers has ever used it as a poetic technique as much as today's writers. It is done with polish. And the audiences love it! Too much signifying can be negative, I think; how-ever, most of today's poets are very conscious of how important positive vibrations are, and few have carried signification to an extreme. In the main, it is being used for constructive destruction.

A quick, or lengthy, look at the poetry of Don L. Lee, Nikki Giovanni, or Sonia Sanchez shows that these three poets signify with their readers and the objects of their poems. *Signify*- fuh days . . .

"wallace for president
his mamma for vice-president"
                        —Don L. Lee

and—

Memorial. The supremes—cuz they dead
                        —Sonia Sanchez

or

ever notice how its only the ugly
honkies
who hate . . .
—Nikki Giovanni

and of course the master of it all, Ameer Baraka (LeRoi Jones), on
wigs starter—

". . . why don't you take that thing
off yo haid
you look like Miss Muffet in a
runaway ugly machine. I mean,
like that."

Signifying is a way of saying the truth that hurts with a laugh, a way
of "capping on" (shutting up) someone. Getting even talking 'bout
people's mammas and such. It's a love/hate exercise in exorcising one's
hostilities. It's a funny way of saying something negative that is obviously untrue like:

"you look like you been whupped wid uh ugly stick"

or saying something that is negative as:

". . . nigger: standing on the corner, thought him was
cool. him still
standing there. it's winter time, him cool."

Signifying is very often a bloody knife job, with a vocal touch. It moves
in progressions sometimes and it is both general and specific. In *Black
Boy,* by Richard Wright, we are taken through a dozens scene or
signifying scene (to me they are the same), and each phrase is labeled
in terms of its significance.

"You eat yet?" (*uneasily trying to make conversation*)
"Yeah, man I done really fed my face." (*casually*)
"I had cabbage and potatoes." (*confidently*)
"I had buttermilk and blackeye peas." (*meekly informational*)
"Hell, I ain't gonna stand near you, nigger!" (*pronouncement*)
"How come?" (*feigned innocence*)
"Cause you gonna smell up this air in a minute!" (*a shouted accusation*)

"Nigger your mind's in a ditch." (*amusingly moralistic*)
"Ditch, nothing! Nigger you going to break wind any minute now!" (*triumphant pronouncement creating suspense*)
"Yeah, when them black-eyed peas tell that buttermilk to move over, that buttermilk ain't gonna wanna move and there's gonna be war in your guts and your stomach's gonna swell up and bust!" (*climax*)

As you see, every line leads up to the cap, the final one. And the last statement is based on a reality that all blacks know. Peas, buttermilk, cabbage and potatoes will cause you to fart! It is a four-to-four balanced way of making love to—while poking hurt/fun at—one's self and one's life-styles.

A great deal of what today's poets do is hit-and-run signifying—or, another way of saying it: spot-signifying. That is, they do not usually sustain the length of a standard signifying circle. But they are traveling too fast. They hit—

yo mamma!

and keep on moving to the next point—

your daddy too!

or

if dracula came to town now
he'd look like daley
booing senator ribicoff
no pretty man himself
but at least out of the beast
category
—Nikki Giovanni

The poets signify with/about a whole lot of people in one poem, hitting one, then another; usually, though not always, one theme holds the poem together.

When two people signify with each other, one feeds the other for progression, dramatic buildup to impact, but the object of ridicule doesn't have to be around or vocal. Responses can be imagined or drawn from the poet's own experiences—

you followed him niggers
all of you—
yes you did,
i saw ya. (*implied response—no, I didn't*)
—Don L. Lee

Now, because signifying often contains such a broad base of truth it has been known to cause—in fact, it is famous for causing—a fight or a death. It can get too down, too real, so true and personal it uncovers too much. If the signifier can really get down (and in grammar school the last word was "yo mama is uh man . . ."), the second party who cannot move his tongue to balance the scale may use his fists to do so—or his knife, or both. And it is a matter of pride. No black person wants to be sigged about or capped all over.

No black person can listen to some signifying without responding in some way. It pulls us in and we identify with the bad signifier. Obviously, this style of poetry has the power to involve black people and to move them. It is a familiar mover, and is probably the most dynamic type of poetry I have mentioned up to now.

I trust that I have initiated here a rather complete incomplete picture of where black poetry is at. Some may quibble with the actual attempt to label what black writers are doing. Others may take issue with the labels.

We do not (it cannot be said too often) want subhumans defining what we be doing. There is no human reference point. And objectivity does not really exist in criticism. There is, perhaps, reason, tempered by a good strong sense of what is reasonable, what is fair. Ultimately, one's life-style is his point of view.

Black poetry is becoming what it has always been but has not quite *beed*. And we have love and the spirit of our ancestors to guide us.

Expressive role behavior

■ Roles and ideologies

R. LINCOLN KEISER

R. Lincoln Keiser is a lecturer in anthropology at Wesleyan University and, for the academic year 1971–72, was a visiting professor at the Institute for Social Anthropology at the University of Stockholm. A specialist in urban anthropology, Keiser has been involved in the urban scene for several years both as caseworker for the Cook County Department of Public Aid and the Municipal Courts of Chicago and as a field anthropologist. He is editor of *Hustler! The Autobiography of a Thief,* by Henry Williamson, and author of *The Vice Lords: Warriors of the Streets,* from which the selection here was taken, and several other articles dealing with the Vice Lords and the nature of doing fieldwork among black urban gang youth. The fieldwork with the "Lords" of the black West Side community of Chicago was done during 1966–67.

The two chapters from Keiser's book on the Vice Lords, incorporated here as a single piece, illuminate much of the perspective of black urban gang youth: the "gang-bangers"; the code

they subscribe to; their obligations and responsibilities to themselves, their peer and nonpeer groups; and their projected self-image. Just the name "street warrior" says a great deal about how the Lords see themselves and how they wish to be seen by others. Consciously concerned with ritual, performance, and style, as expressed through the various roles that they play, the Lords project a life style and value system reflecting the influence both of socioeconomic pressures and of conditions imposed and directed from those power sources outside the community, as well as inner-directed cultural forces. For example, the motivation for "gaming" is clearly linked to the scarcity of or limited access to goods and services; however, the form of manipulation, the skill and ingenuity with which the game is carried off ("whupped," in Chicago) is as much appreciated as success ("scoring") and, as such, needs to be examined from an aesthetic as well as socioeconomic perspective.

An important part of the pattern in Vice Lord social life is comprised of what can be called social roles. In our study of Vice Lord roles we shall use a theoretical framework to help organize and bring sense to the data. Dr. Allen Hoben has written a concise explanation of the role concept in a community study guide for Peace Corps volunteers. Part of this will form a section of our framework, and that portion of his work is included here.

Hoben identifies three general aspects of social roles:

First, there are in any society a number of well-defined and publicly recognized social personalities or identities. Father, son, teacher, pupil, employer, and employee are examples of social identities in our own society. It should be stressed that these are not different kinds of people, but different social identities. The same individual is called upon to assume different identities in different situations.

Second, in any society only in certain social identities can people interact with one another. There are very definite rules of combination—a sort of grammar of possible social interaction. For example, father-son, father-daughter, husband-wife, teacher-pupil, and employer-employee are grammatical combinations of social identities in our own society. Father-pupil, employer-son, daughter-teacher, and son-wife are not. A single social identity (father or professor) may have a grammatical relationship with several other identities (father-son, father-daughter, or professor-student, professor-professor, professor-chairman of department).

Third, there are in any society, for each grammatically possible combination of social identities, agreed-upon rules concerning appropriate modes of interaction. This means, for example, that father and son, teacher and pupil, employer and employee are aware of the behavior they expect from one another.

If we focus on the third aspect—the "agreed-upon rules concerning appropriate modes of interaction"—differences in kinds of rules are found.

1. There are formal rights and duties limiting the behavior of individuals in identity relationships. A Vice Lord who assumes a particular identity expects certain rights, and he owes certain duties to the Vice Lord who assumes the alter identity in the relationship. If either party fails to fulfill his duties, sanctions are imposed.

2. There are modes of behavior that are considered proper between individuals in social relationships. These we can call social etiquette.

3. There are modes of behavior that signal which identities are being assumed.

The final point in our framework concerns role distribution. If the distribution of roles in relation to social contexts is studied, important differences in contextualization are found. While Vice Lords assume some identities in a few contexts, there are, in contrast, other identities that are assumed in a wide range of social contexts.

Vice lord–vice lord

The role Vice Lord–Vice Lord is found in a wide range of social contexts. Whether hanging on the corner, drinking wine, or gang fighting, individuals in the club often assume the identity Vice Lord in relationships with each other. There are a certain set of rights and duties that regulate behavior between individuals assuming this identity. When my informants discussed the way Vice Lords should behave toward one another, the idea of mutual help was a constantly recurring theme. As one person put it, "We may get to arguing and then humbug [fight], but soon as it's over we buy a drink, and we back together. See, the way we see this thing, we all out to help each other . . . really."

Mutual help can be divided into two kinds—help with regard to material things, and aid in fighting and other dangerous activities such as strong-arming. Vice Lords state that members of the club should help each other in any kind of dangerous activity. If a Vice Lord is jumped on by members of another club, all other Vice Lords present should help, regardless of personal risk. Also, if a Vice Lord asks another to help in hustling, he should not turn down the request. When I asked if most Vice Lords actually do usually give physical help to each other, the answer was an emphatic "yes." For example, I asked one Vice Lord what one should do if he saw another Lord getting jumped on. The answer was, "Help him! You not supposed to do this, you going to do this! You a Lord . . . Lords don't fear nothing but God and death. I never seen a Lord cop out [chicken out]—not a true Lord." When pressed, however, some informants admitted that not all Vice Lords act in this manner. Those who don't, however, are strongly sanctioned. A person who does not fulfill the obligations of physical support is derisively referred to as a "punk," or a "chump." According to one informant, if one is judged a punk, other Vice Lords will refuse to have anything to do with him: "They say he's a punk—tell him to go on away from them; tell him to go home; tell him to stop hanging with them." Another Vice Lord stated that a person would actually be physically sanctioned if he "punked out": "Most of the time when a fellow punks out they wait until the person get out of the hospital, get his side of the story, see did the dude really punk out. If the guy say he punked out on him they usually jump on him . . . or take him in Cobra territory and put him out."

It should be pointed out, however, that the obligation of physical support is similar to the commandment "Thou shall not kill." Although this commandment is supported by sanctions, there are certain circumstances when it can be broken with impunity. Sanctions are not imposed for killing in self-defense, or during a war. Similarly, sanctions are not always imposed on Vice Lords who do not give physical aid to other Vice Lords. For example, if a small group of Vice Lords is attacked by a much larger enemy force, it is felt that one Vice Lord should run and get help rather than stay and help the others. Also, if a Vice Lord sees another member being beaten up by an enemy group, he can try to get a weapon before helping in the fight. Even if he returns with his weapon after the fight is finished, he will not normally be sanctioned for punking out. There are also situations where a Vice Lord's obligations to help other Vice Lords in hustling activities is put aside. For example, at 3:00 one morning two drunk Vice Lords came to the house of Doughbelly and yelled in his window asking him to help them hold up somebody. Because of the noise they created Doughbelly's mother told him he could no longer live in her house. He became enraged at the two drunk Lords for getting him thrown out, and told them he would not help them, and further, if he saw them again he would kill them. It was never suggested publicly that Doughbelly had punked out for refusing to help in this situation, and no sanctions were imposed.

Since there are sanctions imposed for failing to fulfill the obligations of physical support, it seems clear that these are part of the rights and duties of the Vice Lord–Vice Lord role. A Vice Lord has the duty to give physical support to other Vice Lords and the right to physical support from other Vice Lords. This set of rights and duties, however, can be tempered by particular circumstances.

The rights and duties of mutual help regarding material things presents a more complicated picture. Although Vice Lords say they should lend money and clothes, share food, and should not try to "beat" (con) each other out of their possessions, many individuals admit that most do not usually act in this way. In fact, when I asked if Vice Lords usually do give material help, the answer was often hoots of laughter. In my observations I found that Vice Lords frequently tried to beat each other out of things, and I saw many cases where individuals refused to lend things to other Vice Lords. There were no group sanctions imposed for failing to live up to this ideal, and when questioned, my informants stated that it was the responsibility of the individual who felt he was wronged to take what action he felt necessary. Can it be said that mutual help with regard to material things is not important in the Vice Lord–Vice Lord role? I don't think so. It is generally felt that individuals who refuse to live up to the ideal of mutual help should not deny the validity of the ideal. Further, there are situations when most Vice Lords usually will extend material help to other members of the club. If they are convinced that a member is really in need, then he usually will be helped. An individual may have been thrown out of his home by angry parents and have to fend for himself on the streets, or he may have recently returned from jail with no money and nowhere to live. In such cases other Vice Lords usually give whatever help they can. I observed an instance where material help was given to a Vice Lord in need. A set had been planned by the Fifteenth Street Lords. Throughout the prior week, the set was a constant topic of conversation. The clothes that were going to be worn and the girls that were going to be present were repeatedly discussed. The evening for the set I met a group of Fifteenth Street Lords at the house of Tex, the Fifteenth Street's president. Everyone was dressed and ready for the set except Old Dude. Old Dude was one of the least important members of the Fifteenth Street Lords. He was thought by everyone to be "light upstairs" (not too intelligent), and he did not have a rep for gang fighting. His family was extremely poor, even by ghetto standards, and his mother gave all her attention to another brother. One of the fellows asked Old Dude, "Say man, why you ain't dressed for the set?"

"I ain't got no pants. It's my own fault. I knew about the set all week, but I just ain't got no pants."

Tex said, "Damn Jack! You should've asked us. You a Lord—we take care of you." Tex then asked his mother to press one of his extra pairs of pants, and another of the fellows went home to get a clean shirt for Old Dude to wear.

It is interesting that in this context Vice Lords sanction individuals who will not help a club member in need. Such a person is referred to as stingy and becomes the topic of derogatory conversation. Certainly anyone with leadership aspirations could not afford to be classified as stingy. From this we can conclude that material help is a binding obligation when it is thought that an individual is in real need.

Looking now at the rights and duties regarding mutual help, a clearer picture emerges. Mutual help, both material and physical, is a binding obligation when Vice Lords feel real need is involved. If a Vice Lord is jumped on by members of an enemy club, he is in danger of serious physical injury. When a Vice Lord has nowhere to live and nothing to eat, he is also in need. The obligations of mutual help become binding in such situations. We can now better understand why Vice Lords feel that even when an individual is not in real need, it is still necessary to uphold the value of mutual help. Life in the ghetto poses many risks; the rights and obligations of the Vice Lord–Vice Lord role provide a kind of social insurance. No one knows when he may find it necessary to bring into play the obligations of mutual help. Thus the ultimate legitimacy of such obligations must be jealously guarded. Publicly denying that these obligations are legitimate would threaten the well-being of all Vice Lords. Therefore, it is felt that individuals should not deny the legitimacy of a request for help, although the request does not always have to be granted.

There are certain forms in the interactive behavior of individuals who assume the Vice Lord identity that can be called social etiquette. Standardized greetings are one example. When individuals pass one another on the street, there are two greetings that are used. In some cases the right hand is raised to the side, the hand balled into a fist, and the arm raised and lowered two or three times. In other instances the club name is yelled out as a greeting.

Upholding the legitimacy of the obligations of mutual help is also a part of Vice Lord social etiquette. For example, if a Vice Lord were asked to loan money to another member and answered, "No man! I ain't your daddy. I ain't going to give you nothing!" this would be a breach of good manners; that is, it would go against social etiquette. It would also be interpreted as a hostile act—a signal not only that he was refusing to assume the identity Vice Lord vis-à-vis the asker, but also that he was assuming an identity as a protagonist. The individual who asked for the money would then have the legitimate right to retaliate by starting a fight; that is, public opinion would support his starting a fight. In contrast, if the person asked for the loan couched his refusal in the form of an excuse, and in a friendly tone, this would constitute proper social etiquette. It would not be interpreted as a hostile act, and public opinion would not support the asker if he started a fight. I observed an instance that provides a good example.

A meeting of the Nation had just occurred, and groups of Vice Lords were standing around talking. I was with Goliath, my major informant, and a few other Vice Lords. While we were talking, Tico walked up and said to Goliath, "Hey man, give me a quarter. I get paid Tuesday, and I'll take care of you then, but I got to get me some jive [wine] tonight." Goliath answered, "Yeah man, I'll take care of you," and turned around and started talking to another Vice Lord who was standing with us. After a few minutes Tico again asked Goliath for the money. "Damn Jack, what about the quarter?" Goliath answered, "Yeah, I'll turn you on." This continued for a short time—Goliath kept assuring Tico he was going to give him a quarter, but made no move to actually do so. Finally he reached into his pocket, pulled out some change, and began counting it intently: "Let's see, I need forty cents for a Polish [sausage], twenty-five for a . . ."

"Shit man, we Vice Lords. We supposed to be brothers. Come on, Jack, I gotta get me a taste."

"I'll take care of you. You know that. Now I need forty for a Polish, twenty-five for carfare, fifty to get my baby some milk . . . shit! I'm fifteen cents short. Say man, can you loan me fifteen cents?" Tico shook his head and walked away in disgust.

I should note that Goliath did not need fifteen cents—he had ten dollars in his wallet—but this was used as an excuse rather than denying that he should loan the quarter. Goliath was, therefore, observing the proper social forms of the Vice Lord–Vice Lord role. (Incidentally, Tico did not need the quarter. I saw him later that evening with two dollars.)

Street man–street man

Another role that is found in a wide range of contexts is what I call the Street Man–Street Man role. The social identity Street Man is one that all male blacks living in the ghetto assume at various times. Vice Lords often assume this identity in their relationships both with other members and with those who do not belong to the club. The essential element in the Street Man–Street Man role is manipulation. It is expected that persons who assume the Street Man identity will try to manipulate (or, as Vice Lords say, "beat") each other out of as much as possible. This manipulation, however, has certain bounds set to it. An example will illustrate.

While driving down 16th Street, Cochise was hit by a woman who had gone through a red light. She did not have insurance, but agreed to pay forty dollars for damages. After two weeks she still had not paid Cochise, and he decided to get the money himself. He asked Jesse, another Vice Lord, to accompany him and help out in case of any trouble. Jesse was to get a share of whatever was collected in return for his help. Jesse and Cochise broke into the woman's house and took a television set, radio, and toaster. Cochise kept the toaster and radio. Jesse got the television set, but gave Cochise twenty dollars so that each would have a fair share. Later Cochise and Jesse were on the corner of sixteenth and Lawndale discussing what had happened. Cochise mentioned that he was going to take the radio home and then try to sell it the next day. Jesse said, "No man, don't do that. The Man liable to come in your house, and if he find the radio he'll bust [arrest] you. Now I know an old building, ain't nobody in there. You can leave it there." Later, when I mentioned this incident to Goliath he laughed and said, "You know why Jesse said that?" I said, "No."

"Well, if Cochise took that radio home, Jesse couldn't go in his house and get it, but if he put it in that old building then Jesse'd sneak back at night and get the radio hisself."

In this instance Jesse was attempting to manipulate Cochise in order to beat him out of the radio. According to the expectations of the Street Man–Street Man role it was acceptable for Jesse to attempt this. However, there are limits to the ways it could be done. If Cochise had taken the radio home, it would not have been acceptable for Jesse to have taken it from there. Stealing from the home of a close acquaintance is considered wrong behavior by Vice Lords, and few individuals would have much to do with a person known to act in this way. On the other hand, if Jesse could have talked Cochise into leaving the radio in an abandoned building, he would have been free to go back and get it for himself. Successfully manipulating others is called "whupping the game." If Jesse had been successful in whupping the game on Cochise, his prestige with other Vice Lords would have increased. It is now possible to isolate at least one of the rights and duties of the Street Man–Street Man role. Individuals who assume the identity Street Man have the right to expect others in the alter identity to follow the rules which set limits to manipulation, and they have the duty to follow these rules themselves. The sanction of public opinion supports this right and duty.

The social etiquette of the Street Man–Street Man role consists of greetings, farewells, and forms of ongoing social interaction. There are two greetings that are generally used. An individual may say either "How you doing?" or "What's happening?" Sometimes "man" or "Jack" is placed at the end of the greeting—for example, "What's happening, Jack?" The person who begins the exchange has the option to choose the greeting he wishes. When one of these greetings is used to initiate a social exchange, the other is usually the response. To terminate a social episode most individuals say simply, "Later."

A form of behavior that is a part of ongoing social interaction is hand-slapping. In hand-slapping a person puts his hand out with the palm up, and another person touches the open palm with his own hand or arm. Although this might seem somewhat similar in outward form to shaking hands, as we shall see, it has radically different social significance. (Vice Lords do not usually shake hands like most middle-class Americans.)

A hand-slapping exchange can begin in two ways. In some cases during the course of a social episode an individual puts his hand out with the palm raised. The proper response is to touch the raised palm with a hand or arm. Other times a hand-slapping exchange is initiated by a person raising his hand with the palm down. The proper response is to put out the hand with the palm raised. The first individual then slaps the outraised palm. In the first kind of hand-slapping exchange there are several kinds of responses to an outraised palm that are considered proper. Some (but not all) of these have different social significance. A person can respond to an outraised palm by slapping it with his own palm either up or down. This has no particular social significance. Touching the outraised palm with the arm or elbow is also a possible response. Further, an individual can vary the intensity of his slap. These last two differences—touching the palm with an arm or elbow rather than the hand, and varying the intensity of the slap—do have significance.

In general, when a hand-slapping episode occurs during social interaction, it emphasizes agreement between the two parties. If an individual has said something, or done something he thinks particularly noteworthy, he will put out his hand to be slapped. By slapping it, the alter in the relationship signals agreement. Varying the intensity of the slap response indicates varying degrees of agreement. A Vice Lord may say, "Five Lords can whup fifty Cobras!" and then put out his hand, palm up. Another club member responds by slapping the palm hard, thus indicating strong agreement. The first Vice Lord might then say, "I can whup ten Cobras myself!" and again put out his hand. This time, however, the second individual may respond with a much lighter slap. This indicates that he does not emphatically agree with the statement. If he barely touches the outraised palm with a flick motion of the wrist, he indicates disparagement. However, if he touches the outraised palm with his arm or elbow, this shows that he respects the person but does not feel his statement is either particularly true or else particularly important. If the second individual raises his hand before the first puts out his hand, this not only emphasizes agreement but also expresses esteem.

It is considered a serious breach of social etiquette to purposely ignore the initial moves of a hand-slapping episode. I was told that to do so is a serious insult. While I observed several instances in which Vice Lords indicated disparagement by lightly touching an outraised hand with a flick of the wrist, I never saw anyone refuse to respond at all in some appropriate way.

Vice lord–enemy

The social identity, Vice Lord, has a grammatical relationship with the identity I call Enemy. An individual who is a member of the Vice Lords can assume either the identity Street Man or Vice Lord in social interaction with males who are not members of the club. If he assumes the Street Man identity, the grammatically proper identity for the alter to assume is also Street Man. However, if he assumes the Vice Lord identity, then the alter is automatically defined as an Enemy. Both parties in such a relationship have an initial option as to which identity they will choose, but if either chooses the identity which defines the situation as one of enmity, then the other must choose the grammatically matching one. In other words, if the individual who is not a member of the Vice Lords assumes the identity Street Man, then the person who is a Vice Lord has an option. He can assume either the identity Street Man, or that of Vice Lord. If he assumes the latter, then the first individual must act as Enemy. In contrast, if the first individual assumes the Enemy identity rather than that of Street Man, then the second person must assume the identity Vice Lord.

Although there is insufficient information to discuss the Vice Lord–Enemy role in terms of rights and duties and social etiquette, I did find both behavioral expectations between individuals interacting in this role and regularized forms of behavior that signal the assumption of the identities in question. There are two kinds of behavior that are expected in situations of enmity. Vice Lords call these "woofing" and "humbugging." Woofing is the exchanging of insults and challenges to fight, while humbugging is actual fighting. Not all situations of enmity end in humbugging. Individuals who assume the identities Vice Lord and Enemy, respectively, can play out their social interaction solely in terms of woofing.

People who intend to assume the identities which define a social situation as one of enmity do not signal this simply by initiating physical violence. There as certain verbal formulas which indicate a person is assuming the enmity identities. One of the most common is to demand a sum of money—for example, "Hey man, gimme a dime!" When put like this, it is not an actual request for money. If a dime were given, then a demand for money would be made until finally the individual would have to refuse. Refusing the demand is the cue that the alter is assuming the grammatically matching identity of enmity, and from there the relationship can be played out in terms of woofing or humbugging.

Another formula for signaling the assumption of an enmity identity is to start an argument. Individuals often argue in the course of social interaction, and these arguments do not always signal enmity. However, when an individual starts a violent argument over something that is considered extremely inconsequential, it does function as such a signal. For example, an individual may be talking about the kind of clothes he likes the best. If another person begins to vehemently argue with him, it is a sign that he is assuming an enmity identity. Of course it is not always clear whether an argument is "consequential" or not, and there are other subtle cues which also indicate if an identity of enmity is being assumed. My informants, however, could not verbalize about these. They said, "Man, you just *know* . . . that's all." Unfortunately, during the time of my field work I was not able to make a systematic study of these subtle cues. Possibly they consist of such things as facial expressions and certain qualities and tones in the voice. Not all people are equally adept at appropriately responding to such cues. Being adept at responding properly is one of the things that constitutes "knowing what's happening," or "knowing how to live on the streets."

Leader–follower

There are several named leadership identities that are assumed in a few social contexts. We have already discussed these and it is not necessary to deal with them in detail here. However, in order to be eligible for these identities—for example, president, war counselor—one must be what Vice Lords call a "Leader." We can, therefore, discuss a Leader identity without necessarily specifying a formal political position. Vice Lords define a Leader as a person who has followers. To a person outside the world of the fighting clubs this may seem overly simplistic, but what defines one as a Leader or Follower is self-evident only to Vice Lords. There are several reasons for this. Leadership is highly contextualized—that is, there are few contexts when an individual's identity as Leader emerges. Further, the same person may assume identities of both Leader and Follower at different times.

A few definitions would help clarify the discussion. A Leader is one who exercises power. Power is the ability to get others to do one's will. The exercise of leadership is thus the exercise of power. Among Vice Lords a person is recognized as a Leader when he has the ability to get others to do his will. In some societies power is often a function of force. Individuals exercise leadership through the use, or threat of use, of physical or mystical force. This fits the popular conception of the gang leader. Among Vice Lords, however, power is not based on force. A Leader exercises power through what we can call influence. Vice Lords follow others because they like them, or respect them, or because they think they will gain something by doing so, but *not* because they fear them.

What are the contexts in which the Leader and Follower identities are relevant? There are two kinds of contexts when people assume Leader and Follower identities—that is, there are two kinds of contexts in which power is exerted. The first kind includes situations that demand physical action. Some obvious examples are: gangbanging, wolf packing, and hustling. An example from the Fifteenth Street Lords provides a good illustration. I had met Tex, the president of the Fifteenth Street Lords, several times before I found out how important a person he was. Observing Tex riding in a car, hanging on the corner, or drinking wine, there was no clue that he was a person with power. He was not particularly assertive, and when demands were made of him, he usually complied. If there was an argument over who was going to sit by the window while we were riding, Tex usually lost. If there was an argument over who was going to buy cigarettes, Tex usually lost. At a party one evening a group of Fifteenth Street Lords stole a large sum of money from an individual who was not a member of the club. When Tex tried to get them to return the money, he was completely ignored. Then one evening there was a fight between a Fifteenth Street Lord and a member of the Cobras. Everyone expected the Cobras would attack Fifteenth Street territory. In this situation Tex's identity as a Leader became relevant. He immediately took charge of planning for the defense of the territory. Not only were his orders obeyed without question, but individuals sought him out to ask what they should do.

I observed other instances which also demonstrated the pattern. Crow was one of the top Leaders in the Nation. Next to Cave Man, he was considered to be the most influential Vice Lord. I was on the corner of Sixteenth and Lawndale one night with Pico talking to Crow. There had been an outbreak of fighting between the Lords and the Roman Saints that evening, and it was expected that the Roman Saints would attack Sixteenth and Lawndale. Pico suggested that he lead a group of Lords into Roman Saint territory, but Crow felt he should stay and help protect the corner. Pico did not even put up an argument, but simply said, "Yeah man, I guess you're right." Another time I was riding with Pico down Lawndale. We pulled up to a corner where there was a group of Lords. Crow was standing in the group, and Pico wanted to talk to him. Pico yelled out the window. "Hey Crow, you skinny mother fucker, get your ass over here!" Crow smiled and said, "What's happening man?" and walked over to the car.

These two examples help us better understand how Vice Lord leadership works. Both Tex and Crow assumed the identity Leader in the gang-fight context, but at other times assumed different identities. The casual onlooker observing their behavior at these other times might think they were not Leaders. He would be wrong. Both Tex's and Crow's failures to exert power in these situations were unrelated to their identities as Leaders, since these were social contexts where the Leader-Follower role was irrelevant.

The second kind of context in which leadership identities are relevant is that defined by public decision-making. Some decisions which affect the club are made during discussions between Vice Lords while hanging on a corner or in an alley. Usually, however, public decision-making takes place during club meetings. These meetings form an arena for leadership competition and demonstrations of power. A major objective of individuals who either are recognized Leaders or who have leadership aspirations is to prove they have power—that is, to demonstrate that others will follow them. Many times the particular decision under discussion is secondary to this objective. For example, Cave Man had long been president of the Nation. During the summer of 1966, however, a group of the Senior Lords met and decided it would be best for the club if someone else took over. Cave Man agreed to step down and let Lonzo be the new president. At this time the executive board was instituted. Cave Man was not even given a place on the board, but was relegated to the formal position of a regular member. However, Cave still had considerable power, and he lost little time in demonstrating it to the new officers. A group of social workers and clergymen from the West Side contacted Lonzo, the new president, to request permission to attend a meeting. They desired to get Vice Lord participation in a project. Several board members told them their request would be submitted to the club, but that the board would support it. When the meeting began, it was evident there was considerable opposition to this group. Cave Man had been hired by the YMCA to help control gang fighting, and he had worked in close cooperation with a social worker who was part of this group. At the meeting, however, he was the loudest voice in the opposition. He said, "What have them social workers ever done for us? Shit man, we don't want them in here!" Cave Man became the rallying point for the opposition, and was able to marshal enough support so that the group was not allowed in the meeting.

After the formal part of a meeting it is customary for Vice Lords to congregate on Sixteenth and Lawndale to drink, sing, and recount past exploits. After this particular meeting, Cave Man called out to Vice Lords who were standing around in small groups: "Come on! We're going to tear up this West Side! We're going to tear down all these signs! [Someone had painted "Black Power" on several buildings.] We're going back to the old days! We're going to gangbang! Those Cobras and Roman Saints, they ain't shit! We're going to run 'em out of the West Side! Vice Lord! Vice Lord! Terrifying, terrific Vice Lords! This whole West Side belongs to the Vice Lords! Come on, let's go!" With that, Cave started out for Sixteenth and Lawndale, and about twenty-five other Vice Lords fell in behind echoing his yells and shouts.

Cave Man's actions, both during the formal meeting and immediately after, can be understood in terms of the way Vice Lord leadership operates. He opposed allowing the YMCA worker to attend the meeting even though he was getting money from the YMCA and had in the past closely cooperated with this same person. He stated that social workers had never done anything for the club, but he had been instrumental in getting Vice Lords to cooperate with YMCA programs. For some time he had been working to limit gang fighting, but after the meeting he called for a resumption of gang wars. All this makes sense if we look at Cave Man's position at this time. He needed to demonstrate that while he was no longer a formal officer, he was still a Leader—that is, a person with power. He needed to show that others would still follow him. An important segment of the new officers had tacitly agreed to letting the outsiders attend the meeting, but many members were against it. This gave Cave Man his opportunity. By mobilizing the resistance and successfully opposing the new officers, he convincingly demonstrated his power to everyone. His later behavior is also understandable in these terms. Arriving at Sixteenth and Lawndale in full view, at the head of a large group, further emphasized Cave Man's ability to gather a following. I do not believe he seriously intended to lead Vice Lords in a new gang war. He simply used an appeal to gang fighting values that are seldom, if ever, publicly questioned to gather a following and validate his identity as a Leader. After Cave Man reached Sixteenth and Lawndale at the head of this group, he made no further move toward initiating gang fighting.

Some Vice Lords who are considered Leaders sometimes assume Follower identities in certain situations. There is a formal hierarchy of leadership positions that partially accounts for this. For example, the president of the Nation is thought to be in a higher position than the president of a branch. Therefore, the president of the Nation assumes the identity Leader in certain situations, while presidents of branches are Followers. The de facto distribution of power, however, fits only partially with the formal hierarchy of political positions. The incident just discussed involving Cave Man provides a good example. Bat Man was a Leader and vice-president of the Fifteenth Street Lords. In the meeting of the Nation he opposed allowing the social workers to attend.

Cave Man, even though he had no formal political position at this time, assumed the identity Leader in the meeting and Bat Man, who was a vice-president, assumed that of his Follower. After the meeting, Bat Man joined the group that followed Cave Man to Sixteenth and Lawndale.

The composition of a Leader's following changes in various situations. One time a Leader may join the following of another Leader (and bring his own following with him), but another time oppose that same Leader. Thus Vice Lords never know ahead of time exactly who will be allied and opposed in any particular instance. In other words, the strength of an individual's power is subject to constant fluctuation. We can now better understand why situations in which public decisions are made are contexts for the exercise of power. Power is based on the number of one's followers, but a Leader's following is constantly changing, and the exact extent of a person's power is not usually known. In situations where public decisions are made, however, lines of opposition are drawn, and power becomes crystallized. In the decision-making process individuals make the choice whether to assume a Leader or Follower identity. Those who choose the latter make the further choice as to whose following they will join. Through these choices power is actualized, and claims to the Leader identity are validated.

So far we have concentrated on social roles—one aspect in the pattern of Vice Lord social behavior that comprises the social system. We have identified certain social roles and discussed these in relation to a particular theoretical framework. Now we shall switch our concern and look at Vice Lord behavior in terms of a cultural system.

Vice Lords define their world and guide their actions in terms of a particular ideological framework. This constitutes Vice Lord culture. Our concern is to describe some of the beliefs and values comprising this framework, and to show how they relate to social behavior. I found four general ideological sets which constitute Vice Lord culture. They can be designated: heart ideology, soul ideology, brotherhood ideology, and game ideology. Each of these sets functions to divide Vice Lord reality into a number of compartments we can call cultural scenes, and to guide and judge behavior within these scenes.

Heart ideology

A Cobra swung on one of the fellows, and he come down with his knife out. That means he's not scared to take that man's life if he wished to. That's what you call a lot of heart—not scared to go to jail and pay whatever the consequences is.

If a group of boys say, going to break into a store or truck, and I tell this boy to do it and he does it, the people say he got a whole lot of heart—he not afraid of anything. He'll just go and do everything the other person tell him to do.

A person who got heart, he not scared to do anything. Like we break in a liquor lounge or something, he not worried about being busted. He's game for it. Or like we in a fight, and we outnumbered say four to two. This man will stand up there and fight with you no matter what. If you all go down, he be there with you. You all both go down together.

If you don't show heart people call you a punk, and they don't want to hang with you. A punk is a person who like get into a fight with somebody and he don't fight back. Or like if say me and you and somebody else, we going to rob somebody, and one of us be scared and won't do it. Then they say he punked out.

From these explanations we can understand what Vice Lords mean by "heart." It is apparent that generally "heart" means bravery, but it means more than just this. It also means bravery in terms of being "game," that is, being willing to follow any suggestion regardless of personal risk. Having heart contrasts with punking out. A person who acts in a cowardly way—that is, who is not game for any suggestion— is a punk. Vice Lords believe that having heart is good, while being a punk or punking out is bad. Heart, in other words, is one of the values of Vice Lord culture.

The heart-punk contrast defines a particular segment of Vice Lord reality. If we look at the explanations given by Vice Lords, it is apparent that the heart-punk contrast is relevant to situations where there is personal risk. Individuals are judged in terms of heart ideology only in situations which involve personal risk, and thus these situations are set off as distinct segments of Vice Lord life. A further look at our Vice Lords' explanations shows a division in risk situations—those involving fighting, and those involving robbing. Vice Lords call fighting "humbugging," and robbing "hustling." Humbugging is further subdivided: fighting between rival clubs is "gangbanging," fighting between individuals is "humbugging," and fighting which results when a group of club members goes out to jump on anyone they can find is "wolf packing." We can show this more clearly by constructing a typology comprised of contrast sets.

Personal Risk Situations				Other Situations
Humbugging$_1$			Hustling	
Gangbanging	Humbugging$_2$	Wolf packing		

Personal risk situations contrast with other situations. Within the former, humbugging$_1$ contrasts with hustling. Within humbugging$_1$ situations, gangbanging, humbugging$_2$, and wolf packing all contrast. I should explain the difference between humbugging$_1$ and humbugging$_2$. Vice Lords refer to all kinds of fighting as humbugging. A fight between a boy and his father, a fight between males and females, a fight between rival clubs, or any other kind of fight can be referred to as a humbug. However, Vice Lords further distinguish between kinds of fighting. Gangbanging refers only to fights between enemy clubs. When individuals wish to distinguish between fights involving two individuals and fights involving rival clubs, they refer to the former as humbugs and the latter as gangbangs. Thus humbugging means any kind of fighting when contrasted with hustling, but means only fighting between individuals when contrasted with gangbanging. Therefore, I have used humbugging$_1$ to designate fighting in general and humbugging$_2$ to specify fighting between individuals.

Situations which involve humbugging$_2$, gangbanging, wolf packing, and hustling form distinct segments of Vice Lord reality that can be called cultural scenes. The use of scene is an analogy to the scenes of a play. As the action of a play is divided into scenes, so the action of Vice Lord behavior is structured into units we can call cultural scenes. My data on humbugging$_2$, wolf packing, and hustling is too limited to provide a detailed description of the pattern of action that takes place within these scenes. We can, however, study the cultural scene gangbang in greater detail. We made the distinction between gangbangs that resulted from accidental encounters between members of an enemy club and those that involved prior planning. Here, we are concerned with the latter.

There are four phases in a gangbang. The first we can call the prefight gathering. Before actual fighting begins, Vice Lords meet in their territory to plan strategy. During this phase there is drinking, singing, shouting, and bragging. Besides planning strategy Vice Lords are emotionally preparing to face the dangers of actual fighting. The second phase is the confrontation between enemy clubs. During the confrontation the groups stand facing each other while the two rival war counselors are in between, exchanging threats and insults. When the rival war counselors begin fighting, the third phase begins. This we can call the encounter. During the encounter the actual fighting takes place. The final phase is the postfight gathering. During this phase Vice Lords again gather in their territory to drink and brag of their exploits. The following account illustrates in greater detail what happens during the second and third phases.

> Now a fight like this really looks funny when it starts, but it turns out to be terrifying. When it's just coming night is when most of the fighting occurs so if The Man come, then everybody can get away.

You get a stick, or maybe a knife, or a chain. And some fools got shotguns. What you really do, you stand there and the counselors are the first ones up. You stand back and wait and see if they come to an agreement and talk. Now everybody standing there watching everybody else to see what's going to happen. And all of a sudden maybe a blow will be passed, and if it is, a fight start right there. Let's say this is what happened. Now nine out of ten you know everybody in your club, or everybody who came with you. You standing just like you'd met in a crowd and you were talking. It's really almost a semicircle. You just standing there and you're looking—you're watching the counselor. And if a blow pass, automatically the first thing you do is hit the man closest to you. After that if things get too tight for you then you get out of there. If it look like you getting whupped, you get out. It's all according to your nerve. The first who runs, that's it right there. Naturally if you're standing there and you're fighting, and you see half the club starting to run, you know the other half going to run soon. All it takes is one to run and the whole crowd breaks up. That's how a club gets its rep—by not running, by standing its ground.

The beliefs and values of heart ideology underlie the action of the gangbang scene. Esteem among Vice Lords corresponds to rep. Rep, in turn, depends on how others judge one's behavior in relation to heart ideology. These judgments are made on the behavior that takes place during the second and third phases of the gangbang scene. Heart ideology is also important in the first and third phases of a gangbang. Here, the beliefs and values of heart are reinforced through expression in ritualistic behavior. The basic tenets of heart ideology are contained in a poem composed by several of the original members of the club:

> From back out to south came the King of the Gestapoes, Lord of the Sabotage, Ruler of the Astronauts, knocking down fifty-sixty lanes.
> I say, for any man make attempt to take a Vice Lord down, he got to first find a rock to kill Goliath, overturn the pillars of Sampson, name the stone that David stood on, name the three little children that walked the burning fires of hell, stand in front of the Lord and say, "I have no fear."
> For the Vice Lords, I say for all Vice Lords, sixty-two across the chest, don't fear nothing, God and death, got a tombstone opportunity, a graveyard mind, he must be a Vice Lord 'cause he don't mind dying.
> Vice Lord! Mighty Vice Lord!

During the first and third phases of a gangbang this poem is repeated by members of the club. The group divides itself into sections and each repeats alternating phrases. The final refrain—"Vice Lord! Mighty Vice Lord!"—is said by the entire group. In this manner the beliefs and values contained in the poem are given public expression, and heart ideology is reinforced.

Soul ideology

There are several aspects to the Vice Lord concept of "soul." In one sense it refers to a general sort of Negritude. One who acts in a "hip" manner is said to have soul. However, it means more than this. Soul also refers to a way of doing something. When someone puts real effort into what he is doing, he is said to have soul. Stripping away superficiality and getting to the essence (or, in ghetto jargon, getting down to the real nitty-gritty) is also involved in soul. Thus, for example, someone who sings with real effort and real feeling, and in so doing succeeds in capturing the essence of black experience, has soul. His musical ability as such is irrelevant to the amount of his soul. Charles Keil has made an intensive study of the soul concept among blacks in Chicago, and his research shows that the Vice Lord meaning of soul is the same as that found in ghetto culture as a whole. For a deeper analysis of the soul concept the reader is referred to Keil's monograph *The Urban Blues*. For our purposes, however, it is only necessary to note these three elements—Negritude, intense effort, and stripping away superficiality, or getting down to the real nitty-gritty—for Vice Lords base their judgments of soul on these elements.

Vice Lords value soul. To tell someone he has soul is a compliment, while to say he has "a hole in his soul" is a definite criticism. There are certain social situations in which judgments are made in terms of soul. These are contexts involving music. Music is an extremely important part of Vice Lord life. Vice Lords closely follow the music from Chicago's black radio stations, and they are constantly singing the songs that are broadcast there. Many have formed their own singing groups which hold regular practices and perform at certain times. Dancing is even more important in Vice Lord life. Almost all Vice Lords take intense pride in their dancing ability, and lose few opportunities to demonstrate it.

Vice Lords judge one another's singing and dancing in terms of soul ideology, and thus that segment of Vice Lord life in which singing and dancing is found is set off from other social situations. Singing and dancing are important activities in two Vice Lord scenes. These are called by Vice Lords "sets" and "hanging on the corner." A set can be translated as a party. Vice Lords usually display their dancing ability in this scene, and it is here that judgments are made in terms of soul. Singing takes place in many situations. Riding in a car, or meeting at a member's house, are examples of when singing occurs. However, judgments about singing are usually made during performances that take place while hanging on the corner. When large groups of Vice Lords gather on the corner of Sixteenth and Lawndale, for example, various groups demonstrate their singing abilities, and soul judgments are made on these performances.

Brotherhood ideology

We noted that the idea of mutual help is an important value in the Vice Lord cultural framework. Vice Lords often express this in terms of brotherhood. "Man, we're just like brothers" is an often-heard phrase. One Vice Lord scene in which the values of brotherhood are especially relevant is drinking wine. There is a special ritual to wine-drinking, and through this ritual the values of brotherhood are expressed and reinforced.

A wine-drinking scene is initiated when a small group of Vice Lords gathers and someone suggests having a taste, or pulling some jive. The next phase is gathering the money. The individual who made the first suggestion usually acts as collector. Everyone in the group donates what he feels he can afford. Often it is necessary to go around the group several times before enough money is collected. Vice Lords passing by are also asked to contribute money and join in the wine-drinking activities. After the money is collected and the wine is purchased, the next phase of the scene begins. This consists of "cracking the bottle." The bottle of wine is given to one of the group, who points it toward the ground and strikes the bottom of the bottle two times with the palm of his hand. This cracks the seal. Next, a small portion of the wine is poured out on the ground either in the letters CVL, or simply the letter V. This is interpreted as a symbolic gift to all the Vice Lords who have been killed or who are in jail. Finally, the bottle is passed around to everyone in the group, and each drinks the same amount regardless of how much money he contributed toward buying the wine.

There are two aspects of the wine-drinking scene that give expression to brotherhood ideology. The first is the wine that is poured out in the Vice Lord letters. Vice Lords place a high value on wine, and pouring out even a little is a form of sacrifice. This sacrifice is interpreted as a symbolic giving to other Vice Lords in need. Vice Lords who are dead and in jail can't get wine for themselves, but this way there is symbolically something for them to drink, too. The second aspect that reinforces brotherhood values is the way the wine is distributed and the way it is drunk. Every person in the group is entitled to an equal amount of wine regardless of the amount of money he contributed. Each gives whatever he has or whatever he can afford, but all, as Vice Lords put it, "share like brothers" in the consumption of the wine. Further, the wine is drunk from the same bottle. Each person does not take his portion in a separate glass, but everyone drinks from the same bottle. To Vice Lords this sharing further symbolizes the unity and brotherhood between members of the group. Thus the wine-drinking ritual expresses and reinforces the values of mutual help—the values of brotherhood.

Game ideology

In the previous study of the Street Man–Street Man role we noted that in certain situations the ability to successfully manipulate others, or, as Vice Lords say, "whupping the game," is an activity which sets off a particular part of Vice Lord life. We can call this segment a "game." The way individuals behave during a game scene is judged by other Vice Lords in terms of game ideology. Individuals who are thought to be good at whupping the game are said to have a "heavy game," while those who are judged to be poor at this activity are said to have a "lightweight game." The technique one uses in whupping the game is called a "front," and the quality of various individuals' fronts is often a topic of conversation.

Vice Lords often tried to whup the game on me with various degrees of success. A few examples will help illustrate the kinds of situations that constitute the game scene. Washington was known for having a lightweight game. He was seldom successful in beating anyone out of anything, but he was often taken himself for various items of value. His attempt to whup the game on me consisted of simply requesting money: "Hey man, can you give me a quarter?" My answer was, "Sorry Washington, I don't have it today." This exchange constituted a game scene in Vice Lord life.

Blue Goose, in contrast to Washington, was known to have a heavy game. Once he convinced me that a group of older men who were not members of the Vice Lords were planning to jump on me. He assured me, however, that I had nothing to fear because he would see to it that they did not bother me. He made a big show of chasing two old wine-heads who he purported were plotting against me down the street. A little while later he asked me to loan him fifty cents and a shirt so he could make his gig (job) the next day. Of course, in gratitude, I was more than glad to help in any way possible. Later I learned I had taken part in a game scene and had been the victim of a successful front.

The greaser is a "bad ass"; the gowster is a "muthah": an analysis of two urban youth roles

HERBERT G. ELLIS AND STANLEY M. NEWMAN

Herbert G. Ellis is currently a corrections counselor and teacher at the House of Correction School in Chicago after several years as a teacher and field adjustment counselor at the Moses Montefiore Social Adjustment School for boys. In his present and past capacities as counselor, teacher, and curriculum designer and co-ordinator, Ellis has had extensive contact with black male urban youth, both within and outside the institution, plus the reason, motivation, and opportunity to study and familiarize himself with their life styles and general value orientations. It was from his role as counselor and on-the-scene participant-observer that he began to systematically investigate and examine various aspects and dimensions of black expressive role behavior.

Stanley M. Newman is associate professor of urban anthropology and coordinator of the Uptown Peoples—Northeastern University Center on Chicago's North Side. Newman is also staff anthropologist at the Mile Square Health Center, a comprehensive neighborhood health center of Presbyterian St. Luke's Hospital on Chicago's West Side. Working in these capacities enables Newman to maintain a continuing involvement in the ethnic urban scene.

The present Ellis-Newman article portrays vividly various characteristics of persons through the images they project to members of their respective cultural groups. A person's "presentation of self" reveals a great deal about the code he lives by and the way in which he can be expected to communicate with others. In portraying counterparts from different cultural groups, the article brings to focus the important (but as yet unsatisfactorily answered) question of the degree to which role behavior is influenced by socioeconomic pressures—i.e., through the offering by society of limited and restrictive options, which thereby make illegal or anti-social roles more attractive—and the degree to which role behavior is motivated by inner cultural forces, such as a masculine code, life style, or other traditional (aesthetic!?) prototypes or features that could be regarded as normative to the culture.

For several years the authors have been concerned with discovering, describing, and analyzing various roles played by black low-income youth in the ghettos of Chicago.[1] From the inception we were interested in determining if similar roles existed among white youth. This need became increasingly apparent as the response to our findings indicated

[1] For example, Newman offered a paper entitled, "He Gowster: A Functional Analysis of a Ghetto Personality," at the annual meeting of the American Anthropology Association in Pittsburgh in November, 1966, and Ellis and Newman offered a paper entitled, "The *Gowster, Ivy-Leaguer, Hustler, Conservative, Mack-*

that of six black roles,[2] one in particular, the "gowster," seemed to have its counterpart among poor white youth. Typical of the kind of feedback we received was, "I never heard of the 'gowster' before, but he sounds like a 'greaser.' " Or, "Put a 'dago-T' on the 'gowster' and you've got a 'greaser.' "[3] It seemed clear to us therefore that comparative research was in order. This paper describes and compares the role of the greaser with the role of the gowster, and it explores how function and role relate to each other in an urban environmental context.

We collected data through questionnaires, participant observation, and other techniques. Over a five-year period a large number of teenage youths and young adults were informally interviewed. Specifically, a questionnaire was administered to two groups of twenty-five youths.[4] The breakdown of the sample is presented in Table 1.

The questionnaire in both cases was basically the same, with additional refinements to include what was learned from the first experience. Items are divided into four categories that permit role description and differentiation to emerge. "Style of Dress" refers to a mode of dress and hairstyle that is generally associated with a particular role. Included here are characteristics such as peculiar postures, stances, and dancing and walking styles. "Social and Economic Prestige" refers to the ability to enhance one's self-esteem by achieving high status within the peer group. Economic prestige, narrowly defined, refers to the individual's skill in obtaining money, irrespective of method used. "Anti-Social Aggression" refers to attitude, behavior, and demeanor. Specifically, it denotes thoughts, feelings, and acts that are viewed as negative according to the standards of the larger society. "Sexual Prowess and Dominance" refers to the ability to control, dominate, and manipulate women for one's own financial and sexual gain. Dominance per se has to do with the extent to which an individual can influence and control the thoughts, feelings, and actions of others.

The data were collected by black and white interviewers from two groups of youths, black and white, representing different sections of Chicago over a period of twenty-four months. No claim is made to having used a "scientific" approach to the sample; rather, we are impressed

---

man, and *Continental:* A Functional Analysis of Six Ghetto Roles," at a similar AAA meeting in Seattle in November, 1968.

[2] Herbert G. Ellis and Stanley M. Newman, "The 'Gowster,' 'Ivy-Leaguer,' 'Hustler,' 'Conservative,' 'Mackman,' and 'Continental': A Functional Analysis of Six Ghetto Roles," in *The Culture of Poverty: A Critique,* ed. Eleanor Leacock (New York: Simon & Schuster, 1971).

[3] In white Chicago parlance a "dago-T" is a white sleeveless undershirt worn with no shirt over it during hot weather. A dago is an Italo-American or someone who looks the stereotype, i.e., swarthy complexion with dark, greasy hair.

[4] The Group 1 questionnaire was administered by Marianne Zeh, a white graduate student and teacher at a Chicago high school.

Table 1. Sample.

Variables	Group I	Group II
Interviewer Role	White female Greaser	Black male Gowster
Instrument	48 item open-ended questionnaire	48 item open-ended questionnaire
Respondents	18 white males 7 white females	25 black males
Age range	14–19	14–21
Mean age	17.5	17.9
Academic status	1 freshman, 7 sophomores, 6 juniors, 7 seniors, 1 graduate, 3 nongraduates	3 freshmen, 1 eighth- grader, 3 sophomores, 1 junior, 15 nongraduates, 2 graduates
Schools represented	4 public high schools located in the North- eastern and Northwestern sections of Chicago	2 social-adjustment schools, one of which is custodial

Sample distribution
according to schools
represented
	19 students from one
	  school,
	4 students from a
	  second school,
	1 student from a
	  third school,
	1 student from a
	  fourth school
		18 social-adjustment
		students were custodial
		and 7 were not

Time duration	Questionnaire administered over a three-week period during 1969	Questionnaire administered over a five-week period during 1970

with the congruence of our findings because the data were collected from a diverse population through time.[5]

Our findings show that the roles of the greaser and the gowster are seen as dominant roles (though not exclusively so) for certain individual youths at a given time. The outstanding clue to identifying the greaser and gowster is style of dress. In both cases our respondents stressed their appearance as characteristic of the role in saying, "He looks like a raggedy gowster," or "Greasers dress different. They don't care about neatness." An ideal description for both reveals baggy pants, big-collar shirts, Italian knit sweaters, pointed shoes, and black leather jackets or coats.

[5] For an insightful discussion on how insisting on retaining the original design prevented the researchers from incorporating significant information during the research period, see Frank Friedlander, "Emerging Blackness in a White Research World," *Human Organization* 29, no. (Winter, 1970): 239–50.

Part of their style has to do with a particular stance, walk, and movement. They walk with a "bounce," "slow and easy with head down and tilted." They stand with "round shoulders, one hand in a back pocket." "They 'bop' when they walk."[6] A point to be noted concerns the emphasis and ambivalence (derogation/admiration) our white respondents placed on the greaser's emulation of black Americans. Statements such as "They [greasers] walk like colored people—loose jointed," or, "They walk like spades, smooth and graceful, snapping their fingers while they are walking." "They dance like niggers, with soul, like James Brown—they dance in a 'dirty' manner."

Analysis of the "Social and Economic Prestige" category reveals that where differences occur they are the result of economics. For example, greasers place a tremendous emphasis on cars. In talking about the greaser's use of leisure time, the automobile is alluded to very frequently. "Cars make them feel cool, flashy, it builds them up," or, "They spend their time hot rodding and working on cars." Other leisure-time activities of the greaser also stress the economic differential: repeated statements such as, "They spend their time at 'dirty movies,' " or, "In the summer you can find them hanging around drive-in movies, airports, and bowling alleys" indicate a different use of leisure time determined (in part) by access to money.[7]

The attitudes of the greaser and gowster toward parents, school, and authority figures in general are similar. They "don't like school—teachers get on their back—they 'cut' classes to be with their friends and eventually drop out." Again and again this sentiment was expressed: "School is a drag." The greasers' and gowsters' general feeling toward adults is that they are "let down" by them: "Home is just a place to sleep." One respondent put it succinctly, saying, "The greaser feels that there are too many people pushing him around." In our earlier study of the gowster, we said, "Gowsters resent adults and feel animosity toward their parents." For both, parents and other adults are seen as authority figures who "don't understand," causing tension and arguments at home and in school. The dominant feeling vis-à-vis adults is that greasers and gowsters "don't like being told what to do" so that school and the home are perceived as "places where they are not welcome."

[6] Walking styles often serve to communicate information about the status of the individual, e.g., in an article about Assistant Secretary of Labor Arthur Fletcher, the following quotation indicates his status as a youth: "By 13, he was diddy-boppin' down the streets of Los Angeles as a youth gang leader from Central Avenue" (Alex Poinsett, "Watchdog for U.S. Labor," *Ebony* 26, no. 6 [April, 1971]:95–104).

[7] We find a strong interest in cars among gowsters as well. However, the gowster generally only can *talk about* them (to own a "Hog" [Cadillac] or a "Deuce and a Quarter" [Buick Electra 225]), whereas the greaser's greater ability to obtain a car results in different leisure-time activities.

Perhaps the most outstanding and visible attribute possessed by greasers and gowsters is antisocial aggression. It is this trait more than any other that determines the greaser's and gowster's reputations with their peer groups and the adult world. In a word, both are fighters. In discussions with blacks and whites about gowsters and greasers respectively, the one theme that developed first, most frequently, and most clearly dealt with violence:

"Don't mess with that cat, he's a gowster."
"Greasers don't waste time, they look for fights."
"The gowster will 'jack you up' " (i.e., strong-arm you).
"They [greasers] must prove that they are 'bad asses'."

Statements applicable to both indicate the similarity of roles:

"They defend the gang."
"They enjoy doing wrong."
"They do not respect the police, teachers, or those in authority."
"They crash parties, will fight strangers, snatch purses, steal, rob homes and their parents."

Underlying the role of the greaser and gowster is a need to project and protect the image. This image is one of toughness, the "street warrior" whose propensity and ability to engage in violence sustains his self-image as an individual who must be respected for what he is.[8] "They feel they are bad," "They don't back down from a fight," "They must show their toughness" are sayings that offer important insights into the function of the greaser-gowster role.

In the area of "Sexual Prowess and Dominance" a comparison between the greaser and the gowster reveals that the similarities are also greater than the differences. In both cases to get drunk, to get high on pot (marijuana), to gamble, and to present a physically tough demeanor are desirable traits used to impress, control, and dominate others. Differences occur in the area of sex. The greaser appears to be more concerned with sexual conquests, though the difference is more one of degree than kind. Greasers are seen as "lovers" interested in "crashing" parties in order to "pick up chicks" for purposes of "making out." Much of their behavior is to attract women. Their reputation in this area is a daring, reckless abandon to impress others. One respondent offered an example of this, saying, "They [greasers] are daredevil lovers, they eat pussy!" No gowster would ever accept such a statement as a compliment.

We are suggesting that the evidence supports two roles, one black

8 See, for example, R. Lincoln Keiser, *The Vice Lords* (New York: Holt, Rinehart and Winston, 1969), and in this volume; Gerald D. Suttles, *The Social Order of the Slum* (Chicago: University of Chicago Press, 1968).

and one white, that function in similar ways. This impression is strengthened in the realization that both the greaser and the gowster represent, in their respective ethnic groups, the "other" part of a dichotomous set of roles. Gowsters are the opposite of "Ivy-Leaguers." The Ivy-Leaguer's style of dress affords the black individual middle-class status. He attempts to dress "Brooks Brothers style," wearing button-down shirts, and behaves in an "Ivy-League" way, joining social clubs or fraternities. The greaser is the opposite of the "duper." White dupers, like black Ivy-Leaguers, do well in school, attend church, and show respect to teachers and parents. Generally they are well liked by, and rarely in conflict with, defenders of the (middle-class) status quo. The roles of the gowster and greaser respectively contrast with the roles of the Ivy-Leaguer and the duper. This becomes clear in listening to teenagers discuss the two opposing sets of roles, as the following composite description points up: "They [gowsters/greasers] hate [Ivy-Leaguers/dupers]." "They'll [gowsters/greasers] fight an [Ivy-Leaguer/duper] to 'rip them off' [i.e., take their money], or just do it for the hell of it." "[Gowsters/greasers] are not like [Ivy-Leaguers/dupers]—they feel that [Ivy-Leaguers/dupers] are sissies and resent being put down by them."

Up to this point we have confined our analysis to a static description of roles. An analysis that takes into account the environment or context in which the roles are played is necessary for an attempt at understanding function. The environment or context that greasers and gowsters are subjected to is harsh, impoverished (literally no or little money), physically severe, violent, and (perhaps most important) extremely limited with regard to available options. One cannot, in our opinion, understand the greaser and gowster without perceiving their worlds from behind their eyes. The "environmental box" they are locked into offers few alternatives; those available are restricted, often institutionally calculated to make escape (upward mobility) difficult if not impossible without the kind of compromise that many would find psychologically castrating.

To the outsider greasers and gowsters are seen as losers. Outsiders describe greasers and gowsters with "nondescriptions"—that is, they tend to talk negatively, to underscore all the things (believed) that greasers and gowsters *do not* possess. Very little effort is made to understand *what is* (as opposed to *what is not*). Frederick Gearing has explicated this problem in another setting in his brilliant book, *The Face of the Fox*. The following quotation refers to the Fox Indians but applies equally well to the greaser-gowster:

> The trouble is . . . that such nondescriptions are so very easy, undemanding of the observer. But the way toward truth is much assisted by a simple rule of thumb: one never describes an alien people by naming what they are not. That is, whenever in a description of an alien other the words "are not" or "lack" or prefixes and suffixes like "un-" or "-less"

come into mind . . . warning bells should ring, for the chances are strong that . . . the people have been left undescribed and perhaps rendered inconceivable.[9]

Thus to describe the greaser-gowster as *non*middle-class, *lacking* restraint, *un*cooperative, *un*able to defer gratification, and *un*controllable, ultimately leads to a description of *un*real people.

When one attempts to look at the world from within the frame of reference of the greaser-gowster, different insights are made available. Greasers and gowsters do not see themselves as losers. Given the school situation, for example, the greaser-gowster perceives himself as resisting an oppressive system. One informant, who identified himself as a gowster, related to us how and why he left school. He did not, incidentally, consider himself a drop-out.

> I missed two weeks of school because I was sick. When I came back they sent me to a counselor who told me that because I had missed so many days this year I couldn't go ahead. I had been sick before, you know. He said, "You don't really like school do you." I mean he said it like he already knew where my head was at—like he was challenging me, you know. So I told him, "No man, I don't dig school." He then told me, "Why don't you quit if that's the way you feel." I said, "Well, O.K. I will," so I split.

The above is meant to illustrate what goes on in the individual's head. Statements like this, along with our observations, discussions, and interactions enable us to infer the "inside" view of the greaser and the gowster.

Another example treats the propensity for violence. Seen from the outside, greasers and gowsters are violence-prone; they are labeled "trouble-makers," persons who constantly resist those in authority. Greasers and gowsters, however, see themselves as "men" who have enough "heart" (courage, bravery) to withstand encounters that challenge and threaten their manhood. A greaser told the following story to his buddies about his being called down to the principal's office for disrupting a class:

> I told him [the principal] that the teacher was always trying to "put me down" in front of the class. I told him that the teacher knew I didn't like math so why did he keep calling on me—just to "put me down," to make me look bad. I'm not as dumb as he thinks so I "turned it around" on him and got the class to laugh at him. See how he likes being the fool.
> The principal said I was a wise guy, thought I was a "smart alec." He said that what I needed was a good old-fashioned talk behind the wood shed. I told him, "Who're you going get to do it: better not try or somebody is going to get hurt, bad!" Man he turned white and started to

[9] Frederick Gearing, *The Face of the Fox* (Chicago: Aldine, 1970), p. 69.

shake. "You're suspended for threatening a school official." "That's good,
I said, this school ain't worth a shit anyway."

In the area of work other examples are instructive. A number of
gowsters expressed the sentiment that "it is better to 'scuffle' [endure
great hardship, struggle] in the streets for pennies than to work for The
Man [white authority figure] for nickles and dimes." One gowster exemplified this feeling in saying, "Shit! I can make more in a day hustling
in the streets than washing Mr. Charley's [a white man, especially a boss]
cars for a week."

What we see here is a response to an oppressive system. Given the
context that greasers and gowsters must live within, they often are highly
vulnerable to outside pressures and exploitation. Their reaction, from
their viewpoint, is to resist the pressure, minimize their vulnerability,
protect their manhood, and hopefully to continue to "walk tall" (maintain dignity).

It seems clear to us that highly comparable roles exist for some low-
income youth, black and white, in Chicago at this time. Description and
analysis of the role of the gowster (black) and the role of the greaser
(white) reveal that both often are seen by outsiders as similar.

Analysis by categories such as "Styles of Dress," "Sexual Prowess
and Dominance," "Social and Economic Prestige," and "Antisocial
Aggression" indicates that the role functions to enable the greasers-
gowsters to cope with specific life-situations in ways which achieve status
within their respective peer groups.

Larger questions, however, remain still to be explored. For example,
while it is a priori to state that only when viewed from within their respective life-contexts can a proper understanding of the lifeways of the
gowster/greaser come about, it still does not explain to what extent their
role behavior is a manifestation of inner cultural forces or a socioeconomic adaptation to circumstances largely shaped and controlled by
outside agencies. For example, we note as an illustration of the latter
that the context in which the gowster and greaser operated offered limited options for change, due in large part to lack of money and to a
continued need to resist exploitative pressures from the larger society.
On the other hand, as an illustration of the former, we have never met
a poor person who did not have middle-class, "mainstream" values and
aspirations. It strikes us, therefore, that if we are ever to get a proper
view of causality, we need to distinguish empirically between behavior
that is a consequence of inner cultural forces and that which is brought
about by pressures from the outside. For that reason, Valentine's present
work in this direction impresses us as being especially meaningful.[10]

[10] Charles A. Valentine, *Culture and Poverty* (Chicago: University of Chicago
Press, 1968).

Another question more specifically related to the present study (and a logical follow-up to it) is: What is the "inside" view of the gowster and the greaser to complement the essentially "outside" view presented here?—which is to ask more directly: What is the gowster or greaser's view of himself? In view of the fact that we can never "get into their heads," such a study poses qualitatively different ethnographic problems from those confronted here. It would seem necessary to begin by putting aside preconceived notions and hypotheses, stressing instead the greaser's and gowster's concepts of self as they talk and live them, if only to acquire the humility and sensibility which would enable us to learn from those we study. The results could produce insights and knowledge that would benefit us all.

Table 2. Similarities and Differences between the Gowster and Greaser as Based on Responses to Four Descriptive Categories

Category A: Style of Dress

Item	Gowster	Greaser	Similarities	Differences
Wear nylon socks	no	yes		x
Wear Italian knits	yes	yes	x	
Wear wide-collar shirts	no	yes		x
Wear suede shoes, Cuban heels, pointed toes	no	yes		x
Wear hair long and slicked down	no	yes		x
Wear "dago-T's"	no	yes		x
Wear V-neck cardigan sweaters	no	yes		x
Wear "continental" pants when dressed	no	yes		x
Wear baggy pants when not dressed	yes	yes	x	
Wear side burns, somewhat short	no	yes		x
Don't care about neatness	yes	yes	x	
Stand with shoulders rounded	yes	yes	x	
Walk with a bounce; drag feet, slow and easy, one hand in back pocket, head	yes	yes	x	

Category A: Style of Dress (*continued*)

Item	Gowster	Greaser	Similarities	Differences
tilted, body loose-jointed, smooth and graceful				
Snap fingers when walking	yes	yes	x	
Wear combat boots	no	yes		x
Wear "black leathers"	yes	yes	x	
		Total	7	9

Category B: Social and Economic Prestige

Item	Gowster	Greaser	Similarities	Differences
Cars make them feel *cool*	no	yes		x
Daring drivers	no	yes		x
Don't let friends down	yes	yes	x	
Stay out late, seldom come home	yes	yes	x	
Like soul music	yes	yes	x	
Come in groups to parties	yes	yes	x	
Belong to gangs	yes	yes	x	
Seldom engage in sports	yes	yes	x	
Dance "funky" ("dirty")	yes	yes	x	
Drink every day	yes	yes	x	
Smoke marijuana	yes	yes	x	
Leisure time at drive-in theaters, bowling alleys	no	yes		x
Leisure time at poolroom	yes	yes	x	
Leisure time at parks and beaches	no	yes		x
Leisure time at "dirty movies," hot-rodding, working on cars, at airport	no	yes		x
Must have "cool" to join gang	yes	yes	x	

Category B: Social and Economic Prestige (*continued*)

Item	Gowster	Greaser	Similarities	Differences
Challenge each other to drinking	yes	yes	x	
Don't like school; cut classes	yes	yes	x	
Dropout from school	yes	yes	x	
Feel middle class let them down	yes	yes	x	
Don't like home	yes	yes	x	
No parent-child communication	yes	yes	x	
Broken homes and large families	yes	yes	x	
Parents work in factories, restaurants	no	yes		x
Work after dropping out of school	no	yes		x
Steal from parents	yes	yes	x	
Sell dope	yes	yes	x	
Sell "hot" merchandise	yes	yes	x	
Gamble, snatch purses, burglarize homes	yes	yes	x	
Live off their parents	yes	yes	x	
Steal cars and sell the parts	yes	yes	x	
Work part-time in factories, parking lots, hamburger joints, dime stores, construction	no	yes		x
Like to "get high"	yes	yes	x	
"Get high" to escape world; for status, to feel manlike, to feel bolder	yes	yes	x	
"Get high" on beer, wine, and whisky	yes	yes		x
Must have group loyalty	yes	yes	x	
	Total		27	9

Category C: Anti-social Aggression

Item	Gowster	Greaser	Similarities	Differences
Fight to defend gang	yes	yes	x	
Don't back down from fights	yes	yes	x	
Show toughness	yes	yes	x	
Crash parties	yes	yes	x	
Don't respect authority	yes	yes	x	
Feel school is a place for squares	yes	yes	x	
Fight in school lunchrooms	yes	yes	x	
Total			7	0

Category D: Sexual Prowess and Dominance

Item	Gowster	Greaser	Similarities	Differences
Don't like to stick to one girl too long	yes	yes	x	
"Pull train on girl,"[11] then have oral sex	no	yes		x
Show body off with T-shirt	no	yes		x
Go steady with girl for sex	yes	yes	x	
Get drunk, smoke pot, to have sex	no	yes		x
Go to parties to make out	yes	yes	x	
Drink to impress girls	yes	yes	x	
Influence friends	yes	yes	x	
Make out at movies, parks, and airports	no	yes		x
Get girls drunk to get a piece	no	yes		x
Dress to attract women	no	yes		x
Total			5	6
Grand Total			46	24

[11] "Pull (a) train"—refers to several men alternately fornicating with the same woman.

■ Aspiration

MELVIN S. BROOKINS

Melvin S. Brookins is a free-lance short story writer. "Aspiration" originally appeared in the *Liberator* in December, 1967, and is included here for its sharply etched portrait of the hustler Big Time, for its use of idiom and examples of expressive language behavior, and for its selective identification of those aspects of the pimp-hustler behavioral role and general life-style which Youngblood wished to emulate and which can be considered value-orienting for many young black urban males.

While sitting round in back of the drugstore having our usual taste of Molly Pitcher dark port, our most pleasant conversation was bodily interrupted by the noisy, yelling, arm-waving approach of Little Willie upon the scene. His eyes were mere slits, heavily weighted down by the mellow smoke—light-green marijuana. Having the jug in hand and clearly in the sight of Willie, I expected the first four words out of his mouth to be "Save me the corner," but instead he pleasantly surprised me by screaming "Big Time is in the poolroom, baby!" Big Time: the magic name that made every young potential pimp, hustler, gamer, mack man, booster, or player tremble with excitement, for he represented all the things that they hoped to imitate or possibly even emulate someday. Big Time was *it*. He was *in,* baby—really what was happening. All you had to do was name it and have the proper amount of collateral and Big Time would score for you, or turn you on to someone in the position to do so. He was sharp, cool, untouchable. To quote Brother Cassius, he was "the greatest." Sharp? This man was really sharp. From his nylon underwear to his two-hundred-dollar imported mohair suit. Cool? No one ever heard him speak above a whisper. Always calm. Never, I mean never ever, in a hurry. Slow and steady. Always seeming to know his next move in advance. Untouchable? He was always a mile further ahead, a pound heavier, or a foot taller than anyone he associated with. Like on a pedestal, but always in touch spiritually, you dig?

Knowing that his appearance on the scene usually meant a handout plus some hip conversation on the art of pimpology, we all proceeded toward the end of the alley with great haste. As we turned the corner, the pace automatically slowed to a crawl, for gamers are never in a hurry, always cool, always cool.

The warm glow of the wine was now leaving the pit of my gut and slowly, pleasantly rising upward toward my head, where it would envelop my brain with that wonderful feeling of don't-give-a-damnism. Through my rose-tinted shades I could see Big Time's piece. A 1968 Eldorado. The top was laid, and sprawled on the front seat was a fine fox. Her platinum hair, teasing tan skin, and white silk dress seemed to coincide perfectly with the all-white leather interior of . . . the big white Hog. Perfection, baby, perfection. As we approached the piece, I could hear the restrained sound of Miles playing (bop bop bop bop dada, bop dada bop dada) "Bye Bye Blackbird." The chick, her head thrown back and eyes closed, was softly singing, "Pack up all my cares and woes. . . ."

I cut her short, saying, "You shouldn't have a care or woe in the world, baby. Your man is the king, and that makes you a queen."

Slowly her heavily made-up eyes opened, and from that voluptuous, moist, delicious-looking mouth came, "Hi young lover, what's happening?"

"You name it, baby, you're the queen. Your wish is my command. May I trim your hedges? Mow your lawn? Or clean your closet, maybe?"

"Ha, ha, you still want to be my handyman, eh youngblood?"

"I've got to start someplace, baby. I've always said the way to the king's riches may be through the queen's drawers."

Noticing the reaction my conversation was getting from the broad, Willie shrugged his shoulders, nodded to the others, and they made it on into the poolroom. Smiling slightly and turning just far and high enough on the bucket seat to expose about a foot of her soft tan thighs and give me a quick glimpse of her bright red panties, she said, "You're cute, youngblood, you're *very* cute. I dig you because Big T. digs you. He says you're different, not like the others, and he's right. You have good looks; you're tall, black, and damn near pretty. You've got the gift of gab and a whole lot of soul. All the makings of being a king, with one exception. You're too young, baby. You're just too young."

Her mouth was moving, and those were the words that came forth, but all the while her eyes seemed to be saying: *Come here, man, take me, devour me, swallow me up. Dinner is served. The table is set. If you are prepared, feast. I'm yours completely, now forever, in any and all ways.* Seduction. A good whore definitely has a way of getting her message across without an actual invitation. My mind started turning over: *It's your move, man. Make it! No. There's always the possibility that she's just teasing, toying, playing as a bitch would with a young pup.* I knew by my nervous, unsure reaction that I wasn't ready. *Inexperience, damn it!* So I smiled at the bitch as if I knew something that she didn't know and then slowly turned and walked away cursing myself for being so goddamn incapable.

As I entered the poolroom I was still somewhat in a daze. I don't know if it was from my brief conversation with the whore or the half fifth of wine I had drunk. But this I do know: I was immediately shocked into regaining my composure by the strange stillness that enveloped me. The poolroom silence was almost audible. I noticed the hell of a change; like a drunk wandering into an old hang-out only to find that it had been changed to a store-front church, I became quiet, humble, almost reverent with respect, for I knew that Big Time had to be playing.

All of the tables were closed with the exception of the one on the very end. This was where Big Time played. The small benches lining the walls were filled to capacity, but I managed to squeeze in between Willie and some other dude. All eyes were on Big Time as he gracefully moved around the table, calmly calling his shots. The game was straight pool. A hundred and twenty-five balls. The bet: two bills a game. Big T. missed a corner pocket shot and cooly replied, "Bet two hundred more I beat the man."

The man he was referring to was Smiley, the East Side champ, now coming to the table. The score was seventy-five to seventy in Smiley's favor. He studied the setup of the table carefully, then proceeded to run thirty balls. All that could be heard was the click of the cue ball against the called ball, the squeaking of the chalk on Smiley's cue stick, and the raspy voice of Smiley calling his shots. He banked the nine ball cross-corner and drew the cue ball back in perfect position for his break shot. "Rack 'em," he said.

From in the corner I heard Big Time say, "Three hundred more I beat the man."

Damn. Smiley only needed twenty balls and it was still his shot. What the hell was Big Time trying to prove? I took a good look at Smiley and then I knew the answer. Smiley was good. One of the best. But he had one weakness: he was a trembler. He couldn't play under pressure. At the sight of four or five bills his game fell apart. His hands would become sweaty. His mouth would get dry. His stroke would become short and jerky; even his face would take on a different expression—one of fear. In short, Smiley had the skill of a champion, but the heart of a chicken. He was a damn good player but not a gambler, and Big Time knew it.

"You're on for two hundred," said Smiley.

"I'll take the other hundred," said the house man.

"Bet, gentlemen," replied Big Time.

Smiley studied the setup of the balls for what seemed like hours. He had the rack man tighten them three or four times, then lit up a fresh cigar, powdered his hands, chalked up, and got down on the table. That's when it must've hit him, because small beads of sweat began popping out on his forehead. His lips were tightly set and his eyes darted quickly from the cue ball to the ball he was trying to make.

Back and forth, back and forth—five, six, seven times maybe. I think that Smiley and everyone in the place knew right then that he was going to miss the shot. He stroked the cue stick several times, took aim and shot. The cueball struck the six ball perfectly, sending it rifling into the corner pocket, and in almost the same instance hit the back cushion and tore the stack wide open. Smiley had made a hell of a shot! The place was now buzzing with excitement, and Smiley, living up to his name, was showing all thirty-two of his teeth. He walked quickly to the end of the table, chalked up, and shot an easy side-pocket shot. The cue ball slid off the five ball and scratched in the corner. Smiley stood there, mouth open, eyes staring with disbelief. He had gotten over the hill only to trip on his way down and break his goddamn neck. He slowly walked to the side, took his seat, and sat there, stunned.

Big Time then came to the table and gave one of the most beautiful exhibitions of playing I've ever seen. He ran fifty-five consecutive balls, and I believe he could have run more had they been needed. Just after he made his last ball he looked over at Smiley and George and asked, "Same bet next game, gentlemen?"

"Yeh man," said George.

Smiley just nodded his head, still dumbfounded with disbelief.

That was it; they were on their way to blowing a grand if they had that much between them. But before the start of the second game, the barber from next door stuck his head in the door and yelled, "Hey Big Time, that goddamn rookie cop'll be by here in a minute and you're parked in a no parking zone."

"Thanks, daddy," said Big Time and almost in the same breath, "Say, youngblood. Move my piece over on Flora's lot and tell Dolly to go in and have herself some ribs. This might take some time."

My goddamn heart jumped in my mouth. Me, driving Big Time's 'Rada. Hoping he wouldn't detect the tremor in my voice, I said, "Sure thing." I don't know if I walked or floated to the door, but I could feel the eyes of all the fellas burning into my back with envy. When I hit the street the day seemed brighter, and Dolly and that Cadillac seemed even lighter. I walked slowly to the piece, snatched the door open, slid under the wheel, and slammed the door. Dolly looked startled, but pleased. Before she could offer any objection, I said, "Big Time told me to move his piece over to Flora's and for you to get something to eat 'cause he might be a while."

She said, "Crazy, baby; let's motor. The keys are in the switch."

I turned the key; there was a slight click, and then the quiet breathing of three hundred horses. I slipped her into the drive, checked the rear-view mirror and then eased away from the curb, doing about twenty. We were on a one-way street, so I had to circle the block in order to get to Flora's, which was behind us and on the opposite side of the street. As we cruised around the block, heads turned, mouths dropped open, eyes popped damn near out and some just stopped and stared. I smiled and thought, *Some day this will be a permanent thing, not just for a hot five minutes.*

As we pulled into the lot behind Flora's, Dolly said, "You look good behind that wheel, youngblood, kind of natural." I parked next to Flora's delivery truck, scooted down in the seat, lit up a Kool and relaxed. Dolly just sat there with her chin in the palm of her hand, staring. Suddenly she reached out, grabbed my hand and placed it on her knee. She said almost in a whisper, "What would you do with this if it was yours?"

A warm tingling sensation started stirring below my belt. My head got light and I could feel the start of a great uprising. I turned on the seat, looked deep into her brown eyes and said, "What would any kid do with an ice cream cone?"

She stuck her tongue out at me, gave a little pout, and was quickly out of the piece and into the back door of Flora's.

Damn cock teaser. All the way back to the poolroom the sweet fragrant smell of her was still in my nostrils. *Well, what the hell. Next month I'll be sixteen. I can get my ass out of school, out from under my daddy's thumb, and out into the streets, where I can fulfil my destiny. I shall become a KING.*

■ Foreword from *Pimp: The Story of My Life*

ICEBERG SLIM

Iceberg Slim, the pen and nickname of Robert Beck, is author of *Pimp: The Story of My Life, Trick Baby,* and *Mama Black Widow.* The selection included here is the foreword of his first book, *Pimp;* it reflects something of the idiom, role behavior, and overall life-style that was Iceberg Slim's own during the years he spent on the "fast track" of Chicago's South Side.

As the pimp life-style has had a pervasive influence on black urban male youth—one sees and hears of "pimp style-books," "pimp walk," "pimp talk," and other expressive forms of behavior deriving or evolving from the pimp prototype—it seemed important to offer Slim's firsthand account, however brief, of the "pimp game," even that aspect of it that speaks to the male-female (pimp-whore) relationship, as contributing to our identification of the black community's normative models or sources in the areas of expressive role behavior and communication.

Dawn was breaking as the big Hog scooted through the streets. My five whores were chattering like drunk magpies. I smelled the stink that only a street whore has after a long, busy night. The inside of my nose was raw. It happens when you're a pig for snorting cocaine.

My nose was on fire and the stink of those whores and the gangster they were smoking seemed like invisible knives scraping to the root of my brain. I was in an evil, dangerous mood despite that pile of scratch crammed into the glove compartment.

"Godamnit, has one of you bitches shit on herself or something?" I bellowed as I flipped the long window toward me. For a long moment there was silence.

Then Rachel, my bottom whore, cracked in a pleasing, ass-kissing voice. "Daddy Baby, that ain't no shit you smell. We been turning all night and ain't no bathrooms in those tricks' cars we been flipping out of. Daddy, we sure been humping for you, and what you smell is our nasty whore asses."

I grinned widely—inside, of course. The best pimps keep a steel lid on their emotions, and I was one of the iciest. The whores went into fits of giggles at Rachel's shaky witticism. A pimp is happy when his whores giggle. He knows they are still asleep.

I coasted the Hog into the curb outside the hotel where Kim, my newest, prettiest girl, was cribbing. Jesus! I would be glad to drop the last whore off so I could get to my own hotel to nurse my nose with cocaine and be alone. Any good pimp is his own best company. His inner life is so rich with cunning and scheming to out-think his whores.

As Kim got out I said, "Goodnight Baby, today is Saturday so I want everybody in the street at noon instead of seven tonight. I said noon, not five minutes after or two minutes after, but at twelve noon sharp I want you down, got it, Baby?"

She didn't answer, but she did a strange thing. She walked into the street around the Hog to the window on my side. She stood looking at me for a long moment, her beautiful face tense in the dim dawn.

Then in her crisp New England accent she said, "Are you coming back to my pad this morning? You haven't spent a night with me in a month. So come back, Okay?"

A good pimp doesn't get paid for screwing; he gets his payoff for always having the right thing to say to a whore right on lightning tap. I knew my four whores were flapping their ears to get my reaction to this beautiful bitch. A pimp with an overly fine bitch in his stable has to keep his game tight. Whores constantly probe for weakness in a pimp.

I fitted a scary mask on my face and said, in a low, deadly voice, "Bitch, are you insane? No bitch in this family calls any shots or muscles me to do anything. Now take your stinking yellow ass upstairs to a bath and some shut eye, and get in the street at noon like I told you."

The bitch just stood there, her eyes slit in anger. I could sense she was game to play the string out right there in the street before my whores. If I had been ten years dumber I would have leaned out of that Hog and broken her jaw, and put my foot in her ass, but the joint was too fresh in my mind.

I knew the bitch was trying to booby trap me when she spat out her invitation. "Come on kick my ass. What the hell do I need with a man I only see when he comes to get his money? I am sick of it all. I don't dig stables and never will. I know I'm the new bitch who has to prove herself. Well Godamnit, I am sick of this shit. I'm cutting out."

She stopped for air and lit a cigarette. I was going to blast her ass off when she finished. So, I just sat there staring at her.

Then she went on. "I have turned more tricks in the three months I have been with you than in the whole two years with Paul. My pussy stays sore and swollen. Do I get my ass kicked before I split? If so, kick it now because I am going back to Providence on the next thing smoking."

She was young, fast, with trick appeal galore. She was a pimp's dream and she knew it. She had tested me with her beef and now she was lying back for a sucker response.

I disappointed her with my cold overlay. I could see her wilt as I said in an icy voice, "Listen square-ass Bitch, I have never had a whore I couldn't do without. I celebrate, Bitch, when a whore leaves me. It gives some worthy bitch a chance to take her place and be a star. You scurvy Bitch, if I shit in your face, you gotta love it and open your mouth wide."

The rollers cruised by in a squad car so I flashed a sucker smile on my face and cooled it until they passed. Kim was rooted there wincing under the blizzard.

I went on ruthlessly, "Bitch, you are nothing but a funky zero. Before me you had one chili chump with no rep. Nobody except his mother ever heard of the bastard. Yes Bitch, I'll be back this morning to put your phony ass on the train."

I rocketed away from the curb. In the rear-view mirror I saw Kim walk slowly into the hotel, her shoulders slumped. In the Hog, until I dropped the last whore off you could have heard a mosquito crapping on the moon. I had tested out for them, "solid ice."

I went back for Kim. She was packed and silent. On the way to the station, I rifled the pages in that pimp's book in my head for an angle to hold her without kissing her ass.

I couldn't find a line in it for an out like that. As it turned out, the bitch was testing and bluffing right down the line.

We had pulled into the station parking lot when the bitch fell to pieces. Her eyes were misty when she yelped, "Daddy, are you really going to let me split? Daddy, I love you!"

I started the prat action to clinch her when I said, "Bitch, I don't want a whore with rabbit in her. I want a bitch who wants me for life. You have got to go after that bullshit earlier this morning, you are not that bitch."

That prat butchered her and she collapsed into my lap, crying and begging to stay. I had a theory about splitting whores. I think they seldom split without a bankroll.

So, I cracked on her. "Give me that scratch you held out and maybe I will give you another chance."

Sure enough she reached into her bosom and drew out close to five bills and handed it to me. No pimp with a brain in his head cuts loose a young beautiful whore with lots of mileage left in her. I let her come back.

When at long last I was driving toward my hotel I remembered what "Baby" Jones, the master pimp who turned me out, had said about whores like Kim.

"Slim," he had said, "a pretty Nigger bitch and a white whore are just alike. They both will get in a stable to wreck it and leave the pimp on his ass with no whore. You gotta make 'em hump hard and fast to stick 'em for long scratch quick. Slim, pimping ain't no game of love, so prat 'em and keep your swipe outta 'em. Any sucker who believe a whore loves him shouldn't a fell outta his mammy's ass."

My mind went back to Pepper. Then back even further, and I remembered what he had said about "The Georgia."

"Slim, a pimp is really a whore who has reversed the game on whores. So Slim, be as sweet as the scratch, no sweeter, and always stick a whore for a bundle before you sex her. A whore ain't nothing but a trick to a pimp. Don't let 'em 'Georgia' you. Always get your money in front just like a whore."

On the elevator riding to my pad, I thought about the first bitch who had "Georgied" me and how she had flim-flammed me out of my "head." She would be old and gray now, but if I could find her I would sure get the bitch's unpaid account off my conscience.

■ The game

WOODIE KING, JR.

Woodie King, Jr., is presently artistic director of the Henry Street Settlement in New York after serving five years as cultural arts director for the Mobilization for Youth. This was the first training program in which young blacks and Puerto Ricans produced their art under professional supervision. As president of Woodie King Associates, King has organized his considerable creative talents as producer, director, writer, editor, and consultant under one rubric. He produced some of the most important writers in black theatre: Leroi Jones, Ed Bullins, Ronald Milner, Ben Caldwell, and William Mackey. While director of plays at Concept East Theatre in Detroit, King was awarded the John Hay Whitney Fellowship for directing (1965–66). King's short stories have often been anthologized, and feature articles of his have appeared in *Variety, Liberator, Black World*, and elsewhere.

"The Game" originally appeared in the Liberator in August, 1965. It is included here for its wealth of cultural information: for vivid portrayals of personality types and roles, for idioms and other expressive language, for illustrations of the various maneuvers and strategies connected with "gaming," and for the sense of a cultural event or happening.

"Someone is always waiting for him," a hipster says to me.

"He is always doing something unusual," says another.

Both describes Sweet Mac to a tee.

I first met Sweet Mac two years ago officially; had heard of him all over town though, especially down Hastings way. You see, Mac was going with Glorie, a babe that lived next door to me. Fact is, everybody was going with her—to her bed or the Foggy Night Hotel (everybody calls it the Foggy Day though). No secret at all, everybody was laying Glorie. And since I was there, Sweet Mac musta been hip to the fact that I was one of the "everybody." Fact is, the most difficult part to making the broad wasn't the shoot-down, but getting there when no one else was around, which was in no way easy. Some of them squares waited for hours. It's a bitch if a stud ain't got nothing else going for him! But me, I was in a mellow position. Had a joint next to her pad; could dig out the window. On this occasion, after I had dug out the window, thinking it safe, I gets high and goes over.

And Sweet Mac was there; legs crossed, showing his Stacies and two-fifty sox. Together! Looking drugged 'cause I done blew his fast cop. He musta got there two-three seconds before I did 'cause it don't take too long to cop Glorie.

Glorie went through a few changes: pretending we were just visitors who were strung out over her; and kinda scared to show too much favoritism, making meaningless chit-chat, you know, like she had both our noses open.

I was getting drugged; Mac sat quiet most of the time, grunting now and then, as though in reply to Glorie's bogue chatter. So I started going through the same changes, hoping Mac would split. Sitting nodding; trying to outwait each other; grunts of conversation. We did this grunting—with Glorie's meaningless yarding between—until three-four A.M., at which time I went unwisely to sleep and Sweet Mac musta wisely went for action.

When I woke Sweet Mac done copped and is almost outa his mind; laying on the couch panting like a mad dog. Between the pants, he is laughing like Wallace Beery. Fact is, he looks like him.

I was disgusted and pretty damn mad. If you ever missed that A-train, you know what I mean. I had just lost six hours which I could have applied to making four-five other broads.

But from those short grunts Mac and me became good friends until this particular Saturday night. Did lots of partying together. The stud is a maniac for broads, doesn't matter if they are fat, ugly, skinny; let them come, Mac'll make them quicker than Speedy Gonzales. And they knock him out. I ain't jiving. I mean he passes out after a bust. Out. O-U-T. Like Liston when Cassius hit him upside the head. But this don't stop Sweet Mac. He takes care of business three hundred and sixty five times a year! (Twice on his birthday, I hear.) That's how he got that name. Naturally, all the fellows would hate a cat like Sweet Mac. But anybody like Mac ain't Mac, 'cause he knows how to stay friends with studs, too. I think it's because of that weird laugh.

Add to this: He also was a booster downtown a little back. Could steal ten-twelve vines in one go round. Sometimes he'd let me cop a V or a Benny for nothing. We became even better friends because of his generosity.

Now, about this particular Saturday night. I was supposed to meet him at Joe's Bar-B-Que to get a hot number. I was told earlier by Sweet Mac: "If you don't, Monday night you will be very hot too."

"But Mac," I said, "I am bare as the cupboard."

"This digit is going to keel over Monday evening before five o'clock," he said. "All the hippies got a bag open."

I got out of bed that Saturday night about midnight. Come Monday, if Mac was right, I would have my bag open, too. Musta been about twelve thirty when I arrived at Joe's. Knew I was too early for Sweet Mac—he is one of them night people, you dig, a hipster at that; he don't show at night anywhere until somewhere near two A.M. (all the bars close at two A.M., you know, and most of the hip whoes around the city eat at Joe's).

While I'm standing outside of Joe's, onto the scene strode Logan X. A stone cynic, refuses to have a last name.

"Some stiff-ass farmer tossed me and my brothers a tag long time ago with a heap others doing same," he says. "And I ain't gonna buy that Jones, Smith, and Williams bull."

This particular Saturday night Logan was very neat indeed. Wearing a 3G; leather benny with a marino lining was laying on his arm, new do; hair laid snug and pretty to that big head of his. Sweet Mac calls him waterhead because Mac says its like a tank. Looking at Logan's head, you can't help but to agree with Sweet Mac 100 percent. Lo immediately pushed out his hand and spouts *"As Salaam Alaikum,* Brother Pierre?"

Slapped his hand as I replied, *"Wa Alaikum Salaam;* waiting for Sweet Mac, Brother Lo." Called him "brother" because he supposed to be a member of this Muslim thing (though I know he ain't 'cause the cat eats pork, chitterlings, hog maws, and anything else he can sink his teeth into) and because I had intentions to hit on him for a pork sausage sandwich. But he interrupts me as I was about to open my mouth. Cat must be psychic as well as cynic.

"Pierre, man, Mac is the cat I'm here to meet myself. Gonna git into something tonight, brother."

"Well," I said, "Mac is where it's at, brother."

By now, two-three other hipsters have also eased in, all planning to cop a beg, since it was evident that Logan X was pretty clean and just might be open to said beg.

"Come here Brother Lo," I said. "Got something I want to run down to you."

We walked off a foot or two.

"Let me cop a Benny Franklin until my whoes brings me some dough," I said. "You can slip it to me while ain't nobody digging us, brother."

"I'm dead, brother," he said. "I need a dime to get some Lipton."

"Jive nigguh! Ain't got a half dollar? Get on way from me, Nigguh!"

Herman started giggling. Stone junky! Giggles all the time. And always wears them black sunglasses. Another Sweet Mac waiter. Very neat, too, not to have a day job.

Herm had a funny-looking little book called *The White Negro.*

"I was running from The Man," he giggled. "Hauling ass man; goes into this gigantic bookstore, hiding and high too; funny as hell, man. Looks up and see this funny looking little book. Ain't that a bitch! So I stole the m . . . f."

Herman sticks out his hand.

Logan slaps it.

"Dig Lo," Herman continued, "if this ofay cat is so set on running down the Rocks, he forgets to mention your movement. If he forgets this he ain't so hip."

"Told you," Logan X replied, "them cats don't know what they talking about most of the time; always running down them spooks who ain't into anything. Always forget to mention that the Rocks have hippies such as Sweet Mac."

Herman laid open his hand.

Logan X slapped it.

"Still it is strange that this grey cat can know so much about the spook," I said, reading a few lines from the book.

"But his knowledge of Sweet Mac's role is truly N.G." Logan X said.

"Mac," Herman yawned, "is into something."

"Sweet Mac is never in a hurry," I said, remembering his many escapades, especially the Glorie affair.

Two stacked broads approached.

Everyone attained a hip position. It consisted of pulling pants high, rolling the Hi-Lo collar, taking silk handkerchief in hand, wetting the lips, getting the body limber, and the natural expressionless face. In his hip position, Herman says:

"Hey mamma, you putty thang . . . shorr look foine. Come mere, let Hoim give you this buzz. Unnnnn Uhh!"

The broads continued on their way expressionless as we gazed wantingly at their big beautiful—

"You sho got a niaz box, baby," Logan X shouted. "The broad got her eyes on you, Pierre. See how she shakes that thang?"

"Dig that thang! Dig man! Broad stacked!! Damn! Dig it man!!" Herman said, jumping up and down, hitting the taps on his Stacies on the concrete, like he was about to wee wee in his pants.

"Yeah," I said, "broad is like that. Knows how to use that weapon."

"Business!" Logan X interrupted. "Mac is supposed to meet me here tonight and turn me on to a number."

"I'm supposed to cop myself," I said. "Mac's copping me a number from hell for a nickel!"

Herman, Logan X, and yours truly had this in common: we all had put a nickel in the hand of Sweet Mac to cop a hot number from a homo prophet. The prophet balls and blasts every Sunday night on a local radio station. One of them Sunday night preachers, you dig. But I hear the numbers he lets out of that gold tooth mouth are sure to keel over. We had no beliefs that Sweet Mac would, in any way, try to beat us for our loot.

"Sweet Mac is on my shit list," a square standing near me thundered to everyone's amazement. "Sweet Mac was supposed to cop me a bag three nights back. I waited all that night in front of Little Sams for the nigguh to show. I waited last night. And I'm waiting here tonight to get my bag of reefer."

"Dan, baby, you been on Mac's list for years," I said, knowing how Sweet Mac feels about Square Dan. Fact is, Mac don't feel nothing for Dan. Ever since Dan and Mac were in the kindergarten together, Mac been putting game on him.

"You a trick Dan—a stiffy," Herman said. "You so square Little Orphan Annie could put game on you."

Dan told us we were some stupid Rocks; he also told all of us to kiss his black —. Square Dan has a nasty mouth, always had one ever since he was a kid at Moore School for Boys.

It was nearing two A.M. I knew this because Joe's began filling. Stacked broads rushed in on the arms of stiffies straight from the corn-fields; you know—them cats with the cowboy hats and ice cream suits. Stone stiffs. I looked through the bug-infested window; broads were laughing everywhere. All them broads with their mouths wide, grinning, barbecue hanging in their teeth, arms greasy to the elbow; them tricks for that night were drinking Lipton tea only. Takes a weird cat to spend all his dough on a broad while he goes without. Half them dizzy broads make more dough than us studs.

I turned from the window.

Sweet Mac!

Hurrying across Mt. Elliott Street to get to Joe's; walking kinda weird like he had to go to the john.

"Rip Van, my man," he said. He called me Van Winkle because of that incident when I fell asleep while he laid the aforementioned Glorie.

"My man," I said. "Everybody got a man and you my man, jive nigguh."

Mac gave that laugh like Wallace Beery when he did the Long John Silver thing. "You O.K. Van Winkley."

Sweet Mac was very dap that night. Sharper than Logan X because he was wearing more jewels; his benny and sunglasses were special made, his lid a stingy Dobbs. And though I believe his feet were hurting because of the narrowness of the Stetsons, he was neat from toe to stingy.

Without a doubt, Sweet Mac was carrying more loot in his pockets than all of us had had that week. And I was about to hit on him for my number so that come Tuesday I could have loot too, but before I could inquire, he said, "Come on in fellows. I got news on something just went down that'll knock you out."

We followed him in and seated ourselves in the back where the money people sit.

"Your orders, please," the waitress said.

"I'd like to have you, sugar," Logan X said. "You foxy thang."

She put her hands on her hips, waited. I visualized her naked.

"Yeah!" I said. "Three coffees."

To which Sweet Mac said, "Give us four pork sausage sandwiches, momma." He turned to me. "Van Winkley, my man, never order Maxwell House when you with Sweet Mac. Get yourself some pork, baby!" Mac's pork is "poke."

"Mellow," we said in unison. I also noted a "mellow" from Logan X.

Then, through the yak-yak, Mac began to tell us the "unusual something" that he had just recently done.

"Dig," he said. "I'm with this Edith broad I been trying to lay on sheets for the past half month."

We puzzled because the broad was definitely unknown to us.

"Edith is the 'saved' broad who can't marry out of her religion," Mac says, "or do anything else out of her religion for that matter, especially what I wanted her to do. A bogue religion, man! So dig, for the last couple of weeks I been quoting the Good Book and all that stuff to her; telling her I am now saved myself, you dig."

"Four pork sandwiches," she interrupted, bending over the table, letting us get a gander at the big June Wilkerson action. Blew some hot air on them; she grinned. Sweet Mac gave her rear a light pat when she turned to leave; she continued to grin.

"*Alaikum-wa-salaam,*" Logan X said. Just goes to show, regarding this Muslim thing, he doesn't know if he is coming or departing.

"Mac? You read this book?" Herman asked.

"Naw, man!" he said, only glancing at the title, "but I'd like to read the Black Caucasian though."

"I ain't hip to that one, Mac," I said.

"Baby," he said shocked, "You ain't hip to the Black Caucasian? All them nigguh politicians is in that bag. Lots of them entertainer cats too. Take that Belafonte cat. Ever hear him sing the Leadbelly songs? Sing 'em like a cat done just left Harvard. Leadbelly never seen the inside of a school. Dig this: Went to see this Belafonte cat at the Fisher, had my number one—six dollar seats, baby! Afterwards I went backstage to get the nigguh's name in his handwriting. He was back there grinning in them ofay broads' faces, speaking hipper than Olivier in Hamlet, not even looking in a brother's direction. Ain't that a bitch, man?"

"Told you, Allah is right," Logan X said.

"But my story is more important," Mac continued. "So tonight I says to her—"

"Where is my loot, Sweet Mac?" Square Dan interrupted.

"Dan, baby!" Sweet Mac shot back, turning a little red in the face. "Sit down, get a pork sandwich, baby."

"You got my loot, jive nigguh," Dan said. "My pocket is dead except for my blade."

Mac grinned like Wallace Beery when he plays a crook.

"Gimme my dough," Dan said.

"The pocket's what—?" Mac said, giving Dan a Benny Franklin, "Here, baby. Go on cop yourself a pig sandwich."

"I gave you two for a cent pack, Mac," Dan said.

Sweet Mac frowned.

"Wait a minute, Dan; I'll give you two dollars, baby. You think I'd put game on you for two cent? I got busted, The Man got me. Let me run this broad down, and I'll give you the cakes."

Dan took the half; sat at a table across from us, drugged. Couldn't argue. 'Cause when a cat gives a bagman dough, he loses everything if the bagman gets copped. Lately, every time you give a bagman dough, he gets copped.

"So what went down with the broad?" I asked.

Sweet Mac ordered two more pork sausages.

"I says to her," he continued with greasy mouth, eating as he talked, "Edith, baby, we can't go on like this. I dig you *but* . . . baby I'm one hundred percent man. And baby, from looking at you, you are one hundred percent woman (the broad went for this evaluation). Do you agree moma? I asked. The broad whimpered, 'Yes, Sweet Mac.' So, I says, if that is the case, something or someone is trying to keep us—two pure American religious people of the same order—apart. At this point, I drop a quote or two from the Good Book on her; *Thou shall not covet thy neighbor's wife;* and baby since you're not anybody's wife, I pleaded, *do unto others as you would have them do unto you.* I got the broad wiggling her legs! Next, I whispered to her secretly, doing the ear bit with the tongue, baby only something like that no-good Satan would want to stop something as mellow as laying naked in the Foggy Night with MJQ or Ravel on the hi-fi, me there playing with you, only Satan, I says. He trying to put game on us, momma. The broad is looking dazed like she done seen the handwriting on the wall. And I think I got the broad. But I'm still uncertain until the broad screams dead in my ear:

" '*It's true.* I been taught it is the Devil that tries to keep good things from us religious people.' Her legs are going like a washing machine; talking to me like she trying to shoot *me* down, breathing hard at the same time.

"I reply to her that *our* religion is definitely correct, many people go through life never realizing this important fact about that no-good Devil.

I said this because the broad is definitely a dogmatist. Wasn't in no mood for any sudden disagreements, like the ones I had been getting for the past two-three weeks. We made a beeline from the oratory direct to the Foggy Night, into one of the most outstanding love sessions of my twenty-one years, starting when I was six years old."

Mac's story was very interesting. The introduction of the Good Book into the game is unique. There are so many religious folk nowadays. And if they listen to Prophet Jones and Sweet Daddy, I can dig why Edith dug Sweet Mac's rundown.

"This will knock you out, I told you this was an unusual session, but I forget to mention this doll is a champ on the sheets! She is brutal; death on sheets, man! Was outa my skull before we even finished the session. The whole room was spinning, twisting and turning, and I'm telling the broad to take it easy; don't want to tell the broad I'm about to pass out, you dig. Then I faints and she screams dead in my ear. That's the last thing I really remembered for a while. I wake up and this fine devil is ready for another go round. Wants more! And I'm dizzy, all outa my head, in a hurry to split the Foggy Night and this brutal broad."

Then he clinched it, not embarrassed either. "I was dizzy and in such a hurry to get out I put the broad's panties on, man."

I expected a Wallace Beery laugh, but instead the cat looked frightened.

We played it cool, since we were eating off him; never can tell how a stud takes to being laughed at.

About that time, in comes the Edith broad—eyes glowing—like she done saved the world. Beautiful shape; cross between Tempest Storm and June Wilkerson, without make-up. I detected right away this was the action. Also noted she was walking kinda weird. She whispered something in Sweet Mac's ear. And at the same time she was rubbing Mac and kissing his ear and carrying on. Her eyes were almost closed like this Monroe doll in that flick *Some Like It Hot*. Could tell she was a natural-born champ.

"Baby, I thought you were dead," she whispered in Mac's ear, kissing him all on the neck and head. A born champ! Could make a ton of money off her!

We sat in complete, expressionless silence.

The broad continued whispering while Mac destroyed the pig. I figured it was about the unusual mistake in drawers by, perhaps, both parties. Then, when Mac had finished the third pork, he broke into that uncontrollable Wallace Beery bag. And we broke our cool and joined.

Even Square Dan joined.

While we were in that cheerful bag, I heard Sweet Mac say: "I'm splittin' fellows. Later."

"Later," I said through hysteria, at the same time slapping Logan X's hand. I was so filled with laughter I forgot to cop my number.

Herman, Logan X, and Square Dan also forgot to cop said digit, or whatever else they were supposed to cop.

Thinking back: Kinda believe Mac's story was a lot of bull. But I just can't imagine Sweet Mac being that hip to Stanislavsky's method.

Think I'll show tomorrow night and wait for Sweet Mac. Yeah, sure, I'll tell him you wanna see him. Say, dig man, let me cop a Benny Franklin 'til my whoe shows. Slip it to me while ain't nobody looking.

■ Lovers and exploiters

ELLIOT LIEBOW

Elliot Liebow is chief of the Center for Studies of Metropolitan Problems at the National Institute for Mental Health. Born and raised in a black ghetto in Washington, D.C., he brings a lifelong familiarity with the black urban scene to his research. *Tally's Corner: A Study of Negro Streetcorner Men,* and selected articles, are products of this synthesis.

"Lovers and Exploiters" from *Tally's Corner* provides ethnographic confirmation for the thesis (advanced by Charles Keil in *Urban Blues*) that the hustler and entertainer are among those who "wear their image in real comfort," and therefore represent "two important value orientations for the lower-class Negro." One of the norms of the hustler, especially as typified by the pimp, is that of exploiter of women, one who has "reversed the

game on whores" as Sweet Jones, the pimp in Iceberg Slim's book states, and as Iceberg Slim, Big Time, and Sweet Mac themselves personify in the literary pieces included in this volume. Liebow's representation of the masculine code of his male street-corner respondents is heavily invested with this theme, if not so much through their actual exploitation of women as through their verbalizations "on the corner" of their exploitation of them. That women should also think and talk of themselves as exploiters of men, for use objects or objects of income, as Liebow states, needs also to be further examined as either a possible adoption of the masculine code with reversal of roles, or of a role norm deriving from some other prototype.

Men and women talk of themselves and others as cynical, self-serving marauders, ceaselessly exploiting one another as use objects or objects of income.[1] Sometimes, such motives are ascribed only to women: "Them girls [whom the men on the corner hang out with], they want *finance, not romance.*" But more often, the men prefer to see themselves as the exploiters, the women as the exploited, as in assessing a woman's desirability in terms of her wealth or earning power or in equating being "nice" with having a job. At a party, Tally waits for Jessie to arrive and grins with anticipation. "She's not pretty,"[2] he said, "but she's got a beautiful job."

[1] This kind of exploitation was also found in a lower-class district of London where "there is also an important exploitative component in the 'love-relationship,' at least on the man's side. . . . The boy may be overtly exploitative, not only of the sexual intercourse which the girl permits, but also of what he can get out of her financially" (Josephine Klein, *Samples from English Cultures,* vol. 1, p. 39).

[2] Other things being equal, the more closely a woman approached her white counterpart, the more attractive she was considered to be, by both men and women alike. "Good hair" (hair that is long and soft) and light skin were the

Lounging in the Carry-out shop, Leroy boasts to the men at the pin-ball machine about the girl he had recently met. She worked in a cafeteria near the hotel where he worked as a bellboy. When they went out, he said, they always used her money.

"She just got herself a government job," said Leroy. "She never misses a day's work. She's a real mule."

"Hell, who wants to live with a mule?" I asked.

"Man, that's the best thing to live with," said Leroy. "When you got somebody who can pull that wagon, you really got something." He turned to Lonny and asked if this wasn't so. Lonny agreed that it was.

Sweets similarly presented himself as an exploiter, boasting that he had a room in another section of town as well as the one near the Carry-out but pays no rent for either one. "Man, I don't pay rent in no places. My lady friends do that." And later, confronted by the choice of whether or not to move in with still another woman who had two children, he weighed aloud the advantages and disabilities. "She's real nice—works two jobs," he said, and he guessed that this would compensate for the disability presented by the children.

---

chief criteria. "Good hair" normally referred to head hair alone, but several of the men also expressed a preference for women with down on their cheeks or long leg hair. In one instance, one of the men explained his strong attraction to a woman by noting that "she has hair all up and down her chest." But a light-skinned woman, while admittedly more attractive than her darker sister, was someone to be avoided, except perhaps as a partner for a couple of hours or one night. With the possible exception of Sea Cat, the men were uniformly afraid of women whose skin color was markedly lighter than one commonly saw on the street. The explanation given was simple and straightforward: "A light-skinned woman will turn on [against] you."

Sweets spoke with intense feeling on the subject. Talking about the woman he had just broken off with, he said that though they had lived together for a few weeks, he never really considered her his woman because she was a "light-skinned girl." He couldn't even like her because of it. One day, just as he knew she would, she turned on him and called him "bad names." (That is, "nigger," "black [something]," and other color slurs.) "I put my fist in her mouth. Now she's living with a friend of mine and he says she's okay. He doesn't know how she turned on me with all those bad names. He'll find out though. All of them, they'll all talk that shit if they get mad enough. And they all get mad enough sometime."

The others agreed with Sweet in principal, differing only in that some would admit there might be exceptions. Tally, Richard, and I had just walked out of a beer joint and I said that the girl who served us was a good-looking woman. Tally said, "She's all right, but she's too light for me." I asked whether all light-skinned women turn on a man.

"Well, maybe not all of them, but eight out of ten of them will. You get in an argument with them and they start talking a lot of shit, calling you all kinds of names, and the first thing you know you're in the police station. Flora [an exceptionally dark-skinned woman], Flora's the kind of girl I like."

"Yeah," said Richard. "You get in an argument with a girl like Flora and she's got to stick to the subject." (That is, because Flora is dark-skinned, she is in no position to resort to color slurs and must restrict her argument to the matter at hand.)

The men are eager to present themselves as exploiters to women as well as to men. The presence of a woman may encourage a man to an even more flamboyant portrayal of himself as the ruthless exploiter. The following (tape-recorded) exchange took place in Richard's apartment among Wesley, Richard, and Richard's twenty-two-year-old half-sister Thelma, who was visiting from New York.

WESLEY: From now [on], if a girl ain't got money and a car, I'm not talking to her.

THELMA: But you don't find very many of those girls.

WESLEY: My buddy next door, he's got one. She's got a '58 Mercury and I hear she's got a whole lot of money.

THELMA: How old is she?

WESLEY: I don't know how old she is but she sure parks that Mercury in front of that door.

RICHARD: She could be sixty if she gave me some of that money, let me drive that new car.[3]

WESLEY (*agreeing vigorously*): What'cha talking about, man!

THELMA: But won't you be embarrassed—to be seen with an older woman?

WESLEY: No. I was dumb one time. This lady, she was about forty-five. She got her own home. She got a white Cadillac, '60. She got a restaurant and she tried her best to talk to me. She told my landlady, told my landlady to get me to call and I wouldn't. But now let her come around! I'll tell the landlady, "Anytime she come around, call Wesley." I was crazy then. All that money! Ooh, I could play a long time! I could cool it. All that money and riding around in a big Cadillac. I'd ride the other women around.

THELMA: She'll have you fixed so you can't ride the other women around.

WESLEY: Uh-uh. I'm smarter than she is. She's got a daughter about nineteen. I'd have her daughter [too]. I'd be stone living!

Men not only present themselves as economic exploiters of women but expect other men to do the same. When other men's behavior does

[3] Within very broad limits, a woman's chronological or relative age does not appear to be a crucial factor in assessing her potential as a sex partner. By and large, sex partners are roughly contemporaries of one another, but this is by no means the rule. The same man may be at once attracted to a girl in her middle teens and to a woman in her mid-forties, as evidenced, for example, by the fact that the mother of one of Tally's children was a teen-age girl and the mother of another of his children was herself a grandmother in her forties. Conversely, one may also find a man in his early twenties and a man in his forties competing for the favor of, say, a twenty- or thirty-year-old woman. Actions and attitudes varied greatly from individual to individual. Tally held that "a man usually likes a older head" (i.e., a woman older than himself) and frequently bore this out in practice. Richard, on the other hand, notwithstanding his "she could be sixty," once "put down" a woman of thirty or so, forgoing the pleasures of her automobile as well, because "She's too old. I like tender meat."

not meet these expectations, they claim not to understand the behavior.

Tally and I were in the Carry-out and I had just told Tally that Sea Cat said he was putting out the woman who had been living with him for the past seven months. Tally's initial disbelief dissolved into puzzlement: "Sea Cat's just talking. He ain't puttin' her out. A bird in the hand is worth two million in the air . . . I can't understand Sea Cat. He's had lots of girls. He treats the goods ones real bad and he's real nice to the mean ones. The girl he's got now, she's real nice, she works every day . . ."

On the corner, with three other men standing around, Sea Cat deplored the fact that not all men were users of women because those men —and he stopped to curse them—who spend money on women are "spoiling the women for the rest of us." Moreover, the thought that many women think nothing of going to "a club" and spending twenty dollars distressed him: "Hell, if I can get that twenty dollars, I can give them all the beer and liquor they can drink and ten dollars will still be in my pocket. They wouldn't know the difference."

Men saw themselves as users of women as sex objects as well as objects of income.[4] Where "pussy" is concerned, a man should "take what he can get when he can get it." Tally earnestly proclaimed that his own motto for dealing with women was "Everything New for '62." Similarly, Sea Cat was angered when a Friday night party at which he expected to meet several new women failed to come off. The thought of his missed opportunities rankled him all the next day. "I could have scored," he kept repeating, slamming his fist into his open hand with annoyance. "I know I could have scored." As several other men on the

---

[4] The sexual exploitation of women does not refer to sex practices. The streetcorner man's heterosexual sex practices are wholly compatible with the observation that "[lower-class] taboos are more often turned against . . . any substitution for simple and direct coitus. . . . [substitutes for intercourse are] considered a perversion" (Kinsey, Pomeroy, and Martin, "Social Level and Sexual Outlet," p. 305). Anal and oral intercourse, for example, are thought of as belonging exclusively to the homosexual world. Even the labels or terms designating or describing cunnilinguism—used so commonly by servicemen and working-class males generally as contemptuous terms of address or in comradely jest—are very seldom used. That such practices stand in clear violation of the heterosexual relationship is strongly suggested by one of the few conversations that touched on the subject. Several of us were standing in a hallway drinking. Upstairs, we could hear an argument between a man and a woman, and the talk moved around to violence between man and wife. Stanton contributed a story about a woman who was continuously abused by her husband, who slept with a gun under his pillow. One night the man came home drunk and forced his wife to perform an "unnatural" act. When he fell asleep, she took a two-bladed ax from the kitchen and held it over his head, closed her eyes, and buried the axe in the middle of his forehead. Screaming, she ran from the house and told her story to the people in the town. She didn't ever come to trial, said Stanton, concluding his story. "They didn't even carry her to court." Tonk, Boley, and everyone else agreed that justice had been done.

corner looked on, Sea Cat promised himself publicly to right the wrong that had been done him: "I'm going to the dance tonight. I don't know and I don't care who's [going to be] there. I'm going to down at least four women in the next twenty-four hours."

Thus the men talked of themselves as exploiters and users of women. But talk is cheap. In practice, in their real relationships with real women, the men frequently gave the lie to their own words. For men and women both, naked exploitation, unalloyed with "liking" or other tempering impulses, was at best a sometime thing. It occurred most frequently as a kind of upside-down ideal statement of how one is expected to behave, as lip service to a public fiction which the individual man or woman is periodically obliged to acknowledge lest he be ridiculed or dismissed as "lame" (a weakling, a sucker, a patsy).

The contention "A man should take anything he can get when he can get it"; Tally's "Everything New for '62"; Leroy's "A mule is the best thing to live with"; Sea Cat's announced intention to "down four women"—any four women—in twenty-four hours were all public expressions of support for the myth or public fiction of man as the uncompromising exploiter of women.

In action, however, the impulse to use women as objects of economic or sexual exploitation is deflected by countervailing impulses and goals, especially the desire to build personal, intimate relationships based on mutual liking or love. It is the interplay of these opposing impulses which accounts, at least in part, for the discrepancy between the way men talk about women and the way they act with them.

Men and women both had to deal with these conflicting impulses and goals. Here, for example, is eighteen-year-old Carol claiming the exploitative ideal for her own and castigating her friend, sixteen-year-old Lena, for making "liking" a precondition for engaging in sex and accepting money from a man. Carol and Lena were unmarried mothers living with their children. This conversation took place on the front steps of the house from which they had just been evicted. Their belongings were piled up on the sidewalk in front of us. I asked Lena whether she was receiving ADC. She said no, she wouldn't have anything like that. On ADC, she said, you can't live your own life.[5] "You can't have any boyfriends or nothing, and I sure like my boys."

"You like your boys, all right," said Carol, "but you better start learning to like some of that money, too."

[5] A reference to Washington's "man-in-the-house" rule which excludes women from receiving Aid to Dependent Children if there is an employable male in the household. This grotesque paternalism was enforced by special investigators who made unannounced searches—at all hours of the day and night—for evidence of a "man in the house." Thus were "cheaters" weeded out; that is, undeserving children whose mothers continued to want love or sex even though they had received a check from the Department of Welfare.

Carol turned to me. "Do you know what she did the other day," she said, indicating Lena with a contemptuous toss of her head. "This man wanted to give her twenty dollars for some pussy and she wouldn't give him any."

"I just didn't like him," said Lena.

" 'Like him,' shit," snapped Carol. "I wish he had asked me for some pussy and him with twenty dollars in his pocket."

Like Carol, the men proclaimed themselves uncompromising exploiters; like Lena, they did not always "take what you can get when you can get it." They sometimes turned down women who were available to them and sometimes took the initiative in breaking off relationships from which they benefited economically. Leroy broke off with Louise, "the mule . . . who can really pull that wagon," to return again to Charlene, who was generally judged to be less attractive than Louise and who, instead of supporting Leroy, was almost entirely dependent on him for her own support. Tally, who was fond of assessing women in money terms and who claimed not to understand how Sea Cat could put out a woman when she was working every day, was no better at exploiting economically his own relationships with women than was Sea Cat. Emma Lou had been living with Tally for a few weeks and wanted to go on living with him. Tally wanted her to leave. Emma Lou offered to turn her weekly pay (about forty-five dollars) over to him in its entirety. Tally refused and shortly forced her out, although he had no other regular woman at this time.

Sea Cat was generally acknowledged as one of the most successful lovers and managers of man-woman relationships, yet it is in Sea Cat's relationship with women that the public pose of the cynical user of women gives way most completely to the private realities. Sally, twenty-one, who lived in the room above Sea Cat's in the rooming house, and Louella, about eighteen, who lived across the street, frequently visited Sea Cat's room. Both were clearly available to him, but he discouraged their advances: Sally, because she was too voluble and unpredictable; Louella, because he was afraid she couldn't sustain a casual relationship and would "be all over me." Wives or girlfriends of his close friends were excluded from his universe of legitimate sex targets. Sea Cat had many times, for example, gone out with Doris, but her subsequent marriage to a friend of his (one of the men on the corner) changed all this. She was, by his own admission, still very attractive to him but Sea Cat stayed away from her until, about a year after her marriage, he learned she was "cutting out" on her husband. Similarly, when a girl who had been going out with his friend Arthur let it be known that she "liked" Sea Cat, he scrupulously kept her at arm's length.

Sea Cat's capacity for self-denial is clearly evident in his relationship with Linda. If his motive was, at bottom, a sexually selfish one, he showed no rancor when the whole thing failed to come off. In April, Sea Cat met and came to like Linda, a twenty-five-year-old waitress. She lived uptown, but after they had known each other two weeks she began coming to his roof after work (2 A.M.) and spending the night there.

"We talk for a while and then we go to bed," said Sea Cat. He said they slept naked, being careful never to touch one another. She had had a bad experience with a man, he explained—he didn't know what[6]— and she was afraid of men. She was afraid of him, too, he added, "but she's learning not to be."

When they had spent four nights in this manner—and occasionally she would also drop in to talk before going to work—Sea Cat had still not kissed her or touched her body because "I like her and I don't want to spoil anything." He felt that he was gradually winning her confidence and that "she'll come to me real soon." Two weeks later, however, she had stopped coming to sleep with him after work. They had not had any sex contact and Sea Cat didn't think they ever would, but they were still "good friends."

This is not to suggest, however, that one must wholly discount men's view of themselves as exploiters and users of women. A poor man who can get hold of some money is that much less poor for the moment he has it. And in a world where sexual conquest is one of the few ways in which one can prove one's masculinity, the man who does not make capital of his relationship with a woman is that much less a man.

If one looks at the varied man-woman relationships as different accommodations to the desire to exploit, on one hand, and the desire for a love or liking relationship on the other, two basic modes of accommodation emerge: an ideal mode and a real mode. In the ideal mode, seldom if ever realized in practice, only one set of impulses—either the exploitative or the nonexploitative—is operative in any given relationship. In the second or real mode, both sets of impulses are operative in any given relationship.

In the ideal mode, the man divides his universe of women into two discrete parts: those who are "nice,"[7] and those who are "not nice."

[6] Talk about sex practices and sex practices themselves are characterized by fastidiousness and reserve. In ordinary, general conversation, the short, blunt words commonly used to designate coitus and genitalia are used freely and easily. But when the subject is sex, as the talk narrows down to one's own person or sex partner, the language becomes less direct and descriptive phrases such as "I really laid some pipe last night" tend to replace the more specific, denotative labels for intercourse. In general, there is a kind of looking away from a close-up of the sex act as if it were a Medusa's head which will not tolerate direct observation. Some of the standard institutionalized techniques for dealing with it directly, as through the use of humor or obscenity, are here weak or unused. Dirty jokes are rare; pornographic pictures are conspicuously absent.

[7] Although being "nice" is perhaps the most desirable quality in a woman, it

One part is reserved exclusively for exploitation; to the other part he is prepared to accord more considerate treatment. Sea Cat makes the distinction and claims to act accordingly, as the following incident reveals.

Sea Cat was changing his clothes preparatory to going out. I flopped on his bed to wait for him and a package of prophylactics fell out from under the mattress. In replacing it, I discovered a dozen or more similar packages. I asked Sea Cat if he always used them. He said no, sometimes he does, sometimes he doesn't: "It depends on the girl. If she's nice, friendly and all that, the kind I wouldn't mind helping out, then I don't use them. But if she's not nice, I don't take any chances."[8]

It is this ideal division of women into two distinct categories, only one of which is designated for exploitation, which permits the man to enter freely and publicly into the more satisfying give-and-take relationships based on liking or love. By claiming to exploit—or actually ex-

---

is a quality that is poorly defined and one that varies according to one or another man's perspective. To say that a woman is nice can, in some contexts, be a specific reference to her sexiness or to some other specific attribute, such as her having a good job or other income. More often, however, when a man says "She's real nice" he means he approves of her as a total person, and "nice" becomes a kind of judgmental distillate of the woman's personal, ethical, social, and aesthetic qualities.

There is, of course, no absolute consensus on who is or who isn't nice, and even one man's opinion may change over time as his knowledge of or relationship with a given woman changes. There are, however, some broad and relatively objective standards which most men would subscribe to. Great importance is attached to a woman's personal appearance and habits. A nice woman does not dress in "raggedy-ass clothes," nor otherwise appear slovenly or unkempt. Her body, her children, if any, and her living quarters are routinely clean and neat in appearance. She is a conscientious wage-earner or homemaker, or both, and not at all like the woman who lounges in a housecoat all day, the bed unmade, the children unwashed and uncombed, and waits for her man to bring her some money or for the mailman to bring her welfare check.

Her ethics bespeak a fundamental honesty and decency. She does not say one thing to your face, another behind your back. She is not sexually promiscuous, and while she may not necessarily remain wholly faithful to her husband or boyfriend, she "cuts out on him" discreetly, with selected persons, and usually only after provocation, such as mistreatment or repeated public infidelity on his part. Honesty means simple honesty in the property sense, too. She does not steal.

In her social relationships a nice woman displays a generosity of spirit; she is friendly, accessible, tolerant, and open and easy of manner. Whatever her "ways" or style, she is fun to be with.

[8] From a middle-class point of view, one would expect the man to protect the "nice" girl against the possibility of conception and to let the "not nice" girl take her chances. Behind this attitude lies the middle-class contempt for the "not nice" (lower-class?) girl who can justly be left to her own devices even if she does conceive. Sea Cat's morality is of a somewhat different order. Acknowledging his responsibility to "help out" any woman whom he gets pregnant, he forestalls having to enter into an ongoing, helping relationship with the "not nice" girl by using contraceptives. There is no such pressing need to use contraceptives with the "nice" girl, since he has no strong aversion to the continuing relationship with her that conception would entail.

ploiting—Sally and Irene, Harry is free to declare his liking or love for Mary without seriously compromising his own or others' image of him as the tough and cynical realist. In this way, romantic love is legitimized in the street-corner world which pretends to use, as one measure of a man, his willingness and ability to take what he can get from women whenever he can get it. Thus Leroy, having publicly established his support of the myth of exploitation by claiming, "A mule is the best thing to live with," by claiming that Louise pays for everything when they go out, and by similar declarations, is free to enter into a mutual love relationship with Charlene with impunity.

Indeed, declarations of romantic love are integral parts of a great many of the man-woman relationships, especially when the relationship has been strained, as after a quarrel, or during the early stages of its growth while enthusiasm still runs high. Here is one of Leroy's letters to Charlene, written about two weeks after their first meeting in the Carryout shop:

> SWEETHEART, time and opportunity spare me no greater pleasure than to take this leisure time to communicate with you the very thoughts that I have at this instant. However, some people go with you because of your beauty but I like you for your intelligence and the wonderful way you carry yourself. These are the things that upset me. The days that I have may have been wonderful and generous days. That is why I can say that the love I have for you is the greatest love a man could ever have for a woman. With this I bring this letter to an abrupt halt. So until the mailman knocks again, be sweet and remain the wonderful Charlene that I shall always remember. LOVE, LEROY ALLEN BROWN

Ten days later, after a quarrel, he writes again, protesting his desolation and his own unworthiness.

> . . . although we have known each other for a few months [in fact it was weeks, not months], I feel as though those few months with you will always remain a wonderful and admirable remembrance . . . I want to ask you for forgiveness . . . I realized you'll find another young man to fill the emptiness in your heart. I wish the both of you the best of luck because when you were mine I didn't treat you right. Just like a king, I've lost everything. I stood all alone on my throne . . . I shall always remember you, Charlene. Love, MR. NOBODY

Leroy was one of the younger men on the corner and by far the most literate, but gallant declarations of romantic love were not limited to the young and the verbally artful. Stanton was twice Leroy's age and illiterate. He was in love with Bernice and also expressed his feelings in the tradition of courtly love, marking her as one whom he would not exploit. He took pride in his concern for her reputation and safety; he declared publicly his love for her and took a public oath to "treat her right," which included, among other things, a willingness to be on the giving rather than the taking end of their relationship.

Bernice was going to leave Edward, said Stanton. The day before, Edward and Bernice had a fight and Edward took back the watch he had given her. Stanton said that this was a stupid thing for Edward to do. Edward just didn't know how to treat Bernice: "She's not going to stay with him anymore. She's coming over to [live with] me and man, I sure do love that woman! I'm going to treat her right, too. When I give her some thing, it's hers, and I'll never take it back."

This idealized mode of man-woman relationships in which there is a clear division between exploitation and nonexploitation is more a wish than a fact. Only exceptionally does this clear division work out in practice, for it is very difficult to keep a given relationship at all times from spilling over the dividing line. The result is that most man-woman relationships fall into the second mode in which both the exploitative and nonexploitative (e.g., "liking") impulses are operative in the same relationships (as they were, in fact, in Leroy's relationships with Louise and Charlene and in Stanton's relationship with Bernice). In this second mode, the man tends to have mixed feelings about the relationship. His attitude and behavior toward the woman tend to appear inconsistent and even contradictory as now one, now the other, impulse takes over. Sea Cat and Gloria are a good example.

Sea Cat's relationship with Gloria was a public affair. The men on the corner, like the chorus in a Greek tragedy, watched its development, analyzed it, and commented on it. They saw—or talked as if they saw—Sea Cat and Gloria as the user and the used, with Sea Cat a kind of Street-corner Everyman who hunts for A Good Thing, finds it, and inevitably loses it. Sea Cat carefully fostered this image of himself and Gloria.

Sea Cat met Gloria in July, 1962, at a recreation and amusement center in nearby Maryland. Gloria liked Sea Cat, and they started going out together. Gloria was a short, stocky, pleasant-faced widow of twenty-five. Her husband had died the year before and Gloria, who was the beneficiary of his life insurance, also inherited his one-half interest in several modest but profitable commercial enterprises. She owned two cars and a beach cottage in Maryland.

Two weeks after their first meeting, Sea Cat and Gloria had become close friends. They had gone to several parties together and spent a Sunday at her beach cottage. Gloria gave Sea Cat the use of her Bonneville convertible. Sea Cat announced—and all the men on the corner agreed—that he "had it made." Sea Cat made no secret of the fact that Gloria was calling the shots in this relationship. He explained that "this [relationship] is a big thing" for him and he didn't want to jeopardize it in any way. He said he was leaving the initiative entirely with her.

As the summer wore on, he and Gloria grew closer together and Sea Cat appeared less and less frequently on the corner. Once, Gloria came to the Carry-out shop with Sea Cat, and once or twice Stanton or one of the other men went along with them to her house or to the beach cottage for a day. But in the main, Sea Cat was drawn into her social circle and maintained only sporadic contact with the Carry-out.

By the end of the year, Sea Cat had moved into a modest but new apartment about five blocks away from the Carry-out. Gloria furnished it and paid the rent. In February of the following year, Sea Cat's oldest child died. His wife and children, together with her parents, had moved to Detroit. Gloria gave Sea Cat the money to go there and to contribute to the funeral expenses.

According to Sea Cat, when he made one of his infrequent appearances on the corner, all was well. But in March and April there were rumors that he was "messing up." Richard said he had seen Sea Cat at the Checkerboard Lounge with another woman. Stanton said that he had heard that Sea Cat had wrecked Gloria's car while riding with another woman and that "Gloria's getting tired of his shit." The men on the corner shook their heads. Some said that Sea Cat couldn't stay away from all those women. Others said that he was a damn fool for letting women "come between him and A Good Thing." In May, Gloria called a halt. She took back her car and Sea Cat was forced to give up the apartment and the furniture. When the men on the corner learned about this, they shrugged their shoulders. "I knew it was coming," some of them said. "It had to happen," said the others.

A short time later Sea Cat appeared at a Saturday night party given by one of the men on the corner. His reserve and self-deprecation were conspicuous among the laughter and shouting of drinking and good fellowship. When he spoke at all, he spoke in a low, quiet voice: "I had it made but I blew it. I blew it. I really loved that woman. She gave me everything she had. Not the money, I don't mean that. She used to say that when a woman gave a man her body she was giving him everything that a woman had to give. I really loved her, and she loved me too."

For the next few weeks, Sea Cat had difficulty in pulling himself together. Gloria finally agreed to his desperate pleas for another meeting, one in which he hoped to effect a reconciliation, but Sea Cat, now the hurt and unrequited lover, spoiled it all by slapping her for reasons which he did not understand himself, either at the time or in retrospect. Now it was over between them. And it was clear to everyone that, however opportunistically Sea Cat had manipulated the relationship in its beginning, the end of it found him mourning his loss more in emotional than in money terms. He had been as much the lover as the user, maybe more.

■ The hustling ethic

JULIUS HUDSON

Julius Hudson was born and reared in Baltimore, Maryland; he received his bachelor's degree from Towson State College. It was as an undergraduate sociology major there that Hudson ventured into the field to systematically investigate and examine the phenomenon known as "hustling" in that part of Baltimore known as "the strip." His role as participant-observer enabled him to derive the ethos and perspective of the hustler, within the overall portrait that he presents to us in his article.

The author has worked in the counseling and manpower area for the YMCA of greater New York since his arrival from Baltimore in 1966 and is presently program director for a Y-sponsored Manpower Training Program (CHOICE) in New York.

This article shows the value system of a person who, as Hudson has reported, has achieved relative success (albeit illegally) in beating a socioeconomic system that was designed to keep him in a subservient position. Thus, as illustrated in other articles and stories included in this volume,

the hustler has become a value-orienting role model for impoverished black male youth for whom legitimate society offers limited, restrictive, and generally unattractive and unrewarding opportunities. Hudson, in his affiliation with the YMCA Vocational Counseling Service in Harlem, is keenly aware of the various segments and elements within the black community with which his service must compete.

Yet notwithstanding the socioeconomic motivation for hustling, whether of the illegal variety described here or of the legal variety practiced daily within the larger society under the heading of "business," this article is also useful in portraying an expressive life-style and behavioral code that, apart from its socioeconomic link, correlates with various aesthetic forms of black culture. "Conspicuous consumption" and "If you've got it, flaunt it," make not only sociological points but aesthetic ones as well; they are compatible with overall black expressive norms governing presentation of self.

The black ghettoes of this country are noted for their conditions of poverty, misery, and despair. Sociologists, city planners, and other social scientists have produced an abundance of literature discussing the problems of the lower-class inhabitants of these slum areas. Some of these works, such as Drake and Cayton's *Black Metropolis,* are indeed excellent ethnographies. Others, such as Kenneth Clark's *Dark Ghetto,* have suggested ways to alleviate poverty in the black ghettoes. The majority of these works, however, share one shortcoming: they focus almost exclusively on the typical, impoverished, black lower class. They fail to give attention to members of the black lower class who are atypical in socioeconomic and other respects. Sociology and other academic disciplines have failed to produce a thorough study of the subculture of the black hustler, to be specific, or the hustler in general.

This is not intended to imply that there is a lack of awareness of this subculture. Quite the contrary, one has only to look at E. Franklin Frazier's *Black Bourgeoisie* or Milton M. Gordon's *Assimilation in American Life* to realize that sociology is not completely ignorant of the fact. More recently, psychologist Kenneth Clark has expressed cognizance of this phenomenon, citing the need for an adequate study of this area. He states:

> Teen-age Negroes often cope with the ghetto's frustrations by retreating into fantasies related chiefly to their role in society. There is, for example, a fantasy employed by many marginal and antisocial teen-agers to pretend knowledge about illicit activities and to a sexual urbanity that models the petty criminals of the ghetto, whose colorful, swaggering style of cool bravado poses a peculiar fascination.

> Some pretend falsely to be pimps, some to have contacts with number runners. Their apparent admiration of these models is not total but reflects a curious combination of respect, of contempt, and fundamentally, of despair. Social scientists who rely on questionnaires and superficial interviews must find a way to unravel this tangled web of pretense if their conclusions are to be relevant.[1]

Clark is correct when he discredits questionnaires and superficial interviews as viable tools for the investigation of this problem. Nevertheless, he seemingly fails to recognize, or to explicitly state, the real difficulty underlying research of this nature. Correspondingly, the previously mentioned dearth of knowledge about economically atypical lower-class blacks, hereafter referred to as "hustlers," shows the deficient nature of studies in the sociology of deviance. Howard S. Becker, a mythopoetic figure in the sociology of deviant behavior, presented this noteworthy observation in *The Outsiders:* "The most persistent difficulty in the scientific study of deviant behavior is a lack of solid data, a paucity of facts and information on which to base our theories."[2] Research such as this should begin to fill some of the gaps.

I anticipate criticism regarding the true "scientific" nature of this study. The study's findings may be classified as generalizations, perhaps categorized as "post factum sociological interpretation."[3] Be that as it may, I maintain that the study and its findings have, at least, a heuristic value. Consider Ned Polsky's comments from his *Hustlers, Beats, and Others:*

> It is all very well to draw a fuller quantitative picture of the numbers and kinds of criminals or criminal acts. But we cannot use this to dodge

[1] Kenneth Clark, *Dark Ghetto* (New York: Harper & Row, 1965), p. 66.
[2] Howard S. Becker, *The Outsiders* (New York: The Free Press, 1963), p. 165.
[3] Robert K. Merton, *Social Theory and Social Structure,* enlarged ed. (New York: The Free Press, 1968), pp. 147ff.

what is the ultimate, qualitative task, particularly regarding career criminals whose importance to any theorist of human behavior, not to mention the rest of society, is so disproportionate to their numbers: providing well-rounded contemporary, sociological descriptions and analyses of criminal life styles, subcultures, and their relation to larger social processes and structures.[4]

What follows, then, is an exploratory-descriptive study of the subculture of the black hustler. I focused my energies and resources on three major areas: the hustler's ethos, types of hustles or games, and leisure-time activities of the hustler. This represents a modest undertaking in this area, but I hope this effort will begin to provide solid data needed to develop theories of deviant behavior. Finally, the study will indeed prove valuable if the research and corresponding methodology ascertain data which at some time prove relevant to problems (such as upward mobility) constantly confronting black Americans.

The study was conducted in Baltimore, which at the time was the seventh-largest city in the United States. According to the 1960 census, Baltimore had a total population of 939,024, 38 percent (325,589) black. The focal point of the study adhered to E. W. Burgess's zonal hypothesis classification as the "zone of transition." Community residents and the participants in this study referred to this area as "the bottom" or the *ghet-toe,* pronounced emphatically. Within "the bottom," I further concentrated my attention on a major centrally located street, similar in many respects to Harlem's renowned Seventh Avenue. In this instance, the street was called "the strip" by the subjects and was the primary locale of their activities. "The strip" extended for approximately two miles and was congested with any number of small, black-owned retail and service businesses. After a cursory observation of "the strip," I spent most of my time in a six-block area which, in effect, was where the action was. Consequently, I spent most of four months frequenting, observing, and to some extent participating in the subculture's activities in the restaurants, pool halls, barbershops, shoe-shine parlors, crap houses, bars, and nightclubs in the "hot" six-block area of "the strip." It was from this participant-observation perspective and from in-depth interviewing of the inhabitants that the following picture of hustling emerged.

Hustling defined

"Hustling" has a variety of connotations for different individuals. Typically, it is defined and perceived by most people in a way that would seem congruent with the following statement: "Hustling, to the degree that it is known to the larger society at all, is classed with that large

[4] Ned Polsky, *Hustlers, Beats, and Others* (New York: Aldine, 1967), p. 122.

group of social problems composed of morally deviant occupations."[5]
In this research, I was more interested in how the hustler defined hustling
than in a definition from the viewpoint of the outsiders. The members
of the subculture, almost to a man, defined hustling in general terms as
a way of "making it" without killing oneself on whitey's jobs. Opera-
tionally, this "making it" encompasses a variety of "games" (i.e., hustles)
run in a smooth, slick manner. Hustlers were quick to point out that
their games do not represent crimes of violence against individuals.
Rather, they are tactful circumventions of the law, and in most cases
success is facilitated by cooperation from police and judicial officials.
Moreover, the respondents stressed the fact that their actions represented, to a certain extent, a taking over of illegal activities operated by
whitey in the ghetto for years. In essence, the hustlers conceived of their
activities as one form of economic black power.

The hustling ethos

The subculture of the black hustler and the concomitant life-style stand
out in contrast to the general socioeconomic level of living in the black
ghetto. Given this sharp contrast and the historical insight of the researcher, cursory observation and interviews discerned one major tenet
of the hustling ethos: "If you've got it, flaunt it." Members of this subculture are indeed conspicuous consumers. The symbols of such consumption are basically clothes, jewelry, and automobiles.

The attire of the hustler represents one of the most significant aspects
of his "front" or *modus operandi*. As one hustler put it to me, "Look
Jim, to make money you've got to look like you have money. I can't
go no place expecting to take off some fat suckers if I look like a grease-
ball." Moreover, numerous interviews pointed out that one's wardrobe
is a factor in the determination of the hustler's peer-established prestige
ranking. Thus, when a hustler starts making money, he immediately
gets his wardrobe together.

The style of dress in the hustler's subculture is flashy and flamboyant.
In fact, it represents the extreme difference from the so-called Ivy
League–Brooks Brothers–J. Press style of dress. The hustlers are conscious about fabrics, and silk, silk-wool worsted, sharkskin, and cash-
mere appear to be most popular. By and large, colorful silk pants and
Italian-knit sweatershirts appear to be the favorite dress combination of
hustlers.

This normative outfit is usually embellished with alligator (or other
reptile) shoes in a matching color. In fact, while I was interviewing one
hustler in his apartment, he showed me seven pairs of alligator shoes
each costing at least eighty-five dollars. Hustlers are also quick to point

[5] Ibid., p. 42.

out that they purchase their clothing from New York's leading men's stores, such as A. J. Lester's, Phil Kronfield's, and Leighton's.

The automobile a hustler drives is a good indicator of his success. Nearly all hustlers express a penchant for large, luxurious, expensive cars. Along these lines, the Cadillac, called "Hog" in hustler jargon, is the most popular car in this subculture. Currently, all three lines of the Cadillac (Coupe de Ville, Sedan de Ville, Eldorado) are in vogue and demand by hustlers. Moreover, a special model Eldorado, renamed El Cavalaro (reputedly designed by Raideman, a deceased hustler who was a prominent figure in Harlem's hustling subculture), is currently the ultimate in hustler's automobile selection. Short of a Hog, an upcoming hustler will settle for a medium-price large car such as a Buick Electra 225, Buick Riviera, Pontiac Bonneville, or Oldsmobile Toronado. In no cases, however, did I encounter hustlers driving economy cars. As a matter of fact, I was frequently the target of good-natured joking for driving a Volkswagen. The hustlers made it very clear that they value and treasure their automobiles. An expensive automobile appears to be one of the major mechanisms by which the hustler shows the ghetto residents and the black middle class that he has made it—or, as the expression goes, "is doing good in this town."

In addition to clothes and automobiles, hustlers spend a great deal of money on jewelry. They usually adorn themselves with gold-diamond rings and watches costing $500 to $2,000. On many occasions I noticed hustlers with two expensive rings on their hands and costly watches on their wrists. One hustler in particular had a ring which he said cost $10,000. Considering the occupational success of this individual, the reported cost was probably pretty close to the truth. In the main, the acquisition of such expensive jewelry was considered ostentatious by the town's middle-class blacks and other outsiders. Hustlers put this attitude down as jealousy and ignorance. Furthermore, they are quick to point out the economic fact that with all the occupational hazards of hustling (i.e., arrests, large gambling losses, bad deals, etc.) the purchasing of expensive jewelry represents security and a good investment.

The hustler's philosophy

Up to this point, this paper has related to material aspects of the hustling subculture. A major dimension of the hustler's life style, however, is the prevalent philosophy of this subculture. This philosophy, which I have termed "the hustling ethic," incorporates two major tenets which are diametrically opposed to certain views espoused in Weber's "Protestant Ethic," usually associated with middle- and upper-class individuals. First, one tenet of the hustling ethic is an obsessive drive to become wealthy and to display such wealth in an ostentatious manner.

In effect, then, hustling from the perspective of the hustler is primarily about making money or (more poignantly) "making heavy paper." The second tenet of the hustler's philosophy is an extreme sense of contempt and disdain for work, particularly those manual-labor and service jobs traditionally available to lower-class blacks.

The tenacity with which the hustler abides by his hustling ethic is most vividly reflected in his "rap." For example, during one interview a hustler said to me, "Boy, all I do in life is sleep late, eat rich cake, read the funnies, and count money." Another hustler expressed his contempt for work in the following manner: "Baby, let me tell you one thing. I shall not work! Do you hear me? Dig, if you ever see me with a pick and shovel in my hand you'd better grab one too, because you'll know that I've struck gold." In the main, this type of rap was used to put down that body of upward-mobile blacks functioning in professional capacities, semi-skilled blue-collar occupations, and white-collar jobs. Hustlers, by the way, refer to this body as "eight-hour chumps." Hustlers also employed this line of rhetoric to impress the female members of their subculture and other females classified by them as "square broads" (social workers, schoolteachers, etc.).

Inherent in the hustling ethic is the frequent tendency of the hustler to glamorize his life vis-à-vis the eight-hour chump. In the course of this study, I interviewed and hung out with one hustler, Sheldon James Henson (known as Slim by his comrades), who employed poetry as the means for his rap. What follows is one of Slim's favorite poems which reflects the philosophy and life style of the hustler. This poem and the other raps mentioned offer great insight into the hustler's definitions, rationalizations, and reasons for his role and related behavior.

THE BACKSTREET HUSTLER

A hustler is a very wise person, but yet he's lost
  he's a person who refuses to "eight,"[6] (for Charlie)
    the white boss.
His life consists of heartaches, a little pleasure
  and no pity
    at times I hesitate to believe that hustlers are very witty.
His profession ranges from dealing seconds to controlling the cue
  from conning, pimping and cheating at crap
    and sometimes after making a misplay, he'll gladly confess
      that being a backstreet hustler is his own mishap.
This cat is cool, smooth, sharp, handsome, dashing and neat
  except his eyes are always red because he doesn't get very much sleep.
Now with the exception of his red eyes a normal face will remain
  but then his nose is always raw, from snorting the best of cocaine.

[6] Work for eight hours a day.

He possesses a lively tongue, the instant gift of gab
  he's a liar and an actor and to the ladies never a drag.
Now when this man has a good day, you'll see him smile,
  hear him say "All bona fide hustlers come forward, all suckers
  stay away."
The moral of this poem is very sad but true
  a hustler's life is not all roses
    most of it is blue
      and chumps you be glad the title "hustler" doesn't mean you.
There will come a time, when great things will seem quite normal
  not unique at all.
    Something standing strong and erect
      will eventually someday fall.
The tall black stallion will get corralled
  or stumble to its own end over a stone,
    well
      The Backstreet Hustler is sure to die
        broke,
          unmarried,
            unwanted
          and
            most of all
            alone.

Games hustlers run

Throughout the preceding pages I have been describing the luxurious
life-style of the hustler. After numerous trips into the ghetto I began to
formulate a clear concept of how the hustler maintains his rich style of
living. I discovered that there are various activities ("hustles" or
"games," in the jargon of the hustler) which provide the hustler's source
of income. Nearly all of these activities are violations of criminal laws.
But they are not brutal crimes like those committed by gangsters and
thugs. The crimes committed by hustlers are tactful circumventions of
the law. In addition, law-enforcement officers are usually bribed to remain oblivious to those criminal offenses.

The various hustles that a hustler engages in run the gamut from pool
hustling to the stuff game. Certain hustles or games have a high rate of
preference because they are extremely lucrative. On the other hand, certain hustles are highly preferable because they entail small jail sentences
or fines. In any event, the major hustles or games in which the hustlers
of this subculture engage in are as follows: the garment game, the pool
hustle, the crap hustle, the digit game, the pimping game, and the stuff
game. The following paragraphs describe each of these hustles.

The pool hustle

The pool hustle is the one hustle in which nearly all hustlers engage. This is probably true because the poolroom is the locus of just about all of the hustler's activities. Virtually all lower-class black male youths hang out in poolrooms at one time or another; consequently, they develop an interest in shooting pool and acquire a certain degree of proficiency and skill in the game. After the neophyte acquires a certain amount of skill, he begins to wager on his ability to defeat his opponents. At this stage the evolutionary process has ceased to operate and the youth becomes a pool hustler.

The primary pool games of the pool hustler are nine ball, point pool, and one pocket. In nine ball the object is to see which opponent can pocket the nine ball first. In point pool the opponents set a discrete number of points, ranging anywhere from ten to one hundred, as the limit of the game. The first player to reach the limit wins the stakes. The object of the game in one pocket is to see which player can first pocket eight balls in one pocket. The pocket choice available to the players is either the right or left corner pocket at one end of the table.

The possibilities for monetary gains in the pool hustle are unlimited. One night I watched a relatively young hustler win $2,500 playing one pocket. But for most hustlers pool is not that lucrative. Therefore, the pool hustle is usually viewed as a means of supplementary income. Equally important, however, is the fact that through pool hustling one develops insight and contacts which later facilitate success in other areas of hustling. In effect, one begins to know what is happening in the streets.

The garment game

In the garment game the hustler uses the expertise of a salesman. In fact, this hustle consists mainly of the acquisition and re-selling of "hot" merchandise. Although this hustle's name designates apparel, it is not limited to this sphere alone. In reality, the merchandise sold in the garment game runs the gamut from ladies nylons to floor-model color television sets.

A hustler usually acquires his stock of merchandise from "boosters." These boosters are professional shoplifters, male and female, who survive solely on this enterprise. Often boosting broads are in a certain hustler's stable. They therefore turn over the wares at no charge to their man. Boosting broads also cop clothes for their man. The hustler also acquires a certain amount of merchandise from drug addicts who have to steal to support their habit.

The hustler buys merchandise from the boosters and addicts at approximately 20 percent of the selling price. He in turn sells it (to middle-class Negroes most of the time) at anywhere from 40 to 60 percent of the selling price. Thus the hustler usually receives a profit of 100 percent or more.

Even though the garment game is highly profitable—a good boosting broad averages no less than $150 per day for her man—it is not popular with a majority of hustlers. It has two negative aspects which most hustlers condemn. First, most hustlers do not like to risk being caught with stolen goods on them or in their cars. Second, most hustlers feel that the acquisition and reselling of the merchandise requires too much time. Therefore, the garment game is also a secondary or supplementary hustle.

The crap hustle

The crap hustle is perhaps the oldest hustle in the ghetto. A great many male inhabitants of the ghetto shoot dice. But, the crap hustler is considerably more skilled than the layman in this area.

Most crap hustlers begin their education in this speciality at some stage in their early teens. This educational process usually starts as friendly crap games among peers for pennies and nickels. Later the potential crap hustler becomes cognizant of all the cheating mechanisms which will allow him to win consistently. Next he acquires a thorough knowledge of the appropriate betting odds and the probability distribution of different points on the dice. At this stage, the youth becomes a fully developed crap hustler.

The mature, experienced crap hustler seeks his fortunes primarily in a crap house. He abstains from participating in floating crap games for fear of violence and susceptibility to arrest. In a crap house the proprietor controls violence and the police. Furthermore, the crap house offers greater possibilities for winning large sums of money and eliminates the obvious cheating element. In the course of this study I visited the crap house on the strip on numerous occasions and witnessed the loss and gain of as much as $30,000 by various hustlers. Noteworthy here is the fact that crap hustling is not solely an in-group game. The crap house on the strip was frequented by blacks from all walks of life (e.g., professionals, entertainers, athletes, etc.). Most hustlers dig a good crap game and always find time and money to participate.

The digit game

The digit game, or numbers or policy racket as it is otherwise known, is one of the oldest hustles in the black ghetto. Its beginning can be traced back to the Black Belt of Chicago and Harlem of New York at the turn of the century. Nearly everyone in the ghetto, and quite a few middle- and upper-class blacks, play the numbers. Consequently, the digit game is a fruitful source of income for the hustler.

The hustler is involved in the digit game at two levels. At the first level of involvement the hustler is primarily a digit-writer; his hustle consists primarily of canvassing the ghetto to record number plays and collect the bets. It is also his responsibility to pay off the winning players. At the second level, the hustler is called a number-backer. He is the individual who covers all the bets.

A digit-writer in this city receives about 10 percent of his total collection. I understand that the rate is as high as 25 percent in other cities. But the digit hustler in this city still manages to derive a good income from the digit game. He is usually paid quite handsomely by winners for delivering their money. In addition many digit hustlers "edge" the smaller number play on their book; they assume financial responsibility for the smaller (five-cent to fifty-cent) plays. This supplements the rate they receive from the number-backer.

The digit game is most profitable to the backer. The odds against a player hitting the number are nine-and-a-half to one. The average backer only pays off at a rate of six to one. Thus the backer is practically assured of a 40 percent profit. Most digit-writers aspire to becoming backers and getting rich. In fact the largest digit-backer on the strip is reputed to be a millionnaire. I was told he owns at least half of all the bars and nightclubs on the strip. He is also said to be the behind-the-scenes owner of a number of legitimate enterprises.

Given the safety and lucrative returns, most hustlers aspire to have a nice thing going for them in the digit game. The major reservation expressed, however, is that if a black cat gets too big with numbers, organized crime will move in on his territory. Historically, this started when Dutch Schultz moved in on Harlem's numbers racket years ago; it still holds true today.

The pimping game

Pimping is a hustler's activity which has a long history in the ghetto. However, pimping in this particular ghetto encompassed much more than deriving one's living from the earnings of a prostitute. It meant deriving ones living from a female regardless of how she earns her money. In this respect, I was able to discern three patterns of pimping in this subculture.

The first pattern involves pimping on employed females. These females cover an age range of twenty to fifty-five in most cases. They are usually single, but some of the older ones are married. Their occupations run the gamut from clerk-typists to schoolteachers to administrators.

The pimp in this case is usually a good-looking, well-dressed, and well-built guy, but the most important characteristic in this type of pimping is the ability to sexually satisfy a female. Thus this pimp is the gigolo type. Once the pimp establishes his superiority in this area, he encounters virtually no obstacles to the attainment of the female's money. He simply waits until her payday for his share, which is usually twenty-five dollars or more on a hundred-dollar base. Often such pimps get their broads to buy them expensive automobiles and other desired goods.

The second pattern involves pimping off professional female shoplifters, or "boosting broads," as they are called on the strip. These females are usually high school dropouts who started shoplifting primarily because they wanted to dress fashionably. After a couple of years' practice and a few arrests, they boost to acquire their income, and maintain status in the hustling community.

To this end, these females adopt or are adopted by a pimp on the strip. What develops thereafter is a relationship in which the pimp receives a great percentage of the boosting broad's goods and income. In return the female receives protection, legal aid, prestige, and sometimes housing. Interestingly different in this pattern of pimping is the satisfaction derived by the female.

The pimp to whom the boosting broads give their money, clothes, and jewelry does not necessarily have to be good looking or have superior sexual abilities. But he must fulfill two important prerequisites. First, he must be a pretty good fighter. This is necessary because people on the strip are always attempting to take merchandise from these boosting broads. Second, he must have a good reputation as a successful hustler. This latter prerequisite appears to be the crux of the whole matter. The female in this case wants a pimp with a great deal of prestige on the strip so she can share it. At this point, the pimping game resembles some form of hero worship; the boosting broads are quite vocal in extolling the virtues of their man and how much money they make for him.

The third pattern of pimping involves the acquisition of money from prostitutes, or "trick broads." Simply stated, a woman sells her body to support her man. In this instance, the trick broad desires and needs all the pimp characteristics mentioned in the preceding patterns. Hence, she wants a pimp who is good looking and highly rated by his peers. She also needs a man who is physically able to protect her from the hazards of customer relations in her chosen occupation. Finally, trick broads desire a competent and satisfying sex partner. As one such trick rapped to me in an interview, "After turning tricks with those jive Johns, I need a dude who can take care of business when I want to have some fun."

The relationship between a pimp and a trick broad is an extremely interesting one from the viewpoint of roles. A great number of the trick broads I interviewed viewed their pimp as a combination lover-father. This quasi-paternal nature of the relationship comes home strongly when pimps discover attempts by their tricks to withhold money. What results is usually a public and/or private beating, with the female quite submissive. On one occasion I witnessed such a beating; the female passively accepted the physical punishment and only pleaded, "Oh daddy, please stop. I swear I won't do it any more." On the other hand, when things are going good for a pimp, he treats his tricks in the manner of a gentleman and is always concerned about their safety.

All hustlers consider the pimping game to be an extremely attractive hustling activity. If the female has a good job, is a good prostitute, or is a good booster, the income derived can be quite lucrative. In addition, if possible most hustlers will combine the types of females they pimp on to enhance their income. Pimping is also attractive because once the pimp establishes rapport with the female it is not too time-consuming. And last but by no means least, pimping does not involve any flagrant breaking of the law for the pimp. In those cases when the broads are arrested, the pimp readily pays the fine and acquires whatever legal assistance is necessary.

The stuff game

The stuff game is hustler's jargon for the selling of narcotics. It represents an extreme case of the breaking of the law, and therefore the probability of arrest is high in this activity. On the other hand, the hustler minimizes the risk involved by his clandestine methods of operation, bribery of law-enforcement officers, and a tightly structured organization. Consequently, the high profits accrued make the stuff game one of the most preferred hustling activities, especially if the individual has a "good thing going for him." In effect, this means that a successful hustler in the stuff game has reliable personnel, excellent contacts to "cop" drugs, and a good front. The proper combination of these factors usually results in lucrative returns on an investment in drugs—especially heroin. A top hustler in the stuff game indicated to me that the net return for an investment of $8,000 to $10,000 for a kilo (2.2 lbs.) of heroin is in the range of $75,000 to $100,000. On such a return his take is approximately 40 percent off the top, with the remainder going to his personnel and other individuals receiving cuts. Also noteworthy is the fact that the time element involved in such a transaction averages out to a week.

The major drugs sold in the stuff game are heroin, cocaine, and marijuana. Heroin is the largest selling and the most profitable. Cocaine yields good returns but does not move as rapidly as heroin. Marijuana is the least-profitable drug and is a time-consuming venture.

Hustlers involved in the stuff game rely on a wide gamut of techniques to decrease the risk of getting busted. At the top level of the stuff game the boss virtually never touches the drugs, and he protects his personnel by bribing law-enforcement officials. Other individuals whose functions are considerably more hazardous invoke additional protective methods. Pushers, for example, refrain as much as possible from keeping drugs in their possession. To this end, pushers develop stashes to hide their drugs while they are not actually making a sale. In this instance, places close to the strip such as telephone booths, bathrooms in pool halls, or parked cars were utilized as stashes. Another technique invoked by stuff hustlers is to affect an esoteric atmosphere through the use of argot. In this respect, virtually all the hustlers in this particular subculture communicated in a language of their own. Typically, terms such as "horse," "smack," "dugee," and "white boy" were used to denote heroin. Even more ingenious is the use of the following sentence to inquire where one can purchase some marijuana: "Have you heard Aretha's song today?" In this case singer Aretha Franklin's name is pronounced as *a-reefer*. The use of argot by hustlers also serves to reinforce their sense of hipness and as a putdown to "squares." During the course of the study I witnessed several situations where hustlers baffled law-enforcement officers and squares with a fast, heavy rap in the language endemic to their subculture.

In the final analysis, most of the hustlers I interviewed expressed a strong desire to make it big in the stuff game. The opportunity to make a great amount of money in a relatively short period of time negates the fear of arrest and incarceration. One hustler I interviewed told me that on his noon pick-up he averages around $3,500, making six stops in less than a half hour. The normative attitude with regard to the stuff game is perhaps best expressed by the following statement: "Well dig man, like the only way a brother can get rich quick in this country is to sing rock & roll or sell dope. Now my singing ain't none too tough, but I can sell some dope."

The activities of the hustler are by no means separate entities as they have been described here. Rather, they are interrelated and interdependent parts of a complex whole. Hence most hustlers do not confine themselves to a single hustling game. It is conceivable that such a restriction may be economically fruitful; more often than not, however, the typical hustler is dealing in a number of games simultaneously. I began to ascertain that the ideally successful hustler was one who was involved in the entire gamut of games. To put it in the hustler's jargon: "A guy has got to make it if he has a lot of things going for him." Moreover, an evolutionary career pattern became discernible when I interviewed a number of hustlers with emphasis on how they became such. Most hustlers begin their careers in pool or crap and graduate to the more lucrative games through contacts developed in their apprenticeships.

In the course of this study I became acquainted with a typically successful hustler. After numerous conversations with this hustler I was able to construct a brief history of his hustling career. He stated that he began shooting crap at the age of eleven. By the time he reached fourteen, he had decided to quit school and make it as a crap hustler. Within the next year, he became closely attached to an elderly hustler. At this point, he embarked on a four-year informal course in the mechanics of crap hustling and pool hustling. At the end of this training period he was a skillful crap hustler and pool hustler. He began to accumulate relatively large sums of money through his hustling activities.

One year later he hit the number and collected $20,000. He then started to bank numbers. Oddly enough, this individual refrained from involving himself in pimping in any form. The next year he hit the number for $50 and collected $30,000. His next step was to venture into the stuff game. The stuff game is now his primary hustle, but he retains his other hustles to supplement his income. At the time of this study he was considered to be the most successful young hustler on the strip, and he was reputedly on the way to becoming a millionnaire.

The social life of the hustler

The social life of the hustler is the primary area in which he displays his acquired wealth and peer group–approved prestigious material possessions. In this sphere the hustler spends his money recklessly and flamboyantly. It is not uncommon to see a hustler treat everyone in a nightclub to numerous rounds of drinks; I saw a hustler pick up a tab for $184 in one of the more popular clubs on the strip one night.

The hustlers also attend all major sporting events quite frequently. At these events they almost always occupy the most expensive seats, and they openly exhibit and wager thousands of dollars. In short, the social life of the hustler is the one area in which he can show society that he also is making it regardless of his educational and occupational shortcomings.

After-hours parties represent another major aspect of the hustler's social life. These parties, as the name denotes, are given after the bars close. They are usually held in one of the hustler's pads. I went to a couple of these parties and found them to be wild affairs. The host provides plenty of food and alcoholic beverages; furthermore, a really hip host will provide a plentiful supply of marijuana and cocaine so that anyone interested can indulge. A number of hosts also bring in girls (two) at an average cost of $400 to entertain their friends with a freak sex show. The opportunities available for entertainment at these parties are unlimited; or, to put it in the hustler's jargon, "A cat can really get into something at these affairs." These activities run the gamut from smoking pot in the bathroom to seducing a chick in the bedroom.

At a point during this study, the hustlers formed an ad hoc club to promote a special social affair. What was interesting here is the fact that the social was a black-tie affair. To a great extent this was an imitation of the city's middle- and upper-class blacks who naturally excluded hustlers from their social-register balls. This particular affair lasted all night and culminated with a soul-champagne breakfast which I attended. When asked how they enjoyed this affair, most of the hustlers responded quite enthusiastically in a positive and boastful manner. Note the following response: "Yeah man, it was out of sight. I guess we really showed those jive ass doctors, social workers, and teachers how to have a ball."

Summary

The evolution of the hustler's society, and of the social type designated as the hustler, accounts for the unexpected (and to a certain extent shocking) wealthy life-styles found in the black ghetto. Although the hustling ethic appears to be diametrically opposed to the Protestant ethic, it is really an outgrowth of it. That is to say, it has been the experience of a number of lower-class blacks that years of hard work on mediocre jobs will in no way mitigate their economic and social problems. Or, stated differently, the inconsistencies in the American social structure make it virtually impossible for most lower-class blacks to achieve any degree of upward social or occupational mobility. In this respect the hustler's society represents an innovation by which lower-class blacks can attain their desired economic and social goal. One might well argue that the social system of the hustler represents a systematized form of deviant behavior, but in the final analysis this behavior could be appropriately classified as adaptive behavior. In effect, the hustler's society represents the lower-class black's original and indigenous means of waging a "war on poverty." Members of this subculture, and numerous ghetto residents, feel that the hustler's anti-poverty effort is considerably more successful than the government's.